BECOMING A **GRAPHIC**

DESIGNER

BECOMING A **GRAPHIC** DESIGNER

A GUIDE TO CAREERS IN DESIGN · FOURTH EDITION

STEVEN HELLER & TERESA FERNANDES

WILEY

JOHN WILEY & SONS, INC.

DEDICATION

To Louise Fili and Nick Heller – SH

To Barry Blitt and Sam Blitt – TF

ACKNOWLEDGMENTS

To Margaret Cummins, our editor throughout all the editions of this book, thanks for your continued faith in this project. To Doug Salvemini, who oversaw the production, we appreciate all you've done to bring this to fruition. To Kat Riehle, who assisted in the layout of the new edition, and Brooke Rane, who assisted in updating the text, thanks to both of you for your attention to detail.

Of course, the book would not exist if not for the contributors to this and all the previous editions. Taken as a whole, they are a who's who of design practice and education. Individually, each has generously provided invaluable insight to all those who are seeking a career in graphic design – or whatever it will be called in the not so distant future. – SH + TF

This book is typeset in Mrs. Eaves and Myriad Pro, and is printed on acid-free paper.

Art Director/Designer: Teresa Fernandes, TFD STUDIO
Associate Designer: Kat Riehle
Research Assistant: Brooke Rane

Copyright © 2010 by John Wiley & Sons, Inc. All rights reserved

Published by John Wiley & Sons, Inc., Hoboken, New Jersey

Published simultaneously in Canada

For general information about our other products and services, please contact our Customer Care Department within the United States at (800) 762-2974, outside the United States at (317) 572-3993 or fax (317) 572-4002.

Wiley also publishes its books in a variety of electronic formats. Some content that appears in print may not be available in electronic books. For more information about Wiley products, visit our web site at www.wiley.com.

Library of Congress Cataloging-in-Publication Data:
Heller, Steven. Becoming a graphic designer: a guide to careers in design/Steven Heller & Teresa Fernandes.—4th ed.
    p. cm.

ISBN 978-0-470-57556-7 (pbk.);
ISBN 978-0-470-63757-9 (ebk);
ISBN 978-0-470-91296-6 (ebk);
ISBN 978-0-470-91297-3 (ebk);
ISBN 978-0-470-91298-0 (ebk);
ISBN 978-0-470-95077-7 (ebk)
1. Commercial art— Vocational guidance. 2. Graphic arts—Vocational guidance.
I. Fernandes, Teresa. II. Title. III. Title: Guide to careers in design.
NC1001.H45 2010
741.6023'73—dc22
2010004729
Printed in the United States of America
10 9 8 7 6 5 4 3 2 1

BACK COVER CREDITS:
top: Passages: Photographs in Africa *by Carol Beckwith and Angela Fisher* CLIENT: Harry N. Abrams *CREATIVE DIRECTOR/DESIGNER:* Michael J. Walsh *PHOTOGRAPHERS:* Carol Beckwith, Angela Fisher *YEAR:* 2000; center: *10 Days in South Africa* CLIENT: Interactive Africa *DESIGNERS:* Hjalti Karlsson, Jan Wilker COMPANY: *karlssonwilker inc.* YEAR: 2007/2008; bottom: *Cloud Cult Gig Poster* CLIENT: High Noon Saloon DESIGNER/ILLUSTRATOR: Travis Cain ART DIRECTOR: Kevin Wade YEAR: 2007

CONTENTS

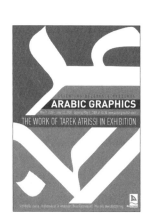

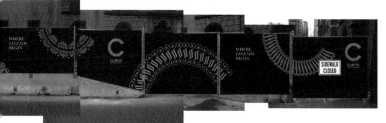

Welcome to the 4th edition of *Becoming a Graphic Designer*; the first edition was published in 1999. In the course of world (and design) history, this meager span of time is a drop in the bucket; in the scheme of graphic design, it is an eternity. The field has shockingly changed but in the process a certain timeworn practice is maintained. While shedding obsolete notions and moving on to technologies and platforms that graphic designers rarely occupied, there is an essential continuity. Type is still the language and typography will always be the voice of "graphic" design. But instead of flat, immovable surfaces (i.e., paper), graphic designers are now increasingly more likely to work on screens of all shapes and sizes, with light, sound, and even touchy tactility to be considered. Interactivity is now a design watchword, and user experience has replaced the more pedestrian words, "reading" and "looking."

This is not your grandmother's graphic design. Nor is it your older brother's or sister's. The rate of speed at which the practice moves is cyclonic. All you have to do is look around to see that the world of design involves media that were inconceivable when grandmas were starting their careers.

Yet the more things change the more they stay the same (*plus ça change*). And this edition of *Becoming a Graphic Designer* is testament to that adage. Throughout the previous editions we have removed sections, sidebars, and interviews that had become obsolete, adding new content that was more con-temporaneous. In the interview section, we included younger practitioners with fresh outlooks, while retaining veterans whose wealth of experience (and at times wisdom) we believed was essential to understanding graphic design. This edition is no exception.

Some of the added voices are those, like Art Chantry, who are legendary for their iconoclastic ideas and artifacts. Others, like Nigel Holmes, Michael Johnson, and James Montalbano, are pivotal figures in their respective disciplines, respective information design, corporate identity, and type and lettering. Still oth-ers are the next generation of veterans, like Rodrigo Corral, Christian Schwartz, and Jason Santa Maria, who are working across the board, respectively in book jacket design, type design, and Web design. Finally, there are the current "next" generation, including Marian Bantjes, Ji Lee, and Randy J. Hunt, who are making their marks in type and letter, advertising, and Web design.

The fundamental design genres have not changed at all from the 3rd edition to this. But the shift in emphasis has been considerably altered to reflect developments in the field. Perhaps the most obvious increase in activity is the move from print to screen. This is so profound that I coauthored with David Womack *Becoming a Digital Designer* in 2007, which covers a broad swath of interaction and information design, as well as the nexus of digital technology and traditional form and content. At this stage, the "digital designer" is more or less a distinct discipline with its own tenets, although the edges are becoming increasingly blurred. More graphic designers are doing both Web and print, and as you will learn in the latest batch of interviews, the Web is becoming the primary medium for many old and new design firms as all businesses and organizations want to establish a virtual presence.

The most significant additions in this edition appear in Section Two: Design Businesses. Many of those interviewed cite "the small studio boom" as causing an increase in freelancers starting their own proprietary concerns with one or slightly more employees. They note that desktop technologies encourage this form of entrepreneurial spirit. Therefore, the majority of recent interviews can be found in this section and run the gamut from highly established firms, like Noreen Morioka's AdamsMorioka to newer studios, like Chris Ritchie and Adam Michaels' ProjectProjects. Most of the newbie studios have been operating for more than two years (and less than five), but there are some fairly recent start-up endeavors too.

The other hot-button, entrepreneurship and authorship, continue as growth areas—and many of those who were engaged from the previous edition are still active. We added Deborah Adler, who created the now celebrated Target SafeRX prescription drug system. She began her project as a thesis for the MFA Designer as Author program at the School of Visual Arts and pursued it into the marketplace. The other addition, David Barringer, a former lawyer turned author, publisher, and designer, is also representative of how design from left-field can be integrated into multi-leveled entrepreneurial practice.

Of the more traditional genres found in Section One: Design Specialties aside from the largest growth area, Interaction, we find that Type and Lettering continues to grow and hold solid fascination for students looking to enter the field. Information design, both

independent of and tethered to Interactivity, is a growth area too, either as a specialty or ancillary part of a business.

Corporate design is slowly shifting from in-house design studios to contracting independent firms, but there are still jobs and careers in large and small corporations. The areas in this edition where we did more pruning than adding are the following: Editorial (print),

THIS IS NOT YOUR GRANDMOTHER'S GRAPHIC DESIGN. NOR IS IT YOUR OLDER BROTHER'S OR SISTER'S.

which is still chugging along but in a state of flux; Book design is continually threatened by "the end of print" doomsayers and the rise of the digital reader, yet book covers and jackets are getting better all the time; Music, which is truly a dying art form in terms of CD or record design, but may have a resurgence through posters and online media; and Advertising and Branding has not been restructured in this edition, not because there is less of it, but we had it pretty well covered in the previous edition.

The requisites for becoming a graphic designer have definitely changed, but a solid design education at a good art college,

university, or design program, both undergraduate and graduate, is still recommended. More programs are offering digital tools, and a few are going beyond just teaching method and technique. The MFA Interaction Design program at the School of Visual Arts as well as the Master of Design in Interaction Design at Carnegie Mellon University are leaders in advance study dealing with the present and future of design in digital media.

We often wonder whether each edition of *Becoming a Graphic Designer* is the last; and yet we are never surprised that we are asked to continue to update and upgrade. Despite the radical shifts and states of flux graphic design—or rather "communication design," as some call it—in which type is the key language and conveying messages to a public is the primary goal, it is here to stay. Even the most standardized and automated formats cannot undercut the need for innovative presentation. Graphic designers are essential in the role of organizing and framing ideas and information, making them readable, accessible, and entertaining. This book continues to offer the art student or design fan a chance to survey the field(s) in order to determine where, if anywhere, they fit in or would like to learn more. Graphic design is here to stay (for now) and as authors (and practitioners) we hope this edition provides you with a readable, accessible, and entertaining guide.

STEVEN HELLER, 2010

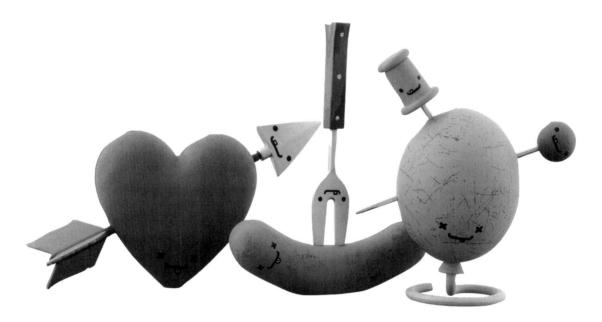

So You Want to Be a Graphic Designer?

The 1960s rock band The Byrds recorded a song that underscored the obsession of its generation: "So you wanna be a rock and roll star / well listen now to what I say / go and get an electric guitar /and take the time to learn how to play." Given the current interest in graphic communications, these lyrics might be rewritten in the twenty-first century to read: "So you wanna be a graphic designer / well listen now to what I say / go and get a Macintosh G5 / and take the time to learn how to play." Okay, it doesn't parse as well, but you get the point. The Mac is to graphic design what the electric guitar was to early rock and roll. The electric guitar changed everything from the sound to the look of music; the Mac has had a profound influence on the look as well as the *sound* of graphic design.

The first lesson for all prospective graphic designers is how to use the computer and its numerous layout, illustration, photo, and type programs. The second lesson is how to make the computer work for the designer, not the other way around. The computer is a tool, just as the ruler, X-Acto, and waxer were tools not long ago. Like the electric guitar, the computer is an expensive machine that, without the intervention of human intelligence and talent, produces noise—so at the outset it is important to establish as fact the graphic designer's need to know how to work (as well as play) with the tool; this is a necessary step toward proficiency.

However, this does not answer the question "How do I become a graphic designer?"

Actually, this is not the proper first question. Given the sea changes in graphic design and visual communications (terms that are used interchangeably) in the early twenty-first century, the initial question should be: "What is graphic design?" Once the many graphic design disciplines—and there are many specialties—are identified, "How do I learn more about them?" can be asked. Only afterward is the question about becoming a graphic designer applicable.

Becoming a Graphic Designer is not going to teach the neophyte how to use the computer. Scores of books and thousands of courses offer basic, intermediate, and advanced instruction. Rather, this book is an introduction—a navigational guide, if you like—to what in recent years has become a complex profession comprising many print, film, and electronic genres. In the music business, it is not enough to play a few chords on the guitar; it is useful to be proficient in R&B, folk, reggae, punk, hip-hop, and so forth. Likewise, graphic design is not simply about the exclusive practice of editorial, book, advertising, or poster design; all these forms can (and even should) be practiced by individuals depending on their relative skill, expertise, and inclination. More important,

with the recent development of desktop publishing as well as computer-driven multimedia, the field has expanded to such an extent that entirely new divisions of labor, unprecedented collaborations, and specializations have emerged. This book describes both traditional and new disciplines.

Before becoming a graphic designer, it is imperative to learn as much about the profession as possible. Knowledge is the key to saving time and energy.

THE IMPULSE TO BECOME A GRAPHIC DESIGNER IS NOT EXCLUSIVE TO THOSE IN THE APPLIED OR FINE ARTS.

Nevertheless, many practitioners naively stumbled into the field through their love of art or letterforms while others fiddled with QuarkXPress or InDesign and were therefore drafted to produce the occasional newsletter or flyer. Becoming a graphic designer does not always require advanced university degrees or years of intense academic training. True, many of the interviewees cited in this book logged considerable time in undergraduate and postgraduate design schools, but others originally held jobs as writers, painters, illustrators, cartoonists, printers,

and typesetters, and one was even a graffiti artist. In fact, the impulse to become a graphic designer is not exclusive to those in the applied or fine arts; anyone interested in "visuals" is a prospective candidate. Once engaged in a graphic design practice, however, in-house or staff designers, freelancers, and principals of independent firms all need a shared fundamental knowledge.

Graphic designers all speak the same basic vocabulary (and use the same jargon), and while some designers are more adept at fine typography than others who may be better skilled at sequential narratives or information management, graphic design is not an intuitive endeavor. It cannot be done without knowledge of the task, genre, or medium in question. Contrary to the now infamous 1987 television advertisement that introduced the first Macintosh by arrogantly announcing that, with the advent of this revolutionary machine, graphic designers were a thing of the past, graphic design must be studied, learned, and continually practiced to achieve even basic proficiency. To go further, to transcend simple service and craft with inspiring work, graphic design must be totally embraced, body and soul.

This sounds hyperbolic, but it is not. For their designs to rise above the commonplace reams of hack work that flood the market, graphic designers must be devoted to as many aspects of the endeavor as possible. They must know who is doing what and how it is done. They must understand the history

IMAGE ON OPPOSITE PAGE:
TITLE: bffs Collectible Vinyl Toys DESIGNER/ ART DIRECTOR/ ILLUSTRATOR: Travis Cain CLIENT: KidRobot YEAR: 2009

of the field to avoid reinventing the wheel. It is not enough to mimic fashions and trends as if they were schematics for success. To practice well means to master the tools and marshal the talent that eschews cliché.

Graphic design is a business (an aspect discussed in detail below), but equally as important, it is a tool of visual expression, a process whereby ideas and products are given concrete forms through the often conceptual manipulation of type and imagery. A graphically designed object—whether a page, package, or screen—can be expressive or neutral, hard-sell or soft-sell, classical or radical. The level of complexity or simplicity is determined either by the nature of the message or the preference of the designer. Graphic design has its share of recurring procedures and repetitive tasks—ask anyone who works within a strictly prescribed book, magazine, or Web page format—but there is always potential for surprising outcomes that are novel and, indeed, innovative. Within the parameters of a given project, graphic design can be anything short of art for art's sake. It is a mistake to think that graphic design is only about positioning type on a page regardless of content and aesthetics. Graphic design may be utilitarian, but it is not void of the creative essence.

Graphic design is indeed a commercial art. Yet contrary to shortsighted notions, the qualifier "commercial" does not diminish the noun "art." The commercial arena is where the graphic

designer performs a difficult balancing act—to sell, entertain, and inform in a manner that also adds aesthetic value to the receiver's (or audience's) experience. Art is what distinguishes the designer's expertise from the layperson's ignorance. With the widespread availability of template software programs, it is easier today than during the years B.C. (before computers) for anyone to compose a layout in a semipro-

> *THE TECHNIQUES OF GRAPHIC DESIGN CAN BE LEARNED, BUT THE INSTINCT FOR MAKING ART NEEDS TO BE NURTURED OVER TIME.*

fessional manner, yet to imbue it with the nuance and uniqueness (as well as imagination) that demands an audience's attention requires the artist's deft touch. The techniques of graphic design can be learned, but the instinct for making art needs to be nurtured over time.

Like painting and sculpture, graphic design is influenced by myriad movements, ideologies, and aesthetic points of view that derive from well over a century

of modern practice. This legacy cannot be imparted through even the most sophisticated computer programs. Neither knowledge nor inspiration is an instant fix. Moreover, knowledge is more than simply knowing the names of a few typefaces, or when to use justified columns, or how to specify colors; a graphic designer must understand both the stylistic and aesthetic options that are available and how to use them for optimum advantage. A good graphic designer is able to adapt existing historical or contemporary models and derive unique approaches; this comes from patient study and dedicated practice. A great graphic designer can apply these unique approaches to solving complex problems in a manner that appears effortless. While in theory prolonged schooling is unnecessary to becoming a graphic designer, forging knowledge and instinct into critical thinking is. More often than not, this comes from the marriage of academics and on-the-job training.

Graphic design was never easy, although veterans sometimes pine for the good old days. Prior to the introduction of digital media, the field appeared simpler than it does today. Back then, one could start a design business with a few low-tech tools on a kitchen table. Today, a major financial investment in hardware and software is required just to be in the position to start learning. Yet even in 1900, graphic design was more complex than positioning type on a page. In fact, it was helpful to be adept at the difficult crafts of printing, hot metal type composition, and hand lettering. Back then, as today, specialties existed, various skills were necessary, and many aesthetic options were possible. The only difference between current and past practice is the type of work available. Early in the century, many more graphic design activities were exclusive to trained specialists, whereas those specialties are no longer exclusive.

Where once type design was the sole province of skilled punch cutters and type designers, the computer makes it possible for anyone proficient in certain font programs to design custom typefaces. Not everyone is skilled enough to design a viable, multipurpose typeface, but the potential exists for those outside the traditional discipline, including many graphic designers (as opposed to professional type designers), to contribute quirky faces that are made available through digital foundries and shareware on the Internet. Another example is desktop publishing; the term suggests a wellspring of amateur activity. Anyone sitting at a computer loaded with a page layout program and a newsletter/periodical/flyer template can pretend to be a graphic designer. At the turn of the century, printers alone did the design. In the 1920s and until recently, it was more or less the exclusive province of art directors and layout persons. In the 1960s, the availability of transfer type and photocopy machines made it easier for amateurs to try their hands at layout, but today,

HOW MANY GRAPHIC DESIGNERS ARE THERE? WHAT DO THEY EARN?

Statistics concerning the graphic design profession are sketchy because the industry encompasses a number of design areas. Studies often lump architects, interior designers, set designers, furniture designers, industrial designers, and even floral designers together with graphic designers.

According to U.S. Department of Labor data (provided by Research Division, National Endowment for the Arts), there were 212,000 designers in the United States in 2002. The Bureau of Labor Statistics weighs in with a staggering 682,000 designers, including architects, and projects that the number grew at a rate of 30 percent through the year 2000. But in a report by Strategies for Management, Inc., in cooperation with Creative Access, of the total number of designers in the United States, 160,000 are *graphic* designers (although this changes from year to year).

According to the American Institute of Graphic Arts (AIGA), annual salaries range from $16,000 for a junior designer to $32,000 to $60,500 for an art director to $124,000 and upward for a creative director. Each design specialty has its own salary range, which can vary greatly. For example, the magazine publishing industry starts off junior designers with much lower salaries than advertising agencies do.

all the tools of editorial design are at the amateur's disposal, which opens up unfettered access to every possible mistake.

As the boundaries between professional and amateur break down, it is more important than ever for graphic designers to maintain standards that distinguish the two. Becoming a graphic designer means accepting, promoting, and, perhaps, eventually helping to change the existing standards.

The dissolution of certain specialties coincided with the emergence of new ones. Career guides published only a decade ago do not mention the handful of new disciplines that currently fall under the graphic design rubric or are areas where graphic designers are currently finding work as collaborators in broader design activities. Among them, information architecture (the design of data-driven charts, maps, graphs) is a genre of graphic design open to those with a penchant for conceptual thinking. Another is Web page design, which has become an entry point for a wide range of artists and designers. Some Web designers come directly from print media, while others bypass print entirely. In the attempt to redefine graphic design, the Web has become a pivotal realm because it involves traditional graphic applications, such as type and page layout, wed to nontraditional graphic design components, such as sound and motion. With these expanding new options, becoming a graphic designer requires neophytes to thoughtfully decide on the media in which they will devote the time and energy to acquiring expertise.

New venues, like the Web, and interactive forms, like handhelds and iPad, do not remain wide open for long. After an initial surge to fill the new jobs, standards tighten, openings constrict, and competition becomes tougher. It is axiomatic that in the early stages, until the dust settles, new media attract the lion's share of students and neophytes because it is cool to be involved. But graphic design is not a fly-by-night endeavor; it's a venerable profession with enough facets to keep a practitioner absorbed for a lifetime. Nonetheless, graphic design is also more and more a springboard to enter other communications industries—especially in this cross disciplinary era.

Becoming a Graphic Designer is a survey of many aspects of the profession: traditional print media, including type, book, periodical, advertising, and corporate; new media, including wireless media, Internet, and film and video; and cross-disciplinary practices, including collaborations with architects and environmental designers. In recent years, the increased availability of high-end production tools that, in many cases, eliminate production middlemen has allowed graphic designers who were once only cogs in the wheel to become involved in the total conception and manufacture of designed products. Through the

> THROUGH THE AID OF THE COMPUTER, A GRAPHIC DESIGNER IS NOT RELEGATED TO FRAMING CONTENT BUT CAN NOW DETERMINE, CONCEIVE, AND PRODUCE IT AS WELL.

aid of the computer, a graphic designer is not relegated to framing content but can now determine, conceive, and produce it as well. A designer is now capable of being an auteur, entrepreneur, or "authorpreneur."

Meant for those who have not been introduced to or have had only a passing understanding of graphic design, this book showcases a multileveled profession that is as accessible as it is intricate. The numerous voices reveal through interviews both the commonalities and the differences among disciplines. And because this is a profession populated by individuals, we have also included iconoclasts whose conflicting viewpoints underscore the healthy diversity that contributes to making graphic design a rich, creative profession in addition to practitioners in the accepted movements, styles, and schools of contemporary design.

Once upon a time, graphic designers grumbled that the world ignored their contributions. "Not even my parents understand what I do," was a common complaint. Today, graphic design is less arcane and more mainstream than in any other period. Thanks, in large part, to the computer, graphic design is not only an integral component of the communication, retail, and entertainment industries but also an entrepreneurial activity that allows for, and contributes to, cultural advancement. These are exciting prospects for those who decide to join the continuum of graphic design at this juncture. Beginners who use *Becoming a Graphic Designer* to identify their first career step (or long-term niche) may not wind up running a successful studio or producing a unique design product, but for those who master the skills, possess the talent, and have the drive, graphic design offers the potential for a creative future.

GLOSSARY

JOB DIVISIONS

Graphic designers are employed in virtually all kinds of businesses, industries, and institutions. Here are some of the typical terms used interchangeably for "in-house design department."

> Art Department
> Art and Design Department
> Art Services Department
> Design Department
> Design Services Department
> Creative Services Department
> Creative Group
> Graphics Group

Different companies are organized differently depending on their focus and goals. A large corporation may distinguish package design from promotion design, or editorial design from advertising design; a smaller business may keep all design activities under one umbrella such as, design department.

Likewise, proprietary or independent design firms, studios, or offices—design businesses that service large corporations and small businesses—may or may not distinguish among design functions, such as a print design department separate from a multimedia design department, or promotion and collateral separate from editorial departments.

JOB TITLES

The titles given to specific jobs and tasks throughout the design field vary according to the hierarchy of the specific company, institution, or firm. For example, an art director for one company may be a design director at another; a senior designer at one may have different responsibilities than a senior at another. Starting from the top, here are typical job titles as used by in-house art departments in publishing, advertising, corporations, and proprietary design firms, studios, and offices.

1. **The managerial level**, where jobs may or may not involve hands-on design work in addition to the oversight of the designers:

> Creative Director
> Design Director
> Corporate Art Director
> Creative Service Manager
> Design Manager
> Brand Strategist

2. **The creative or design level**, which involves directly serving clients. These titles embody different responsibilities depending on the organizational hierarchy of particular business:

> Senior Designer
> Designer
> Senior Art Director
> Art Director
> Graphics Editor

3. **The support level**, which involves working directly with the seniors in both design and production capacities:

> Junior Designer
> Assistant Designer
> Deputy Art Director
> Associate Art Director
> Assistant Art Director
> Production Artist
> Art Associate

4. **Entry level**:

> Assistant Designer
> Junior Designer
> Intern

(This category is temporary—a stepping stone, perhaps—and is often unpaid.)

NEW JOBS

Since this book was first published, Interaction Design has become a dominant career choice for designers. Although communication is the common denominator between the graphic design and interaction designer, there are profound differences. For more detailed information see *Becoming a Digital Designer* by Steven Heller and David Womack (Wiley, 2004). In addition to familiar titles, like "art director," new jobs in this field include the following:

> Service Designer
> Web Designer
> Information Architect
> Interaction Designer
> Freelance

Freelancers, as opposed to principals of proprietary studios or firms, do not manage businesses with additional employees (although they may hire assistants as needed). They often take on individual, finite freelance projects either on the premises of the client or in their own studios. Freelancers usually do not use titles but rather advertise themselves as "Jane Doe, Graphic Designer," or "John Doe, Design Production."

MILTON GLASER | On Being an Influence

Graphic Designer, Milton Glaser, Inc., New York City

Many of the designers we interviewed for this book mentioned you and your work as an influence on them. This is a big responsibility. How do you see your influence on the design community?

Any practitioner wants to be influential, fundamentally. I've always seen myself as someone who worked in the realm of ideas and who was susceptible to influence. My own practice is one where I consciously try to absorb and be influenced by many of my experiences, so the idea of influence and being influential is important to me. My entire vocabulary, you might say, could be analyzed as a series of influences. The idea is being in the stream of artistic ideas, as someone who sees himself not so much as somebody who has a private vision but rather who is in the stream and who wants to continue that stream, and who wants to participate in disseminating ideas. I imagine it's the same impulse that keeps me teaching. The idea of teaching is basically for students to see themselves as part of the continuity of ideas and visual history, rather than as a deviation from that. So if, in fact, I have been influential, it's extremely pleasing to me.

What were your early influences?

One of the big influences was the comic strip. The comics were our academy, in effect. Drawing from

life casts is what we would have been doing if we were growing up as an art student in Europe—but we copied the comic strips. Most of the American artists that I have talked to—of a certain generation, obviously—whether they ended up as painters or illustrators or interior designers, got their start copying the comics. And the comics were, in fact, one of the most profound influences, in many ways. One influence, I'm quite sure, is the idea that comics were linked to narration; two, they had a particular sense of form, sort of a bounded form, designed in black and white, and then filled in with color—they were graphic rather than tonal. Particularly things like *Dick Tracy*, *Terry and the Pirates*, and certainly *L'il Abner*, and even to some extent, *Mickey Mouse*—all those were, I would say, in terms of early influence, very strong elements.

Your work encompasses many areas of design. Did you have a plan early in your career to cross all these disciplines?

No. When I started, my greatest objective was to be a comic strip artist. That's all I wanted to be when I was a kid. Then I went to the High School of Music and Art, and there I awakened to the idea of both painting and design. By the time I left Music and Art to go to the Cooper Union, I knew

TITLE: *Experience Uncoated*
DESIGNER/ILLUSTRATOR: *Milton Glaser*
COMPANY: *Milton Glaser, Inc.*
CLIENT: *Fraser Papers*
YEAR: *1998*

TITLE: *Brooklyn Brewery*
DESIGNER: *Milton Glaser*
COMPANY: *Milton Glaser, Inc.*
CLIENT: *Brooklyn Brewery*
TYPEFACES: *Copper Plate Gothic, hand-lettering*

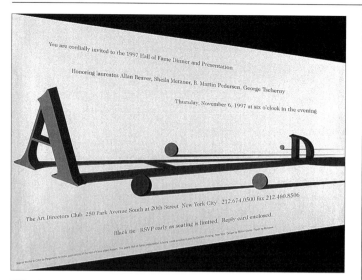

TITLE: Art Directors Club Invitation DESIGNER: Milton Glaser COMPANY: Milton Glaser, Inc.
CLIENT: Art Directors Club YEAR: 1997

TITLE:
Trattoria Dell
'Arte
(restaurant)
DESIGNER:
Milton Glaser
COMPANY:
Milton Glaser,
Inc.
CLIENT:
Sheldon Fireman
YEAR: 1988

TITLE: Picasso
DESIGNER/
ILLUSTRATOR:
Milton Glaser
COMPANY:
Milton Glaser,
Inc. CLIENT:
New York Times
Book Review
YEAR: 1996

there was this thing called design and another called typography. By the time I got into Cooper I was already interested in those things. Then at Cooper I got a pretty good foundation in sculpture and architecture and so on.

After all your years in this art and craft, what would you say is the most important concern upon entering the design field?
A real question for many of us, if we have an artistic vision, is how to reconcile our sense of artistry and the pleasure we get from making things with the demands of a business that very often is not interested in that. So the advice I would give somebody is to think in the long run because if you have a long career—it can span thirty, forty, fifty years—you have to think of what will sustain you and keep you interested for that length of time. One of the great problems of being a designer is that you get parochialized and you find yourself increasingly narrowed, doing more and more specialized things that you've done a hundred times before. For me, the way out was to broaden the canvas, to try to do things that I was not very experienced doing, to try to develop a range of activities so that I couldn't be forced into a corner and left to dry. While that is not the solution for everyone, that is a consideration people must at least examine before they embark on a course, for once they have mastered the professional requirement it may no longer have any interest in it for them.

What skills and attributes are ideal in an employee?

"I like to be able to take employees to see clients and know that they have already done their research without me having to ask. I want to work with people who listen well, who can explain their work clearly and who can also stand up and sell it."

— Raquel Tudela

"The intellectual honesty to work until the work is right. They also must like dogs and babies."

— Josh Liberson

"GREAT TALENT. GREAT THINKING. GREAT SENSE OF HUMOR. LITTLE EGO."

— Noreen Morioka

"I always look for people who are not only good communicators—people who can talk and write intelligently about their work—but also people who can manage themselves. I have little interest in being anyone's keeper, so I expect anyone I work with to be responsible for their portion of a project."

— Jason Santa Maria

"I LOOK FOR IMAGINATION, A SENSE OF THE ABSURD AND BEAUTIFUL, AND AN INTEREST IN WORDS, BOOKS, AND WRITERS."

— Leanne Shapton

"Intelligence, ideas, self-sufficiency, speed, and an understanding that design is a service-oriented business and not an art project."

— Ethan Trask

"Eagerness, willingness; 'raw' and 'proven' talent. 'Raw' because that's where you can anticipate and dream of someone's potential, this might come in the form of sketchbooks or experimental work; nothing is better than seeing a talent flourish under your watch. 'Proven' because you want to see real examples of smart thinking and ability to solve nearly any problem."

— Michael J. Walsh

"Not only do they need to be talented, they need to carry with them hunger, drive, and optimism, to rebound quickly from an idea that goes nowhere and get to the idea that will deliver everything." — Rodrigo Corral

"I look for a thirst for making. I love to see a designer who can't help but design. I also tend to look for designers with varied backgrounds. When a person has a wider life experience, I think that comes through their design ideas. Thirdly, organization is very, very important. Being able to keep within a studio's workflow, file conventions, communication patterns, etc. can make a huge difference in how smoothly a project unfolds."
— *Randy J. Hunt*

"TOP FOUR: AN UNDERSTANDING OF TYPOGRAPHY, THE ABILITY TO CREATE SOMETHING OUT OF NOTHING, A SENSE OF HUMOR, AND BEING ABLE TO COMMUNICATE WELL VERBALLY AND IN WRITING. NOT NECESSARILY IN THAT ORDER."
— *Criswell Lappin*

"We hired our current designer because he seemed to have the right combination of raw talent and drawing ability, mixed with a general curiosity about type and graphic design and a respect for the craft of type design. He was also someone we thought we could get along with on a personal level." — *Christian Schwartz*

"In our office we need open minds. People that are willing to try something they've never attempted before. And when it doesn't work, they try again and again." — *Sam Eckersley*

"Curious, and interested in the world; an instinct for design and design thinking; a great sense of typography; self-motivated; able to communicate clearly to me, fellow employees and to our clients; a willingness to take on any task; relaxed, with a sense of humor. "
— *Mark Randall*

"Passion, curiosity, and a desire for a well-rounded understanding of the world. Also, being able to play an instrument really fast and loud helps." — *Jean-Marc Troadec*

"There are really two types of graphic designers I have found I need in a team. First is the image-maker. This person has to be incredibly productive and restless. Someone who can come up with ten completely different directions in a couple of hours even though there might be a million typos and no real thought to the details of how this would be executed across an entire project. This person is like the id of a design team. I try to protect them from editing or tedious assignments and just let them rip. The second type of designer is the 'system' or 'type' designer. This person can take twenty half-finished things and make them all look good and solid and cohesive. This takes a level of maturity and people like this are generally good at larger projects like books and identity systems. They are like the super-ego of the design team."
— *Dmitri Siegel*

"An employee needs to keep a strong interest in the design profession and in trends and technological developments constantly affecting our work. " — *Tarek Atrissi*

"PASSION, DESIRE, AND AN ABILITY TO LEARN BY OBSERVATION AND PRACTICE." — *Craig Frazier*

THINK LON

TITLE: *Think London* DESIGNERS:
Michael Johnson, Julia Woollams
DESIGN FIRM: Johnson Banks CLIENT:
Think London YEAR: 2004–2005

M ost art schools wisely teach graphic design as a general practice, the theory being that the orchestration of type and image, whether on paper or screen, is always based on the same fundamental formal principles. Different media, however, have different requirements. Editorial design is not the same as advertising; advertising is not the same as book design. Each has a unique focus and target. In most cases, the tools are similar but the methodologies are not.

Many graphic designers perform a broad range of tasks, switching media as clients and jobs demand. A designer cannot always afford to specialize because the volume of work in a specialty may not warrant it or competition may be too intense. Therefore, it is prudent at the outset of a career to learn about and practice all the disciplines that strike your interest and fancy as well as those that are growth areas for employment. Although it is not necessary to be expert in everything, it is useful to be fluent in as many forms as possible, at least while you are looking for a career niche.

SECTION 1

Design Specialties

How is this accomplished? For those bound for art school, there may be no choice. The average design program provides instruction in the basics while spotlighting specialties such as magazine layout, book and record covers, posters, advertising, and Web design in order to provide students with a well-rounded professional portfolio. Once out of school, however, specialization usually calls. If you are hired by a general design firm, exposure to a variety of disciplines is very likely. But if you are hired by an in-house art/design department, specialization is inevitable.

A junior designer at a design firm usually assists on different aspects of various projects, from annual reports to brochures to Web pages. Even if you do not feel entirely confident with a particularly new medium, never refuse an opportunity—in fact, volunteer for as much extra duty as possible within the limits of monetary remuneration (learn as much as you can, but do not allow yourself to become financially exploited in the process).

A junior designer at an in-house corporate or business art/design department is often given a single task. While it is important to build expertise in whatever field this may be, it is also consequential to expand your potential knowledge base. If possible, volunteer for additional jobs that depart from your basic assignment. If the company art department has several divisions, such as print, Web, and exhibition, attempt to assist outside your own area; there is a very good chance you will be given the opportunity to do so.

This advice is not aimed exclusively at neophytes. Experienced designers must also continually broaden their range of expertise, if only to thwart impending obsolescence. For example, when digital technology entered the realm of graphic design, many dedicated print designers turned their attention toward CD-ROM and Internet opportunities. A few enrolled in graduate schools to get more intensive training; others gave up senior print jobs to apprentice or assist others already working in the digital arena. Moving from print to electronic media is not the only possible career change. Many designers who fall into a specialty without previous exposure elsewhere want new challenges and so switch from, say, advertising to editorial, perhaps accepting a lower position to get on-the-job training until achieving proficiency in the new discipline.

Ultimately, the majority of designers pick a specialty (or specialties) and stick with it (them) until the learning curve flattens out or the projects become routine. Of course, depending on their comfort level, some designers spend their entire lives in one job either moving up the corporate hierarchy or, if content with the status quo, remaining at the same basic level. Everyone's ambition is individual and depends on personal needs, wants, drive, and ability. If one hungers for creative challenges, then general practice is preferred; if one longs for consistency, then specialization is a good option.

Your decision to practice in a specific discipline should be considered thoughtfully. While it is true that many designers stumble into a specialty simply because a particular job is available to them, others carefully reconnoiter the job market for the position that most appeals to their passion or interest. Then there is the hip factor: Some job seekers simply want to be hired by the hippest firms—MTV and Nickelodeon Networks rate high among that demographic. There is nothing wrong with this goal—except, of course, that you must be aware that these sought-after companies receive hundreds of applications for comparatively few openings.

It is axiomatic that more is much better than less knowledge, which means that it is important to know what disciplines are available, what they require of a prospective candidate, and how to apply for the job. This section examines genres that hire the greatest number of graphic designers and offers basic information concerning the nature of each at the entry and senior levels. Becoming a graphic designer in any of these showcased disciplines is based on skill and accomplishment—graphic design is nothing if not a meritocracy. When your portfolio is professional (no loose or disorganized scraps of paper), well edited (the number of pieces is limited to the few that show how proficient you are), and smartly paced (showing that you know how

to make ideas appear dynamic), then you have a greater likelihood of influencing a prospective employer, if not for the job being considered, then for other possibilities and referrals. Even if you don't get the job, it is important to make a positive impression

IF ONE HUNGERS FOR CREATIVE CHALLENGES, THEN GENERAL PRACTICE IS PREFERRED; IF ONE LONGS FOR CONSISTENCY, THEN SPECIALIZATION IS A GOOD OPTION.

so that you are remembered for future positions.

Knowing the field is one important way to maximize your chances of entering it. Each specialty has unique needs and wants. Job candidates who desire to make a good impression should design a portfolio that indicates interest, and at least a modicum of expertise, in the selected area.

1. EDITORIAL

FACTS AND FIGURES issued by the United States Department of Labor are sketchy about exactly which medium is the largest employer of graphic designers. Nonetheless, it is a sound assumption that magazines and newspapers give opportunities to a large percentage of junior and senior designers and art directors.

Within a magazine or newspaper infrastructure, design duties are often divided into two fundamental groups: editorial and promotion. The latter, which administers advertising and publicity, including the conception and design of ads, billboards, and collateral materials such as advertising rate cards, subscription campaigns, and promotional booklets and brochures, may be large or small, depending on the priorities of the specific company. The former, however, is the creative heart of an institution. Editorial designers are the people who give the publication its aura, image, and format. And yet the editorial art department is configured differently from publication to publication, so it is not always possible for a job candidate to know the makeup of specific departments before interviewing for a job (which may or may not help anyway). The following are typical scenarios that illustrate the variety of editorial opportunities.

MAGAZINES

Magazines come in various shapes, sizes, and frequencies. In any given year, thousands are published on such a wide range of subjects that it is difficult to list them all here. The quality of their design also ranges widely from high to low, with a great deal in between. While this book is not a critical guide to design quality, one important part of any professional equation is indeed the publication's design standard. Does the publisher expect the highest and most rigorous quality or merely competent work? The evidence is usually clear from the look of the magazine itself. The job seeker should decide whether working for a particular publication is going to enhance or detract from future prospects—and from compiling good portfolio samples. Of course, this is ultimately a personal decision. Sometimes acquiring experience is more important than any other concern; sometimes working on the best not only encourages the best but results in greater opportunities later.

Design positions at magazines are frequently available for all experience levels. The intense and constant work flow that goes into periodical design and production demands many participants. A typical hierarchy begins at the top with a *design director* or *art director*, who manages the overall design department and design of the magazine, including the format (which either he or an outside design consultant originally designed); this may include overseeing the work of senior and junior page designers and designing pages and covers himself. It may also involve assigning illustration, photography, and typography. (When the budget allows, custom typefaces are also commissioned.) In addition, the art director is involved in meetings with editors (and sometimes authors) concerning article presentation. Some of these duties are invariably delegated to a deputy or *associate art director*, who does many of the same design tasks as the art director and also may manage, depending on the workload. The deputy or associate may be on a track to move into the art director's position, should it open, or, after acquiring the requisite experience, move on to an art director position at another magazine.

On the next-lower level, *senior* and *junior designers* are responsible for designing components of a magazine (features, columns, inserts, etc.). Some design entire spreads or pages and commission the artwork and photography; others design elements of a feature and use the illustrations supplied to them by the art director or the deputy. Some are better typographers than users of art. The difference between senior and junior is usually the degree of experience and talent. The former may have been a junior first or may have been hired directly as a senior from another

THE CASE OF THE DEFAULT ART DIRECTOR

In the art department of small publications, such as a neighborhood newspaper, it is possible to rise from production artist to art director in a short time. A veteran art director relates his phenomenal accession: "I was hired right out of high school for what I thought would be a summer job as a mechanical artist for a small New York newspaper. Within a month, after the art director taught me the job—at that time, doing pasteups—he was hired to be the art director of a larger, more prestigious magazine. With barely two weeks' notice, I was plunged into the role of art director while the publisher looked for a replacement. I don't know why, but fortuitously, no good applicants emerged and by default I was given the job. It was an incredible experience—a frightening one, too, as I knew absolutely nothing about art direction. But I was forced to learn very quickly.

I remained art director for a year, until the newspaper folded, by which time I was hooked on publication design. I decided not to continue with my liberal arts studies at college, briefly enrolled in art school, and continued to get increasingly better art directorial jobs at magazines and newspapers."

job; the latter is often right out of school or was an intern while a student. Based on achievement, a senior or junior designer can be promoted to a deputy or associate position. There are no codified rules of acceleration other than merit and need. Therefore, it is not impossible for a junior to be so professionally adept that promotion to the next level is fairly swift. Conversely, merely competent progress in a job is rarely rewarded.

The junior designer position is often at the entry level. Some magazines have additional entry-level jobs, such as unpaid *interns* or paid *assistants* who do less critical, yet nevertheless necessary, support work. The most common task is production, such as scanning images into the computer or maintaining electronic files; occasionally, a minimal amount of layout or design work on tightly formatted pages may be assigned. In addition, the intern or assistant is invariably required to act as a gofer, attending to all the odd jobs that need to be done. This is actually a critical juncture for the wannabe because an employer can measure the relative competence or excellence of a worker. Even the lowliest job can result in significant advancement.

The art department is only one nerve junction of a magazine. In some environments, it is on a par with the editorial department (editors and writers), while in others it is the handmaiden. The relative importance of art and design is often linked to the comparative strength and power of the design or art director. Whatever the hierarchy, it is important that editorial designers (at any level) be aware of the editorial process—not merely the schedule but the editorial philosophy of the magazine. Too many bad relationships between design and editorial departments exist because their missions are not in sync. The two

THE INTENSE AND CONSTANT WORK FLOW THAT GOES INTO PERIODICAL DESIGN AND PRODUCTION DEMANDS MANY PARTICIPANTS.

departments must complement each other; achieving this is one of the jobs of the design or art director. But even the lowest-level designer must have a precise understanding of what is being editorially communicated in order for the design to not only carry but enhance the content of the publication.

NEWSPAPERS

Although financial analysts report that, due to fierce competition with television and online services, newspapers are currently a faltering industry, nonetheless there is an increased demand for art directors, designers, graphics editors, and production personnel at newspapers today. The reasons are fairly simple. Once many newspapers (afternoon, morning, and evening editions) competed in the same locales for the same readership and advertisers. That number has been radically reduced (for example, from their peak in the 1950s, New York City's dailies have been reduced from twelve to three). In most cases, this means that the remaining few papers are larger in size and offer more extensive coverage. In addition, over the past two decades, newspapers have augmented hard news with soft news features, such as lifestyle and home sections. At the same time, printing technology has significantly advanced to allow more innovative visual display (including full-color reproduction). In the past, newspaper composition was carried out by editorial makeup persons who were not trained as artists or designers; today, art directors and designers are responsible for the basic look and feel of the average newspaper.

Another paradox that makes newspapers a welcoming job market is the precipitous decline in the number of art directors and designers specifically trained for this medium. Despite the newspaper's ubiquity, few art schools and colleges offer courses dedicated to its design. If they exist at all, they are folded into a general publication design curriculum. Many who work in newspaper design departments never formally studied the discipline in school classes—they came through school newspapers, internships/apprenticeships, or junior or senior design positions at magazines—hence the current demand for designers exclusively trained in the newspaper environment. Various journalism schools have started news design courses, but getting a newspaper job and learning from hands-on experience is still a viable option at the entry-level stage.

Over the past decade, news-papers have introduced new job categories unique to this industry. One notable entry is the graphics editor, a hybrid of editor and designer, who is responsible for the information graphics (charts, graphs, and maps) that appear regularly in most newspapers. This new sub-genre has become essential to contemporary newspaper content.

The newspaper industry has distinct hierarchies, but each newspaper has different jobs and job descriptions; the following are typical. Beginning at the entry level, the best way to start is as an *intern*. All newspapers employ seasonal (usually paid) interns as junior copypersons, who act as assistants-in-training to the various news desks. Likewise, the art department (which is often under the wing of the news department) employs a design intern to work directly with designers or art directors. The *New York Times*, for example, hires one intern a year for a ten-week stint. Often, art department interns are selected from art schools or universities with publication design programs (the candidates need not have had newspaper experience, although some newspaper work is a definite advantage). The tasks given the intern vary depending on the publication; one newspaper may offer intensive training in design, production, and information graphics, while another may have the intern do gofer work (scanning, making copies, or whatever clerk-like tasks are necessary). Internships sometimes lead to permanent employment; some-

CONTINUING EDUCATION

A certain amount of design know-how can be obtained by osmosis on the job. The ambitious neophyte who lands a production job at a periodical is in an excellent position to learn practical skills as well as the procedures involved in that specific publication. But the likelihood of promotion to a design job is minimal without additional design experience. One way to convince an employer that your ambition should be rewarded is to enroll in continuing education classes specializing in publication design. Most art schools and some colleges offer intermediate and advanced courses. Some are under the desktop publishing umbrella; others are components of broader graphic design programs. Most classes of this kind are at night, but some of the larger art schools offer intensive editorial design workshops during the summer months. Supplementing on-the-job experience with classroom instruction pays off in the long run.

TITLE: Student on a Half Shell Visual Arts Press
CLIENT: School of Visual Arts Billboard (proposed)
ART DIRECTOR/DESIGNER: Michael J. Walsh
CREATIVE DIRECTOR: Anthony P. Rhodes
PHOTOGRAPHERS: Carolyn De Riso, Michael Visconti YEAR: 2008

times they do not. An internship is a kind of test for an employer to ascertain how well an individual fits, professionally and personally, into a specific art department.

The next level is usually more permanent. If a newspaper has *junior designer* or *design assistant* positions, these are often full-time jobs with various responsibilities. The experience necessary may be an internship at a newspaper or magazine or a junior position, preferably at a newspaper. Regardless of experience, juniors may be hired on the formal and conceptual strength of the portfolio.

Every newspaper art department is organized differently, so the assistant in one may work closely with the senior designer or art director actually designing some of the pages of a hard or soft news section, or the junior may assist many designers in the daily process, which might include doing routine production chores (such as electronic mechanical, color preparation, and photo processing). The degree of responsibility is based on the volume of work *and* the art director's desire to delegate.

In many newspapers, the junior or assistant is a union job, which means that salary, benefits, etc., are governed and job security is ensured by the union contract. Membership in a guild or union is mandatory at this level, and the security offered is both good and bad—good for the obvious reasons and bad because it encourages people to stay in their jobs for a long time, which is not always

FREELANCERS ALWAYS WANTED

Most magazines and newspapers hire freelance designers and support personnel to meet excess creative and production needs. Over the past fifteen years, freelance employees have become prevalent throughout the publishing industries, especially because seasonal shifts in editorial emphasis (special issues and sections) add to the workload. Freelancers are hired to do secondary design and production tasks, and skilled freelance designers are often assigned to work on primary components of a publication. For the junior, this kind of work is experientially important; for the senior, it can be creatively (and financially) beneficial. Freelance assignments can be either long- or short-term and are perfect for designers who are not yet, or have no desire to be, committed to any specific discipline. Most freelancers work in the art department of the publication on their equipment.

THE TECHNIQUES OF GRAPHIC DESIGN CAN BE LEARNED, BUT THE INSTINCT FOR MAKING ART NEEDS TO BE NURTURED OVER TIME.

good for creativity. In fact, in many union shops there is so little movement that the junior may be stuck with the same title for an excessively long time—and this is an important consideration in joining a newspaper art department.

The next job designation is senior designer or art director. (In some newspapers the title *graphics editor* is also given to those who design hard and soft news sections.) Experience required is almost always a periodical design job, whether as a junior or a senior at a magazine or newspaper. Designers without this experience or training are rarely qualified. Nonetheless, opportunities exist in locales where few newspaper or magazine design specialists are found. The responsibilities vary depending on the size of the newspaper. An art director may design a specific section of a newspaper, assign the illustration and photography, and design the so-called dress or feature pages. (An *assistant designer* or, at many newspapers, a makeup editor, may design the more routine pages.) The senior designer or art director works with text editors, picture editors, and graphics editors (when that designation applies only to information graphics). Usually, a production person or production editor works in concert with the senior designer to translate the design layouts into a final electronic or mechanical form. The senior designer may work on one or more sections of a newspaper; at a small paper, the job may involve many subject areas.

Parallel to the senior designer or art director is the *graphics editor* responsible for information graphics. The experience required is a combination of reporting and graphic expertise. In many instances, the prospective candidate must pass a test that determines news judgment and editing skills as well as the ability to consolidate raw data into accessible visual form. The requirements are no less rigorous than for designers and, in fact, are more complex because of the intersection of news and art disciplines. In some newspapers, this job involves page design; in others it is limited to information design alone. The graphics editor works with the news and feature editors, who decide on the daily news report, to conceive and shape a particular graphic presentation. The graphics editor coordinates work with the senior designer in order to achieve a seamless overall page design. For those who are interested in typography, graphics, and research and reporting, this is a wide-open area in which to seek employment.

The top level at a newspaper is called the *design director*, *senior*

art director, *senior graphics editor*, or, in some places, the *managing editor for design*, who is supported by a *deputy*, *assistant*, or *managing design director*. Extensive experience is required for this job, including the administration and management skills needed to oversee a staff of designers and production personnel. The design director is usually responsible for maintain-

THE SENIOR DESIGNER MAY WORK ON ONE OR MORE SECTIONS OF A NEWSPAPER; AT A SMALL PAPER, THE JOB MAY INVOLVE MANY SUBJECT AREAS.

ing the overall design quality and is often the original designer of the formats within which senior designer and art directors work. Sometimes the design director has a hands-on role in the design of special features, but often the demands of a newsroom require that such work be delegated to others under watchful supervision.

Newspaper design is essentially different from magazine design.

First, it is expressed on a larger scale—more editorial components must be balanced on the broadsheet pages. Second, it occurs at a different frequency—the luxury of a weekly or monthly magazine deadline allows for more detail work, whereas at a daily newspaper, little time is available for the nuances of design. Third, the production values are not as high—working with newsprint on Web-offset presses does not allow for the fine printing common to most glossy magazines. And yet the newspaper is every bit as challenging and offers equal creative possibilities for the designer who is interested, indeed passionate, about editorial work. While one can use a newspaper job as a stepping stone to other job opportunities, a majority of newspaper designers find that this medium provides a good place to build a career.

TITLE: Visual Arts Journal *Visual Arts Press* CLIENT: *School of Visual Arts* ART DIRECTOR/DESIGNER: *Michael J. Walsh* CREATIVE DIRECTOR: *Silas H. Rhodes* YEAR: *2005*

Entry Level

Most entry-level portfolios include a large percentage of school assignments, often one or two redesigns of existing magazines or fantasy magazines. This work exhibits original thinking unfettered by the constraints of a real job, and yet the solutions are realistic. The editorial portfolio should include mostly editorial work, but general samples (posters, brochures, letterheads) are useful to gauge typography and layout skills.

CONTENTS

Ten to twenty samples:

  a. Feature pages and spread designs (showing range of stylistic and conceptual thinking)
  b. Cover designs (showing two or three logo and illustration approaches)
  c. Department pages (to show how routine editorial material is designed)
  d. Two to four noneditorial examples

TITLE: Once There Was a Way… *by Harry Benson CLIENT: Harry N. Abrams CREATIVE DIRECTOR/DE-SIGNER: Michael J. Walsh PHOTOG-RAPHER: Harry Benson YEAR: 2003*

Junior/Senior Designer

By this stage, portfolios should include a large percentage of published work. The junior may continue to include school projects, but the senior should jettison them. The samples should be of high quality. Not everything in print rates showing in a portfolio. Through these samples, the important thing is to show your taste, talent, and expertise.

CONTENTS

Fifteen to twenty-five samples:

  a. Feature pages and spreads from published periodicals
  b. Cover designs (if available)
  c. Examples of illustration and photograph assignments (if available)
  d. Department pages (if available)
  e. Two noneditorial examples

Format

35mm slides (in tray) are still applicable, but increasingly this method is being phased out in favor of CD and DVD in the following formats: Flash, PowerPoint, and iPhoto. Online portfolios are also encouraged. Avoid digital tricks. Keep the presentation as straightforward as possible. Anything that crashes the viewer's computer will hamper appreciation of your work.

TITLE: Curiosa: Celebrity Relics, Historical Fossils, and Other Meta-morphic Rubbish *by Barton Lidice Benes CLIENT: Harry N. Abrams CREATIVE DIRECTOR/DESIGNER: Michael J. Walsh ARTIST: Barton Lidice Benes PHOTOG-RAPHER: David Corio YEAR: 2002*

CRISWELL LAPPIN | Collaborate as Much as Possible

Design Director, *Metropolis*, New York City

How long have you been a graphic designer/art director?

I started undergraduate studies in 1990 and finished graduate school in 1997, so nineteen years if you count school, twelve if you don't. I have been the head of the *Metropolis* art department for about ten years.

What are the changes in practice (and form) you have seen and experienced since you began?

My first design projects were made on a stat camera with cut paper and gluestick. My first year at *Metropolis* [2000] almost all our art was submitted in hard copy form, now I might get ten pieces a year like that. Most everything is done onscreen. Except generating the ideas.

How have these changes impacted your work?

It has made access to imagery and artist easier. More work is expected faster. Technologies have expanded the definition and capabilities of design—for both good and bad.

Would you say that you have a particular style or character to your design? If so, how would you define it?

I hope what I do responds to content in an engaging and accessible way. Since I am not always the right person to design everything, part of the character of what I do is determined by who I choose to work with. That is the part I find most engaging.

What about graphic design is the most challenging for you?

The word *graphic*. That word defines what we do to the uninitiated, but I find it limiting and superficial. Once you figure out how to design beyond the boundaries of "graphics" or the surface, then I think the potential for being productive expands.

What are the projects that most satisfy your aesthetic sense?

The projects where many people contributed to a solution that helped solve a problem.

How important is type and typography in what you do?

Crucial. Most of the work I do centers around a magazine, which the editors generally like people to be able to read.

What, in this current technological and economic climate, does the future hold for you specifically, and graphic design in general?

Graphic designers should look to collaborate as much as possible, not only with others in design and arts-related fields, but with smart people in general. Make yourself indispensable through knowledge and broaden your skill set.

TITLE: *Rural Studio Builds the $20,000 House*, Metropolis *Cover* CREATIVE DIRECTOR: *Criswell Lappin* ART DIRECTOR: *Dungjai Pungauthaikan* PHOTOGRAPHER: *Timothy Hursley* YEAR: *2009*

TITLE: *Pinning Our Hopes on Wind*, Metropolis *Cover* CREATIVE DIRECTOR: *Criswell Lappin* ART DIRECTOR: *Dungjai Pungauthaikan* DESIGNERS: *Brian Collins, John Fulbrook III, Timothy Goodman, Jason Nutall* YEAR: *2009*

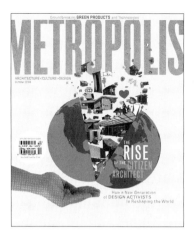

TITLE: *The Rise of the Citizen Architect*, **Metropolis** *Cover*
CREATIVE DIRECTOR: *Criswell Lappin*
ART DIRECTOR: *Dungjai Pungauthaikan*
ILLUSTRATOR: *Christopher Ro*
YEAR: *2008*

TITLE: *A Look Inside*, **Metropolis** *Cover*
CREATIVE DIRECTORS: *Criswell Lappin, Erich Nagler*
PHOTOGRAPHER: *Albert Vecerka/Esto*
YEAR: *2007*

TITLE: *What Is Good Design*, **Metropolis** *Cover*
CREATIVE DIRECTOR: *Criswell Lappin* ART DIRECTOR: *Dungjai Pungauthaikan*
DESIGNERS: *SpotCo, Gail Anderson, Jeff Rogers, Amanda Spielman* YEAR: *2009*

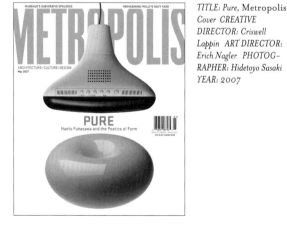

TITLE: *Pure*, **Metropolis** *Cover* CREATIVE DIRECTOR: *Criswell Lappin* ART DIRECTOR: *Erich Nagler* PHOTOG-RAPHER: *Hidetoyo Sasaki* YEAR: *2007*

TITLE: *Dubai Rising*, **Metropolis** *Cover* CREATIVE DIRECTOR: *Criswell Lappin* ART DIRECTOR: *Dungjai Pungauthaikan* PHOTOGRAPHER: *Nousha Salimi* YEAR: *2007*

Designing the Story

Former Art Director, OP-ED Page, *The New York Times*, New York City

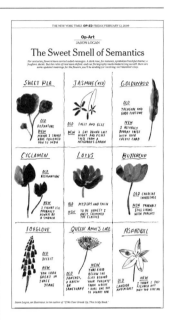

TITLE: *Valentine's Day* CLIENT: The New York Times DESIGNER: *Leanne Shapton* ART DIRECTOR: *Leanne Shapton* ILLUSTRATOR/PHOTOGRAPHER: *Jason Logan* YEAR: *2009*

» How long have you been working as an art director?

On and off for ten years.

What are the changes in practice you have seen and experienced since you began?

When I began illustrators were still sending finals and sketches via courier and fax, now everything is done entirely over email. Also, the editors I work with have become more design savvy, knowing what is possible within a short amount of time. In terms of content, Google Image and photoshop technology have also expedited the research and execution processes. I've seen an increase in the use of photography and text in illustrations. In some ways I think people are reading things more, and differently, and reading faster.

How have these changes impacted your work?

Due to the velocity of email and scanning, I tend to see more sketches, which is a good thing. Sometimes someone will send the genius germ of a half-baked idea which, with collaboration, can be quickly turned into a solution. I think emails have loosened up the process and allowed for more collaborative and cooperative work. Also, I can get a final very easily from an illustrator halfway around the world.

Would you say that you have a particular style or character to your design? If so, how would you define it?

Visually I favor really strong, dark line work, or something that has a narrative line-through. I like when illustrators can both write and draw. As I'm limited by time, fonts, and word counts I don't have too much room to design on the page—though often the more limitations I have the better I work. Sometimes, if I can, I let the illustrator's sketch dictate how the image is paired with the text. Or try to do something to help the reading of text. I might define it as [making it] "more readerly."

What are the projects that most satisfy your aesthetic sense?

I like content-driven work where the design and story work simultaneously. This is why I like book covers, contributors who can both write and draw, and the op-arts that I get to do on the op-ed page. I don't like very passive, overly decorative or mood-driven work.

How important is type and typography in what you do?

I love it when someone solves an illustration problem with type. Sometimes this stymies the editors, but often it helps sharpen the point and plays off of a different kind of thinking, sort of a reading illustration—where, in

TITLE: *Economy Stimulus* CLIENT: The New York Times ART DIRECTOR: *Leanne Shapton* ILLUSTRATOR: *August Heffner* YEAR: *2008*

TITLE: Saturday Night *Magazine Covers* CLIENT: National Post *ART DIRECTOR/ DESIGNER: Leanne Shapton ILLUSTRATORS/PHOTOGRAPHERS: Various - Christopher Woods, Jelle Wagenar, David Shrigley, Barbara Kruger, Nicholas Blechman YEAR: 2000–2002*

TITLE: Avenue *Pages Client: National Post ART DIRECTOR/DESIGNER: Leanne Shapton ILLUSTRATORS/PHOTOGRAPHERS: Various - Benoit, Blex Bolex, Seth, Emmanuel Pierre, Dave Eggers YEAR: 1998–2000*

the process of reading, you get the "get" rather than an imagined depiction of a concept.

What, in this current technological and economic climate, does the future hold for you specifically, and graphic design in general?

A consistent attention to graphic design has, I believe, helped me in this climate, as an understanding of "how" people read, rather than "what" or "where" they are reading, will help me figure out what to do next. I do believe magazines and newspapers have a limited life. I think opportunities for graphic design are increasing, there seems to be a sort of frontier quality to the media landscape, and so much can be improved in what we look at and experience online (and off, for that matter). The more choices we have the more we'll rely on thoughtful systems of priority and direction.

TITLE: Barbie Op-ed *CLIENT:* The New York Times *ART DIRECTOR/ DESIGNER: Leanne Shapton ILLUSTRATOR/PHOTOGRAPHER: Ruth Gwily YEAR: 2009*

MICHAEL J. WALSH | The Designer as Juggler

Art Director, School of Visual Arts Press, New York City

» What does it mean to be a graphic designer?

I've learned that to be a solid graphic designer you need to develop the skills to be involved in the editorial or content development to be able to consistently play a positive role or else you can simply be a victim of someone else's ideas. This is not always a bad thing, as I've had the great fortune to work with, learn from, and answer challenges from some of the best writers, editors, and creative directors. I've also had to step into that role in order to truly activate a project. I've learned how to produce the content, outline a strategy, rather than to take a hand-off and react to what's given to me. These capabilities build trust in others, trust that you can help solve problems with enlightened solutions.

Would you say that you have a particular style or character to your design?

No, not exactly. But I'd like to think that I bring a certain level of energy to my work. Each project usually has different circumstances that require very different kinds of solutions. Having a style can be helpful in some ways, when one is striving for consistency in developing a "look" for an ongoing project. But flexibility of thinking, and possession of a wide range of interests, would

make a reliance of a "style" sort of routine or less inspired... .

What about graphic design is the most challenging for you?

I tend to want to consider so many ways to solve something that I get off on tangents sometimes. This, and juggling lots of different types of projects. Trying to convince people of ideas, especially far-fetched ones. It's a challenge making every aspect of a project, from beginning to end, complete. Many times projects "sit" in a very close state of "near completion" and by the time it's finalized (shipped to a printer, files posted to a server, etc.) you start thinking of new ways to try something and then you worry if you explored enough.

What are the projects that most satisfy your aesthetic sense?

Books will always hold a special appeal for me, art books, unusual materials. Sometimes the consideration of all materials—binding, typography, ink, paper—is extremely satisfying, creating first a two-dimensional surface design that takes form as a three-dimensional object. The satisfaction of wrapping a new dust jacket design around a book dummy is wonderful!

How important is type and typography in what you do?

It's critical yet sometimes in different ways. Making type choices to start up a new publication serve a very different purpose than book jackets or posters. Sometimes I start with a type design and evolve the idea away from type alone and sometimes it's an idea that has very little to do with type. I think that many graphic designers get so caught up in typography issues that they end up creating very similar ideas to one another, since they may be choosing the popular typeface of the moment.

What, in this current technological and economic climate, does the future hold for you specifically, and graphic design in general?

Man, a loaded question. I think it's an opportunity personally for me to utilize my experiences to my advantage by being a "thoughtful" designer with many forms of media to express myself in. The economic forces make for some "thinking" on your feet, bending and questioning what you know into other creative ways to satisfy what is needed on a given project. It's time to be the one who has informed and unique ways to take design to a new level. Every one of us.

TITLE: War Scare—Nuclear Countdown after the Soviet Fall CLIENT: Turner Publishing Inc. ART DIRECTOR/DESIGNER: Michael J. Walsh YEAR: 1996

NOTE: Turner Publishing suspended publishing early 1997 and the rights to War Scare were sold; the book was eventually published in 1999 with a different cover.

TITLE: American Flags: Designs for a Young Nation by Nancy Druckman CLIENT: Harry N. Abrams DESIGNER: Allison Henry CREATIVE DIRECTOR: Michael J. Walsh YEAR: 2003

TITLE: Loving Picasso: The Private Journal of Fernande Olivier by Fernande Olivier, Afterword by John Richardson CLIENT: Harry N. Abrams CREATIVE DIRECTOR/ DESIGNER: Michael J. Walsh ARTIST: Artwork from Fernande Olivier's sketchbook YEAR: 2001

TITLE: Industry, Architecture, and Engineering: American Ingenuity 1750–1950 by Louis Bergeron and Maria Teresa Maiullari-Pontois CLIENT: Harry N. Abrams CREATIVE DIRECTOR/ DESIGNER: Michael J. Walsh YEAR: 2001

TITLE: Dear Dave—Issue 4 Visual Arts Press CLIENT: BFA Photography Department/Stephen Frailey, Editor-in-Chief ART DIRECTOR/DESIGNER: Michael J. Walsh CREATIVE DIRECTOR: Anthony P. Rhodes PHOTOGRAPHER: Daniel Weiss YEAR: 2008

TITLE: Sports Illustrated Cover CLIENT: Time Inc. ART DIRECTOR/ DESIGNER: Michael J. Walsh CREATIVE DIRECTOR: Steven Hoffman ILLUSTRATOR: Philip Burke YEAR: 1998

Design Director, GQ, New York City

>> **You have been art director for various magazines—*Texas Monthly*, *Rolling Stone*, and *GQ*. What determines how you design each one?**

It's primarily a response to the material, but all kinds of things play into it: What's my editor like? How much autonomy do I have? What's my staff like? How's the magazine doing? The most important job is to create a look for your book that is singular, its own. The worst thing possible would be to look like somebody else. This goal tends to set you off on a contrary path from the start. When I arrived at *GQ*, although long regarded as an industry leader, it was generally perceived to be "your father's magazine" and was losing readers and advertising. Nobody told me to make the magazine look younger; I just thought that's what was needed. I didn't go in thinking I was going to redesign, but as I tried to put the first issue together and make personal sense of what I was doing, understanding the content and structure of the book . . . well, I ended up changing that first issue completely. Michael Hainey, the executive editor, said it was like changing the tires on a moving vehicle.

With *GQ*, you've created a very distinctive design environment. What would you say is its most important trait?

Simplicity. The exercise I set for myself was to see how far I could strip it down—how simple could the page be and still be interest-

ing. After fourteen-plus years at *Rolling Stone*, I was eager for a fresh start. I didn't want to repeat myself. It wouldn't have been fair to either magazine. I was looking for something like reinvention and said at the time I was hoping to shed a skin. It was a little like being that newly divorced guy who finds himself moving from a comfortable, rambling Victorian (with lots of additions over the years) into a small, spartan, white box of an apartment. I was happy to throw everything away, even the stuff I loved most, in the hope of feeling lighter and for the chance to build something fresh and new.

Illustration and photography serve very different functions in your magazine. How would you describe the difference?

I have always considered myself a Champion for illustration, but I must admit here that *GQ* is a photo-driven magazine. In this company [Condé Nast], photography is king. Generally, if we can shoot somebody, we do. In addition to the commissioned portrait and fashion work, the product shots are sweated over, and great effort is put into photo research. Illustration is used to solve specific problems, and the choice of illustrator must mesh stylistically with the overall vibe of the magazine—masculine, modern, graphic, smart, sexy,

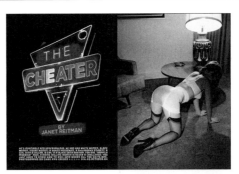

TITLE: The Cheater DESIGN DIRECTOR: Fred Woodward DESIGNER: Sarah Viñas PUBLICATION: GQ PHOTOGRAPHER: Chas Ray Krider PHOTO EDITOR: Bradley Young YEAR: 2004

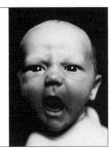

TITLE: Baby Einstein DESIGN DIRECTOR: Fred Woodward DESIGNER: Ken DeLago PUBLICATION: GQ PHOTOGRAPHER: Amy Arbus PHOTO EDITOR: Jennifer Crandall YEAR: 2004

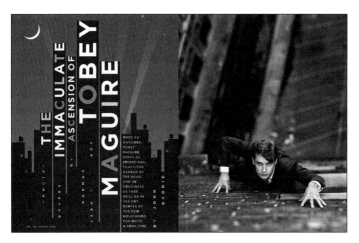

TITLE: Tobey Maguire DESIGN DIRECTOR: Fred Woodward DESIGNER: Paul Martinez
PUBLICATION: GQ PHOTOGRAPHER: Norma Jean Roy PHOTO EDITOR: Jennifer
Crandall YEAR: 2004

TITLE: Jamie Foxx DESIGN DIRECTOR: Fred Woodward DESIGNER: Ken
DeLago PUBLICATION: GQ PHOTOGRAPHER: Mark Seliger PHOTO
EDITOR: Bradley Young YEAR: 2004

TITLE: Chris Kattan
DESIGN DIRECTOR:
Fred Woodward
DESIGNER: Ken DeLago
PUBLICATION: GQ
PHOTOGRAPHER:
Mark Seliger PHOTO
EDITOR: Jennifer
Crandall YEAR: 2004

and sometimes funny. Illustrators like Christoph Neiman, Zohar Lazar, and Tavis Coburn are the prototypes for *GQ* at the moment.

You cannot design every page, so what are the most important components in *GQ* that you must design yourself?

Every page matters, but I have always been most interested in the design of the feature stories and the cover. I always work with the other designers. We are an ensemble cast, a design team. More than anything else about my job, I enjoy this collaboration. When the chemistry in a group like this is right, we are all better than anyone would be individually.

Given your strong design personality, what must an associate or assistant designer have that will make you want to hire them?

Well, it helps if they like my work. I'm most interested in chemistry—for myself and for the team as a whole. It's all about the exchange—someone who adds spark, personality, humor, intelligence. Generosity of spirit. A quick mind and a good heart; people I'd like to spend time with; a good work ethic. Hunger.

How do you find these people?

I rarely advertise an open position on my staff. It's usually word-of-mouth, a referral, or someone's portfolio I had seen when there was no opening. A couple of the best hires were the result of receiving a heartfelt letter. I like to promote from within, so I'm usually looking for the most junior position. I prize loyalty above everything else.

Something Out of Nothing

Principal, Frost Design, Sidney, Australia

>> **As a magazine designer, what do you think is the most important part of the design process?**

The most important thing for me is doing the right magazine. They take up a lot of your time, life, and energy, so it is important that you have infinity with the subject matter and the editorial team, especially the editor. I like to listen to the content, and I get the editor to tell me what each article is about, as often the article I need to start thinking of illustrating has not been commissioned or written.

What are the influences for your typographic styles?

I have always liked fairly bold typography. As I am constantly trying to make something out of nothing, I use typography to do most of the expression of the content. I try to create the magazine's aura, its look and feel. Fonts each have their own personality, and choosing them is an enjoyable process.

What determines what typefaces you use? Is it a personal aesthetic or a more rational decision?

I suppose for me it is an intuitive organic process. Once I know what the brief is and the kind of person it is aimed at, I start to play with the blank page. I start by playing with combinations of fonts, paper,

formats, rules, grids, hierarchy, images, pace, etc.

Can you learn how to be a magazine designer, or is it an instinctual process?

I learned how to do it mainly by being chucked in the deep end. I never have and still don't find it easy. Like all my other work outside of publishing, I go through the same process, and the way I work is definitely using my intuition. I am always aware that each and every dot of ink will be seen by hundreds of thousands of people. So I try to make the right decisions, as any mistake is seen all over the world.

What is the relationship between a magazine art director and an editor?

This relationship is the most important one for me. Magazines are stressful enough without having poor communications between the art director and the editor. You need to share the same vision and have mutual respect for each other's skills. My point of view is that it's my role to support and visualize the editor's vision.

What is the best way to become a magazine art director?

Make sure that is really what you want to do! I think the best thing is to try to get work experience in different publication companies that create magazines that

TITLE: The Independent *Magazine* *DESIGNER/CREATIVE DIRECTOR:* Vince Frost *STUDIO:* Frost Design *PHOTOGRAPHER:* Matthew Donaldson *CLIENT:* The Independent *YEAR: 1995*

TITLE: Zembla *Magazine, Issue 3* *DESIGNERS:* Vince Frost, Matt Willey (London), Anthony Donovan (Sydney), Tim Murphy (Melbourne) *CREATIVE DIRECTOR:* Vince Frost *STUDIO:* Frost Design *CLIENT:* Simon Finch Rare Books *YEAR: 2004*

TITLE: Zembla *Magazine, Issue 1 and Issue 2* DESIGNERS: *Vince Frost, Matt Willey (London), Anthony Donovan (Sydney), Tim Murphy (Melbourne)* CREATIVE DIRECTOR: *Vince Frost* STUDIO: *Frost Design* CLIENT: *Simon Finch Rare Books* YEAR: *2004*

interest you. There is no point getting stuck on a publication that you don't enjoy. Magazines are relentless and bloody hard. You work long stressful hours and your social life reduces to zip. The way that I work is outside that world, and we design the magazines that we work on in the studio. I believe that you can be more versatile when you work from or in a design studio. The variety of work keeps you fresh, and you don't get consumed in the world of publishing politics.

Perhaps I sound negative about my experience working on magazines. That is not the image I want to create. They are incredibly rewarding. I thrive on the pace, and the opportunity to play on the page is wonderful. I still get a buzz out of the whole process, and I can't wait each time to be the first person to hold the complete printed magazine, even knowing that I now have to go through the whole process again.

TITLE: Zembla *Magazine, Issue 3* DESIGNERS: *Vince Frost, Matt Willey (London), Anthony Donovan (Sydney), Tim Murphy (Melbourne)* CREATIVE DIRECTOR: *Vince Frost* STUDIO: *Frost Design* CLIENT: *Simon Finch Rare Books* YEAR: *2004*

Working for the Reader

Design Director, *The New York Times Magazine*, New York City

You've designed monthlies *[Spin and GQ]* and now a weekly magazine. Creatively speaking, what is the biggest difference between the two, other than time frame?

Starting on a weekly was incredibly intimidating at first, until I learned that it was a hell of a lot more organized then a monthly. With monthlies, editors have more time to make decisions, which inevitably means that the art department has about a week to design the issue. Therefore there is no difference, but creatively speaking you do not have as much time for experimentation. You have to make a decision and adhere to it. This can often work in your favor, considering that gut reactions are usually the best and most honest.

Obviously, designing *Spin* has different priorities than a news/feature magazine. What are they?

The type play is a little different. At a music magazine, your type solutions can be consistently flippant if you choose. You do not always feel the pressure to define your design; sometimes it's just about having a good time and doing something cool or weird. At a news magazine, especially *The New York Times Magazine*, I feel like every story is so incredibly important to the entire world that the pressure almost dictates my decisions. I tend to work a little harder for the reader and not just for other designers. I still get results that I feel good about; I just take a different path to get to that point.

What is the key element in the design of a periodical? Is it organization, aesthetics, or conceptualization?

I would have to say aesthetics. Organization is good, but disorganization can be quite enjoyable when done right. Concepts are great but not always necessary. Sometimes it's just about creating a beautifully designed page. No concept, no real grid, just great intuition.

How important is the cover to a magazine?

Extremely. It dictates so much. It tells the reader whether or not it's worth picking the magazine up. It defines what you should expect on the inside. However, there is nothing in the world more disappointing then to pick up a magazine that has an absolutely beautiful cover and the inside does not hold up. The photograph grabs you, the type is done in some sick and interesting way, the colors are just right, not all bright and color wheel—like but just right. And then you open the magazine expecting the second coming and it immediately crumbles, taking your expectations with it. That's just plain wrong, man... .

What do you look for in a designer who wants to work with you as an associate, junior, or senior designer?

There is nothing like a brilliant designer who is humble. Good design, to me, is based on good intuition and an acute understanding of small detail. I also like people who experiment. I hate holding hands. I would rather see a study of seven layouts with seven different directions, with only one having potential, than a single layout that needs a full critique. Having to give detailed instructions on how to make a layout work should not be my job. I prefer to mold rather than rebuild.

TITLE: Spin *Cover: Red Hot Chili Peppers*
DESIGNER: Arem Duplessis PHOTOGRAPHER:
Norman Jean Roy PUBLICATION: Spin

TITLE: *Fear and Laptops on the Campaign* DESIGNER: *Arem Duplessis*
PHOTOGRAPHER: *Chris Buck* PUBLICATION: The New York
Times Magazine

TITLE: *Icons—Two Spreads* DESIGNER: *Arem Duplessis*
PHOTOGRAPHER: *Norman Jean Roy* PUBLICATION:
The New York Times Magazine

TITLE: *John Kerry
Cover* DESIGNER:
Arem Duplessis
PHOTOGRAPHER:
Taryn Simon
PUBLICATION:
The New York
Times Magazine

TITLE: *Almodóvar's
Women* DESIGNER:
Arem Duplessis
PHOTOGRAPHERS:
*Sofia Sanchez &
Mauro Mongiello*
PUBLICATION: The
New York Times
Magazine

Design Is Essential

Editor, Art Director, Designer, *Esopus*, New York City

>> **You are an editor, not a trained designer, but you have become a publication auteur, which means you write, edit, and design. What is the advantage of wearing all three hats?**
The greatest advantage is, of course, having control over all aspects of publication, which can—when it's working—lend a consistency of focus to the material. Because *Esopus*'s stated goal as a nonprofit is to provide a space for artists and the public to interact with minimal interference, it just made sense for there to be only one person for contributors to deal with, and rely on, in getting their work to an audience. Also, if you've spend weeks editing a piece, engaging in a back-and-forth with the author, you know much more about it and him or her and can reach beyond the final text (say, to a specific reference in a first draft that was later cut) for appropriate, if not obvious, visual solutions. Another great reason to take on everything is the fact that you can save yourself an enormous amount of money.

As a nondesigner designer, what are your typographic strengths and limitations?
I studied graphic design for a year or so in college, so luckily I haven't been working completely from scratch. That limited knowledge has been bolstered by the proliferation of font sites on the Web that are so well-organized according to styles, families, etc., that you can really learn as you go. As far as strengths and limitations are concerned, I think it's like any situation in which one lacks formal training—in some ways, you're handicapped because the knowledge most people take for granted you have to acquire during the creative process, which can be time-consuming and distracting, but in others, you may be better able to think out of the box because you're not starting with any limitations or givens about how things should, or must, be done.

Presumably, starting a magazine is like starting any business; you need capital and customers (or audience). What have you done to ensure that this business succeeds?
The only way *Esopus* can and will succeed is by placing it squarely within the nonprofit world, where one can depend on a combination of public and private grants to sustain the enterprise. The magazine is deliberately sold for less than it costs to produce in order to reach a wider, more diverse audience, and we are dependent on donations from organizations and individuals to make up that difference. As far as reaching an audience, we depend on several distributors, each specializing in a particular market (museum

TITLE: Cover, Esopus 1 *DESIGNER/ART DIRECTOR: Tod Lippy PUBLICATION: Esopus PHOTOGRAPHER: Anonymous YEAR: 2003*

TITLE: Cover, Esopus 2 *DESIGNER/ART DIRECTOR: Tod Lippy PUBLICATION: Esopus PHOTOGRAPHER: Anonymous YEAR: 2004*

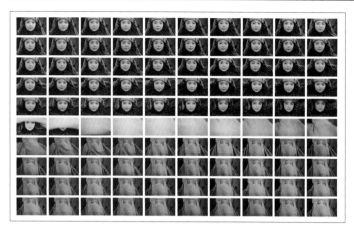

TITLE: 100 Frames: Majid Majidi's "Baran" DESIGNER/ART DIRECTOR: Tod Lippy
CINEMATOGRAPHER: Mohammad Davudi PUBLICATION: Esopus YEAR: 2003

TITLE: Alex Shear's Object Lesson #2
DESIGNER/ART DIRECTOR/
PHOTOGRAPHER: Tod Lippy
OBJECTS: From the collection of Alex
Shear PUBLICATION: Esopus
YEAR: 2004

TITLE: Cover, Esopus 2
DESIGNER/ART DIRECTOR:
Tod Lippy PUBLICATION:
Esopus PHOTOGRAPHER:
Anonymous YEAR: 2004

stores, or newsstands, or large chains like Barnes and Noble, or smaller independent bookstores) to get the magazine into the hands of as many readers as possible. And, of course, the Internet is an enormous help.

How important is design to the success of your magazine?

Design is essential to the success of *Esopus* because the magazine is meant to attract visually those people who might normally shy away from much of its material—contemporary art (often conceptually based), critical writing on culture and the media, etc. The idea was to make the design appealing enough to attract readers, who would then, hopefully, take it home and actually read its contents. That said, the design is never meant to overwhelm or obscure the material it frames.

What does it take to be an auteur? Do you advise this path to everyone?

It takes: (1) a clear vision you are compelled to share with others; (2) enough drive, resilience, and commitment to realize it; (3) an ethical consistency that is clear to both contributors and supporters/investors; (4) a willingness to compromise up to a point (without mitigating that vision). I advise the path to anyone who feels capable of all of the above.

II. CORPORATE DESIGN

THE GREAT PATRONS of graphic design traditionally have been found among powerful businesspersons—for example, the Medici family of Renaissance Italy. Multinational corporations have the resources and wherewithal to fund interdisciplinary design and in many cases also to encourage progressive architecture, industrial, interior, and graphic design. Beginning in the 1950s, IBM, Westinghouse, Cummins Engine, General Dynamics, and Mobil, just to name a few of the biggest companies at that time, sponsored design programs that not only produced emblematic corporate identities but also modernized the very practice of corporate identity.

The discipline known as CI (corporate identity) began in the early twentieth century in Germany, where architect and industrial and graphic designer Peter Behrens developed the earliest inclusive, coordinated design system for the leading German electrical company, A.E.G. What Behrens did that no designer previously had done was develop a consistent design scheme consisting of standard typefaces, layouts, and colors, the application of which was governed by rules put forth in a design systems manual. This ensured a uniform approach to design regardless of who was designing the individual components of the corporate communications—catalogs, brochures, posters, instruction guides, etc. The touchstone of this identity was the logo or trademark—the three initials of the company designed in the form of a honeycomb—the typeface of which determined all other design forms. Behrens determined that a strong and consistent mark should be the anchor of any CI, and while such graphic identifiers were used in the past, never before was one so integral to the overall graphic system.

Since then many world-class identity systems have expressed a wide range of formal approaches, but they are almost always governed by the same fundamental concerns. For example, a corporate logo—which must identify the company clearly, instantaneously, and memorably—must be fairly reductive. In the nineteenth and early twentieth centuries, business trademarks were comparatively complex; like heraldic shields, different visual symbols were condensed into one square, circle, or triangle in order to illustrate the nature of the business or express some aspect of its history. The modern logo, as developed in Germany, was simplified to include only the initials of a company or abstracted into a kind of symbolic brand that has a mnemonic effect (one associates the abstract form with the name of the business, which may or may not appear in conjunction with the mark itself).

Much has been written about the philosophy and psychology of logos and marks. Marks have value when associated with good companies and are valueless when attached to bad ones. The swastika is a case in point. Prior to its adoption as the Nazi party symbol in 1926 (and German national symbol in 1933), the swastika's history dated back to antiquity, when it signified good fortune. In the early twentieth century, it was a very popular commercial mark used on scores of products. But once it was adopted by a heinous regime, it was inextricably wed to evil. The design of the swastika is simple, pure, and memorable, while its symbolic meaning is forever tainted.

The logo or trademark is the cornerstone of CI. The reason for developing a particular mark is often based on research into a company's mission and the synthesis of its ideals into a symbol or brand. The mark itself might be so abstract that no obvious connection can be made, but, simply, the imposed relationship between it and the company imbues it with meaning. The logo is usually the most charged design element of a company, sometimes inviolate, other times mutable, depending on the client's faith in the mark's symbolic power. Therefore, a logo or trademark might take a long or short time to develop and be accepted by the CEO, board of directors, management team, entrepreneur, or whoever else is empowered to make a final decision. Regardless of whether the company is large or small, the time it takes, from start to finish, to conclude the logo portion of the design process cannot be precisely projected; many rational and irrational concerns contribute to making logo design one of the most variable procedures. A logo must appeal to the client (and the public) on cognitive and emotional levels; it is not simply a graphic device to denote one business from another, but, like a national flag, a charged symbol of corporate philosophy. Therefore, it is treated as a kind of totem that does not come cheaply.

Some designers present only one or two iterations of a logo; others bombard the client with many. While too many ideas might confuse a client, too few (unless the presenter has incredible self-confidence or charisma) may frustrate the client. Nevertheless, once the logo is decided upon, then designing the other elements of CI proceeds. This routinely includes the standards manual, which establishes the strictest do's and don'ts for the maintenance of the entire system, such as how, when, and where the logo will be used and what additional typefaces will represent the company. The manual further presents the grid, the invisible page architecture on which type and image is composed, which forms the infrastructure of any coordinated system. Grids are used for such quotidian items as stationery, business cards, mailing labels, hang tags, instruction manuals, etc. The manual shows the permitted type sizes, weights, and colors.

A complete CI system is usually contracted to a consulting

FROM IN-HOUSE TO OUT-OF-HOUSE

The corporate environment can offer invaluable experience. Working within conservative constraints contributes to professional discipline that will hold a designer in good stead, even if later one does more free-form work. Corporate experience from the inside is also a valuable credential when making the switch to the outside. Not all corporate work is done by in-house art departments. Quite a bit is commissioned to design firms that specialize in corporate communications, from public relations to environmental signage. In-house experience only contributes to networking capabilities but also gives out-of-house designers a better understanding of what clients need.

TITLE: One World. Many Voices. ART DIRECTOR: Chris Hacker DESIGNERS: Aveda In-House PHOTOGRAPHER: Ruvan Afandor YEAR: 2002

or external design firm working in conjunction with the internal design department of a particular company. These CI specialists are focused on every detail of the overall system infrastructure and consult with corporate leaders on its applications. The in-house designers strictly follow the manual and other guidelines to produce the lion's share of corporate materials—from business cards to annual reports, from newsletters to packages. Often, however, external design firms are commissioned to produce special components of the corporate communications program, such as advertising, promotion, and, notably, the annual report, which is a corporation's primary outreach to its stockholders. The annual report is often an elaborate piece of design and production that, while following CI system guide-

lines, is usually more conceptually elaborate. Because it is meant to stand out among the standard communications of a company, it is farmed out to design firms that specialize in conceptual thinking, visual creativity (smart and stylish photography and illustration), and high-end printing.

An internal (or in-house) corporate design department is referred to variously as the art department, the design department, and, frequently, the corporate communications department, among the most common names. A company that views design as integral to its success may also support an even more ambitious design laboratory or design center as a hothouse of experimentation in the service of its core mission. Entry- or junior-level designers are hired for these departments and labs based on the quality of their school portfolios; in-house design departments like to hire juniors immediately out of the better undergraduate and graduate design departments. Senior designers and design managers (art directors and design directors) are often hired through job placement services. Although it is possible to get a job in the corporate sector through referrals or recommendations, headhunt-ers are often called upon to search for executive-level employees.

CI is not a design discipline that can be picked up on your own or acquired by osmosis. While a CI designer must not be void of imagination or intuition, knowing the procedures, rules, and standards of the profession is a prime requisite. Most American art and design schools do not offer exclusive majors in CI, but they do provide courses that focus on logo design and systems maintenance. Those who want the security of the corporate environment should pursue academic programs that focus on CI in the broadest sense. The portfolio that results from such a program is the foot in the door of an in-house art department. From then on, learning the job from the inside is the most beneficial.

HOW MASSIMO VIGNELLI INFLUENCED ME

Massimo Vignelli, a preeminent designer, founded Unimark, one of the early design firms devoted to corporate communications, and, later, Vignelli Associates. Some of today's leading designers worked for him. Here they talk about the impact he made on their work:

"I worked for Massimo for ten years. It was my first job out of school. Massimo was like a father to me. I learned three things:

1. Your work matters. Have a point of view and be passionate about it.

2. Although graphic design is ephemeral, you can never go wrong by striving for timelessness.

3. When in doubt, make something really big. He never said these things to me exactly, but this is what I learned."

—*Michael Beirut, Pentagram, New York*

"Vignelli's guiding dictum, *Discipline, Appropriateness, and Ambiguity*, has influenced me continually in all my creative endeavors."

—*Allesandro Franchini, Crate and Barrel, Chicago*

"Massimo has a perpetual passion for design, and he has always been amazingly accessible, energetically engaging in discussion with anyone who shares his enthusiasm."

—*Katherine McCoy, McCoy and McCoy, Buena Vista, Colorado*

"After all these years, I still have Massimo's illustrated recipe for Spaghetti Al (Presi) dente, where he recommends cutting up the cheeses in little pieces about the size of 36 points uppercase letter H. He was always the consummate designer, even down to his attention to cheese size."

—*Tamar Cohen, Slatoff + Cohen, New York*

"Massimo is supremely confident in his own vision. He taught me to be clear, concise, and direct. He was and is intelligent, with a keen ability to quickly distill a problem. I'm grateful to have him as a teacher, model, and friend."

—*Michael Donovan, Donovan & Greene, New York*

Entry Level

School assignments should exhibit a well-rounded sense of design in general—typography, logo/trademarks, publications, posters. This is one area to show a broad range of talents as well as the ability to work within formulas. Present a balance of free-form and strictly formulated work. Do not include published pieces, even if you have them, if they are not of a high standard. A good student assignment is better than a bad professional one.

CONTENTS

Ten to twenty samples:

    a. Letterheads, to show both trademark design and application

    b. Brochures with covers and interiors displayed

    c. Conventional and unconventional typography

    d. Miscellaneous school assignments showing a range of imaginative solutions

TITLE: MFAA Stationery CREATIVE DIRECTOR/DESIGNER: Bobby C. Martin Jr. ACCOUNT MANAGERS: Laurel Richie, Dara Marshall, Daniel Langlitz CLIENT: Ogilvy & Mather YEAR: 2008

Junior/Senior Designer

Portfolios must include a large percentage of printed or fabricated three-dimensional work. The junior may retain a few of the better school assignments, but the senior should have only professional work. Both junior and senior should exhibit a keen ability to solve design problems and to develop design systems.

CONTENTS

Fifteen to twenty-five samples:

    a. Complete annual reports (or any part that was worked on)

    b. Logo/trademarks (including letterheads and design guides)

    c. Newsletters, in-house publications, and other collateral materials

    d. Special presentation kits

    e. Exhibition or display work

    f. Audiovisual presentations for corporate meetings (if available)

    g. Web pages (if available)

TITLE: Abyssinian Stationery DESIGNER: Bobby C. Martin, Jr. YEAR: 2003

Format

35mm slides (in tray) are still applicable, but increasingly this method is being phased out in favor of CD and DVD in the following formats: Flash, PowerPoint, and iPhoto. Online portfolios are also encouraged. Avoid digital tricks. Keep it as straightforward as possible. Anything that crashes the viewer's computer will hamper appreciation of your work.

An Object in Space

Senior VP of Global Marketing & Design for Aveda Corporation, New York City

>> **How did you become the design manager for Aveda?**

I was living in California managing a consulting design business. A woman I had worked with at Estee Lauder earlier in my career approached me and asked if I would be interested in being creative director for Aveda. My initial answer was "no" until I learned more about the company and its interesting and unique approach to design and the environment. I closed down my business and moved to New York.

How do you maintain the corporate brand while not making it too rigid?

We have a small design team that does most of the creative work. Consistency comes from a core team of people working with a clear vision of design based on simple design rules and an environmentally responsible process.

How do you design so that your packages are environmentally friendly?

We set parameters before design work begins and look for unique or high recycled content materials. We also use Merge, which is a computer-based assessment program for determining the most environmentally responsible choice of materials and processes.

How do your packages define or target the audience you are aiming for?

Our packaging approach is a

TITLE: Aveda Magalog—Front and Back Covers
DESIGNERS: The Valentine Group
PHOTOGRAPHERS: Christopher Baker, Enrique Badulescu, Torkil Gudnason YEAR: 1996

TITLE: Aveda Magalog DESIGNERS: The Valentine Group PHOTOGRAPHERS: Christopher Baker, Enrique Badulescu, Torkil Gudnason YEAR: 1996

TITLE: Aveda Magalog DESIGNERS: Dist. Inc. Design PHOTOGRAPHERS: Karen Collins, Graham Brown YEAR: 2002

TITLE: Aveda Magalog DESIGNERS: The Valentine Group PHOTOGRAPHER: Christopher Baker YEAR: 1996

TITLE: Aveda Magalog DESIGNERS: Dist. Inc. Design PHOTOGRAPHER: Karen Collins YEAR: 2002

TITLE: Aveda Magalog DESIGNERS: Dist. Inc. Design PHOTOGRAPHER: Graham Brown YEAR: 2002

simple, clear, and environmentally responsible direction.

Would you say there is a common packaging language?

Yes. Consistent typography and shapes; few colors and environmentally responsible process.

What is unique to package design not apparent in other print design?

It is, of course, the three-dimensional aspect of the work. Package design at its best considers the idea of an object in space and how to use that dimensionality to make an object interesting and unique.

Is it difficult to define the "Aveda style" while also promoting the idea of conscious, responsible consumers?

No. The two are linked in our design process and the resulting designs support both.

Do you find that your training in industrial design has provided you with a different perspective than those who studied graphic design?

My training revolved around solving problems, and the resulting designs are infused with the idea that they were approached with a sensitivity to the resulting function.

What do you look for when hiring new design staff?

Talent, sensitivity, environmental consciousness and interest, and, most important, they must be warm, positive, and enthusiastic.

MICHAEL JOHNSON | Resolutely Pluralist

Michael Johnson, Principal Johnson Banks, London, England

≫ How long have you had your own studio?
I started Johnson Banks in 1992.

What are the changes in practice you have seen and experienced since you began?
Well we haven't grown much—the biggest we ever got was seven people. The biggest changes have come with ever more powerful computerization, and the fact that we now do some truly vast, international projects. In 1992 we had to take out a hefty bank loan to buy two very slow computers and a black and white printer—now we could update the whole studio for about the same amount of cash.

How have these changes impacted your work?
The advent of the Web and email has significantly changed the speed at which we work (and sadly the speed at which clients sometimes expect results). The advent of ever more powerful machines mean, in theory, our mock-ups are better and our work is better. Is our thinking better? I'm not sure. Probably the only thing that isn't really any different is the coming up with ideas. That still involves a train journey, a longish run round the park, a pencil, a sketchbook, or sitting in a café somewhere with a mild, creeping sense of panic.

Would you say that you have a particular style or character to your design? If so, how would you define it?
I've worked pretty hard at being resolutely pluralist, so I'll work in many different ways, whichever is most suitable for the problem at hand. At my core I'm probably a closet minimalist, in that I'll reduce and reduce and reduce an idea to its simplest form. But then we'll design something hideously complicated, almost for the hell of it sometimes (when we did our Think London logo we managed to include 44 separate symbols in one logo).

I know that other people seem to think we're pretty strategic, and we do use a lot of words and wordplay in our communications, and sometimes use witty concepts and ideas. I think that "wordy" reputation may have come about because of my extra-curricular writing (books, articles, and blogging) coupled with the general lack of interest in words emanating from most graphic designers (who seem to see words as the gray bits of lorem ipsum in between their images). **≫**

TITLE: Think London DESIGNERS: Michael Johnson, Julia Woollams DESIGN FIRM: Johnson Banks CLIENT: Think London YEAR: 2004-2005

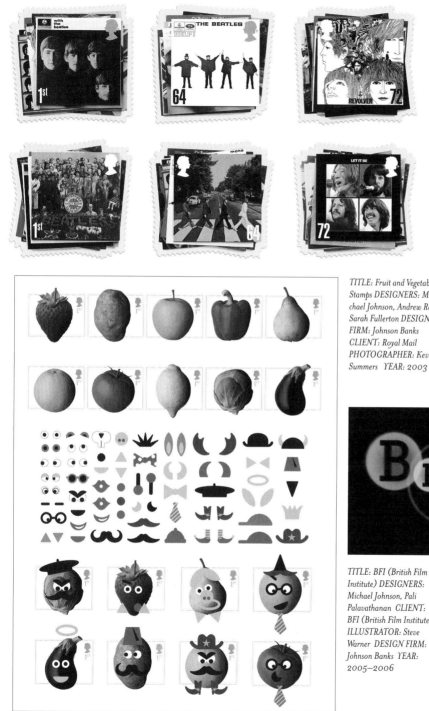

TITLE: Beatles Stamps
DESIGNER: Michael
Johnson CLIENT: Royal
Mail PHOTOGRA-
PHER: Kevin Summers
DESIGN FIRM: Johnson
Banks YEAR: 2006

TITLE: Fruit and Vegetable
Stamps DESIGNERS: Mi-
chael Johnson, Andrew Ross,
Sarah Fullerton DESIGN
FIRM: Johnson Banks
CLIENT: Royal Mail
PHOTOGRAPHER: Kevin
Summers YEAR: 2003

TITLE: BFI (British Film
Institute) DESIGNERS:
Michael Johnson, Pali
Palavathanan CLIENT:
BFI (British Film Institute)
ILLUSTRATOR: Steve
Warner DESIGN FIRM:
Johnson Banks YEAR:
2005–2006

≫

There's an almost zag-zig, counterintuitive approach to our work sometimes as well. Luckily our clients seem to have worked us out and never sit in our boardroom with any expected solution in mind. They never say "can we have what you did for them" —they come ready for a design journey that could go in any direction (but hopefully an appropriate one). If they're not ready for that, or they're nervous, they don't ask us to do their project, it's as simple as that. Design-group client choices seem to have become pretty self-selective, it seems.

What about graphic design is the most challenging for you?

Currently, we're growing up, so I'm getting to grips with branding theory (in a verbal sense). Large identity projects need a verbal start before a visual middle and end. I don't mind it, in fact I started life as a consultant, but navigating a way through the morass of brand-essence-values-beliefs-psycho-babble is tricky. I refuse to use any of the jargon in our projects, just easy concepts like "who are we" and "what do we do." "Brand essence" sounds like the kind of stuff you drip into cake mix. I'd like to think our work had a little more longevity than your average Victoria sponge.

What are the projects that most satisfy your aesthetic sense?

I'm most at home with a poster or a logo, or I guess stamps too. If I could do those all day I'd be the happiest pig in the paddock. But just as important to me are these large identity schemes we do now—finding a way for an identity to flex and change and adapt to the myriad twenty-first-century requirements is the toughest brief, but incredibly rewarding, if you get it right.

How important is type and typography in what you do?

It's pretty much the cornerstone of everything we do. Without a good eye for type a designer is just an image-maker, or illustrator. The complete graphic designer has to be able to deal with type, or they're in trouble (or they'll get found out, eventually). Luckily I trained when type was still drawn by hand, and I'm sure that helped me get inside the shape of letterforms and curves much more than graduates today, who just pick a font and start their layout. Choosing the right typeface can sometimes take me weeks to decide, it's so critical to my projects.

What, in this current technological and economic climate, does the future hold for you specifically, and graphic design in general?

Bizarrely, we're worked off our feet. Our decision earlier in the century to focus on identity seems to be paying off—I was happy as a print designer fifteen years ago but you didn't need to be a rocket scientist to see that had no great future. Our role in projects is usually to start them off then oversee them, so as long as people like us are needed, we'll be busy.

As regards graphic design, it's fairly obvious that the boundaries between graphic design, Web, moving image, and image-making will continue to merrily blur. That's fine, and a good challenge. But the strategic part of our life will always be there—I think that clients will always need help to be verbally memorable then visually unforgettable, and we're happy with that as a starting point. Just as long as we keep looking for a different finish, I think we'll be fine.

Shelter

TITLE: Shelter
DESIGNERS: Michael Johnson, Luke Gifford, Kath Tudball
CLIENT: Shelter
DESIGN FIRM: Johnson Banks   YEAR: 2003

TITLE: Swanswell
DESIGNERS: Michael Johnson, Miho Aishima
CLIENT: Swanswell Trust
PHOTOGRAPHERS: Alex Kent, Pete Gay   DESIGN FIRM: Johnson Banks
YEAR: 2008

BOBBY C. MARTIN Jr.

Creative Director, Nokia, London, England

Across the Pond

>> **How long have you been a graphic designer?**
Growing up my father took me to lectures and exhibitions by prominent African-American artists like Jacob Lawrence and Aaron Douglas. Their work introduced me to the basic principles of scale, color, and simplicity. Wanting to be like them, I studied art and illustration at Virginia Commonwealth University. By chance I took a history course taught by Phil Meggs and was introduced to graphic design. I was powerfully drawn to work that utilized clarity and scale, but also integrated provocative and persuasive messages, like Tomi Ungerer's "Black Power/White Power" and George Lois' Esquire covers. Ever since, I have been obsessed with heartfelt visual communication. Thanks to my dad, I think I've always had a little graphic designer in me.

What prompted you to move from New York to London?
London has been incredible because I'm exposed to a very different design perspective. Working as a creative director for Nokia has given me the opportunity to collaborate with a vast array of design disciplines: graphic designers with rigidly modernist principles, textile designers with "more is more" mentalities, and industrial designers who are like modern-day sculptors that fill the studio with contagious creativity.

London's creativity pours out of the studios and onto the streets. Walls of buildings and overpasses are covered in typographic graffiti, while Banksy's witty paintings pop up on East end corners. Recently, Jonathan Ellery spoke at a D&AD lecture about the importance of building "Points of Reference." London is full of inspiration and inspiring people, these are points of reference that I'm collecting to influence and shape the future of my graphic design.

Was this a hard or easy transition?
The first couple of months were challenging because I was living outside of the United States for the first time, there was a learning curve both in and out of the office. In the office, my first task was to redesign all of Nokia's packaging. The project involved leading a team of designers spread across three different countries. I had to quickly learn how to manage large teams and also accept that I couldn't design every single item myself. I had to step back a bit and trust what has turned out to be a team of some of the best designers I've ever met. Outside of the office, I am still trying to get used to people driving on the other side of the street.

What are the changes in practice you have seen and experienced since you began?
The dotcom era created a youthful exuberance in design, especially in corporate branding. Unfortunately, after 9/11 and the recession that followed, risk-taking brands became much more conservative. Now, during yet another recession, brands are falling even further back to their original foundations, their core assets. >>

TITLE: *Abyssinian 200th Logo* DESIGNER: *Bobby C. Martin, Jr.* YEAR: *2007*

TITLE: JALC Congo Square CD
CREATIVE DIRECTOR: Bobby
C. Martin, Jr. DESIGNER:
Bobby C. Martin Jr., Erika Lee
PHOTOGRAPHER: Frank Stewart
YEAR: 2007

TITLE: Abyssinian Lead Billboard
DESIGNER: Bobby C. Martin,
Jr. PHOTOGRAPHER: Jason
Tanaka Blaney YEAR: 2004

TITLE: JALC Subscribe
Poster CREATIVE
DIRECTOR/
DESIGNER: Bobby C.
Martin, Jr.
PHOTOGRAPHER:
Frank Stewart
YEAR: 2006

Designers have to work harder to create distinct executions within tighter boundaries. Out of hard times, the heart of the brand is renewed.

How have these changes impacted your work?

I find the heart of a brand by researching its visual history and historical context. Then I use those fundamental elements to tell a bigger story. For instance, while developing the identity for the Museum for African Art, I did extensive research of African alphabets, iconography, architecture, and art. I developed a series of shapes that create movement and form patterns like textiles, and then designed a typeface based on those shapes to create the foundation for a robust and unique graphic identity system.

Would you say that you have a particular style or character to your design? If so, how would you define it?

Over a period of time, when I've built a body of work, I hope you'll see a level of honesty that becomes my calling card. My style comes through my process: understanding the goals, then charting a path to a particular audience experience. People don't hire me because my work looks a certain way; they hire me because my work provokes a certain response.

What about graphic design is the most challenging for you?

Thinking it. Selling it. Making it. The biggest challenge for me is convincing a client to go with a strong idea, then making it come to life.

What are the projects that most satisfy your aesthetic sense?

The projects that satisfy me the most are when smart strategy, excellent design, and the right amount of organizational support create a cultural movement, whether it's the internal culture of a company or the culture of a whole neighborhood, seeing your work touch someone's heart is very satisfying. Often times, these are also the most beautiful projects.

How important is type and typography in what you do?

Having worked on both sides of the pond, I see two distinct approaches to typography. Expressive typography is more of a New York thing. It breaks rules to create excitement and emotion. In European graphic design, disciplined and structured type is more common. Both styles are beautiful and effective. What's more important is using type to communicate the right message, at the right time, in the right way.

What, in this current technological and economic climate, does the future hold for you specifically, and graphic design in general?

Living abroad has opened my eyes to different cultures and their ways of working, but even more so, their ways of living. Design is very important to me, but so is enjoying the company of friends and family and making time for the things that I care about. It's essential to both creativity and well-being to take a step back, observe, read, visit, play, and attend. As for the future of graphic design, the best part is that—no matter what the technological or economic climate may be—we will continue to have the ability to create something from nothing. Those who can't, envy it; those who criticize, admire it; and those who are the audience, live it. I love it.

TITLE: JALC Season Brochure CREATIVE DIRECTOR: Bobby C. Martin, Jr. DESIGNERS: Bobby C. Martin Jr., Matthew Poor PHOTOGRAPHER: Clay Patrick McBride YEAR: 2007

TITLE: MFAA Logo CREATIVE DIRECTOR/DESIGNER: Bobby C. Martin, Jr. ACCOUNT MANAGERS: Laurel Richie, Dara Marshall, Daniel Langlitz CLIENT: Ogilvy & Mather YEAR: 2008

The Competitive Market

Principal, The Carbone Smolan Agency (CSA), New York City

>> **What made you launch your own business? What kind of business is it?**

I come from a family of entrepreneurs, so business is in my blood. Initially, I took a job at an annual report house in New York City, but I quickly left to start my own freelance business in Philadelphia. A year later I got a call from Ken Carbone, who had recently established a New York office for Gottschalk and Ash and was looking for a strong designer to collaborate with. When Fritz Gottschalk decided to return to Switzerland in 1980 we bought Gottschalk, and Ken and I have been together ever since. Our goal was to be design generalists—to be able to work on all media and in all industries. Twenty years later, we've managed to maintain a business that represents a full range of design disciplines: branding and corporate identity, marketing communications, architectural graphics, book publishing, packaging, product design, exhibits, and interactive design. Some of our work has now started to extend to video and advertising.

Has the business changed since you began?

In today's competitive environment, clients are no longer willing to make an investment in educating you about their business. They expect you to come to a project with a depth of expertise in their business and your design application. As a result,

TITLE: Skadden DESIGNER: Carla Miller CREATIVE DIRECTOR: Ken Carbone COMPANY: The Carbone Smolan Agency (CSA) CLIENT: Skadden Arps Slate Meagher & Flom PHOTOGRAPHER: Erica Frudenstein YEAR: 1998

TITLE: NWQ DESIGNER: John Nishimoto CREATIVE DIRECTOR: Leslie Smolan COMPANY: The Carbone Smolan Agency (CSA) CLIENT: NWQ Investment Management Company PHOTOGRAPHER: Dan Winters (brochure) TYPEFACES: OCKB, OCRA, Bell Gothic, Letter Gothic, Trixie YEAR: 1997

TITLE: The Image Bank DESIGNER: Carla Miller CREATIVE DIRECTOR: Ken Carbone COMPANY: The Carbone Smolan Agency (CSA) CLIENT: The Image Bank TYPEFACE: Thesis YEAR: 1998

TITLE: Bond Brochure DESIGNER/ CREATIVE DIRECTOR: David Barnett COMPANY: The Barnett Group CLIENT: PSA: The Bond Market Trade Association ILLUSTRATOR: Guy Billout TYPEFACES: Berkeley, Meta YEAR: 1997

TITLE: PBS—The Business Channel DESIGNER: Janette Eusebio CREATIVE DIRECTOR: Laurel Shoemaker COMPANY: The Carbone Smolan Agency (CSA) CLIENT: PBS—The Business Channel PHOTOGRAPHER: Doug Menuez TYPEFACE: Thesis YEAR: 1998

TITLE: Putnam Investments CREATIVE DIRECTOR: Leslie Smolan COMPANY: The Carbone Smolan Agency (CSA) CLIENT: Putnam Investments PHOTOGRA-PHER: John Still YEAR: 1993

we have recently reorganized our business around four major business segments—luxury goods, children's products and services, financial services, and media and entertainment—and brought on senior marketing talent to provide an even greater internal resource for clients. This, coupled with our breadth of experience in all areas of design, has kept us a viable competitor as many design organizations grow to compete with both Web groups and advertising agencies.

Have you seen a shift from service to collaboration in recent years?
Yes and no. It really depends on the client—how much they know about design and how secure they are in their own role.

Are you experiencing the kind of growth that requires new skills of your employees?
Things continue to change at an ever faster rate. Technology has totally transformed what we do, and I believe it will continue to do so. The nature of design requires one to learn new things every day. That's what makes it such an interesting career.

What kind of designer do you look for as an employee?
I look for someone who brings a high level of intelligence and resourcefulness to any project, combined with strong design aesthetics and good drawing skills. It has to be someone I enjoy being with, someone who can make me think and see things in a new way.

Former Senior Designer, Pentagram, New York

>> **What are the changes in practice you have seen and experienced since you began (and now run your own studio)?**

Right now I'm trying to sort out the movement away from print. The economy and the environment and the "flat world" have come together to create a perfect storm that rages against paper.

How have these changes impacted your work?

Moving away from paper allows for new expression. Movement, materials, and even sound are increasingly important. It's not just a digital revolution; it's a signage, branding, letterhead, architecture, experience, e-signature, merchandise, publishing, packaging, production coup. Clients are savvy. They want to be presented with work that will succeed across all media, and PR. Perhaps they are just being frugal, but I like to think they are better understanding the capabilities of graphic design and so better leveraging all that designers can bring to the table. Paper is now just one of many available solutions.

Would you say that you have a particular style or character to your design? If so, how would you define it?

Design process is most important to me. I like to heavily research both the client and the audience, then finely tune the work to their unique history and relationship. New York City's Bid for the 2012 Olympic Games had several very different audiences. For skeptical New Yorkers, we developed an advertising campaign driven by heartfelt but surprising copywriting. For visiting International Olympic Committee (IOC) members, we built a classic and fairly staid conference room in the Plaza Hotel's ballroom. And for IOC members that didn't get to come to New York City, we sent New York City to them. The NYC2012 identity addressed the whole world (literally), but each piece of the campaign could be very targeted. My hope is that I can continue to build brands that are finely tuned to their audiences.

What about graphic design is the most challenging for you?

Having fun. Being serious is easy. But being human is memorable. Funny, imperfect, soulful work is the stuff that will touch your heart. The polished pieces just solve a problem. It's scary but essential to bring honesty and passion into a board room.

What are the projects that most satisfy your aesthetic sense?

I most love a really smart project. If the aesthetic is appropriate to the idea and the audience, then it's perfect. If you are designing an exhibit for the Museum of Sex and you want to educate and entertain a broad audience, then you turn kink, pink, and playful. If you want only "practitioners" to >>

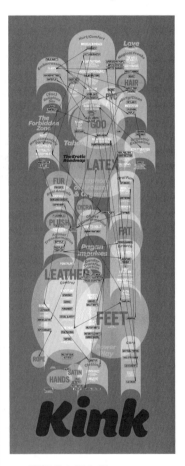

TITLE: Kink, The Erotic Roadmap
CLIENT: The Museum of Sex SENIOR DESIGNER: Michael Bierut, Pentagram
DESIGNER: Jennifer Kinon CONTENT: Katharine Gates YEAR: 2007

TITLE: Kink, Exhibit Identity
CLIENT: The Museum of Sex.
SENIOR DESIGNER:
Michael Bierut, Pentagram
DESIGNER: Jennifer Kinon
YEAR: 2007

TITLE: New York City's 2012 Olympic Games Bid Committee DESIGNERS: Jennifer Kinon, Kristin Johnson, Christine Koroki, Erika Lee YEAR: 2005

TITLE: Saks Fifth Avenue Shopping Bags CLIENT: Saks Fifth Avenue SENIOR DESIGNER: Michael Bierut, Pentagram DESIGNERS: Jennifer Kinon, Kerrie Powell © Saks YEAR: 2006

>>

attend, then you appeal to their niche with hints at fur or leather, maybe even mud or angora sweaters. The best aesthetic fits the purpose.

How important is type and typography in what you do?

My mother always told me, "It's not what you say, it's how you say it."

What, in this current technological and economic climate, does the future hold for you specifically, and graphic design in general?

More people know what graphic design is, sort of. They pick fonts. They self-publish. They self-brand. They don't quite know what makes design good or bad and they aren't sure why their nephew probably shouldn't "do" their brochure, but as money gets tighter and technology better streamlines processes, people will seek out and be able to access better understanding of how graphic design works and our profession will only benefit.

TITLE: NYC2012 Times Square Billboard Summer 2005 CLIENT: New York City's 2012 Olympic Games Bid Committee DESIGN DIRECTOR: Jennifer Kinon CREATIVE DIRECTORS: Brian Collins and Rick Boyko TYPOGRAPHY: Giampetro&Smith COPYWRITING: Charles Hall LOGO DESIGN: Ogilvy BIG DESIGNERS: Kristin Johnson, Christine Koroki, Erika Lee © NYC2012 YEAR: 2005

TITLE: NYC2012 IOC Visit Meeting Room CLIENT: New York City's 2012 Olympic Games Bid Committee DESIGNERS: Jennifer Kinon, Kristin Johnson, Christine Koroki, Erika Lee © NYC2012 IOC Decisions Day Collateral YEAR: 2005

TITLE: Graphis, Library 2003 Graphis PUBLISHER/DESIGNER: Martin Pedersen DESIGNER: Jennifer Kinon YEAR: 2003

TITLE: Graphis, Article Introduction PUBLISHER/ DESIGNER: Martin Pedersen DESIGNER: Jennifer Kinon YEAR: 2003

DMITRI SIEGEL | Watching the Trend Cycle

Managing Director of Direct Business, Urban Outfitters, New York City

» How long have you been working for Urban Outfitters? And what is your job?

I joined Urban three years ago. I am currently Managing Director of the Direct business, which means I oversee all aspects of the Web site and catalog businesses. This includes design, photography, video, content, PR, marketing, development (programming), as well as operations and merchandising. I have responsibility for the sales and profitability of the Web business. I think the fact that someone with an MFA in Graphic Design was given this level of responsibility speaks to what a creative-driven company Urban is.

What are the changes in practice you have seen and experienced since you began?

I'm not one of those people who remembers doing paste-ups and hand-setting type in the "old days." I missed the seismic shift that took place in the '90s when design moved onto the computer. The "old days" for me was basically a slightly slower Mac, and no wi-fi. That said, the ongoing digitization of our culture has continually opened up new formats and opportunities for graphic designers: video, interactive, mobile, even blogging.

Any difference in form?

I have been around long enough to see several formal trends come and go in the rarefied world of "design for designers." When I started out,

the technical look from the likes of Designers Republic was very hot. Since then I've seen hand-drawn type go from Kevin Lyons et al to ubiquity. Recently I keep seeing the formerly academic Dot Dot Dot or "default" style moving into the mainstream. It's actually kind of nice to watch the trend cycle happen, and get more comfortable with that.

How have these changes impacted your work?

Graphic design's ability to adapt to the digitization of culture has meant that I have a very diverse skill set and practice. I write; I work in video and motion and interactive.

I feel very fortunate to have had the opportunity to engage with not just how things look, but in creating the context in which my work will be experienced.

Would you say that you have a particular style or character to your design?

There are elements that crop up over and over again out of habit (or desperation), but I try not to have a consistent visual style. Instead I really try with each project to have one big idea or gesture—I usually try for something big and dumb or big and wrong. This allows me to be flexible about the details with clients and with technological limitations **»**

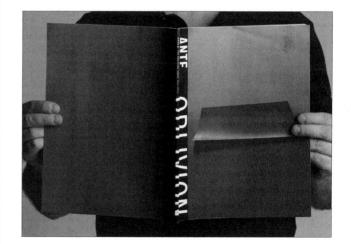

TITLE: Oblivion (Ante #4)
CLIENT: Ante Projects DESIGNER/
ART DIRECTOR: Dmitri Siegel
ILLUSTRATOR/PHOTOGRAPHER:
Mathew Monteith YEAR: 2006

TITLE: Urban Outfitters Blog CLIENT: Urban Outfitters ART DIRECTOR: Dmitri Siegel DESIGNERS: Dmitri Siegel, Andy Beach, Peter Tressler, Dan Keenan WEB DEVELOPER/PROGRAMMER: Joshua Lane YEAR: 2007

TITLE: Urban Outfitters Blog CLIENT: Urban Outfitters ART DIRECTOR: Dmitri Siegel DESIGNERS: Dmitri Siegel, Andy Beach, Peter Tressler, Dan Keenan WEB DEVELOPER/PROGRAMMER: Joshua Lane YEAR: 2007

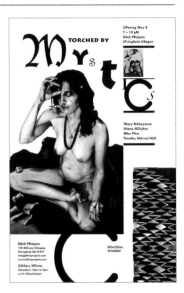

TITLE: Torched by Mystics Poster CLIENT: Ditch Projects Gallery/Ken Miller, Curator DESIGNER/ART DIRECTOR: Dmitri Siegel ARTISTS: Tracy Nakayama, Shana Moulton, Mike Pare, Timothy Marvel Hull YEAR: 2009

TITLE: Anathema *Magazine* CLIENT: Anathema *Magazine* DESIGNER/ART DIRECTOR: Dmitri Siegel PHOTOGRAPHER: Noah Shelley YEAR: 2006

TITLE: Russian Art in Translation CLIENT: Ante Projects/DAP ART DIRECTOR: Dmitri Siegel DESIGNERS: Dmitri Siegel, Peter Tressler ARTIST: Ivan Brazhkin TYPE DESIGNER: Tagir Safayev YEAR: 2007

without losing my voice or authorship. Also, if the big gesture is extreme enough it makes many of the smaller decisions for you. For example, deciding that the Urban Outfitters blog was going to be horizontal scrolling, dictated a very limited height which drove the rest of the layout of posts and navigation, etc.; or deciding to run article titles down the gutter of a magazine meant I had to figure out another way to call-out the beginning of an article. I feel like if I can preserve that big gesture and make it work, then I am less precious about the rest of the design.

What about graphic design is the most challenging for you?

Choosing typefaces and choosing music are really daunting for me. The process can just be very tedious and I'm perhaps over-aware of the impact of those decisions. When I worked at Sundance Channel we used two typefaces for like three years. One had no lowercase and the other was Clarendon, which I can't stomach in anything but title case. It was incredibly limiting but also very freeing. There were so many other things to spend the time on.

What are the projects that most satisfy your aesthetic sense?

The work I do for Ante Projects is probably the most creatively satisfying because I can generally do anything I want. But aesthetically I like the work I do with Urban Outfitters much better. I have my own little set of ideas and hang-ups as a designer (and as a human) so the talent that I get to work with in terms of design, photography, and programming always blows me away. It takes things to an aesthetic level beyond what I could accomplish on my own.

How important is type and typography in what you do?

It is a bit of a cliché to say it, but type and typography really are what separate good graphic design from bad. The hard part is there is no easy way to explain or teach this. I used to think it was about a set of rules but I have seen so many of the orthodoxies I learned in school quite successfully upended. The other day I found myself approving a campaign with Optima—a typeface that I thought of as untouchable. I've learned that the difference between type done well and not done well is not about rules really. It's very subtle; you just know it when you see it. It certainly requires knowing type history and knowing how to set type optically, but there's a million little things that can make type look clunky and it takes finesse to avoid all those little pitfalls.

What, in this current technological and economic climate, does the future hold for you specifically, and graphic design in general?

As far as technological changes, I think there will continue to be new opportunities for designers with an analytical or technical streak. I just hope that design schools can keep up. I still find that a great deal of students coming out of school just want to work on museum catalogs or record covers. These are very small and not terribly lucrative areas of design.

TITLE: Oblivion (Ante #4) CLIENT: Ante Projects DESIGNER/ART DIRECTOR: Dmitri Siegel ARTIST: Josiah McElheney PHOTOGRAPHER: Tom Van Eynde YEAR: 2006

The Art of Involvement

Partner, VSA Partners, Chicago

>> **What kind of work are you doing at VSA Partners?**

We are gravitating toward what I would term integrated marketing. We still do a lot of traditional print communication, but about 40 percent of our work now is in the area of brand marketing, brand positioning, licensing products, and retail. We are even into event planning, whether it's a Harley rally or some large stage program for Potlatch Paper, which are clients of ours. Design today has a much bigger definition and a much more strategic activity.

What do you look for when hiring designers?

Generally, we're fortunate to be at a level where a lot of people are attracted to the work of the office, but it's still hard to find talented people. It's always been hard because our standards are high and we look for the rounded individual. Resumes don't carry a lot of weight. They are important and we need them as a level set, but when the person actually arrives for the meeting, if she doesn't have verbal skills, we nix her immediately. Applicants also have to present a portfolio that tells me that they are not sloppy. Most importantly, their design has to be absolutely arresting. We still give the most weight to solution-oriented work that's expressed in a powerful way. It does no good for us to see a book jacket if all that was solved were colors and the texture of the paper.

TITLE: *Steve Goodman Poster* DESIGNERS: *Ken Fox, Fletcher Martin* CREATIVE DIRECTOR: *Dana Arnett* CLIENT: *Old Town School of Folk Music* PHOTOGRAPHER: *Goodman Archives* TYPEFACE: *HTF Champion* YEAR: *1997*

TITLE: *Harley-Davidson Eaglethon* POSTER DESIGNER: *Dan Kraemer* CREATIVE DIRECTOR: *Curt Schreiber* CLIENTS: *Harley-Davidson and Muscular Dystrophy Association/ © Quadrillion Publishing* TYPEFACE: *Champion Gothic* YEAR: *1997*

*TITLE: Tech Weenie
DESIGNER:
Fletcher Martin
CREATIVE
DIRECTOR: Dana
Arnett CLIENT:
Type Directors
Club ILLUSTRA-
TOR: Max Cannon
TYPEFACE: Hel-
vetica Condensed
YEAR: 1997*

*TITLE: Potlatch
McCoy Logo
DESIGNER: Jason
Eplawy CREATIVE
DIRECTOR: Dana
Arnett CLIENT:
Potlatch Corpora-
tion, Minnesota Pulp
and Paper Division
ILLUSTRATOR:
Jason Eplawy
YEAR: 1997*

*TITLE: Life/If Poster
DESIGNER: Ken Fox
CREATIVE DIRECTOR:
Dana Arnett CLIENT:
Diffa (Design Industries
for AIDS Foundation)
YEAR: 1995*

Do you hire interns?

We have two to three interns every summer. It's important that an intern learn how the production process works. By the nature of our structure, they get to see how teams work and how work is conceptualized, and if there's time and room for their involvement on that side, we utilize them. I would say once every couple of years someone comes along who is good enough to contribute on a conceptual level, but what they really need to learn is the mechanics at that stage. We all had to cut our teeth. It is important for any young person to know that in this office at least, you don't walk right in and start designing your first day. As an intern, you walk in and you learn the mechanics and procedures of the practice.

How would you describe a good work environment?

One that always allows open participation in the process. We've kept an open environment where point of view is as important to success as getting here on time and getting projects done. I believe that if you've made a decision to hire somebody, you can't just slot them. You have to give them enough open ground when they start so that you can discover, as well as they can, where they are going to fit in and contribute. Our teams are set up so that there's very little rank. It's more like you bring as much as you can and are prepared and smart when you bring what you've got.

In-House, High-End

Art Director, Kiehl's, New York City

≫ Where do you work now?

At In-House Full-Time for a high-end hair care and skin care products company designing window displays for their 100+ stores around the world. I did run my own studio for about six years.

What are the changes in practice you have seen and experienced since you began?

I'm dating myself by saying this, but my first job in college was designing flyers and brochures for an office at the university. We still used rub-down letraset type and a hot-waxer to layout images and text on a page. When we did get our first Macintosh, we used it mostly to set type because the printer output for photos was too low-res to use for printing purposes. It was all very lo-fi and hands-on. Of course today the whole layout can be executed on the computer and has put the ability to a make work look much more polished in the hands of anyone with a computer and a good visual sense.

What about changes in form?

In terms of form, I have seen design work change from very hand-done to enthusiastically computer-generated (using bitmap fonts and artwork—see Émigré and April Greiman) to clean and slick to grungy experimental anti-computer-generated work (see Art Chantry, Raygun/

TITLE: Talking Jazz Box Set CLIENT: Ben Sidran/Unlimited Media Limited DESIGNER: Travis Cain ART DIRECTOR: Kevin Wade PHOTOGRAPHER: Lee Tanner YEAR: 2007

TITLE: Andre Williams Gig Poster CLIENT: High Noon Saloon DESIGNER: Travis Cain ART DIRECTOR: Kevin Wade ILLUSTRATOR: Travis Cain YEAR: 2007

TITLE: Various Logos CLIENT: Various DESIGNER/ART DIRECTOR/ILLUSTRATOR: Travis Cain YEAR: 2005-2009

TITLE: Fever Brand Hot Sauces CLIENT: Fever Foods DESIGNER/ART DIRECTOR/ILLUSTRATOR: Travis Cain YEAR: 2005

TITLE: Cloud Cult Gig Poster CLIENT: High Noon Saloon DESIGNER: Travis Cain ART DIRECTOR: Kevin Wade ILLUSTRATOR: Travis Cain YEAR: 2007

TITLE: Biodegradeable Body Cleanser Window CLIENT: Kiehl's Since 1851 DESIGNER: Travis Cain ART DIRECTOR: Victoria Maddocks PHOTOGRAPHER: Stephen Lewis YEAR: 2008

TITLE: Cooper Hewitt Triennial Dunnys, CHEEZE and RIBEYE (official museum souvenirs) CLIENT: KidRobot/Cooper Hewitt Design Museum DESIGNER/ART DIRECTOR/ILLUSTRATOR: Travis Cain YEAR: 2006

David Carson), to roughly where we are today: a bit of all that together. I think on the whole, we have come to terms with the computer and what it can and can't do for us. We know what it is good for and what is still done better by hand—we don't need to rebel against it anymore.

How have these changes impacted your work?

I am glad that I had the experience with the rub-down type and hot waxer. I learned so much about the printing process by going through those steps—now you turn over a disk to your printer and a nice printed piece shows up in the mail—you never really get to see the gritty steps in between. I integrate a lot of hand-drawn type and illustration into my work, which is a holdover from the days when that was how you had to do it. Sometimes a clean, flawlessly drawn Adobe illustrator image is what is required, but I much more prefer it when the lines aren't clean.

Would you say that you have a particular style or character to your design? If so, how would you define it?

I guess I would say that I don't really have a style. I have some typefaces that I like and some visual themes that I reference on a regular basis, but when I work on a project I like to work in a style that fits the project. I have found that the style I do something in is part of solving the design problem—my personal visual preferences shouldn't get in the way of that. »

What about graphic design is the most challenging for you?

It's the quest to solve a client's design problem while creating something original. And then to sell the idea to the client so he/she can see that doing something original is the best solution. Being a good designer isn't just about having amazing ideas or making amazing images—you have to sell the ideas too, or those amazing images will never see the light of day.

What are the projects that most satisfy your aesthetic sense?

A project that I can really push myself and experiment are always fun. When I worked at Planet Propaganda, I had the opportunity to design and screen-print posters for local music venues. On these projects we could pretty much do whatever we wanted (we did them in exchange for admission to the shows). I could draw, paint, make my own typography—whatever. Then, of course the screen-printing part was fun too—always good to get your hands dirty every once in awhile.

That must be true with windows?

I get to collaborate with great photographers and illustrators to make a vision come to life—and then to see the work in store windows all over the world is satisfying on a different level.

How important is type and typography in what you do?

Typography is design. You must be good with type to be a good designer. You need to take every opportunity

you get to learn more about type. You need to work at a magazine or a book publisher and learn to work with large bodies of type. You need to learn to make a beautiful headline. You need to learn to draw type. You need to learn to make type dance. You need to love type.

What do you look for in a student?

Some of the same things I discussed above, with an emphasis on the initiative part. When you're in school potential employers aren't going to expect you to have a lot of experience producing real-world work. However, just having class assignments in your book isn't enough. Know a friend that's in a band? Design their logo, t-shirt, posters, CD package. Are you into photography? Design and make a book featuring your photographs. Make posters for a local theater or nonprofit. Make art and put some of it in your book.

What, in this current technological and economic climate, does the future hold for you specifically, and graphic design in general?

I like to think that design is still the secret weapon for any company's success. A product that is well-designed and built to last will always be in demand. Great designers that can do that work will also always be in demand. Personally, I will continue to push myself to try new things—design more products with great companies like KidRobot and further my interests in print-making and art.

III. BOOK DESIGN

THE PUBLISHING INDUSTRY, despite the confusion resulting from the shift from print to digital, is a major employer of graphic designers. Publishers use design to package and sell their merchandise, and while it may seem crass to discuss books as products, this is exactly how they are conceived and marketed. Despite the cultural significance of books, even the finest literature is nothing more than pages of worthless pulp until it is packaged in a form that attracts readers. It is the book designer's job to cast the text and images in an accessible and pleasing manner; it is the book jacket designer's job to create an alluring wrapper. Like any product, the jacket must attract the customer's attention and impart a message. Certainly, book and book jacket designers have more creative license than most food and hardware package designers, but the goal is the same: to move a product off the shelves. As shelves become less important, there will be a change in the way book jackets and covers are designed, but the industry is not yet sure what that will be.

The book design profession is divided into two basic categories—book interior and book jacket—that have a number of subsets. These two disciplines are tradiionally separate but, depending on the nature of the publishing company, the roles can intersect.

The book designer is responsible for the interior design of most textbooks (books with few or no pictures, such as novels and biographies). The jacket designer is responsible for the hardcover dustjacket, paperback cover, or paper-over-boards wrapper.

When introduced in the early nineteenth century, book jackets were unadorned protective coverings for leather book bindings. Later in the century, jackets were used as advertisements, routinely removed and discarded after purchase. Today, illustrated and typographic jackets are integral to the overall allure of a book and intensely scrutinized by marketing departments. Only purists still denounce book jackets as unwanted appendages. Indeed, most designers who seek jobs in publishing want to become jacket designers.

Book designers are typographers who understand the nuances of type and are skilled at presenting a page in the most elegant and accessible form possible. Interior design is a less glamorous job than jacket design, but without this design discipline a book would be anarchic at best. In addition to interior pages, book designers design bindings or casings (cover and spine) as well as endpapers (the decorative paper pasted inside the cover of some hardcover books). Book designers must also be skilled at production because a large part of type's success is how well it is set and printed. This cannot be learned from a manual—merely flowing type into an InDesign template

does not make a good book designer—but rather considerable study and often intense apprenticeship is needed to hone the designer's aesthetic sensibilities.

In some publishing houses, this job division is as it was a hundred years ago—the interior design and the jacket design have little relationship to each other. In other houses, the work intersects either from the outset or somewhere during the process. Increasingly, more nonfiction visual books are designed as total packages, with one designer responsible for the entire design. The book in your hands—the paperback cover and interior pages—was designed by one individual to ensure its cohesiveness.

Before discussing the roles of designers in the book industry, it is useful to explain the genres

of publishing, for each requires a different kind of design. Industry sectors are conventionally categorized as follows: trade or commercial, which produces fiction and nonfiction books aimed at a general audience; professional, which caters its products to the needs of specific professional groups; and textbook, which produces educational books for school- or coursework. Within these basic categories publishers might specialize in areas such as pop fiction, military biography, graphic design how-to books, etc. Perhaps the largest publishing genre, however, is mass-market paperback—cheaply produced novels (romances, mysteries, science fiction, Westerns, etc.) that are marketed not just in bookstores but also in airports, drug-

SEPARATION OF BOOK AND JACKET

Like church and state, there has long been a distinction between interior book design and cover design. Until recently, it was rare for the designer of one to cross into the other's territory. The reason: The book (cover, spine, endpapers, and text) was the essential entity; the jacket (the dustcover or wrapper) was advertising that sold the entity. Usually, the cover image and typography bore no relation to the interior typography—and, in some cases, the cover illustration exaggerated the plot and misled the reader. Book designers come from a proud tradition of craftspeople with roots in the sixteenth century. The jacket designer is not only a Johnny-come-lately (illustrated jackets did not exist until the 1900s) but is presumed to answer to a different set of qualitative standards. Today, the forms are increasingly merging. Interior book designers are a little less rigid in this distinction, and jacket designers are more general in their skills and talents. Designers who do both are more common in publishing houses and useful to publishers.

stores, supermarkets, etc. Some publishers are known for highbrow content, others for middle- or lowbrow content. Some publishers are enormous conglomerates that release hundreds of titles in a season (usually fall, winter, and spring); others are comparatively small proprietorships with a limited number of books.

The approaches to graphic design used by different publishing enterprises are as different as the books they produce. Some publishers have a tradition of fine classical typography; others promote contemporary sensibilities, and a number do not have any house style or overarching design philosophy at all. Some publishers doggedly follow conventions imposed on their specific genre, while others are more inventive. When seeking employment in a publishing house art department, be familiar with the house's method (or lack thereof) in order to tailor your portfolio accordingly.

There are many ways to become involved in book design. The two most common are as an in-house or freelance designer.

A publishing house art department includes a creative director or art director who manages other designers and also designs book jackets and interiors. In some houses, there are separate art directors for interiors and jackets; in others, one art director manages both. In some publishing houses, design services come under the aegis of the production department, where a production manager is responsible; in others, the production manager

MARKETING, SCHMARKETING

Book publishing is a product-oriented industry, and book jackets are the first line of persuasion in the attempt to win over the consumer. Therefore, jackets are often closely scrutinized by marketing departments and sales representatives. Don't think that just because you have designed a visually resplendent jacket that it will get printed. Sometimes the most original designs are deemed unsalable by individuals who know nothing about design but do know what sells. The constant complaints emanating from art directors, staff, and freelance designers include "The marketing people say the author's name is too small," "The marketing people say the color pink won't sell," "The marketing people say they can't see the image from twenty feet away." For the young jacket designer, the first encounter with marketing may be a shock. Often a savvy art director can save or salvage a good cover, but just as often the best work never sees the light of day. In this genre, however, there is always the next project.

only oversees prepress production. An average art department may employ two or more senior designers and two or more juniors. The seniors design the more critical books on a list. The juniors assist them and may design a few projects as well. At small publishers, the designers may also handle the production—the oversight of printers, color separators, typesetters, etc.

The larger trade publishing houses, such as Knopf, Simon and Schuster, and Farrar Straus and Giroux, can release as many as 150 or more titles per season, each requiring interior and jacket design. In instances where the art director and staff designers cannot handle the workload, or the art director requires a unique or special approach, freelance designers are commissioned. The freelancer may be the principal

or an employee of a design firm or studio or an independent contractor who specializes in book design. Most publishing houses maintain an expanding stable of freelancers, who are selected according to the appropriateness of their individual illustrative or typographic style. To become a freelancer specializing in book design, it is necessary either to show a portfolio or send a promotional mailer (each with mostly book-related work) to the art director. On average, almost 50 percent of all trade book interiors and jackets are done by freelancers. In fact, many smaller trade book publishers (who average between five and twenty books per list) use only freelancers. Designers may be retained for a fixed number of books or seasons or hired on a book-by-book basis. It is therefore useful for freelancers to interview at or send promotional mailers to the full spectrum of large and small companies.

Mass-market paperback houses often produce three times as many books as the average trade publisher, usually on a monthly or bimonthly frequency. Their book covers are invariably more hardsell than those of trade books, with screaming titles, authors names set large and in garish colors or metallic embossing, and seductive illustrations that leave little to the imagination. Most paperback art departments employ a few staff designers responsible for a specific number of covers on a list. Staff production persons routinely handle the interiors, which follow a more or less strict typographic format. Paperback designers often commission freelance illustrators to render cover illustrations and sometimes the lettering as well. Realistic or narrative paintings, mood photographs, and custom lettering are the usual design components for mass-market paperbacks, and specialists in these areas are often in demand for fairly fast turnaround work. Again, a stable of freelancers is retained for this work. To be considered, your portfolio should show your understanding for and talent in this distinct publishing genre.

Publishing houses that produce professional, textbook, and subspecialty books more often than not use in-house art departments for the majority of design and production work. On the whole, these houses produce less adven-

THE APPROACHES TO GRAPHIC DESIGN USED BY DIFFERENT PUBLISHING ENTERPRISES ARE AS DIFFERENT AS THE BOOKS THEY PRODUCE.

turesome (creative) products but rather follow house styles and standards developed over time. For the neophyte, working in this environment offers considerable experience and perhaps an interesting assignment or two per

season, but most of the work is fairly routine.

One other sector of publishing, book packaging, has exerted a strong influence on design. Book packagers are independent producers of books and related products who sell complete packages—text, illustration, design, and sometimes printed books—to publishers and distributors. Increasingly, large publishing houses purchase a certain number of book packages—usually the visual books on their lists. The larger packagers are likely to have their own art department staffed by a creative or art director, staff designers, and production persons. These positions are excellent opportunities to do creative work because there is little or no separation of labor; a visual book must be designed from jacket to index by a single designer to ensure the integrity of the package.

MAKING BOOK

Bookmaking is not as illicit an activity as it sounds—rather, it is a venerable craft that dates back centuries. Even with the computer as their tool, many interior book designers follow the same typographic traditions as the bookmakers of earlier centuries. Although technology and commerce have conspired to alter the book industry, one of the common methods of becoming a book designer is to produce handmade books in school, workshops, or on one's own. Learning typesetting (often by hand), bookbinding, and papermaking may seem somewhat arcane in this digital world, but the tactility of the process can inspire even the desktop practitioner to explore book design and production. While you should know the latest techniques, never underestimate the importance of learning about the past.

Smaller book packagers use a fair number of freelancers and select candidates based on the quality of a portfolio and experience in total book design.

Any designer can design books or book jackets—the same fundamentals of design apply. But, in truth, not every designer can do book design well, just as not every jacket designer can create an effective or inspired interior. Different skills and talents are required, and although many designers have both, desire must be supplemented by knowledge. A book jacket is a mini-poster, but an interior is, in the case of text, a matter of knowing the nuances of type, and, in the case of a visual book, understanding the nature of visual flow. And flow is not as easy as following a grid in placing pictures on a page; it involves knowing what elements complement each other, which picture crops contribute to the dynamism of the page, and how the pages should flow to achieve melody, harmony, and dissonance. To learn this, sometimes on-the-job-training is adequate, but intensive study in school or a continuing education program is best.

Ultimately, a designer in book publishing might choose to stay in this specialty for a long or short time depending, of course, on the nature of the job. Many art directors and designers devote their lives to the field because challenges are ever-present; others find the specialties too limiting and, after a while, look for new opportunities in other creative media.

RANT AND RAVE: WILL THE BOOK SURVIVE?

The book's continuing vitality as a form of communication can be traced from the Good Book to the PowerBook, from the invention of movable type (Gutenberg's bibles) to the silicon chip (laptops). New media prosper because of the book—witness the continued success of Amazon.com (currently the industry standard). Books by or about media moguls and Silicon Valley sheiks such as Bill Gates and Andy Grove proliferate. Even media events, such as the O.J. Simpson trial, are summarized in books.

Today's book designers can trace their lineage to Gutenberg, for what is Quark or Pagemaker but a sophisticated typesetting technology? Designers have adapted to each generation of technology: to hand-set metal type, to Linotype, to phototype, to cutting and pasting on the desktop. Although tasks are now accomplished with a keystroke or mouse click, today's book designer still must observe traditions of book design such as copyright page protocol, folio placement, and indexing. There are potential pitfalls, however, for designers who rely too heavily on page layout software. Long before Steve Jobs and Steve Wozniack invented the Macintosh, the nuts and bolts of text design—line length, line leading, text block proportion, margins, and kerning—were prerequisites to good critical judgment of legibility and readability. These elements of typographic style are not built into the software. No matter how fast or sophisticated the technology becomes, the computer is only a tool aiding the designer.

And yet as Kindles, Nooks, and the iPad revolutionize how books are sold, presented, and ultimately read, designers must find a way to be ahead of the curve (or at least neck and neck with it). All forecasts point towards the iPad as revolutionizing how books will be seen on "readers," but only the future knows what that will truly be at this stage. To its credit, some of the newer technology is more participatory in nature. For example, email, interactive Web sites, and chat rooms may contribute to a renewed interest in communication in written form, albeit electronic. The *lingua franca* of technology has borrowed freely from that of typography, books, and printing: desktop *publishing*, *printer*, *fonts*, *kern*, Web *page*, *bookmark*, and, best of all, *PowerBook*. The computer has opened up opportunities for designers in new media. The difference between Web page and printed page may continue to narrow as the technology of one and the craft of the other evolve. If history is any guide, the book, in all likelihood, will survive.

—Michael Carabetta

It is possible to get a book design job without having had experience. A smart portfolio with good samples may be enough to spark an employer's interest. Nevertheless, it is advantageous to include at least some book-related material. That said, the following is recommended.

Entry Level

School assignments should exhibit an ability to design book jackets and interiors. Emphasis on typography, photography, and illustration is important. Samples should exhibit both formal taste and conceptual acuity. They do not have to be published works, but should be fairly professional comprehensives produced as color lasers or Iris prints.

CONTENTS

Ten to twenty samples:

    a. The majority should be book jacket designs on a range of themes, both fiction and nonfiction, exhibiting typographic and pictorial skill and talent

    b. A few interior book pages

Junior/Senior Designer

Junior designers may show exemplary school assignments but should include as much printed work as possible. Senior designers should show only printed book covers and interiors, as well as complete bindings, if available.

CONTENTS

Fifteen to twenty-five samples:

    a. The majority should be book jacket designs on a range of themes, both fiction and nonfiction, exhibiting a variety of printing techniques

    b. One or two speculative projects (self-generated comprehensives) to show a range of conceptual ability

    c. Interior book pages (if available)

    d. Two or three entire projects (interior, cover, jacket)

Format

35mm slides (in tray) are still applicable, but increasingly this method is being phased out in favor of CD and DVD in the following formats: Flash, PowerPoint, and iPhoto. Online portfolios are also encouraged. Avoid digital tricks. Keep it as straightforward as possible. Anything that crashes the viewer's computer will hamper appreciation of your work.

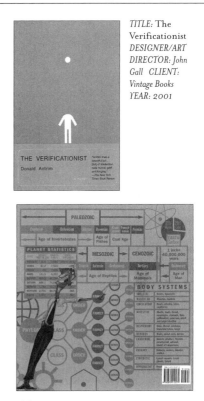

TITLE: The Verificationist *DESIGNER/ART DIRECTOR: John Gall CLIENT: Vintage Books YEAR: 2001*

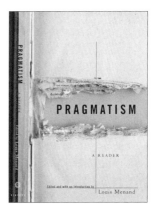

TITLE: Science Verse – *back cover CLIENT: Penguin Group DESIGNER/ART DIRECTOR:Molly Leach ILLUSTRATOR: Lane Smith AUTHOR: Jon Scieszka DATE: 2004*

TITLE: Pragmatism *DESIGNER/ART DIRECTOR: John Gall CLIENT: Vintage Books YEAR: 1997*

| # Makes You Pick Up the Book

Art Director, Vintage/Anchor Books, New York City

» Did you study to be a book jacket designer?
Not specifically, but I did study graphic design. Having gone to school in New Jersey, I felt I was at a bit of a disadvantage competing against all the SVA/Parsons/Pratt graduates when it came time to look for a job. My professor gave me a list of designers I should show my portfolio to. Not really knowing much about New York design offices at this point, I made a ton of cold calls—ones I could never imagine making now. "Uh, hello, is Massimo Vignelli in?" "May I speak with either Mr. Chermayeff or Mr. Giesmar?" So I dropped my portfolio all over town, got some nice callbacks and responses—but no jobs.

Eventually, I answered an ad in the *New York Times* for a book cover designer. Unfortunately, it was a mass-market publisher. But a foot in the door is a foot in the door. Coming out of design school and into this world of ultra-condensed type, gold seals, and romance paintings was a cold slap in the face. So I left after ten months, vowing never to work in book publishing again. And we know how that worked out.

What would you say differentiates your designs from those of other book designers?
I like to think that the work I do, when it's good, makes you want to pick up the book. Simple as that: I hope they are striking, witty, beauti-

ful, weird, surprising, all that stuff, and have a clarity of idea that is true to the book. Some people have told me that my covers don't seem to have a particular style, and others have told me they recognize my covers all the time…so who knows.

Even though the primary function of the cover is to be noticed in the bookstore, I like to think I'm designing for that teeny audience of readers who are going to take the time to appreciate what is going on with the cover. It's a contradictory life.

What is the relative importance of images in jacket design, as opposed to all-type solutions?
This is a tricky question because as a designer I feel that either method can be used in a given situation. Generally speaking, all-type covers are reserved for certain kinds of nonfiction and image-related covers can work for both fiction and nonfiction. To approach, say, a novel with an all-type solution is a bit of a risk—well worth taking, but it may not go over well with everyone else. There is also an emotional tug that an image can supply that is much harder to get with an all-type cover. This is a slippery slope—appealing to emotions—as it can get into manipulative marketing areas, but there's no denying the power that a cover like, say, the one that Chip Kidd (or maybe I should choose a cover of my own here?) did for the

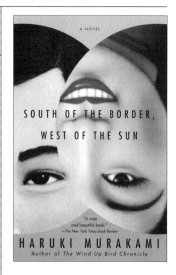

TITLE: South of the Border, West of the Sun DESIGNER/ART DIRECTOR: John Gall CLIENT: Vintage Books YEAR: 2000

TITLE: The Theater of the Absurd DESIGNER/ART DIRECTOR: John Gall PHOTOGRAPHERS: Assorted CLIENT: Vintage Books YEAR: 2003

TITLE: The Vintage Series—Hughes, Amis, Didion, Naipaul DESIGNER/ART DIRECTOR: John Gall PHOTOGRAPHERS: Corbis (Hughes), Michael Birt/K2/CPi (Amis), Ted Streshinsky/ Corbis (Didion), John Minihan/Hulton Archive (Naipaul) CLIENT: Vintage Books YEAR: 2003

TITLE: Zeno's Conscience DESIGNER/ART DIRECTOR: John Gall CLIENT: Vintage Books YEAR: 2002

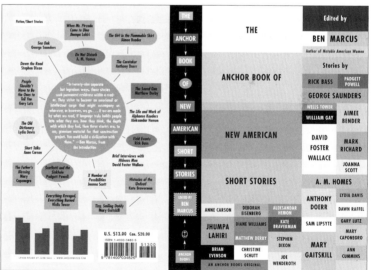

TITLE: The Anchor Book of New American Short Stories DESIGNER/ ART DIRECTOR: John Gall CLIENT: Vintage Books YEAR: 2004

TITLE: The Box Man DESIGNERS/ILLUSTRA-TORS: John Gall, Ned Drew ART DIRECTOR: John Gall CLIENT: Vintage Books YEAR: 2000

≫

TITLE: A Box of Matches
DESIGNER/ART DIRECTOR:
John Gall CLIENT: Vintage
Books YEAR: 2003

TITLE: Up in the Air
DESIGNER/ART
DIRECTOR: John Gall
PHOTOGRAPHER: Steven
Swintek/Getty Images
CLIENT: Vintage Books
YEAR: 2002

New Testament, with the vividly bloody Andreas Serrano photo. This could never be conveyed with type, not with this immediacy. I think that images offer another level of communication — a more immediate one.

What is your process? Do you work with authors or editors, or is yours a sole creation?

The way we work at Vintage is that we will have an informal meeting at the beginning of our list, and editors will present their books and then we'll discuss general directions we might want to go in or avoid. Some of this discussion will also mention comparisons to other known covers. This meeting usually happens before I have had a chance to peruse any of the manuscripts, so it's more of a listening session for me. At this point, I promptly forget (for the time being) everything that was said and read the book and see what ideas might emerge. This is not that I am intentionally disregarding the opinions of editorial or marketing (who know a lot more about publishing a book than I do), but it allows me the freedom (in my own head) to develop ideas and designs that were unimaginable at first. Now this approach may seem loaded with hazards (and it is, and has left me scrambling at the last minute, many times) but if we're after something new and fresh, starting with comparisons to other book covers isn't really going to help. It may help locate the niche market but not the design. Next, the gauntlet of approvals must be run. Editors, publisher, marketing, people standing in the hall, authors, agents—each one

trying to take a little bite. Different adjustments may need to be made, but if it becomes too much I'll go back to the drawing board.

When I do freelance work, I'm usually sent a manuscript and left to my own devices. The difference between a freelance job and in-house work is that if a freelance job just isn't working out, I can remove myself or be removed from the case. In-house, I'm there until the bitter end. So, I do approach the cover as a personal creation, and the best ones are the ones that get through unscathed, but this is an industry of negotiation, compromise, and working with others, which is fine with me, and I am willing to do what's best for the book. Sometimes what's best is to get the book into as many airport bookstores as possible; other times it's just going to be a cool cover.

Would you say that book cover and art direction has enough challenges for you?

Well, every day I look at a brand-new blank 6 x 9 or 5 x 8 panel and wonder what in the world I can possibly do that hasn't been done. Somehow it gets done and my new life as a short-order cook gets put on hold again.

What would you suggest to designers who want to pursue this design form?

First of all, an enjoyment of reading is paramount. I think it is also good to develop a range of design skills, since book themes are all over the map and being knowledgeable in design history and style is helpful. And if you want to design books and book covers, have some examples in your portfolio.

The Classic Style

Art Director, Roxbury, Connecticut

>> **How long have you had your own studio?**
Since 1988.

Why did you select children's book design?
It selected me, really. My husband, [illustrator] Lane Smith, was having trouble with an early book of his and recruited my help. Prior to that I'd been working as a magazine art director and I think my editorial sensibility brought something different to children's books. One of my first books was *The Stinky Cheese Man*. The design is closer to magazine than book design and that was fairly unusual back in 1992. Eventually I gave up magazine work altogether for books—most of them children's—Lane's and others. It's much nicer than working very late Sunday nights at *Sports Illustrated*.

What are the changes in practice you have seen and experienced since you began?
When I began designing, we were doing paste-ups with rubber cement, using ruling pens and sending out for photostats. Also, the rules have changed for children's book designers. It was quite a challenge to convince Viking that the design of *The Stinky Cheese Man* (in 1992) was even acceptable—let alone a good one. The book contains traditional stories with a twist. My idea was to use a traditional typeface (Bodoni) and use it in a whacky way. So

I thought to fill each page with type regardless of the amount of words. Whether the page had twenty words or two hundred twenty, the type filled it. And it melts, expands, and shrinks. Prior to that, most books had to have a certain point size in a very traditional font and layout. But, even then, in those precomputer days, children were visually literate and in many ways more visually sophisticated than their parents. Today, of course, everyone designs on a computer and it's given designers more freedom to experiment.

How have these changes impacted your work?
Certainly I can do a lot more in one day. And I love that I can live in the country and get work to clients just as quickly as I could if I still had my studio in Manhattan. And, designing children's books is more fun these days because there aren't as many restrictions. For example, when I started, all type in a book had to surprint in black. This was because when it was translated into other languages, the particular country would only have to swap out the black plate on press. Today books have a rainbow of colored fonts that can drop out.

Would you say that you have a particular style or character to your design? If so, how would you define it?

TITLE: Fantastic Mr. Fox *and* The Twits— *covers, reissued Puffin edition*
CLIENT: *Penguin/Puffin Books*
DESIGNER/ART DIRECTOR: *Molly Leach* *ILLUSTRATOR*: *Quentin Blake* *AUTHOR*: *Roald Dahl* *DATE*: *1998*

>>

Yes, I do. I think it's a classic style, rather than anything trendy.

What about graphic design is the most challenging for you?

Explaining what I do to my relatives! Often people don't know what designers do and therefore don't find it important or valuable. Respect is hard to come by in design. Occasionally I've had the experience where I've turned in my work and the publisher realizes they need to add a line or two and someone in the art department will open your files, add the type and throw off the whole balance of the design—one of the pitfalls of the digital age.

How important is type and typography in what you do?

Extremely important. In kid's books the type, along with the art and words, is an important component. Jon Scieszka and Lane did a book called *Math Curse* about a kid's day where everything turns into a math problem. Using Franklin Gothic, I boxed the math problems like a text book would and added odd tangencies to enhance the frantic feel of the book. I also did a series of books for Maria van Leishout (*Bloom*, *Peep*, *Splash*). These books were illustrated in a very soft, delicate style. I wanted the type to be bold without obliterating her fragile work so I chose very soft pastel colors in very large Officina Sans. *John, Paul, George & Ben* took place in colonial America so I studied old broadsides and chapbooks and created an eighteenth-century look with antique fonts.

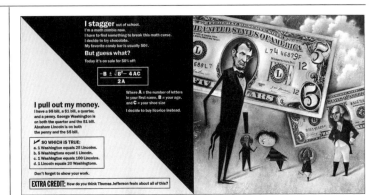

TITLE: Math Curse *CLIENT: Penguin Group DESIGNER/ART DIRECTOR: Molly Leach ILLUSTRATOR: Lane Smith AUTHOR: Jon Scieszka DATE: 1995*

TITLE: Peep! A Little Book About Taking a Leap *CLIENT: Feiwel and Friends Books DESIGNER/ART DIRECTOR: Molly Leach ILLUSTRATOR/AUTHOR: Maria van Lieshout DATE: 2009*

TITLE: Splash! A Little Book About Bouncing Back CLIENT: Feiwel and Friends Books DESIGNER/ART DIRECTOR: Molly Leach ILLUSTRATOR/AUTHOR: Maria van Lieshout DATE: 2008

TITLE: Bloom! A Little Book About Finding Love - cover CLIENT: Feiwel and Friends Books DESIGNER/ART DIRECTOR: Molly Leach ILLUSTRATOR/AUTHOR: Maria van Lieshout DATE: 2008

What, in this current technological and economic climate, does the future hold for you specifically, and graphic design in general?

I worry for graphic design because I think some publishers believe their in-house folks, with perhaps not as much design mileage, are as capable as a professional. Some are. Many aren't. I fear freelancers will be a luxury that publishing houses might feel they can do without. As I said earlier, people don't always know—or appreciate—what designers do.

TITLE: John, Paul, George & Ben CLIENT: Hyperion Books for Children DESIGNER/ART DIRECTOR: Molly Leach AUTHOR/ILLUSTRATOR: Lane Smith DATE: 2006

TITLE: The Really Ugly Duckling from: The Stinky Cheese Man and Other Fairly Stupid Tales CLIENT: Penguin Group (Viking) DESIGNER/ART DIRECTOR: Molly Leach ILLUSTRATOR: Lane Smith AUTHOR: Jon Scieszka DATE: 1992

The Escalating Importance of Sales

Art Director, New Directions, New York

>> **How long have you been a graphic designer?**

I've been a graphic designer for thirteen years and counting, primarily as a book jacket designer.

What are the changes in practice you have seen and experienced since you began?

The most prominent change is the escalating importance of "sales" in book publishing. Book publishing as a whole was driven exclusively by editors/authors and the publishers. Today each book can be influenced and scrutinized by the marketing and sales departments to meet the expectations of the major book buyers (i.e., Amazon, Barnes & Noble).

How have these changes impacted your work?

I hear the words "big book look," "human element," and "fresh perspective," so regularly from clients that it becomes difficult not to allow them to influence my design. These words translate into bright colors, easy to see artwork for new mediums such as Amazon.

Would you say that you have a particular style or character to your design? If so, how would you define it?

If you lay out my designs on a table you probably wouldn't find "a style" because it comes from how I approach projects and from the ideas themselves. My style is derived from the way I think and the ideas I generate, not the individual executions.

What about graphic design is the most challenging for you?

The most challenging part is scaling my work so I can produce more projects, for more clients, faster and still maintain the quality.

What are the projects that most satisfy your aesthetic sense?

That's a tough one. I guess a new type of project that makes me have to explore new aesthetics?

How do you feel education has changed in the past decade?

The Internet provides limitless sharing and increased exposure to ideas. Increasingly education must play a role to help students navigate through the noise that is the Internet to find the important trends that they can really learn from.

What, in this current technological and economic climate, does the future hold for you specifically, and graphic design in general?

For graphic designers in general, technology inspires the idea of "limitlessness" while the economy creates "limits." Technology allows limitless sharing of ideas, tools to create with, and platforms to work across (interactive, mobile, print). At the same time, the

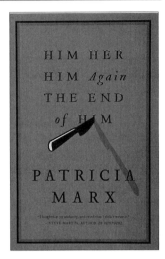

TITLE: Him Her Him Again the End of Him *by Patricia Marx* ART DIRECTOR: *John Fulbrook III* DESIGNER: *Rodrigo Corral* CLIENT: *Scribner Books* DATE: *2007*

TITLE: The Best Creative Nonfiction, Vol. I, *Edited by Lee Gutkind* DESIGNER: *Rodrigo Corral* ART DIRECTOR: *Ingsu Liu* CLIENT: *WW Norton* DATE: *2007*

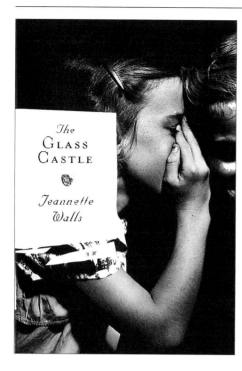

TITLE: The Glass Castle *by Jeanette Walls ART DIRECTOR: John Fulbrook III DESIGNER: Rodrigo Corral CLIENT: Scribner Books DATE: 2005*

current economic constraints could limit the demand for these ideas. The economic constraints seem to create boundaries and make us question everything. This questioning hopefully results in increased quality, a slower pace, smarter development, and forces us to pay closer attention to the details.

TITLE: Lullaby *by Chuck Palahniuk CLIENT: Doubleday DESIGNER: Rodrigo Corral ILLUSTRATOR: Judy Lanfredi DATE: 2002*

TITLE: The Brief Wondrous Life of Oscar Wao *by Junot Diaz ART DIRECTOR: Lisa Amoroso DESIGNER: Rodrigo Corral CLIENT: Riverhead Books DATE: 2007*

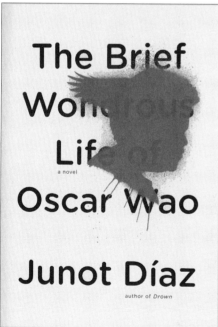

TITLE: Bush on the Couch *by Justin A. Frank, M.D. CLIENT: Reagan Books ART DIRECTOR: Michelle Ishay DESIGNER: Rodrigo Corral DATE: 2004*

| # Books Last Forever

Partner, Marshall & Delesert, Lakeville, Connecticut

>> **Why did you decide to go into book design?**

I worked for four or five years as a graphic designer in a limited market in Colorado; then I went to Denver and got a job in an advertising agency. I worked in the design studio for two years, and then I worked for about six or seven years as an art director. I think that really taught me how to think and how to come up with ideas and how to sell ideas. Then I moved to Europe and I got a job in advertising, but it was almost impossible to do that in a foreign culture. I quit and started designing books on a freelance basis.

What is the most satisfying aspect of your job? The least?

The most satisfying is that when you produce a book, it lasts forever, whereas in advertising you do a TV commercial and you have a great time in Hollywood working on it, working with a lot of nice directors, models, but the commercial runs for two weeks. A few weeks in different markets and it's gone, or it becomes a print ad. But a book can really influence a lot of people for many, many years. So I think that's the most satisfying. The least satisfying is that now the publishing industry, almost internationally, has been so taken over by marketing people that a lot of the creativity is getting lost.

How much of your work is educational books?

The company that I'm doing a huge percentage of my work for does publish school and library books, but they're not necessarily textbooks. They have a small percentage of trade books and a large percentage of school and library, so I'm doing quite a bit of those. They can be short stories, or illustrated classics, or a series of nature books. These are obviously discussing educational topics, but they're not necessarily textbooks.

Do you work closely with illustrators?

Yes. There's a huge collaboration. I would like to start writing books because, in a way, I'm writing them already. Many of the books I'm working on began because the illustrators came to me to help them work out their ideas. By the time I work out the storyline of the pictures, I feel like I've contributed to that book as if I were an editor. The same is true for the text. A lot of illustrators now don't have many outlets. The magazines are really cutting back on the use of illustration. A huge percentage of book jackets are now being done in Photoshop with stock photos. But I think that there is still this glorious illustrated children's book market for illustrators.

TITLE: La Fête des Enfants
DESIGNER/ CREATIVE DIRECTOR:
Rita Marshall COMPANY: Marshall
& Delesert CLIENT: Editions Script
PHOTOGRAPHER: Marcel Imsand
YEAR: 1984

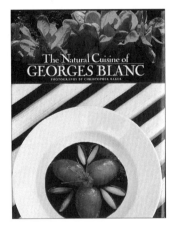

TITLE: The Natural Cuisine
of Georges Blanc DESIGN-
ER/CREATIVE DIRECTOR: Rita
Marshall COMPANY:
Marshall & Delesert CLIENT:
Stewart, Tabori and Chang
PHOTOGRAPHER: Christopher
Baker TYPEFACE: Nicholas Cochin
YEAR: 1987

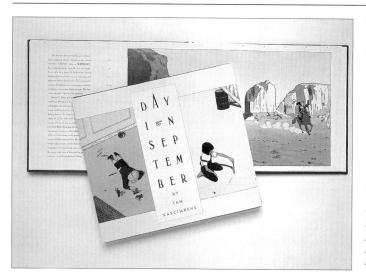

Does it take a certain personality to work well with illustrators?

I think it does. Once again, you have to be able to have an idea of how you want this book to tell the story. If the illustrator also has an idea, you have to work with her to get it right. It's basically her book. After many years of doing that, I've gotten better at it.

TITLE: A Day in September *DESIGNER/ CREATIVE DIRECTOR: Rita Marshall COMPANY: Marshall & Delesert CLIENT: Creative Editions ILLUSTRATOR: Yan Nascimbene TYPEFACES: Blackfriar, Bodega, Opti Packard YEAR: 1995*

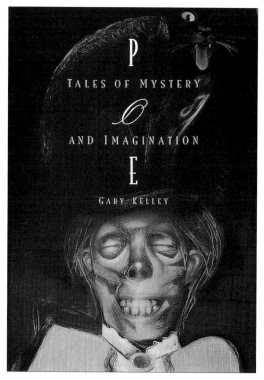

TITLE: Poe/Tales of Mystery and Imagination *DESIGNER/ CREATIVE DIRECTOR: Rita Marshall COMPANY: Marshall & Delesert CLIENT: Creative Editions ILLUSTRATOR: Gary Kelley TYPEFACES: Bodega, Mona Lisa Recut, Lucia YEAR: 1996*

TITLE: Dance *DESIGNER/CREATIVE DIRECTOR: Rita Marshall COMPANY: Marshall & Delesert CLIENT: Creative Editions TYPEFACES: Copperplate, Piranesi YEAR: 1994*

Trials of Trade Publishing

Creative Director, Chronicle Books, San Francisco

≫ As the creative director of a primarily illustrated book publisher, what are your primary concerns?

Chronicle Books is a publisher of illustrated books. My criteria, and those of our designers, are twofold: practicality and aesthetics. Practically speaking, we strive to communicate what the book is about: its title, its content, and its spirit. Aesthetically speaking, we aspire to design books with captivating, original visual content. In the crowded world of book retailing, where the eye encounters scores of titles in seconds, it's imperative to arrest the browser's eye. In the case of a bestselling name author with a stack of books on display, this alone will catch your attention. But what about the unknown first-book author? This is where design can provide the means to get your attention, compel you to pick up the book, read the flap copy or back cover blurbs, and take it to the cash register. It's by design that this last bit of marketing is accomplished and the sale made.

You have a full-time staff, but you also commission freelance designers. How is that division of labor accomplished?

The first division of labor occurs when books are assigned to our designers on staff. We divide the book projects to balance the workload and see that our design-

ers have an opportunity to work on different types of books of varying levels of complexity. Next, the designers can decide, based on their workload and preferences, how they would like to proceed with a given project, either as sole designer or as a project director, which entails hiring a freelance designer, photographer, illustrator, or other talent.

What do you look for in a designer's portfolio for a staff job?

The qualities we look for in a designer's portfolio, whether for a staff position or freelance assignment, are essentially the same: namely, originality and a sound approach to the basic elements of design—in particular typography. A book, above all, is meant to be read. We're looking for a designer's proven ability to compose text and visuals into an integral whole, to give the book a sense of continuity and personality. A working knowledge of materials and printing processes is a given.

With new media as a major aspect of design, do you see the role of the book, and book design, changing in any significant manner?

It is obvious when you think about it, but we often forget that the book has withstood the innovations of radio, movies, TVs, VCRs, CD-ROMs, and now

TITLE: The Body *DESIGNER: Lucille Tenazas CREATIVE DIRECTOR: Michael J. Carabetta COMPANY: Chronicle Books CLIENT: Chronicle Books PHOTOGRAPHER: Tono Stano TYPEFACE: Bodoni YEAR: 1994*

TITLE: Star Wars Chronicles *DESIGNERS: Earl Gee, Fanny Chung CREATIVE DIRECTOR: Michael J. Carabetta COMPANY: Chronicle Books CLIENT: Chronicle Books TYPEFACE: Centaur YEAR: 1997*

TITLE: The Blues Album Cover Art *DESIGNERS: Sarah Bolles, Michael Carabetta CREATIVE DIRECTOR: Michael J.Carabetta COMPANY: Chronicle Books CLIENT: Chronicle Books PHOTOGRAPHER: David Gahr TYPEFACE: Bell Gothic YEAR: 1996*

the Internet. With each successive medium, the doomsayers predicted the book's demise. Long before the development of new media, books were fought over, collected, burned, banned, and passed down from century to century. Books remain the backbone of education, reference, literature, and, ironically, technology. Virtually all computer and software manuals are printed in book form because they offer what no hardware can—comfort, accessibility, and absorbability of highly technical literature.

TITLE: Chronicle Books Trade Show Booth DESIGNER: Earl Gee CREATIVE DIRECTOR: Michael J. Carabetta COMPANY: Chronicle Books CLIENT: Chronicle Books PHOTOGRAPHER: Andy Caulfield TYPEFACE: Copperplate Gothic YEAR: 1992

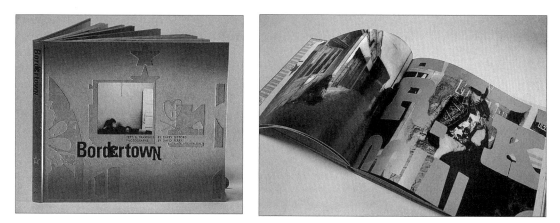

TITLE: Bordertown *DESIGNER: Martin Venezky CREATIVE DIRECTOR: Michael J. Carabetta COMPANY: Chronicle Books CLIENT: Chronicle Books PHOTOGRAPHER: David Perry TYPEFACE: Univers YEAR: 1998*

CHIP KIDD | Exterior Man

Senior Designer, Alfred A. Knopf Publishing, and Principal, Chip Kidd Design, New York City

>> **You are known as a prolific book jacket and cover designer. Have you done many interiors of books?**

I've only done a handful of interiors. In terms of text and novels, I've done several, including *The Secret History* with Barbara de Wilde. In terms of picture books, I did a book with Chuck Close, the artist, that was an overview of his work since 1988, when he became a paraplegic.

How do you feel about doing covers and not interiors?

I think the interior designers at Knopf get beaten up a lot by editorial, far more than I do. They are considered the ugly stepchildren of design here, which is really a shame. But every once in a while somebody there does something really nice and really wakes me up to what is possible. What usually happens is that I get a jacket approved very early on, something that I am really excited about, and I have to go through all of the political channels in order to be able to design the interior. But personally, I think the two should be unified; there's no reason for the jacket to have one kind of personality and the inside to have another. It just doesn't make any sense.

Do you have a personal style?

I don't consciously try and design

that way. People have said, "I can tell if you did something in the bookstore but I can't really put my finger on why." You don't need to define it; not being able to put it into words suits the medium of graphic design perfectly. Certainly I can say I prefer that things are usually on a straight line instead of curved—the simpler the geometry, the better. The publisher here thinks I'm a minimalist. But I think I'm a minimalist only in the sense that I look at a jacket and ask, does this element need to be here? If I can put my thumb on it and not miss it, then I get rid of it. But certainly I think I've done jackets where there's a lot going on. Sometimes that is needed.

How has the computer affected your work?

It's allowed me to do a lot more in a much shorter amount of time. It's seductive, and I have to fight it in order to keep reminding myself that it doesn't have to be the starting point of everything. It can be involved somehow, but going from doing everything by hand to doing everything by machine makes you have to remind yourself that you can do things by hand again, if you want. I think the computer is great and has completely changed everything, but if I was in charge of the graphic design program at a college, I would make all the kids spend their first year not using it at all.

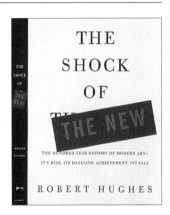

TITLE: The Shock of the New
DESIGNER/CREATIVE DIRECTOR:
Chip Kidd PUBLISHER: *Knopf Publishing*
CLIENT: *The New York Times* TYPEFACES:
Bodoni, Trade Gothic YEAR: *1996*

TITLE: American Illustration
Annual #14 *DESIGNER/ CREATIVE
DIRECTOR: Chip Kidd PUBLISHER:
American Illustration ILLUSTRATOR/
HANDLETTERER: Chris Ware
YEAR: 1995*

TITLE: Print *Magazine cover* DESIGNER/ CREATIVE DIRECTOR: *Chip Kidd* PUBLICA-TION: *Print Magazine* YEAR: *1995*

How involved are you in the final production of your work—the separations, paper, printing? Do you get involved in that aspect at all?

I get involved only to the extent that I can deal with. One of the really nice things about working someplace like this is that we have a really terrific production department, and I would much rather defer to them on this stuff. This is why when I'm sitting around designers and they're talking about paper stocks and things like this, I'm really at a disadvantage because I have no idea what they're talking about. Which is probably bad for me, because I'm not always going to be here.

THE NEW TESTAMENT

translated by

RICHMOND LATTIMORE

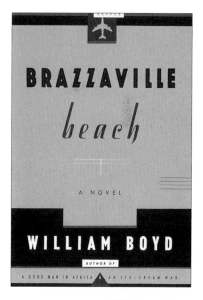

TITLE: Brazzaville Beach *DESIGNER/ CREATIVE DIRECTOR: Chip Kidd* PUBLISHER: *William Morrow* YEAR: *1994*

TITLE: The New Testament *DESIGNER: Chip Kidd* CREATIVE DIRECTOR: *Michael Ian Kaye* PUBLISHER: *North Point Press* PHOTOGRAPHER: *Andres Serrano* TYPEFACE: *Times Roman* YEAR: *1996*

IV. MUSIC/CDs

GRAPHICALLY DESIGNED album covers were not used by the recording industry until the late 1930s, but from that moment on original cover art changed the courses of design and music history. The first record album designed by pioneer Alex Steinweiss for Columbia Records increased record sales by an incredible 800 percent over nondesigned covers. After the first year or so, sales no longer depended entirely on the quality of album design, but during the ensuing decades, graphic design for LP and now CD covers has contributed to the overall allure of the music package as well as the identities of musicians. Indeed, certain recording artists are forever remembered as much for their emblematic album art—for example, The Beatles' *Sgt. Pepper's Lonely Hearts Club Band*—as for their performances. Although the quality of the music (and the airplay it gets) ultimately determines whether a record succeeds or fails in the market, album design definitely tips the purchasing scales. Creative packaging has long been an integral component of the marketing equation. Yet today, with online music sources surging in dominance and popularity, the old paradigms of music design are rapidly changing. Type and image continue to be important, but the lavish presentations of the past are now more rare.

The recording industry is nonetheless a wellspring of graphic design. It may no longer be one of the design field's most viable career niches, but it is still a viable area for specialization. Music will remain a key entertainment industry.

Although various codes are imposed on the design for different kinds of music, within these constraints is great potential to do innovative work. In addition, the

> THE EASE OR DIFFICULTY OF DESIGNING RECORD ALBUMS AND COLLATERAL MATERIAL CAN BE MEASURED IN DIRECT PROPORTION TO THE STAR QUALITY OF THE RECORDING ARTIST(S).

recording industry offers the designer a modicum of cultural cachet and public visibility.

Large record labels have sizable art and creative services departments that are responsible for CD and tape cassette packaging as well as all collateral material (including lyric booklets, special collectors' packages, and in-store displays). A typical design department is supervised by a *product manager* or *creative director*, who may or may not have a background in design. If a recording company has multiple divisions and separate labels (such as classical, pop, rock and roll, hip-hop, etc.), a single design director may oversee individual art directors assigned to each division. Within this hierarchy, in-house designers are assigned to work on projects within either one division or a few. These designers are usually responsible for typography and imagery (they may commission freelance illustration and photography or execute it themselves). Sometimes freelancers are temporarily hired to assist senior staff designers. Additionally, the seasonal release of many new and repackaged records often necessitates commissioning seasoned freelance designers with studios or firms to design entire record packages.

The recording industry operates much like the book industry. New records are scheduled for release during a selling season, which must be coordinated with promotional materials and performances. Designers must strictly adhere to these schedules lest the coordination of release and promotion be sacrificed. Nonetheless, design and conceptual packaging ideas are always subject to change, sometimes owing to the whim of a recording artist, who may not like a particular solution, or the marketing department, which may prefer an entirely different approach.

The ease or difficulty of designing record albums and collateral material can be measured in direct proportion to the star quality of the recording artist(s). The most popular not only retain the contractual right to approve or reject design but can also recommend a preferred graphic designer, artist, or photographer. This is not rare, but neither is it common practice. Most record albums are designed in a routine manner without the recording artist's involvement. Scheduled releases are determined by product managers, who transmit the monthly or seasonal list to the art director, who, in turn, makes specific design assignments to the staff or freelancers. Once budgets are determined, these designers develop ideas that must be initially approved by the art director and, after comprehensives (or dummies) are completed, go to the product manager and marketing departments for final acceptance or rejection. Unfortunately, the process does not always stop there. Graphic design is not an exact science—it is not even a science—and various non-design-savvy people in the recording industry, like any industry, some-times weigh in with opinions that can affect the final outcome.

In a large recording company, this kind of interference is fairly common; in a comparatively small company, where low budgets prevail, more creative license is often the rule. The recording industry has long included many small or independent companies that cater to a wide range of musical tastes and talents. Of course, the job hierarchies in these precincts are not as strict as in the larger compa-

ARTIST VERSUS ARTIST

The most popular recording artists often retain the contractual right to approve their album covers and promotion. The really big stars may also have the power to decide who designs their record packages. For example, the Rolling Stones have total control over their identity, and Mick Jagger and Keith Richards act as art directors. This can be frustrating for the record company art director, whose input is thus limited, yet who is still responsible for the production of the total package. But it is, at the same time, a tremendous opportunity for the anointed designer to work with legendary musicians.

Sometimes, however, the collaboration between recording artist and graphic artist is not satisfying in the least, particularly if the latter is on staff at a recording company.

Because it can be difficult to get a good idea passed through the marketing department in any case, when it is for a high-visibility act, the stakes are even higher. Having to

TITLE: *Sting "Brand New Day— The Remixes" CD Packaging CREATIVE DIRECTOR: Joe Mama-Nitzberg ART DIRECTOR/ DESIGNER: Stefan G. Bucher COMPANY: 344 Design, LLC CLIENT: A&M Records © A&M Records YEAR: 2000*

negotiate ideas with the musicians or their managers can be a further stumbling block. And then ego kicks in. Graphic design is not an anonymous endeavor, and no matter how much a designer might appear to believe that her work is solving someone else's design problem, in the end the designer has to have some ego satisfaction, too. In the record industry, the balance between individual ego and professional responsibility is often tough, but in the end it must be reconciled in a professional manner.

nies; in fact, many independents employ only freelance designers to fulfill their design needs. Some freelancers work on a project-by-project basis, while others are hired on retainer to give consistency to an entire record label's particular identity. Small record companies' budgets are invariably tight, which challenges the enterprising designer to develop innovative approaches and allows for more ambitious solutions. Moreover, independents are not always tied to conventional marketing presumptions and, therefore, encourage designers to take chances that larger companies would not consider.

CDs are still being produced these days by large and numerous small independents. Some alternative indie labels even release 7" x 7" vinyl records with sleeve covers. Designing for these companies offers little remuneration in exchange for invaluable freedom. The work offers a good entry point into the album design field.

Designing for a standard CD package means that the designer is confined to a square plastic jewel box (or, in some cases, a cardboard sleeve that is protectively wrapped in plastic). The box is usually clear, but occasionally colored plastic is used. A small multipage booklet inserted between the front of the box and the CD serves as the album cover. On the front of the booklet is emblematic cover art or a photograph with the typeset or custom-drawn album title; inside are the liner notes describing and crediting the music, artist, producer, etc., along with lyrics, photographs, and other pertinent information. The verso side lists the contents of the album and is also a continuation of the design motif. The front side of the disk itself is also usually emblazoned with type or image.

Recording companies are still releasing boxed sets—in fact, more and more —containing two or

---

THE KEY TO BEING A GOOD DESIGNER FOR MUSIC PACKAGING IS TO HAVE PASSION FOR MUSIC REGARDLESS OF STYLE OR FORM.

---

more CDs, that comprise many more printed materials than a single album, including printed inserts that are often ambitiously designed and produced. In addition, the box that holds the CDs is often fairly unconventional—for example, a casket-shaped box for Goth music, a guitar case for Elvis Presley's entire oeuvre. This kind of assignment offers great opportunities to test a designer's skill with two- and three-dimensional media. Although product managers usually determine when and for whom these packages are produced, an enterprising designer can suggest and experiment with approaches that might be accepted.

The key to being a good designer for music packaging is to have passion for music regardless of style or form. One can approach music as just another job, but the results usually betray such indifference. Also, one should appreciate the musical genre that is being packaged. Think small and think simple. An effective design must somehow underscore the essence of the musical content, help to project the ideas therein, and apply an emblematic image to the sounds. This can derive from individual interpretation or conversations with the musicians. Whatever the means, a record album design must not be a set of rote solutions. Of course, the demands of marketing are at odds with the instincts of art. But designers must nevertheless begin each project with confidence that their proposed design is indeed the best way to graphically frame their subject.

TITLE: Heyday Review Sample Panel CLIENT: Barnes & Noble ART DIRECTOR/ DESIGNER/ILLUSTRATOR/ PHOTOGRAPHER: Ward Sutton DATE: 2009

It is possible to get a design job in the music industry without previous experience designing album packages. A portfolio that exhibits stylishness and conceptual intelligence may entice a potential employer. Nevertheless, it is advantageous to include at least some music-related material, even if that includes comprehensives.

Entry Level

School assignments are useful. Emphasis on typography, photography, and illustration is important. Samples do not have to be printed, but they should be fairly professional comprehensives produced as color lasers or Iris prints.

CONTENTS

Ten to twenty samples:

    a.   CD packages on a range of musical genres to show versatility and interest in music

    b.   Two or three compilation or gift boxes, to indicate an ability to think conceptually and employ printing variations

    c.   One or two non-music-related pieces

Junior/Senior Designer

Junior designers may retain a few school assignments but should include as many printed pieces as possible. Senior designers should show a variety of printed pieces representing a range of music genres.

CONTENTS

Fifteen to twenty-five samples:

    a.   CD packages (and one or two cassette packages) exhibiting a variety of printing techniques

    b.   One or two speculative projects to show a range of conceptual ability

    c.   As many special packages as available

    d.   A range of collateral materials—posters, flyers, point-of-purchase displays

Format

35mm slides (in tray) are still applicable, but increasingly this method is being phased out in favor of CD and DVD in the following formats: Flash, PowerPoint. and iPhoto. Online portfolios are also encouraged. Avoid digital tricks. Keep it as straightforward as possible. Anything that crashes the viewer's computer will hamper appreciation of your work.

TITLE: Solar Twins "Rock the Casbah" CD Packaging DESIGNER/PHOTO-GRAPHER: Stefan G. Bucher COMPANY: 344 Design, LLC CLIENT: Maverick Recording Co. © Maverick Recording Co. YEAR: 1999

TITLE: 16th Anniversary Weekend DESIGNER: Art Chantry COMPANY: Double Down Saloon TYPEFACES: Custom YEAR: 2008

STEFAN SAGMEISTER | An Artist's Vision

Principal, Sagmeister, Inc., New York City

>> **How did you become such a specialist in music packaging?**

I thought that it would be a great combination of my two favorite things: design and music. I get a bigger kick out of meeting some of my musical heroes than sitting in meetings with marketing directors (which I did a lot before I opened my own specialized studio). I love record stores. I love coming up with an idea just by listening to music.

What challenges or obstacles are involved in music packaging?

· The package is small; like most challenges, this can be turned into an advantage.
· The format never changes but still should be filled with something new every time.
· In general, the budgets are smaller than in regular graphic design.

What were some of your most challenging projects?

As in general graphic design, the bigger the project, the more people involved, the harder to get anything through, the wetter the tears, the louder the cries, the bigger the challenge.

Do you have to answer to the artists, or an in-house art director, or both?

We present to the artists. In-house art directors are often helpful

*TITLE: H.P. Zinker
DESIGNERS: Stefan Sagmeister, Veronica Olt CREATIVE DIRECTOR: Stefan Sagmeister COMPANY: Sagmeister, Inc. CLIENT: Energy Records PHOTOGRAPHER: Tom Schierlitz TYPEFACES: Peignot, Franklin Gothic, News Gothic, Hand Type YEAR: 1994*

TITLE: Jazz Festival "Konfrontationen" DESIGNER/CREATIVE DIRECTOR: Stefan Sagmeister COMPANY: Sagmeister, Inc. CLIENT: Nickelsdorfer Konfrontationen MECHANICAL: Christian Hochmeister YEAR: 1990

TITLE: David Byrne Feelings DESIGNERS: Stefan Sagmeister, Hjalti Karlsson CREATIVE DIRECTORS: Stefan Sagmeister, David Byrne COMPANY: Sagmeister, Inc. CLIENT: Luaka Bop, Warner Bros. MUSIC MODEL MAKER: Yuji Yoshimoto PHOTOGRAPHER: Tom Schierlitz TYPEFACES: Hand Type, Franklin Gothic YEAR: 1997

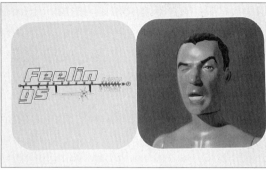

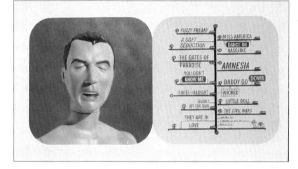

(they are designers themselves and know that it's counterproductive to have one more opinionated person on the project) but occasionally there are other groups involved: on the record company side, product managers, marketing people—if the band is very important, the president or CEO; on the management side, band manager, business manager, tour manager.

In the face of the artist's creative vision, how do you maintain your own?

We try to take on jobs only from artists whose visual sense we admire—David Byrne, for example.

Do you want to continue in this specialty, or do you foresee a much more general practice?

I want to continue; there are still quite a number of CD covers to be designed.

TITLE: Rolling Stones' Bridges to Babylon DESIGNERS: Stefan Sagmeister, Hjalti Karlsson CREATIVE DIRECTOR: Stefan Sagmeister COMPANY: Sagmeister, Inc. CLIENT: Promotone B.V. ILLUSTRATORS: Kevin Murphy, Gerard Howland, Avan Auers PHOTOGRAPHER: Max Vadukul TYPEFACES: Hand type, Mrs. Eaves YEAR: 1997

TITLE: Record Playing Postcard DESIGNER/CREATIVE DIRECTOR: Stefan Sagmeister COMPANY: Sagmeister, Inc. CLIENT: Sagmeister, Inc. TYPEFACE: Spartan YEAR: 1993

The Key to the Soul

Creative Director & Principal, 344 Design, LLC, Pasadena, California

≫ What is the most challenging aspect of designing CD packages?

Coming up with an idea, with a design that properly represents the music and is entertaining in and of itself. The most politically challenging aspect of the process is persuading the record company, the artist, and the artist's girlfriend that your solution is the right solution. CD packages, covers in particular, are scrutinized by hordes of people at the label and in the artist's circle. They come at the tail end of the recording process and at that point there's a lot of anxiety in the air. That said, great ideas almost always sail through. It's the ones that are only pretty good that make everyone's life difficult.

How do you come up with an appropriate visual representation of the music?

Ninety percent of the time the label hands me a stack of photos that are flagged for the cover, usually a portrait of the artist or band. In those cases I try to make run-of-the-mill material into something special through added illustration, typography, color— anything I can do to get away from the standard format. When the label and the artist both agree that I should have the freedom to play, well, then I go play. I'll listen to the music on a continuous loop for a few days and start scribbling

into my sketchbook. Or I'll take a walk and look at the world to see what reminds me of the music. Something always stands out.

Given that you design for music, how deeply is music part of your nonprofessional life?

I love music. It's the breath of the gods and the key to the soul. I listen to music constantly. A lot of nights I let it run while I sleep. I still go to concerts every once in a while, though not as much as I used to. I got spoiled when I worked in-house at a record label. Once you've been on the guest list and got to amble past the lines it's hard to stand in line again. (I'm a snob, I know.) But I'll always turn out for Prince. And for the L.A. Philharmonic. And for the KCRW pledge drive.

How much of the process of designing CDs is dependent on the recording artists' whims and desires?

It depends on the artist. They seem to be most open after they've released one or two albums that did OK. They're confident, but they're not divas about it. The big-name acts seem to rely on their managers when it comes to choosing artwork. Managers generally fall into two categories: former lawyers and former bouncers. Both have big egos and need to let you know they're the boss. But if you can get them on

your side, you're usually home free. Oddly, the most capricious clients are artists about to release their first album. In their mind, they're already superstars. They just know they'll sell ten million records, and they want you to treat them accordingly. (About one in five of those albums get dropped

TITLE: All Access—The Making of Thirty Extraordinary Graphic Designers AUTHOR/DESIGNER: Stefan G. Bucher COMPANY: 344 Design, LLC CLIENT: Rockport Publishers © 344 Stefan G. Bucher YEAR: 2004

TITLE: Oliver Peoples 3 CD Packaging ART DIRECTOR/DESIGNER: Stefan G. Bucher COMPANY: 344 Design, LLC CLIENT: Oliver Peoples Eyewear © Oliver Peoples Eyewear YEAR: 2006

TITLE: *Solar Twins CD Packaging* ART DIRECTOR/DESIGNER: *Stefan G. Bucher* PHOTOGRAPHERS: *Geoff Moore, Ann Short, NASA/CalTech/JPL, StGB* COMPANY: *344 Design, LLC* CLIENT: *Maverick Recording Co.* © *Maverick Recording Co.* YEAR: *1999*

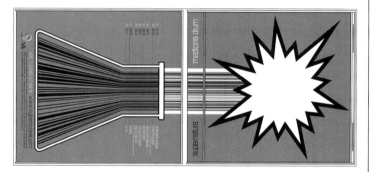

TITLE: *Medicine Drum "Supernature" CD Packaging* ART DIRECTOR/DESIGNER: *Stefan G. Bucher* COMPANY: *344 Design, LLC* CLIENT: *Higher Octave Records* © *Higher Octave Records* YEAR: *2001*

TITLE: *John McCarty "Plans We Made" CD Packaging* ART DIRECTOR/ILLUSTRATOR: *Stefan G. Bucher* COMPANY: *344 Design, LLC Client: Burst Records* © *Burst Records* YEAR: *2005*

from the roster before they even get released, by the way.) But I understand those artists. They don't know the boundaries yet, and they're full to the brim with ambitious glee. Which is a great and wondrous thing. They're out to change the world, and they want my help. When I make a connection with these artists, all the jaded industry knowledge goes out the window and I drink their Kool-Aid. I become part of their band for a little while, and I do whatever I can to help them make it. It doesn't happen that often.

Do you have a preference among pure type, type and photo, or illustration?

As long as it's beautifully done and serves to bring a great idea to life, I love it all. I love working with great photographers. I adore a simple type-driven cover. I started out as an illustrator, so whenever I get a chance to put pen to paper, I'm happy. (Illustration is probably the most difficult to handle, particularly if it's a portrait of the artist. They tend to want a photo of themselves, because this will be their calling card for at least a year, often longer. Few artists are secure enough to live with an illustration of themselves.)

Can one design for record labels without having previous experience? In other words, is it all just design?

In my experience, record labels are like all clients: They think that their projects are totally unique and their problems complex. In reality, it is all just design.

End of the Golden Era

Principal, Art Chantry Design, Seattle, Washington

≫ How long have you had your own studio?

I've been on my own since I started professionally in 1978. I rented in-house studio space from another designer for two years before going out into space of my own. I highly advise avoiding "in-house free-lance." Ultimately, it's a financially abusive arrangement for the novice.

What are the changes in practice you have seen and experienced since you began?

The changes in practice (and form) since I started have been dramatic. When I began, I view that period as the end of a golden era where the design/advertising industry was in its last formal glory. Large agencies and studios dominated the industry collaborating with major corporations and having a large hand in the say and direction of the identities and branding of those corporations.

Since then, with the advent of the computer, all the peripheral support services of the design/advertising industry have been centralized into the desktop computer and we now have to provide everything ourselves. Think of it—when we wanted a photograph or an illustration or proofreading or great typography, we hired other professionals to do it for us and directed their activities. Then we would even profit from the practice by marking up their services and making a small profit by actually hiring them.

TITLE: Queens of the Stone Age DESIGNER: Art Chantry COMPANY: Lotto Arena TYPEFACES: Custom YEAR: 2008

TITLE: The Supervillians DESIGNER: Art Chantry COMPANY: Social Pavillion TYPEFACES: Custom YEAR: 2007

TITLE: The Sadies DESIGNER: Art Chantry COMPANY: 3B Tavern TYPEFACES: Custom YEAR: 2007

TITLE: *Jucifer* DESIGNER: *Art Chantry* COMPANY: *Head of Femur* TYPEFACES: *Custom* YEAR: *2008*

TITLE: *Monsters are Waiting* DESIGNER: *Art Chantry* COMPANY: *Club at Firestone* TYPEFACES: *Custom* YEAR: *2008*

TITLE: *Queens of the Stone Age* DESIGNER: *Art Chantry* COMPANY: *Lotto Arena* TYPEFACES: *Custom* YEAR: *2008*

TITLE: *Black Moth Super Rainbow* DESIGNER: *Art Chantry* COMPANY: *The Pavillion* TYPEFACES: *Custom* YEAR: *2008*

So what about today?

Today, we provide *all* of that our-selves and then have to compete with in-house staffs of hourly employees with minimal skills on price point to even land the project. At the same time the large number of people of all ages entering the field simply relying on what the computer can do for them has reduced the work available to a small fraction of the design field that I originally entered.

The bottom line, we do far more work and take on far more responsibilities for far less money and far less quality. In a sad way, I sometimes feel I'm watching the decimation and ultimate ending of a brave and beautiful craft industry. From my current point of view, I really see no more need to actually hire the freelance graphic designer any more. Why should they? We cost too much and the computer guy in the basement working for minimum wage can do "good enough" work to pass.

But you do get work, don't you?

Currently, I make more money by clients that hire me for my name and not for what I do. Essentially, as the market changed (and what I do stayed the same) I was edged into a different category. I'm now hired as an "artist." People want "Art Chantry" to do something for them and to promote it as such. Very seldom do I get hired because a client wants real "design" work.

How have these changes impacted your work?

I have to work much harder and longer and for far less money just to get the work. Then I have to turn it around very fast and not be ≫

too intellectually challenging or it will be rejected outright (dumbeddown). And I have to expect the work to be drastically altered by the client after it leaves my hands. I can no longer control the creative process of my own work.

You have a particular style or character to your design; how would you define it?

It's an intellectual style based on attitude and knowledge and not on appearance—even though appearances are affected by the style. For years I've had to compete professionally with people adopting my "style," or at least what they think my style appears to be. What they actually seem to do is grasp a momentary idea that my style is working around and simply copycat it as if it were "art chantry look." But because they don't really understand my style at all, it simply looks like their work trying to ape somebody else.

What is the essence of your style?

I explore the subcultural language forms of American graphic design. If you see this work as language as it should be, then what I do is very clear. If you see it as "art" or something like that, you won't be able to read my language form.

What about graphic design is the most challenging for you?

The most challenging part of design is getting to know the client—the history, the personality, the ideas and the philosophy, the market, the function, the product, the quirks— everything. Without that knowledge of the client and his project, you really can't do graphic design. It's

extremely challenging to do the research and human interaction to get the basic info out of a client. But, once you do, the work you create for them is close to perfection.

What are the projects that most satisfy your aesthetic sense?

I really enjoy projects that are so directly linked to the viewer that it's almost as if I'm talking directly to their faces. I think the closest I've ever come to that is with the crummy B&W Xeroxed telephone pole punk poster. But, even that has several layers of clients between you and the viewer.

How important is type and typography in what you do?

Back when the world of typography was strictly the province of the professional typographer as directed by the designer, it was all important. Most of the rules of classic design processes derived from the strict rules of typography. However, today, with typography being more and more the province of the DIY (do it yourself) designer with a computer, I find classical typography less important. If anybody can simply type out "good enough" typography out of their desktop system, then (again) why hire me? So, as typographic availability and quality has oozed into our everyday experience, I find that I step back and get less and less "clean." I find that what I do by hand as an individual is the only thing I can offer that can't be done by a desktop computer system (yet). So, I guess as technology gets better and better, I get lousier and lousier. Simply

because it's so hard to do "lousy" on a computer. I find people now hire me to do work that was once considered "lousy" —because they can't do it themselves any more.

What, in this current technological and economic climate, does the future hold for you specifically, and graphic design in general?

I've become more and more acting the role of "artist" rather than "designer." In popular culture, the two words have virtually become interchangeable and the distinctions are almost broken down. Any action "creative" is "artist." And designers have become media stars as if they were actual artists. However, I still can't divorce my thinking from the idea that design and art are extremely different disciplines with different function, knowledge, and histories. In the past I used to joke that I was an artist masquerading as a designer. I think the roles have now officially reversed into a designer masquerading as an artist. Go figger.

TITLE: Roller Con '08 DESIGNER: Art Chantry COMPANY: Double Down Saloon TYPEFACES: Custom YEAR: 2008

WARD SUTTON

Rock, Theater, and Politics

Illustrator and cartoonist, Sutton Impact, New York City

How long have you had your own studio?

I began working freelance after college, in 1989. By 1992, I was able to let go of my part-time jobs as I was making a full living from my illustration, cartooning, and design.

Are you happy with what you do?

I love it.

Are you happy with what is going on in the design field?

The shift from print to online work has some very exciting aspects. I've enjoyed creating work exclusively to appear online. In terms of exposure, now anyone can see it, not just those who happen to purchase a certain publication. But I'm sad to see so many fine magazines and newspapers folding, and people I've enjoyed working with losing their jobs. Plus the online world is still figuring out its financial model, in terms of paying for content and control of copyright, etc., and that is cause for anxiety at the moment.

Comics play a large part in what you do. Why?

As a freelancer, I enjoy getting to do lots of different things—it keeps me from getting bored. As time goes by my interests wind in different directions. For awhile I had a focus on rock posters, then illustration, then animation, then political cartoons (and often these overlapped). Right now I am really

TITLE: The Heyday of the Insensitive Bastards *CD case CLIENT: Barnes & Noble DESIGNER/ART DIRECTOR/ ILLUSTRATOR/PHOTOG- RAPHER: Ward Sutton DATE: 2009*

TITLE: Obama as Spiderman CLIENT: Entertainment Weekly *DESIGNER: Dwayne Shaw ART DIRECTOR: Brian Anstey ILLUSTRATOR/ PHOTOGRAPHER: Ward Sutton DATE: 2008*

interested in finding new ways to communicate with cartoons. I've worked as a "cartoon reporter," covering the 2008 political conventions and 2009 Inauguration, and am currently creating Illustrated Reviews of books for the Barnes & Noble Review Web site. I think there are so many possible uses for comics that haven't been explored—it's exciting. And I've been experimenting with my style—combining photos and illustration to add more depth visually.

What are the changes in practice you have seen and experienced since you began?
I had some harrowing races to the FedEx office years ago when meeting a deadline meant meeting the FedEx deadline. And the computer has revolutionized the way I work. I've gone from creating everything on paper, to creating linework on paper and scanning to color on the computer, to now often creating everything directly on the computer. I'm a big fan of the Wacom tablet.

How have these changes impacted your work?
Email and the computer afford more opportunity for back-and-forth with art directors, more ability to tweek things, more ability to create and offer variations and experiment artistically.

You have a particular style or character to your design; how would you define it?
I read a quote recently that said that those who run out of inspiration fall back on technique. The quote resonated with me—I realized there have been times in my career when this has happened.

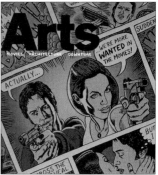

TITLE: Wanted — Arts Section Opening Illustration CLIENT: Time Magazine DESIGNER: Chrissy Dunleavy ART DIRECTOR: Arthur Hochstein ILLUSTRATOR/PHOTOGRAPHER: Ward Sutton DATE: 2008

TITLE: Pearl Jam Poster — Prague and Budapest CLIENT: Pearl Jam DESIGNER: Ward Sutton ART DIRECTOR: Amesbros Design ILLUSTRATOR/PHOTOGRAPHER: Ward Sutton DATE: 1996

TITLE: Freak Broadway Show Poster CLIENT: Freak DESIGNER: Kevin Brainard ART DIRECTOR: Spot Design ILLUSTRATOR/PHOTOGRAPHER: Ward Sutton DATE: 1998

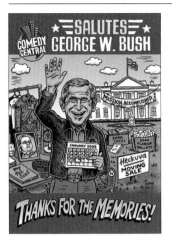

TITLE: *Thanks for the Memories! DVD Cover and Pull-Out Poster* CLIENT: *Comedy Central* DESIGNER/ILLUSTRATOR/PHOTOGRAPHER: *Ward Sutton* ART DIRECTOR: *David Derrick* DATE: *2008*

TITLE: *Village Voice Star Trek Cover* CLIENT: *Village Voice* DESIGNER: *Jesus Diaz* ART DIRECTOR: *Ivy Simones* ILLUSTRATOR/PHOTOGRAPHER: *Ward Sutton* DATE: *2009*

When I'm no longer inspired to work a certain way but am asked to by an art director, or when I just don't have any new ideas. That's why I constantly try to challenge myself and push what I do in new directions. Through all that I do believe there is a certain style that I have, but it evolves over time. Sometimes I think others can see my style more easily than I can see it myself.

What about graphic design is the most challenging for you?

My strengths lie in working with visuals and hand-drawn elements. Working with fonts and type that I haven't created myself—and incorporating them into my drawings and designs—is a challenge that I don't necessarily enjoy, so I try to avoid it.

What are the projects that most satisfy your aesthetic sense?

The projects that begin with my idea, which I then pitch to a potential client. These are the most artistically rewarding in the end, since it all came about through my own inspiration and initiative. But working this way is also stressful and tiring as I often have to do a lot of work on the front end not knowing if the project will go anywhere. It's a lot easier to simply illustrate an article on assignment than create a whole project myself and sell it.

How important is type and typography in what you do?

It's crucial for my comic work.

When I'm doing comics, as opposed to illustration, I'm both a writer and artist. I've created my own hand-written font that I use in my comics, and I'd like to create more. Having a font makes editing so much easier than just writing everything by hand, which is what I used to do. When creating a poster design, I treat the type (which I do by hand) as important a visual element as the other parts of the illustration.

What, in this current technological and economic climate, does the future hold for you specifically, and graphic design in general?

Right now I'm thrilled about the work I'm doing, but I'm also exhausted. I feel like I'm working much harder for less money than I was ten years ago. This is surely related to the economic climate, but likely due to other known and unknown factors as well. But I think we're at an exciting moment partially because nobody knows what's going to happen. What happens when there are no more newspapers? You can approach it all with fear but I prefer to keep my eyes open for the exciting possibilities of what comes next. Is everyone going to walk around with a Kindle, or some spin-off thereof? If so, that will present a whole new design field. Just think about how many Web designers, photographers, and animators there are today—and those jobs didn't exist fifteen years ago. I'm excited to see what's coming next.

V. INFORMATION DESIGN

YOU MAY ASK isn't all graphic design about packaging information? In a word: No. Graphic design is about framing ideas, projecting attitudes, promulgating styles, *and* managing information, but not always at the same time. We have already touched on those disciplines, such as editorial and corporate design, where presenting information is a key but not the only concern of the designer. Yet in recent years, information design, or what architect/designer/author Richard Saul Wurman calls "information architecture," has grown not only in importance in these particular media but also into a specialized discipline under the graphic design rubric. Although information architects argue that theirs is a field unto itself, far from being subsumed by graphic design, it is discussed here as a graphic design sub-genre with its own defining characteristics.

Information design, at its most rudimentary, employs type and graphics to clarify and concretize mostly nonvisual information, such as facts and figures. This is not an entirely new form; after all, pie charts and fever-line graphs have been used throughout the century in all kinds of arcane and public documents, from scientific reports to high-school textbooks. Yet usually these visual aids have been minimally designed, if designed at all. Over fifty years ago, however, a movement began to improve such material by making it more visually accessible. What has been called the pictograph revolution, launched

THE ROLE OF THE INFORMATION DESIGNER IS TO GUIDE USERS AWAY FROM CONFUSION INTO UNDERSTANDING, REGARDLESS OF SUBJECT.

by German designer and social scientist Otto Neurath in the late 1920s, introduced universal graphic symbols that stood for common words, terms, or concepts and were used in charts, maps, and graphs to represent specific ideas and notions. These images evolved into what are known today as *pictorial sign symbols*, the icons used in public spaces like malls and airports to identify rest rooms, restaurants, telephones, etc. But even more important, they developed into an extensive lexicon of icons used to clarify all kinds of data, from television listings to annual corporate profit and loss statements. Thus they have become the proverbial picture that speaks a thousand words.

Pictorial sign symbols are used in graphic design disciplines—editorial, corporate, environmental, etc.—and are ubiquitous on computer screens and as Web site navigational buttons. But the sign symbol is only one small part of information design. Type and image are the primary tools of graphical information management. As in any design discipline, information designers must have a mastery of these fundamental tools, but unlike in decorative design, the focus is not on style and fashion but rather function and utility. The role of the information designer is to guide users away from confusion into understanding, regardless of subject.

Information can be communicated in many ways. For example, introduced in the post–World War II era, the Swiss School or International Style of graphic design proffered the reduction of graphic design to a few typefaces built on tight grids and based on mathematical proportions. All text and

visual information fit into strict formats void of nonessential or decorative graphic accoutrements. Breaks in text, indicated by added space or different type weights relieved daunting masses of text, and generous amounts of white (or negative) space lessened the clutter of most high-density visual material. It was correctly assumed that the reader would focus on the essential aspects of the printed matter and, in the end, simplicity wed to rigidity would enable greater comprehension of what was usually dry information.

The International Style continues to hold sway when designers have to assemble massive amounts of textual information for publication, but owing to the sharp increase in the volume of information during this "information age," concurrent with the decrease in available time for the average user to digest these data, additional presentation alternatives have been introduced to both ease and simplify information flow. The current information design specialist must be fluent in all methods of presentation and expert in decidedly visual or graphic approaches. What's more, the clear and entertaining communication of data is surging with more need on the web for digestible charts, maps, graphs, and interactive graphics.

This is not an area that a designer can acquire only through instinct (although some people are better suited to visual organization than others). Yet this does not mean that instinct does not play a part in the day-to-day process of design. Information designers are in various

THIS IS NOT AN AREA THAT A DESIGNER CAN ACQUIRE ONLY THROUGH INSTINCT (ALTHOUGH SOME PEOPLE ARE BETTER SUITED TO VISUAL ORGANIZATION THAN OTHERS).

proportions typographers, statistical analysts, mapmakers, and reporters, and must constantly draw upon their instincts in these areas to make correct design decisions. However, while the combination of all or some of these attributes is important, to become an information designer one often begins as a renderer of others' ideas. Most designers start as,

and many continue to be throughout their careers, translators of writers', analysts', or reporters' nonvisual material into graphic form. To do it well—to make intelligent interpretations—is invaluable because often what passes for information design is merely the overlay of a few decorative graphics that may relieve eyestrain but fail to add substantive cues that help the user obtain or retain the information.

Effective information design looks good, but it also adds an intellectual dimension to the subject that increases the user's understanding. It must eliminate, again in the words of Richard Saul Wurman, "information anxiety." The ability to achieve this goal takes time and practice. Although information design is an expanding area of graphic design and practitioners are always in demand, an even greater demand exists for those with outstanding qualifications. The way to attain these is, first, to pursue a good education; second, to start practicing at any level and in any medium that is available; and, third, to explore different ways of presenting information—to not follow tired formulas.

TITLE: Eating the Recipe - Desk Topography DESIGNER: Alicia Cheng COMPANY: mgmt CLIENT: Yale University Graphic Design MFA Class YEAR: 1999

This is a comparatively new field, but one with fairly rigorous standards. Portfolios should be tightly edited and professional.

Entry Level/Junior

School assignments should emphasize the marriage of research, reporting, and design. Samples need not be published, but they should be quality laser or Iris prints.

CONTENTS

Ten to twenty samples:

> Charts, maps and graphs that show drafting and conceptual strengths are good examples.

Senior

Printed work showing a wide range of problems and solutions designed for periodical, textbook, audiovisual presentations, and annual reports is preferred.

CONTENTS

Fifteen to twenty-five samples:

> a. Charts, maps, graphs, and information graphics that exhibit typographic acuity and conceptual strength
> b. Online or CD-ROM graphics (if available)

Format

35mm slides (in tray) are still applicable, but increasingly this method is being phased out in favor of CD and DVD in the following formats: Flash, PowerPoint, and iPhoto. Online portfolios are also encouraged. Avoid digital tricks, keep it as straightforward as possible. Anything that crashes the viewer's computer will hamper appreciation of your work.

TITLE: Tour de Force CLIENT: Sports Illustrated ART DIRECTOR: Steve Hoffman DESIGNER/ ILLUSTRATOR: Nigel Holmes DATE: 1997

TITLE: Icon System for Information Graphics CLIENT: Network World DESIGNER/ ILLUSTRATOR: Nigel Holmes DATE: 2002

TOUR DE FORCE

Cyclists are about halfway through the three weeks of the Tour de France. 198 riders started from Rouen on July 5 (the route is different each year); 19 are already out of the race with injuries. Here are the peaks and valleys of their 2,403-mile ride, compressed into nine inches.

- One stage per day
- The 19 road stages range in length from 92 to 163 miles
- Crashes through July 14

Information Is the Basis of Everything

Principal, Explanation Graphics, Westport, Connecticut

>> **How long have you had your own studio?**

From 1967 to 1977 in London, my company was called Musgrave House; (then I worked at Time magazine in New York until 1993, but continued to do lots of freelance work while there); from 1994 to present in Westport, Connecticut, the company is called Explanation Graphics.

What are the changes in practice (and form) you have seen and experienced since you began?

The speed with which jobs can be done. Then: slow, now: faster (and easier). Then: all by hand, now: start by sketching with a pencil as before, but completed with a computer. Then: art-work/mechanicals with multiple overlays and type repros stuck into position with glue, and the whole package (often very large and heavy) delivered by courier to a printer, by commercial airline. Now: from computer straight to printer. Then: office with enough space for plan chests, type books, reference books, materials (mounting boards, acetate, mylar, amberlith, letraset letters, patterns and graduated screens, inks, rotrings, tape, rulers, straight edges, cow gum, compasses, mechanical pencils, electric pencil sharpener, oval templates, ship's curves, propor-tion wheel, lightbox, magic tape).

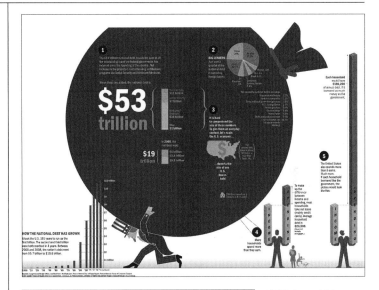

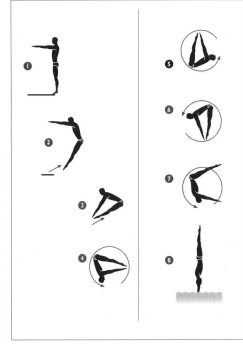

TITLE: America's Debt CLIENT: American History ART DIRECTOR / DESIGNER/ ILLUSTRA-TOR/PHOTOGRAPHER: Nigel Holmes RESEARCH: Lorraine Moffa DATE: June 2009

TITLE: How to Do a Reverse Inward Pike CLIENT: Bloomsbury Press/ Wordless Diagrams ART DIRECTOR /DESIGNER/ ILLUSTRATOR: Nigel Holmes DATE: 2005

>>

Now: sketchbooks, pencils, scanner, computer (and I kept all the reference books, despite google and wikipedia).

How have these changes impacted your work?

I can do more: "set" my own type, as opposed to getting proofs from a repro house; do my own research; the computer is my courier service. And I can do multiple versions of any job, often paring the imagery down to the right amount that gets the message across most efficiently, right up to deadline.

What is the allure of information design?

Information is the basis of everything I do, so it's not so much allure as a given, a necessity, before starting any job. The exact choice of information or data is important, however. That's why data can be seen as a slippery thing, merely promoting someone's agenda. Certain kinds of *faux* information are very appealing: the sort of thing that Jon Stewart and Stephen Colbert do on TV. This is different from *false* information—it's more of a friendly, funny, popular way to introduce people to greater truths. It's interesting to note that many people get their news from these programs. Given the bias in many "real" news outlets (newspaper, Web, radio, cable or network TV), these people are probably better informed, and can have a laugh at the same time.

Would you say that you have a particular style or character to your design? If so, how would you define it?

Nowadays I mostly use a very simple, stripped-down style,

that's flat (as opposed to three-dimensional); linear in its approach to story-telling, with little color and (where appropriate) a sense of humor.

What about graphic design is the most challenging for you?

Mixing illustration (or something visual) with information so that *both* play their part properly. I want to mix pictures and data because I believe that most of us are attracted to visuals first and will read on later, once hooked. If I abuse this, people will just call it trivializing the information (and they have done that). I'm not trivializing information, I am trying to interest readers so they will pay attention to the data.

What are the projects that most satisfy your aesthetic sense?

The ones where I have achieved the principle outlined above—pictures and data working properly together. I like this quote from American painter Hans Hoffman: "Simplification means eliminating the unnecessary so that the necessary may speak."

How important is type and typography in what you do?

It's very important, but in a limited way: I'd use one font all the time. That is not because I don't care about type, it's because it should be invisible in information graphics. My preferred font is Gill Sans (actually Gill Sans Alt I). It is based on classic roman letterforms, but is a sans. Eric Gill's use of historical precedent

gives his typeface both readability and character, something that is lacking in the more neutral sans faces that are often specified for my kind of work.

What, in this current technological and economic climate, does the future hold for you specifically, and graphic design in general?

A move away from print to the Web. Animation (in my case with my son Rowland, who has helped me make short animated films for ten years now). Two kinds of books: First, carefully produced books with lots of attention to graphic detail, binding, paper, printing, probably short runs and expensive; objects that demand to be picked up and handled. Second: print-on-demand books (to my mind the way of the future) for mass-market fiction and non-fiction, paperbacks, textbooks, all with immediate spin-offs into other media: videos, formatted for i-phones, kindle and other electronic readers.

TITLE: Spread from Red Hat (Wordless Story) CLIENT: Self ART DIRECTOR /DESIGNER/ ILLUSTRATOR: Nigel Holmes DATE: 2008

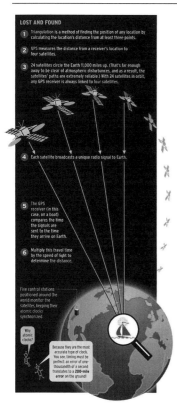

TITLE: How GPS Works CLIENT: Attaché ART DIRECTOR: Holly Holliday DESIGNER/ ILLUSTRATOR: Nigel Holmes DATE: 2004

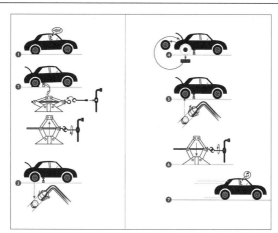

TITLE: How to Change a Tire CLIENT: Bloomsbury Press/Wordless Diagrams ART DIRECTOR /DESIGNER/ ILLUSTRATOR: Nigel Holmes DATE: 2005

TITLE: How to Conduct CLIENT: Bloomsbury Press/ Wordless Diagrams ART DIRECTOR /DESIGNER/ ILLUSTRATOR: Nigel Holmes DATE: 2005

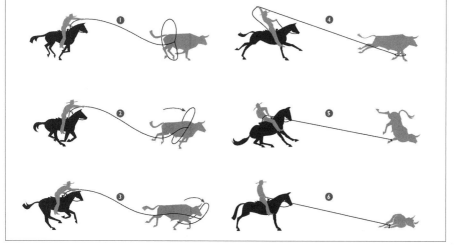

TITLE: How to Lasso a Steer CLIENT: Bloomsbury Press/ Wordless Diagrams ART DIRECTOR / DESIGNER/ ILLUSTRATOR: Nigel Holmes DATE: 2005

Data Visualization

Principal, Feltron, New York City

» How long have you had your own studio?

I started gathering my own clients while I was still employed, and went out on my own in 2002.

What are the changes in practice (and form) you have seen and experienced since you began?

I began as a generalist, doing work in advertising, identity, and editorial and Web design. I also enjoyed having projects in several different mediums happening simultaneously. The influence of personal projects like my "Annual Report" series has been the most surprising twist in my career. While I lost sleep and sweated every detail of notable professional projects that were largely overlooked, the smaller projects I made for myself have had a profound affect on my career.

How have these changes impacted your work?

A few years ago, I saw my expertise growing as an identity designer, and thought that brand-oriented design work would be the future trajectory of my career. The first Annual Report I printed was a great self-promotional tool, and was useful in securing various identity and print commissions. Following the publication of the 2007 Annual Report, the types of work that found me began to change. Through a combination of awareness of me and an increased general interest in data

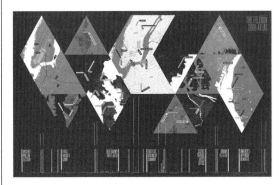

TITLE: Feltron 2008 Annual Report DESIGNER: Nicholas Felton DATE: January 2009

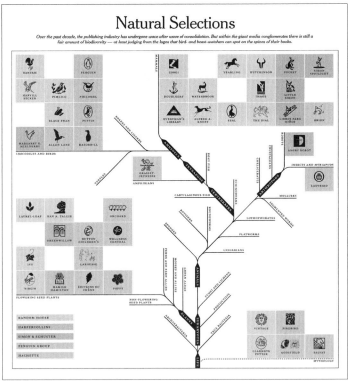

TITLE: Natural Selections CLIENT: New York Times Book Review DESIGNER: Nicholas Felton ART DIRECTOR: Nicholas Blechman DATE: June 2009

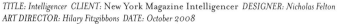

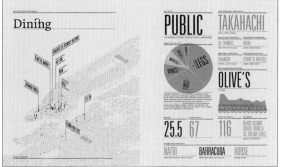

TITLE: Intelligencer CLIENT: New York Magazine Intelligencer DESIGNER: Nicholas Felton
ART DIRECTOR: Hilary Fitzgibbons DATE: October 2008

TITLE: Feltron 2007 Annual Report DESIGNER: Nicholas Felton DATE: January 2008

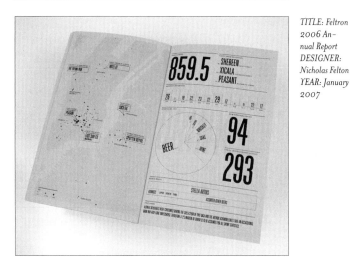

TITLE: Feltron 2006 Annual Report DESIGNER: Nicholas Felton YEAR: January 2007

visualization, I am now primarily known and hired as a designer of data-driven layouts, which suits me extremely well.

What is the allure of information—and faux information?

I appreciate this quote on the matter:

> "I often say that when you can measure what you are speaking about, and express it in numbers, you know something about it; but when you cannot measure it, when you cannot express it in numbers, your knowledge is of a meager and unsatisfactory kind; it may be the beginning of knowledge, but you have scarcely in your thoughts advanced to the state of Science, whatever the matter may be."
> —Lord Kelvin, 1883

I find that pseudo-information is even more amusing when considered under this mantle.

Would you say that you have a particular style or character to your design? If so, how would you define it?

I would describe the character of my work as systematic, rigorous, balanced, and at times obsessive.

What about graphic design is the most challenging for you?

I find the business side of design fairly difficult. I would much rather be doing the work than tracking down a payment or writing a proposal.

What are the projects that most satisfy your aesthetic sense?

The projects that manage to bundle simplicity, obsession, and a clever idea are always the most satisfying to me.

≫

How important is type and typography in what you do?

Type and typography is critical. In the most reductionist view of my work, I believe that I bring high typographic standards to pie charts. I obsess over typographic texture and line breaks in a realm where the norm is established by Microsoft Excel.

What, in this current technological and economic climate, does the future hold for you specifically, and graphic design in general?

It is my hope that the current climate will free clients and designers from some of the restraints of the previous decade and that we will discover some visionary new ways of working along the way. I look forward to corporations using technology and a newfound sense of responsibility to create more work without a primary interest in self-promotion.

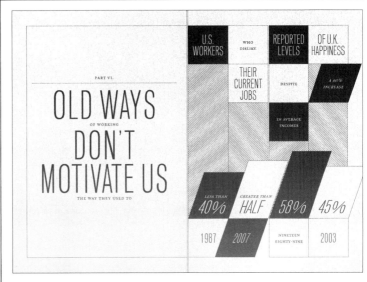

TITLE: We Tell Stories: Hard Times CLIENT: Penguin DESIGNER: Nicholas Felton WRITER: Matt Mason DATE: March 2008

TITLE: The Obsessives CLIENT: Print Magazine DESIGNER: Nicholas Felton ART DIRECTOR: Kristina DiMatteo DATE: April 2007

For the Public Good

Principal, MetaDesign, San Francisco

≫ **What are your responsibilities as project director at MetaDesign?**

I put together creative teams to solve problems. I work simultaneously in the role of creative director and producer in that I help clients under-stand what problems design can solve and then put together the editorial resources and the visual resources and the design resources to execute them.

What kind of clients do you have?

I've been involved with publishing clients as well as clients in soft-ware development, principally for network environments. These are two very different kinds of clients, but representative of my interests in design, in that I'm interested in all kinds of things as opposed to any one thing in particular.

What is the best aspect of being involved with information design and management?

The consequences of the work that I do. I think I help people do things for themselves. As a designer, to do that means being sensitive to the things that people want to do for themselves, the choices people would like to be able to make, and giving them the tools or the resources to do those things. Also, not pushing my agenda of what is hip or cool, not making presumptions of how to do that, but actually listening to clients and working with them.

TITLE: *Conference Flag and Postcard* DESIGNER/CREATIVE DIRECTOR: David Peters COMPANY: GDA, Inc. CLIENT: The Halifax Conference: A National Forum on Canadian Cultural Policy YEAR: 1985

TITLE: *Tommy CD-ROM (unpublished)* DESIGNER: Jerry Lien CREATIVE DIRECTOR: David Peters COMPANY: Two Twelve Associates, Inc. CLIENT: Kardana Productions ILLUSTRATOR: Jerry Lien YEAR: 1994

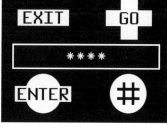

TITLE: *ATM Touchscreen Interface* DESIGNER/ CREATIVE DIRECTOR: David Peters COMPANY: Two Twelve Associates, Inc. CLIENT: Citibank, N.A. YEAR: 1992

ALICIA CHENG

Partner, mgmt, Brooklyn, New York

Explicitly Quantifiable

>> **How would you define information graphics?**

A visual reduction of a complex experience into a graphic representation.

Apart from clarity and understandability, what is the most important component of data-driven graphics?

Authorship and expression. The challenge of information design is not only to create graphics that are clear and accurate but also visually articulate, aesthetically pleasing, and that communicate some aspect of the designer's sensibility.

What appeals to you about info graphics, compared to other graphic design media and genres?

I have always been intrigued by the graphic representation of information, from the humble arrow, to diagrams of military stratagems, to the notation systems of Rudolph Laban. To me, information design expresses the ultimate communicative powers of graphic design: a tangible, data-based problem solved with a descriptive visual strategy that still uses basic formal principles of color, weight, and scale.

Can information be abstract?

Information design can be simultaneously abstract and informational. The works of Ladislav

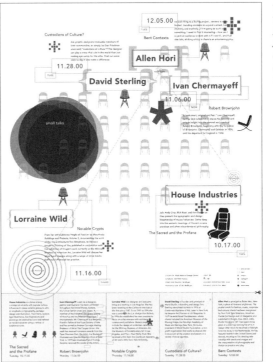

TITLE: *AIGA Small Talks 2000 Poster* DESIGNER: *Alicia Cheng* COMPANY: *mgmt* CLIENT: *AIGA* YEAR: *2000*

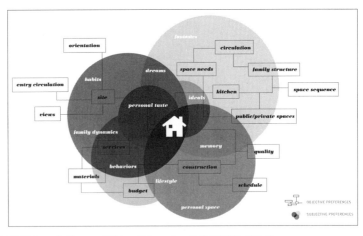

TITLE: *Living for Tomorrow (MIT's prefab "smart house")* DESIGNER: *Alicia Cheng* COMPANY: *mgmt* CLIENT: Metropolis Magazine YEAR: *2002*

TITLE: Eating the Recipe—
Flow Chart DESIGNER:
Alicia Cheng COMPANY:
mgmt CLIENT: Yale
University Graphic Design
MFA Class YEAR: 1999

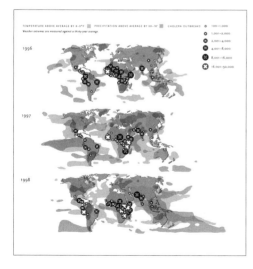

TITLE: Under the Weather
DESIGNER/ILLUSTRATOR:
Alicia Cheng COMPANY:
mgmt Client: Harpers
Magazine YEAR: 2001

Sutnar and Erik Nistche are beautiful abstract compositions in and of themselves. The fact that they also are content bearers makes the visual experience even richer. By investing basic geometric forms with data, a line can represent a movement, a circle the angle of a head, and even a gathering of people could be used to chart the stars. Using these untraditional conceptual forms as a method of record-making to me has boundless possibilities.

Can a designer be ornate and decorative and still produce effective information?

If you include expression and abstraction within that definition, I believe that information can be communicated through a multitude of untraditional graphic elements, applied in unconventional ways. When faced with content that is less explicitly quantifiable (like measuring an esoteric emotion or how technophobic you are), these "decorative" elements can often be the most appropriate means of graphic representation.

Does information graphics require an educational background different from other design disciplines?

A sensitivity to the content and a highly attuned aesthetic awareness is all the special background you need. It helps to see information and data as a palette from which you can create a clear and expressive piece of graphic design.

VI. ADVERTISING & BRANDING

THERE IS NO BIGGER mass communications producer than the advertising industry. More than any other discipline, advertising is so completely intertwined with American life that one cannot even peel a banana without confronting a "Got Milk?" ad. With the exception of public television and radio (which do feature sponsor advertisements), advertising is indeed everywhere and on virtually every surface. While television and radio command the largest budgets and address the highest audience share, print (publications, flyers, brochures, direct mail, and billboards) is the most ubiquitous of the advertising media. Before entering the advertising profession, therefore, it is important to know both the divisions of labor and distinctions among approaches.

The center of advertising production is an advertising agency (or shop, as it is colloquially called). Mega-agencies, midsized agencies, and small agencies sometimes vie for the same accounts as well as service different niches. Some agencies are so big they can afford to accept only megaclients, while others, the so-called boutique agencies, handle lower-billing accounts. The mega-agencies are often media-capital-based conglomerates that also own subsidiary advertising agencies in several cities and around the world. Some of these agencies own graphic design firms that service the creative needs, and produce the collateral materials for, the clients of the larger agency. The midsize agency usually handles midsize accounts, those that do not have tens of millions to spend on saturated national

AN ADVERTISING ART DIRECTOR IS THE ARBITER AND CREATOR OF THE VISUAL MESSAGE OR STYLE; THE COPYWRITER DEVELOPS THE THEMES AND CREATES THE WORDS THAT SELL THE MESSAGE OR THE PRODUCT.

media blitzes, but rather have a few million to spend on targeted areas. The small agency usually gets local accounts with limited budgets (but may have one or two highly visible accounts as well). In addition, countless smaller all-purpose agencies serve small local businesses. Finally, some graphic design firms also handle advertising for their own clients.

The size of an agency is determined by the number of its clients divided by its annual billings. Without getting deeply into the complex financial structure of advertising agencies, which is a book in itself, the larger the agency, the more money it spends on placing advertisements in mass media; the more money it spends, the larger its commission or return. For each ad placed on, say, network TV during the Super Bowl, the agency will get a larger fee than at other less visible time periods. These fees or commissions are tied to the amount it costs to buy ad space. In a sense, the creative services of an agency are a loss leader. The number of employees in an agency is directly proportional to the number of clients that it services as well as the number of accounts that it is attempting to add to its roster. The largest amount of staff work is devoted to existing accounts, but in many agencies some staff is devoted to attracting new business, which often involves creating entire spec (or proposed) campaigns. An agency, regardless of size, may spend hundreds of thousands to capture a prized multimillion-dollar account.

The size of agencies varies from a few hundred employees (and additional freelancers) to two or three persons (and freelancers). An agency is typically headed by two or more *partners*, who are the names on the shingle (for example, Lord Geller Federico and Doyle Dane Bernbach). Whereas a design firm need only have one creative principal, an advertising agency routinely has creative *and* business partners. Under the creative rubric is typically an *art director* and *copywriter*; under the business rubric is an *account executive*. An advertising art director is the arbiter and creator of the visual message or style (either for print or television); the copywriter develops the themes and creates the words that sell the message or product. These "creatives" often work in tandem, in creative teams, and constitute a symbiotic entity. The account executive manages the account. Sometimes this is the person who sold the agency to the client in the first place; at other times this is the liaison between the client and the creative team. This three-way combination is integral to the workings of the agency.

Below the partner level are various jobs and job categories. The principal level is the *creative team*, which is assigned to an aspect of or an entire account. A team may include three or more principals; the number is determined by the scope of the account. Below this level are *creative* and *production assistants* who fabricate the work. In addition, creative teams may call upon freelancers and subsidiaries to attend to the diverse components of the basic campaign. For certain kinds of printed matter, for example, an agency might subcontract to a subsidiary or independent graphic design firm. For television commercials, an independent production house

might get the call. The larger agencies employ their own graphic designers, while the smaller ones may not. The larger agencies may have a house director for TV or radio, but most hire freelance directors from a large pool of itinerant talents. Some agencies directly handle only one aspect of a campaign, like national TV

TITLE: *Bringing Out the Dead* DESIGNER: *Kevin Brainard* ART DIRECTOR: *Drew Hodges* CLIENT: *Paramount Pictures* YEAR: *1999*

spots, and routinely subcontract all other components to independent firms or studios. There are, obviously, many places for a graphic designer to get a foothold in the advertising industry.

Legend has it that art and copy people are not the best collaborators—in fact, sometimes they are too concerned with their turf to meld into one. In advertising, the copywriter once ruled supreme, but for decades art and copy have

been more or less balanced in importance—depending, of course, on the nature of the product. Yet a memorable jingle or tag line— something that forever sticks in the consumer's head—is quantifiably more valuable than the smartest layout or wittiest picture. So, it is important for art directors and designers to pursue writing as well. A talent for writing crisp copy invariably makes the visual idea much stronger. Most schools that teach advertising wed the two disciplines. Incidentally, it is rare that entry-level advertising designers are hired without some kind of formal education.

In the agency hierarchy, television is the pinnacle. Print is, as agency people say, "below the line." Nevertheless, designing for print is a good way to enter the agency structure. Print art directors are usually responsible for a large percentage of creative output, and art and design schools continue to emphasize print as the most important component of a campaign. If an advertising campaign is seen as a strategic military action, television and radio are the first wave of attack, but owing to the expense of mounting such an offensive, print is the second wave of land troops. After saturation bombing to soften up the audience through electronic media, print captures the high ground by providing constant reminders in the manner of a continual assault on the consciousness of consumers.

Starting out in advertising requires some historical deep

background. At root is knowing the function of advertising and how its goals are attained. But the neophyte's true calling card is the portfolio, and this important container must, like an ad itself, contain enough material to convince the interviewer that the interviewee is devoted to making smart advertising. A few years ago, art directors wouldn't even look at portfolios that were not dedicated entirely to advertising campaigns. In fact, graphic designers were thought of as people who make letterheads. However, graphic design is integral to the look and feel of contemporary advertisements. Indeed, a large percentage of advertising today is less about the so-called big idea, driven by the marriage of terse copy and stark image, than about mood, feeling, and attitude. Graphic designers and, specifically, skilled typographers, are routinely hired as staff or on a freelance basis to massage components of or to develop entire advertising campaigns.

Whether or not an agency employs its own graphic design specialists or subcontracts to independent firms, there is no doubt that the graphic designer's role in advertising has measurably increased during the past decade. Among the most typical assignments (for which samples should be represented in a portfolio) are promotion pieces (booklets, flyers, mailers, press kits, etc.), point-of-purchase displays, (easel-back standups, countertop objects, etc.), and package designs. This last has emerged because more

TITLE: Toulouse Lautrec
DESIGNER/ILLUSTRATOR/
HAND LETTERER: Seymour
Chwast CLIENT: Le Nouveau
Salon des Cent YEAR: 2001

TITLE: 947 Years Poster
CLIENT: The Innocence
PROJECT DESIGNER:
Masood Bukhari
ART DIRECTOR: Masood
Bukhari SPONSOR: Sappi
Ideas That Matter, 2007
DATE: 2008

agencies are not only selling already conceived products but also packaging and repackaging old and new products. The value of the so-called full-service agency to a client is its capacity to engage in many advertising and design services.

Designers have a significant role in the advertising industry—particularly these days in terms of design for the web and conception of guerilla (or non-traditional) campaigns. Yet it is nevertheless important to caution that this is a very volatile profession. Even the fortunes of established advertising agencies may tumble when clients pull their accounts—and they invariably do. A client engages in agency reviews when it feels the performance of its current agency is no longer selling the goods, or when it simply wants a change. Moving a multimillion-dollar account can be a devastating blow—if not to the agency as a whole, then at least to many of its employees. Entire creative staffs, including veteran employees who worked years for the same agency, are laid off when accounts are switched. Sometimes the competing agency will hire them—often not. Advertising is a high-pressure profession; its practitioners must creatively serve the client's whims and needs. Many creatives are, therefore, peripatetic, frequently moving from agency to agency. Given this uncertainty, the entry-level designer might be wise to consider starting at a midsized or small agency, one with a variety of relatively stable clients, and spend a few years learning and experiencing the advertising business before moving on.

Advertising is a multimedia industry, and designers and art directors are sought after for print, television, and online work. A typical advertising design portfolio is not very different from a general graphic design portfolio, yet there must be due emphasis on ads and promotion materials.

Entry Level

School projects, including entire ad campaigns for real or imagined products, are useful for showing insight into advertising methods.

CONTENTS

Ten to twenty samples:

TITLE: Code Warrior Packaging
CREATIVE DIRECTOR: Paul Lavoie
DESIGNER: Joanne Véronneau
COMPANY: TAXI CLIENT:
Metrowerks Corp. YEAR: 1994

   a. Two complete campaigns (three or more ads showing headlines and visuals), including logo, print advertisements, and collateral material. (Additionally, show the product, if that was part of the school problem.)

   b. Single ads or posters for different products

   c. Marker-drawn storyboards, to show technical skill

   d. Web example, whether or not done for an advertising project

Art Director

Show samples that exhibit experience with a firm or agency.

CONTENTS

Fifteen to twenty-five samples:

   a. One speculative campaign (for school or otherwise)

   b. Print ads done individually or as part of a two-person team

   c. One or two storyboards, to show technical and conceptual skills

   d. Various ads done by you alone

   e. Web examples, whether or not done for advertising clients

   f. Examples of logos, packaging, and branding (if available)

Format

35mm slides (in tray) are still applicable, but increasingly this method is being phased out in favor of CD and DVD in the following formats: Flash, PowerPoint, and iPhoto. Online portfolios are also encouraged. Avoid digital tricks. Keep it as straightforward as possible. Anything that crashes the viewer's computer will hamper appreciation of your work.

TITLE: Seussical DESIGNERS: Drew Hodges, Sandra Planeta
ART DIRECTOR: Drew Hodges PHOTOGRAPHER: David LaChapelle
CLIENT: National Artist Management Company YEAR: 2000

Branding, Branding, Branding

Principal, Third Rail Holdings LLC, New York City

» How long have you had your own studio?
Two years.

What are the changes in practice you have seen and experienced since you began?
Technology continues to shape and change the discipline of design. The online environment has shortened the lifespan of brands, and companies are rebranding at a faster rate. Style often prevails over substance and new styles are quickly consumed and discarded in an effort to seem current. You can now have a logo designed for $99 online, but there is much more involved in branding than just a logo. The software we use in the practice of design has been completely democratized—even my mother is semi-fluent in Photoshop now. Whether this is a good thing is up for debate.

How have these changes impacted your work?
I do a lot of branding and identity work and the Internet allows me to research more quickly, yet it's harder to create new forms because there are so many people doing design.

Would you say that you have a particular style or character to your design? If so, how would you define it?
A personal style is difficult to avoid and why would you want to? It's who you are! Many designers say

that they do not have a particular style, yet we can always identify their work when we come across it in contests or in publications. I try to approach each project differently but within that frame work I often employ typography or vector graphics in the solution.

What about graphic design is the most challenging for you?
Deadlines! I was a graffiti artist for over two decades and often worked under extremely stressful circumstances: painting in the dark, dodging moving subway trains, and hiding from the police. These skills transferred over well to the field of graphic design—especially the hectic nature of editorial design. I come alive under "mission impossible" projects with "do or die" deadlines. Yet given too much time, I find it difficult to make decisions. I 'think I am alone in this and it's something I'm working on.

What are the projects that most satisfy your aesthetic sense?
Work that allows me to research and revive previous design movements is also something that I find fulfilling.

How important is type and typography in what you do?
Graffiti art is based on the stylistic manipulation of letter forms so first

and foremost I am a typographer. I believe that there is a typographic solution to every design problem. Words deliver their message instantly and often carry a more concise message than an image.

What, in this current technological and economic climate, does the future hold for you specifically, and graphic design in general?
My crystal ball was stolen last week, so it's hard for me to say. In the meantime I'm taking Stefan Sagmeister's advice: "Keep the studio small and pick and choose your clients."

TITLE: Sportmax Signage Logotype CLIENT: Max Mara DESIGNER: Masood Bukhari ART DIRECTOR: Masood Bukhari DATE: 2008

TITLE: Burgweid Identity AGENCY: BDWHS CLIENT: Halter Immobilien DESIGNER: Masood Bukhari ART DIRECTOR: Roger Sandmeier DATE: 2003

TITLE: *Reds BBQ Identity*
CLIENT: *Reds BBQ*
DESIGNER/ART DI-
RECTOR: *Masood Bukhari*
DATE: *2006*

TITLE: *Realabilities Film Festival Program Guide* AGENCY: *Empax Inc.*
CLIENT: *JCC in Manhattan* DESIGNER/ART DIRECTOR: *Masood*
Bukhari CREATIVE DIRECTOR: *Martin Kace* DATE: *2008*

TITLE: *Illhouse Identity* CLIENT: *Illhouse*
DESIGN DESIGNER/ART DIRECTOR:
Masood Bukhari DATE: *2007*

TITLE: *Phenix Centre Identity* AGENCY: *BDWHS*
CLIENT: *Peikert Immobilien AG* DESIGNER:
Masood Bukhari ART DIRECTOR: *Roger Sandmeier*
DATE: *2003*

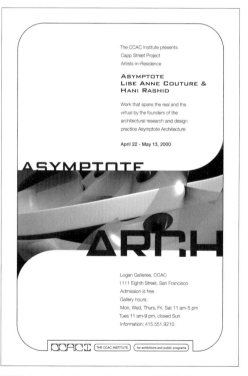

TITLE: *Lolo's Cottage Identity* CLIENT: *Lolo's Cottage* DESIGNER:
Masood Bukhari ART DIRECTOR: *Masood Bukhari* DATE: *2009*

TITLE: *Asymptote Architecture Advertisement* CLIENT: *CCA Wattis In-*
stitute DESIGNER/ART DIRECTOR: *Masood Bukhari* DATE: *2000*

Nonstarving Art Director

Senior Art Director, DeVito Verdi, New York City

>> **How did you get into advertising design?**
I received a B.F.A. from the
School of Visual Arts, and as an
SVA undergraduate, you get exposure to the major communication
fields. I took a strong liking to
advertising.

**Do you have a strong personal style? Is
it important to have one in advertising
design?**
The agency I work for has a style,
but I try to avoid being pigeonholed into any one style. Madon-
na would be a great art director.

**How would you describe a good working
environment?**
One that is open to new ideas—an
environment where people are
not threatened by the unfamiliar;
an environment where people are
willing to take chances.

**What is the most fulfilling aspect of your
job? The least?**
Having your ad stand out among
the millions. Having an ad
remembered and appreciated by
people not in the industry. Least
fulfilling is having an ad you know
is great never see the light of day.

**How much of your time is devoted to art
direction versus business matters?**
You never get enough time to design an ad. I currently work at an
agency that's more concept-driven
than it is driven by design.

TITLE: *Beer Can* DESIGNERS/ART DIRECTORS: *Aaron
Eiseman, Abi Aron Spencer* CLIENT: Esquire *Magazine*
YEAR: 1997

TITLE: *Siskel & Ebert*
ART DIRECTORS:
*Abi Aron Spencer, Rob
Carducci* CLIENT:
Time Out New
York *YEAR: 1998*

What do you look for when hiring designers?
It helps to have connections, but a great portfolio is a great portfolio. Good agencies don't have to look for art directors; art directors have to look for good agencies.

What advice would you give to someone interested in becoming an advertising art director?

My advice to anyone who wants to be an advertising designer is to either do great ads or don't bother. The field is already saturated with mediocre art directors. The good advertising designer remembers that an advertisement is more than a piece of art—it must clearly communicate an idea. An overdesigned ad can be worse than an underdesigned ad. Knowing this is more important than any skill.

What would you like to attain in your career?
Money, power, respect. Let's not forget, this isn't a career for people aspiring to become the next Mother Teresa.

TITLE: Multiple Personalities DESIGNERS: Aaron Eiseman, Abi Aron Spencer ART DIRECTORS: Abi Aron Spencer, Aaron Eiseman CLIENT: Digital City YEAR: 1998

TITLE: T-Shirt DESIGNERS/ART DIRECTORS: Aaron Eiseman, Abi Aron Spencer PUBLICATION: People Magazine CLIENT: Daffy's PHOTOGRAPHER: Steven Hellerstein YEAR: 1996

TITLE: 77% (Inspired by Barbara Kruger) ART DIRECTORS: Abi Aron Spencer, Aaron Eiseman CLIENT: Pro-Choice Public Education Project YEAR: 1998

The Poster as Advertisement

Director, The Push Pin Group, Inc., New York City

≫ Is designing a poster different from any other kind of graphic design?

The principles of design apply whether you are designing a poster or a chewing gum wrapper. The function of posters that are posted for the multitude demand a certain immediacy, graphic impact, and clarity not required for design to be read at one's leisure.

You have designed many bus-shelter posters for TV and theater. What is the most important goal of designing one of these posters, and how do you achieve that?

Aside from the requirements I mentioned, I have to know how and where the poster will be used. Of course, the goal is to convey the message (in the broadest sense) of the client with a unique graphic presentation. Unique in the sense that my work would not confuse the viewer and an idea that has meaning for me. Posters must grab attention.

When you sit down to design one, do you have an existing toolbox of rules, regulations, and standards that you follow?

I work on instinct and experience. My eye goes for books and old posters for inspiration while my hand has a life of its own when I start to sketch. My hand tends to fall in the same rut as it has many times before. I have to castigate it and slap it with my other hand. Any good designer goes against expectation while the client's message stays fixed in the back of the head.

TITLE: End Bad Breath DE-SIGNER/ILLUSTRATOR: Seymour Chwast CLIENT: Personality Posters YEAR: 1968

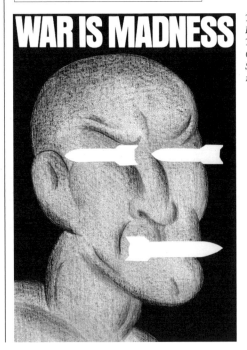

TITLE: War Is Madness DESIGNER/ILLUS-TRATOR: Seymour Chwast CLIENT: The Shoshin Society YEAR: 1986

What makes a fantastic poster? And which of your posters fit that bill?

I save the word *fantastic* for things like sex, music, and a rare piece of architecture. Posters I consider *great* tend to be those of the first half of the twentieth century (the golden age) and a few after that. While great posters successfully wed metaphors of the message, a poster could be just beautiful as well.

What makes a bad poster? And have you ever designed one that made you cringe after it was done?

Bad posters have clichéd images badly presented. If posters must have impact, weak posters are bad. Since design is an art, so much is subjective. A poster may be good for its time and place of origin and a failure for another time and location. My poster promoting a Judy Garland show was awful and embarrassing, but the Museum of Modern Art in New York wanted it for its collection. Go figure.

When you teach students the art of poster design, what do you stress?

I get them to listen to the brief and take it seriously. I have them come up with their own ideas and help in refining them and proposing methods of execution. I try to get students to conceptualize with thumbnail sketches before exercising their proclivity for going online. Scale, which is a valuable tool in poster design, seems to be difficult for some students to grasp and take advantage of. I stress the glory with the great possibilities in the mystery of design.

TITLE: *Scoop* DESIGNER/ILLUSTRATOR: *Seymour Chwast* CLIENT: *Mobil Oil Corp.* YEAR: *1986*

TITLE: *What Is Design?* DESIGNER/ILLUSTRATOR: *Seymour Chwast* CLIENT: *Cooper Hewitt National Design Museum* YEAR: *2004*

Adman Designer

Principal, J&M Martinez Ltd., Los Angeles

What differentiates advertising design from graphic design?

I've done advertising, design, and illustration. Everything in advertising has to contribute specifically to the one message, goal, concept. In graphic design, there is often more flexibility and independence.

Are there more compromises in advertising than other areas of design?

There is more collaboration. Everything is carefully considered and tested because, usually, much more is at stake. A lot of capital and many livelihoods can be tied to a campaign for a large enterprise.

As a freelance art director, what kind of clients do you have?

In advertising, hit and run. We're brought in to solve particular problems quickly. The clients are mostly luxury goods and image campaigns. In design, there is more time, less pressure, and the clients are mostly publishers or manufacturers.

What is the most fulfilling aspect of your job?

Having clients who give good guidance and trust me implicitly.

And the biggest problem?

Short deadlines; not having sufficient time and budget.

How much of your time is spent on design and art direction, and how much on business matters?

All to the first and none to the second (I have a good agent and a willing partner). Thanks to FedEx, time and distance have been completely altered. Except for production, I work entirely from home now. I no longer need full-time assistants. I email much of my work. Clients expect fewer meetings and replace them with faxes, email, and conference calls (I usually attend only for presentation or if a briefing is particularly involved).

What do you look for when you do hire designers?

I look for people who have ideas and understand concepts; design skills are secondary. We have hired students and beginners but always pay them. Even if they are learning on the job, they are getting work done for us.

TITLE: *Noritake—Rehearsal Dinner, Coffee, Takeout* ART DIRECTOR: *John Martinez* ADVERTISING MANAGER: *Floyd Sullivan* COPYWRITER: *Nancy Tag* COMPANY: *Dentsu* CLIENT/COPYRIGHT: *Noritake* PHOTO-GRAPHER: *Alan Richardson* YEAR: *1994*

BRIAN COLLINS

Principal, COLLINS, New York City

Branding Is Storytelling

As the leader of the Brand Integration Group at Ogilvy, you complement, supplement, and lead advertising campaigns. How is this accomplished?

With our agency counterparts, who examine existing media, like TV, our team explores the more experiential expressions of a brand. Where does a brand really come to life? On the street? In stores? On-line? In architecture? In events? In packaging? On a cell phone? In gaming? In fashion? How do people recognize it? Use it? What makes it meaningful to them? We try to understand how a brand really expresses itself—and how it mutates across communications, environments, and products. Then we invent new expressions and new ideas as well as try to bring greater meaning and cohesion across all of them. Sometimes this means our work can lead an overall campaign. That's how it worked when we did the "What's Your Anti-Drug?" campaign. Other times it means we focus on the visual design of the puzzle, from identity to envi-ronmental design, as we did with Motorola. And sometimes we work independently, as we did with Her-shey's on the design of their Times Square chocolate factory.

What does the term *branding* mean to you?
Branding is storytelling. It's that simple. And storytelling is always interesting because it's driven by

TITLE: Brill's Content
COVER DESIGNERS: Luke Hayman, Brian Collins

TITLE: Hershey
DESIGNERS: Ed Chiquitucto, Roman Luba, Clear Channel Spectacolor, JGA Associates, Brian Collins

TITLE: NYC2012
DESIGNERS: Bill Darling, Brian Collins

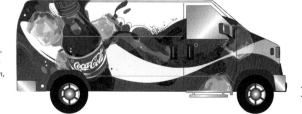

TITLE: Coca-Cola DESIGN-ERS: Leigh Okies, David Israel, Sa-tian Pengsathapon, Brian Collins

TIMES SQUARE CENTENNIAL

TITLE: Times Square Alliance
DESIGNERS: Alan Dye, Bill
Darling, Brian Collins

TITLE: Sprite DESIGNERS: Iwona
Waluk, Weston Bingham, Brian Collins

TITLE: Times Square Alliance DESIGN-
ERS: Alan Dye, Bill Darling, Brian Collins

one question: What happens next? That's what people want to find out. It's why they turn the page, why they enter a store, or click online—to see what happens next. And whether our roots are in graphic design, advertising, architecture, interactive, or environmental design, we are all in the what-happens-next business. People lose interest, fast, when nothing interesting happens next.

So you tell stories to retain the public's interest?

Stories are fundamental to us. Human beings are genetically designed for them. Stories are how we understand the world and how we create meaning for ourselves at the deepest level. The way I see it, it's the job of advertising and design to help shape brand stories into something truthful, meaningful, and useful. When branding is done with sincerity and imagination, the outcome can bring understanding and enjoyment. Or it can just help people navigate through their lives a little better.

In my view, design is a tangible, immediate kind of storytelling because it touches people's actual experience. It isn't the promise of experience—like an ad. It *is* experience. Design is a brand's promise made visible, and ultimately, personal. And once an experience becomes personal, it can become a meaningful part of someone's own story.

How does design work with branding?

When you crystallize a brand promise with strong design, you can harness extraordinary power. I love the example of pirates and their skull and crossbones flags. That black flag was the pirate brand identity, if you will. When they raised it, it sent an unmistakable brand promise to the crews on the ships sailing through the Caribbean: "You're dead." The sight of that flag summoned a very specific set of brand expectations—ones which the pirates consistently delivered. Each time they acted ruthlessly, the pirates delivered on their brand promise—and deposited more legends and meaning into their flag. In fact, they were so bloodthirsty so consistently that by the eighteenth century, all

a pirate ship had to do was hoist its Jolly Roger and the crew of the victim ship would often drop their cargo and flee. The outcome the pirates wanted materialized simply by waving, in effect, their logo.

How does a young designer, used to doing brochures or posters, become a practitioner of brand integration?

Designers should broaden their perspective beyond the creation of a single artifact (a book cover, a poster, a Web site, etc.) and learn to see such artifacts as the start of a much larger continuum of connected experiences. Ask bigger questions and follow the answers out the window. They should push to create as much of that broader experience as they can. If someone asks them to design a package, for example, they should try to create such a big idea—a big story—that it could inspire the design of a great store, an ad campaign, a film, an event, a game, or a series of books all based on the product idea. It can be terribly fun.

Stoking the Campfire

CEO, Chief Creative Officer, TAXI, Montreal/Toronto/New York City

>> **You started your firm, TAXI, with the idea that a small, select team of experienced experts should take responsibility for every dimension of a brand. Have you been able to maintain this approach?**

We started out by tearing down the traditional departmental walls that existed and replacing them with more collaborative, more empowered, and more accountable work groups. The result is consistently more vibrant work along with better morale. As we have grown in size we have, for the most part, maintained this approach, with the main difference being that with larger mandates we have surrounded some of the Taxis with more support staff. In our industry, I've noticed there is a natural tendency, as a group gets larger, etc. for people to build walls between each other. You notice this happening between creative and account people, clients and agencies, management and staff, or between separate offices. You have to be vigilant. To counter this, part of the solution is to limit the size of the company. Primitive tribes realized that beyond a certain number the community dynamic was lost, and the U.S. Army avoids units larger than 150 because they become dysfunctional, and in war, that's dangerous. At TAXI, we decided to limit the population of any given office to that number.

When we get there, we put a no-vacancy sign in the window.

What is your process when combining the disciplines of advertising and design to create a new brand?

The process starts with a very disciplined but highly creative exercise that identifies the brand's essence and dimensionalizes it into a simple architecture that everyone understands and can build on. We call it a campfire. It becomes something that everyone from the client CEO to the delivery guy can rally around. This is the brief of all briefs. From there, working separately or together, the design, interactive, entertainment, and advertising disciplines will respond with directions. At this point there is sharing and a cross-pollination of ideas that in turn gives rise to more ideas and conceptual synergies. The creative

TITLE: Pizza CREATIVE DIRECTOR/DESIGNER: Paul Lavoie COMPANY: Cossette Communication Group CLIENT: McDonald's Restaurants of Canada Ltd. YEAR: 1990

TITLE: Coach CREATIVE DIRECTORS: Paul Lavoie/Zak Mroueh ART DIRECTORS: Ron Smrzek/ Paul Lavoie WRITER: Zak Mroueh COMPANY: TAXI CLIENT: See You in Fund PHOTOGRAPHER: Ron Fehling YEAR: 2003 >>

Title: Bus Shelter Creative Directors: Paul Lavoie/Zak Mroueh Art Director: Paul Lavoie Writer: Donna McCarthy Company: TAXI Client: Covenant House Agency Producer: Louise Blouin Director: Paul Lavoie Year: 2000

spark can come from anywhere. Once there is a consensus on direction, the teams then go back to drilling deep into their respective disciplines to craft their part of the overall solution. It's a very organic, collaborative approach, but there is always clear leadership in one creative director.

You have also directed your own commercials. Do you find that versatility is key to your success?

I love directing and would do it more often if I could find the time. I wrote and directed a short film that made a few festivals. When you think of it, it's much like running a company. Bringing different disciplines together under one vision to create a product. The difference is you cannot yell "Cut!" in a new business meeting and demand more enthusiasm from the client.

You want to create a new national image for Canada. What started this interest in the ultimate branding challenge?

Report on Business magazine asked me to write an article on Canada's international image and perception, and I found that Canada is not a country people think of. According to the most reliable research, we are invisible. And we have no one to blame but our brand architects at the federal government and the agencies they have hired. Because we have never successfully managed this aspect of our country, the international perception is a default to the outdated and cliché (snow-covered mountains, RCMP, beavers, and hockey players). This image, I might add, does not live up to the current reality of our nation or its ambitions. The solution, I'm convinced, will not be resolved in one magical ad campaign and certainly not in a new logo. Did you know our federal government has already commissioned and paid for well over 800 logos? I wish they would stop terrorizing us with more logos. We already have a great symbol. It's a maple leaf. That leaf should come to symbolize more than just our natural beauty but who we are and what we have to offer to ourselves and to the world.

You've said that you "hire courageous people who speak their minds and try new things." How can you tell?

Courage is important because it can unleash everything, including true innovation. The courageous are rare, but that makes them easy to spot. They are generous, confident, and curious. They are the first to challenge convention and the first to accept blame. They accept failure as part of a natural path to innovation.

Principal, SpotCo, New York City

>> **You found a very special niche for yourself—theatrical posters and advertising. How did you come to focus on this area of design?**

We had made a career of entertainment design—movies, records, and cable TV. One of our clients—Geffen Records creative director Robin Seibert—asked us to design the album package for *Rent*. This subsequently led to working on all aspects of *Rent*. I think their goal was to market the album in the rock racks at the front of the store rather than the show-tune bins. After that we were asked to do *Chicago*, and the rest just followed. It's been a fast eight years. I think the skill set we had just was a good fit for Broadway. We were doing both pure design as well as advertising, and the culture was just beginning to see the emotional promise of design as a kind of ad. Also, Broadway was looking to get younger and move into the contemporary market.

Your company has grown in extraordinary ways in a relatively short time. How did you successfully build your design firm?

Very simple—no big promos, no press agents hired (well, one—when we made the move to ad agency). We just found each job led to a next one. Also, you really are building relationships with people rather than completing a project at a time. And I learned a great lesson from my first intern,

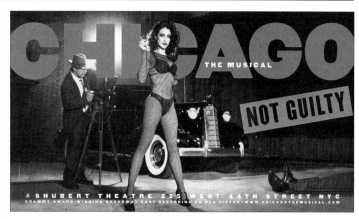

TITLE: Chicago DE-SIGNERS: Drew Hodges, Naomi Mizusaki ART DIRECTOR: Drew Hodges PHOTOGRAPHER: Max Vadukul CLIENT: National Artist Management Company YEAR: 1996

TITLE: The Good Body DESIGN-ERS: Gail Anderson, Jessica Disbrow ART DIRECTOR: Gail Anderson ILLUSTRATOR: Isabelle Derveaux CLIENT: The Good Body, LLC YEAR: 2004

>>

TITLE: *Harlem Song* DESIGNER: *Gail Anderson* ART DIRECTOR: *Drew Hodges*
CLIENT: *Harlem Song, LLC* YEAR: *2002*

James Spindler. He told me, "Never talk design to a client—they are terrified you will go there." Talk marketing, or problem solving. Then they are reassured you are working for their needs, not yours. Of course, in the end you are trying to solve yours as well; you just don't need to talk about it. And I hired some very strong people in the beginning (we were five people as a design studio, and leaped to twelve as an agency. We are now thirty-six people strong.). And they began to hire their own departments. It actually became easier for me in terms of how many jobs I had to do when I had the revenue to have more people do them.

Does designing for theater and film require a different mindset than for other media markets?

Nope. But doing advertising does. You need to know how the business works, recommend budgets, and have some sense of history as to what has worked in the past. Real-world case studies help. The only thing different about Broadway advertising is convincing twenty people to like a design rather than five. But at least you get to stand in front of the twenty rather than hear later that one of the five hates green.

This work demands a lot of collaboration and probably compromise; how do you balance such activity with your aesthetic and artistic vision?

Paula Scher taught me "pick your spots." Know when the design has the chance to really be special, and hit it hard. The others, say your opinion, plead a little, but let it

go. And my favorite achievement is to figure out what look, what line, what presentation will allow the client to feel they got what they wanted and needed and still leave me with what I wanted and maybe needed a little. And I truly believe almost every problem has many, many solutions, I just have to find the one that does both. Also, let it go a little—sometimes the solution you were sure was genius wasn't—it just took a year to see it. And the thing you thought was just so-so turned out to be pretty good.

How much do you actually design these days? Or have you become more the impersario?

Not much. OK, hardly any. I get to guide Gail Anderson (formerly of *Rolling Stone*) and Vinny Sainato (of Comedy Central) as much as they will let me, and I get to do the same on radio and television, which we also make. And my job now is to create the best environment internally to create the best work. And try to help get a client to like it.

Is this kind of design field open for young designers?

Sure, but there is a catch—there are a small number of agencies in the country who do this work. Three in New York do Broadway, and maybe five firms in Los Angeles specialize in film. So that probably adds up to fifteen design positions in New York working on Broadway. So those jobs don't turn over often.

DEBBIE MILLMAN

Brands That Change Behavior

President, Sterling Group and Chair MPS Branding, School of Visual Arts, New York City

>> **What is the most critical concern when designing a brand that will represent a mass-market product?**

It is not politically correct to say this in some circles, but I believe that people like brands. In this day and age, consumers have come to feel protective about their brands. Brands not only simplify choices and guarantee quality, but now they add fun and interest. In an often irreligious world, brands provide us with beliefs. They can define who we are and they immediately signal our affiliations. With this wave of brand appreciation has come a new breed of marketers, people who will proudly inform you that "your brand" is no longer a "product" but a way of life, an attitude, a set of values, a look, an idea. They believe that this is better than that—"your brand" is "just" a power drill, or a hamburger chain, or a pair of jeans, or even a massively successful line of coffee drinks. This is where fundamental issues like truth and authenticity are paramount, at least for me.

So what is the most critical concern when designing a brand that will represent a mass-market product?

1. Can the brand change behavior in a positive way (i.e., make consumers' lives better or easier)? (Sony Walkman, Apple iPod, America Online, Levi's Jeans)

TITLE: *Burger King* CREATIVE DIRECTOR: *Marcus Hewitt* DESIGN DIRECTOR: *Stephanie Godkin* MANAGING DIRECTOR: *Debbie Millman* YEAR: 2004

TITLE: *Givaudan* CREATIVE DIRECTOR/ DESIGNER: *Marcus Hewitt* YEAR: 1999

>>

2. Can this brand or this design become embedded in our day-to-day life in a genuine and beneficial way? (CNN, Microsoft)

3. Is the branding telling a compelling story that is truthful and accurate? (BP, FedEx)

4. Does it have the potential to become part of society's lexicon? (MTV, eBay, Google)

5. Can this brand express a lifestyle that is aspirational? (Nike, Starbucks)

What does it take to be a brand designer, as opposed to a book, record, or other form of designer?

Actually, I think there is no difference between a brand designer and a book, record, or annual report designer—or really, any type of graphic designer. If a designer is not aware of the cultural, psychological, marketing, and creative aspects of how his/her design will be perceived, then I think it is simply an arts-and-crafts project.

Presumably, there is considerable client input and consumer testing because the stakes are high. How as a designer do you balance this with the creative impulse?
Testing, more than ever before, has given marketers a sense of validation and security about their choices. I have never seen so much fear in our industry. And it is not industry

specific, per se, with a particular type of brand or company. I have often found that the companies you would expect to be conservative—financial institutions, insurance companies, and so forth—are often the most graphically progressive. And some of the most trendy, culturally relevant clients are very often quite conservative in the way they approach creative. (Example: 3M, a largely conservative company, has changed their logo numerous, numerous times over the course of their existence, whereas Nike and MTV have never changed their logos.) Right now, change is seen as a threat to security. Research suggests that people will actively fight or resist any new direction in

TITLE: Krinos
CREATIVE DIRECTOR: Simon Lince
DESIGN DIRECTOR: James Grant
YEAR: 2001

TITLE: Invigor8
CREATIVE DIRECTOR: Marcus Hewitt DESIGN DIRECTOR: Richard Palmer MANAGING DIRECTOR: Debbie Millman YEAR: 2004

TITLE: IO (cablevision)
CREATIVE DIRECTOR: Marcus Hewitt DESIGN DIRECTOR: Stephen Dunphy YEAR: 2003

interactive
Optimum

their work environment unless they are convinced that this change will benefit "everyone." And that simply isn't possible! People don't fear the actual changes. What they fear is a loss of security with something new.

Are there any taboos that have been busted?
Yes! There was a time when you never saw green on a package (aside from Green Giant). Conventional thinking was that green represented spoiled. Healthy/no-fat (Healthy Choice, etc.) packaging changed that. Also, blue was not a big packaging color (aside from soft drinks); now low-carb packages all feature blue as the primary color to communicate that attribute. Currently there are cultural taboos that are slow in busting—for example, there are some colors and imagery that you can't use in certain countries (cows in India, purple in parts of Asia, green in Thailand). One of the last taboos that has not been busted is provocative language and/or photography on packaging. You are much more likely to see that in advertising or logos (for example, the FCUK identity or Calvin Klein billboards).

What would you say to a young designer who wants to become a branding expert?
Run for your life. (Joking!) As we compose our branded stories, as we weave our myths and hopes and dreams into our brands, let's remember our frailty and strengths and foibles and failings. Let's remember our humanity.

VII. ENVIRONMENTAL

GRAPHIC DESIGNERS have engaged in some aspect of what is currently known as *environmental graphic design* since the 1800s. Back then it was called *sign painting*—which is not to imply that the new discipline is exactly the same as the old but rather suggests that it evolved from a venerable craft into a sophisticated specialty (that employs sign painters, among other craftspeople, in the process). Today, environmental graphic designers are involved in a wide range of design activities, from billboards to wayfinding to interactive kiosks. Indeed, virtually every aspect of design that deals with an outside or inside physical environment is fair game for the environmental designer. For those with an interest in architecture and interior design, this specialty is a point of intersection. Environmental graphic designers are routinely included in design and planning teams that must solve problems endemic to defining and marking cultural, commercial, and residential space.

On the most rudimentary level, environmental designers are concerned with the look and feel of signs, which might include anything from a simple retail shop shingle to an entire directional system for a hospital, theater, or museum. The former might be one board that bears little or no relationship to the rest of the

architectural or interior design, while the latter is often a major component of a coordinated overall identity—an institution's logo and related graphic elements are carried through the environmental aspects of an entire program. To achieve success at this kind of design is not as easy as flipping a switch that causes one or two dimensions to become three. Rather, it involves a keen ability to make something that is ostensibly flat into dynamic three-dimensional objects. Moreover, this is not an abstract process; the environmental designer must have experience with and current knowledge of numerous new materials and fabricating processes that transform ideas on paper into functional objects. In recent years, increasingly more digital display is used in the environment. This will doubtless continue to be a growth segment of the industry.

Two-dimensional graphic design is a decidedly utilitarian applied art, but environmental graphic design demands even more attention to function because of the direct impact it has on the public. The old saying that graphic design, unlike architecture, will not collapse and therefore never harm an individual is not necessarily true in this genre. A badly built or installed sign can do considerable physical damage. In fact, official ordinances and codes govern at least the minimum requirements for this kind of design, so environmental designers—many of whom begin their careers as print designers—must have extensive training and apprenticeships with design firms that devote the better part of their time to practice in this area. Most art and design schools include environmental courses within a graphic design curriculum, but for those who want to seriously pursue this specialty, more rigorous course work should be sought.

Environmental graphic design is an umbrella term for various design activities, of which wayfinding is among the most common. Everyone has found himself lost within a sprawling confine where, most likely, directions were either confusing or nonexistent. Without a map (and even with one), successful navigation relies on a system of integrated signs. This is the job of wayfinding, and the graphic designer's responsibility (often working with environmental planners) is to devise systems that are not only easy to follow but aesthetically pleasing within the environment. It is not enough to design a sign with an arrow pointing in one direction if no complementary signs are spaced at just the right intervals as further guides. Wayfinding is as much about engineering efficient traffic flow as it is making functional design. Yet wayfinding is also often just one component of a larger scheme.

The environmental designer is

URBAN BLIGHT/ADVERTISERS'RIGHTS

Critics argue that billboards are a blight on the environment, but this is not always true. While roadside beautification is a *cause célèbre* that few would argue against, billboards and electronic spectaculars are also invaluable means of mass communication. A billboard in the middle of a sylvan setting certainly has an adverse impact on the sanctity of nature, but on the urban streetscape, in areas zoned for such things, these signs are perfectly acceptable, particularly when environmental graphic designers exercise responsibility. Times Square would be a drab canyon if not for the spectaculars that give the Great White Way its glimmer and sheen. Likewise, commercial strips around the nation benefit from well-designed outdoor advertising that sells a product, conveys a message, and provides entertainment. Not all these displays are blights when designers make it their business to act responsibly.

responsible not only for directing traffic but also for education and illumination. Take a zoo, for example: Not only must the public be directed where to go in the maze of displays and attractions, but it must also be informed about the contents of the displays. The job of creating informational signs and panels often resides with the environmental designer. This, like any graphic design activity, is not as simple as stapling a piece of paper with a block of text to a wall beside an attraction. Because individuals read differently—and some do not read at all—it is important to present information in an engaging and aesthetically pleasing manner consistent with the overall identity of the zoo. Sometimes the designer builds a format typographically; at other times, type and image are combined. Sometimes illustrators are employed to render details of the flora and fauna; sometimes

photographs are the principle visual ingredient. Of course, maps and charts play important roles in showing where species derive and migrate. The smart designer knows how to marshal these elements and who to commission to do the best possible work (often within a tight budget).

Creating information graphics in a physical environment is fundamentally not all that different from doing it in a print environment. However, three-dimensional space allows for more media options than does print. Among the most common are interactive displays—kiosks with touch-screen computers, videos, or CD-ROMs—that can be effectively employed to complement the more traditional text media. Environmental designers must be trained to determine which of these is most effective in a particular context (and within a concrete budget).

In addition to education, environmental design involves creating and establishing an aura or mood for events, places, and institutions, such as baseball stadiums, Olympic arenas, theme parks, commercial malls, industrial parks, and urban arts and culture zones, as well as entire city and town business districts. The materials employed may include banners and flags, signs and guideposts, stands and kiosks, billboards and electronic spectaculars—both temporary and permanent. Working in tandem with architects and planners, the environmental designer does not just provide a service but contributes to the content of the project.

Some corporations hire in-house environmental designers under the rubrics of graphic, interior, or architectural design, but, more often, outside design firms are commissioned on a project basis. Some of the larger architecture firms maintain environmental design divisions, but the medium- and small-sized offices also commission outside design firms. Some graphic design firms include environmental design as part of their repertoire, while other firms dedicate themselves exclusively to environmental design. Finally, some environmental design firms subcontract parts of a job (interactivity, for example) to specialist firms. To enter this field, you are advised to identify a design firm, office, or studio where environmental design represents a significant amount of the work and tailor a portfolio to this growing specialty.

Graphic designers who work in this area must have two- and three-dimensional acuity. An effective portfolio shows a variety of typographic and problem-solving skills, as well as an ability to design effective way-finding and navigational systems.

Entry Level

School projects including signs and graphics for real or imagined buildings, shops, and events are useful in showing insight into how design works in the environment.

CONTENTS

Ten to twenty samples:

    a. Two sign ideas

    b. Two to three drawings of signs, banners, etc., in the context of the environment

    c. One to three coordinated sign systems

Advanced

Show samples that exhibit experience either assisting or initiating environmental projects.

CONTENTS

Fifteen to twenty-five samples:

    a. One speculative campaign

    b. Any work that exhibits prowess with three-dimensional media

    c. Plans for signage or wayfinding systems

    d. Real or prospective exhibition or event design materials

Format

35mm slides (in tray) are still applicable, but increasingly this method is being phased out in favor of CD and DVD in the following formats: Flash, PowerPoint, and iPhoto. Online portfolios are also encouraged. Avoid digital tricks. Keep it as straightforward as possible. Anything that crashes the viewer's computer will hamper appreciation of your work.

TITLE: Chicago Park District Signage Program DESIGNERS: David Gibson, Andrew Simon, Cesar Sanchez ART DIRECTOR: David Gibson COMPANY: Two Twelve Associates, Inc. CLIENT: Chicago Park District Maps ILLUSTRATOR: Gerald Boulet PHOTOGRAPHER: Erik Kvalsvik TYPEFACE: Scala YEAR: 1998

DEBORAH SUSSMAN | Vision Matters Most

President, Sussman Prejza, Culver City, California

» **How did you decide on environmental design?**

A natural evolution from fine art to visual communication and a feel for environmental (dimensional) work.

Do you have a personal style in your design?

A personal standard and vision matter most. Style is to be avoided; one's imprint is what counts. My approach is contextual, free, tending toward boldness. I thrive on large-scale programs, collaboration, and teamwork.

How much of your time is devoted to design and art direction, and how much to business matters?

Art direction: 25 percent; design: 15 percent; conceptualizing: 25 percent; dealing with clients and collaborators: 25 percent; business matters: 10 percent.

What would you like to accomplish in your career?

Permanent civic and cultural aspects of the urban landscape or streetscape. The best product for the most people, accessible to all.

TITLE: East Washington Boulevard Revitalization ASSOCIATE IN CHARGE: Scott Cuyler DESIGNERS: Sharon Blair, Holly Hampton, Paula Loh CREATIVE DIRECTOR: Deborah Sussman COMPANY: Sussman Prejza CLIENT: Culver City Redevelopment Agency PHOTOGRAPHER: Jim Simmons, Annette Del Zoppo Photography YEAR: 1998

TITLE: Walt Disney World, Orlando, Florida Associate in Charge: Robert Cordell DESIGNERS: Scott Cuyler, Corky Retson, Kyoko Tsuge CREATIVE DIRECTORS: Deborah Sussman COMPANY: Sussman Prejza CLIENT: Disney Development Co. PHOTOGRAPHER: Timothy Hursley YEAR: 1990

TITLE: 1984 Olympic Games
DESIGNERS: Debra Valencia, Mark Nelsen, Scott Cuyler, Luci Goodman, Susan Hancock, John Johnston, Charles Milhaupt, Charles Reimers, Corky Retson, Stephen Silvestri, Eugene Treadwell, Fernando Vazquez CREATIVE DIRECTORS: Deborah Sussman, Paul Prejza COMPANY: Sussman Prejza CLIENT: Los Angeles Olympic Organizing Committee PHOTOGRAPHER: Jim Simmons, Annette Del Zoppo Photography YEAR: 1984

TITLE: City of Santa Monica DESIGNERS: Deborah Sussman, Debra Valencia, Paula Loh CREATIVE DIRECTOR: Deborah Sussman COMPANY: Sussman Prejza CLIENT: City of Santa Monica PHOTOGRAPHER: Jim Simmons, Annette Del Zoppo Photography

TITLE: Walt Disney World, Orlando, Florida ASSOCIATE IN CHARGE: Robert Cordell DESIGNERS: Scott Cuyler, Corky Retson, Kyoko Tsuge CREATIVE DIRECTORS: Deborah Sussman COMPANY: Sussman Prejza CLIENT: Disney Development Co. PHOTOGRAPHER: Timothy Hursley YEAR: 1990

Architecture and Design

Principal, Hunt Design Associates, Pasadena, California

>> **How did you decide to become an environmental graphic designer?**

I've always loved architecture and have a sense for three-dimensional spaces and design. I'd rather read an architecture magazine than any graphics publication. Environmental graphics is the logical result of marrying architecture and graphic design—signage, exhibit design, placemaking, and wayfinding design. At Hunt Design, we practice environmental graphics with an emphasis on entertainment spaces.

Is it more difficult doing environmental work or print?

Each has good and bad points. Some designers are good at both. However, as each discipline grows more technical, it is less likely that any one person can be effective at both—there's just too much to know.

How do you go after clients?

The best is when they go after you. That doesn't happen too often, especially at first. We try to be a source that is automatically considered for the good EGD projects, certainly in Southern California. That's a result of reputation, public relations, being active in the field. Of course, we go after specific projects, architects, and clients. We contact them and try to wangle an interview. It's pretty basic, really.

TITLE: *Children's Zoo Exhibit* DESIGNER: *John Temple, Christina Allen* CREATIVE DIRECTOR: *Wayne Hunt* COMPANY: *Hunt Design Associates* CLIENT: *LA Zoo* PHOTOGRAPHER: *Jim Simmons/Annette Del Zoppo* YEAR: *1996*

TITLE: *View of Rocket Plaza at Apollo Saturn File Center—Exhibit Design* DESIGNERS: *Brian Memmot, Christina Allen* CREATIVE DIRECTOR: *Wayne Hunt* COMPANY: *Hunt Design* ASSOCIATES PRODUCER: *BRC Imagination Arts* CLIENT: *NASA* PHOTOGRAPHER: *Jim Simmons/Annette Del Zoppo* YEAR: *1997*

TITLE: Airport Welcome Sign DESIGNER: John Temple CREATIVE DIRECTOR: Wayne Hunt COMPANY: Hunt Design Associates CLIENT: McCarran International Airport PHOTOGRAPHER: Jim Simmons/Annette Del Zoppo YEAR: 1998

TITLE: Panda Panda Restaurant Identity DESIGNERS: Jennifer Bressler, Christina Allen CREATIVE DIRECTOR: Wayne Hunt COMPANY: Hunt Design Associates CLIENT: Panda Management Inc. PHOTOGRAPHER: Jim Simmons/Annette Del Zoppo YEAR: 1998

Do you have a personal style in your design?

I hope not. We try to avoid it at all costs. Graphic designers generally should not have a personal style.

What is the most fulfilling aspect of your job? The least?

I enjoy the dialog with enlightened clients (when we have them) —presenting, selling, promoting, persuading. The best part of all is bringing good work, work I believe in, to a meeting of sophisticated, demanding clients. I also enjoy broad overviews, strategy, and organizing complex situations. I'm not good at the details. The least fulfilling part is the ever-increasing noncreative part of large environmental graphics projects: mountains of paperwork and reports, insurance, legal issues, recordkeeping, etc. I also don't enjoy firing people—so I hire extremely carefully.

What does someone who is interested in environmental design need to know?

It helps to love architecture, cities and neighborhoods, museums and theme parks, airports and public spaces of all kinds. It helps to love maps, systems, and complex communication challenges. However, if you're an uncompromising perfectionist, EGD may be frustrating for you.

TITLE: Gateway Sign DESIGNER: Jennifer Bressler CREATIVE DIRECTOR: Wayne Hunt COMPANY: Hunt Design Associates CLIENT: City of Pasadena PHOTOGRAPHER: Jim Simmons/Annette Del Zoppo YEAR: 1998

DAVID B. GIBSON

The Built Environment

Principal, Two Twelve Associates, New York City

>> **What is environmental graphic design, and how is it different from graphic design?**

Environmental graphic design is graphic communication in the built environment, a.k.a. signage. Environmental graphics is a confusing term; people often assume it refers to something ecological, which it does not. It is quite different from classic two-dimensional (and four-dimensional) graphic design. The projects are usually much bigger, the client teams more complex, the issues more diverse, but the sensitivity to design and good typography and layout is similar. The key is to understand communication in three-dimensional space and the creation of three-dimensional objects.

How competitive is the field of environmental graphic design?

EGD is a less mature field than conventional print graphic design. As such, fewer firms are doing the work, and even fewer are working on the big high-profile projects. This is quite unlike the situation where countless smaller print design specialists compete for a standard print project. On the other hand, for high-profile and large-budget projects, there may be a national search for a design firm and therefore competition from the key players across the country. As a result, as many as ten or fifteen firms may go after such a project. Getting the job requires a submis-

TITLE: *Chicago Streetscape Signage* DESIGNERS: *David Gibson, Jill Ayers* CREATIVE DIRECTOR: *David Gibson* COMPANY: *Two Twelve Associates, Inc.* CLIENT: *Chicago City Government Maps* ILLUSTRATOR: *Gerald Boulet* PHOTOGRAPHER: *Erik Kvulsvik* TYPEFACE: *Transit* YEAR: *1999*

TITLE: *Central Park Zoo Signage and Graphics Program* DESIGNERS: *David Gibson, Juanita Dugdale, Sylvia Harris* CREATIVE DIRECTOR: *David Gibson* COMPANY: *Two Twelve Associates, Inc.* CLIENT: *The New York Zoological Society* ARCHITECTS: *Kevin Roche, John Dinkeloo & Associates* PHOTOGRAPHERS: *Jim D'Addio, Peter Aaron/Esto* TYPEFACE: *Bodoni* YEAR: *1987*

sion of qualifications, possibly a visit to a remote site, the preparation of a detailed proposal, and the conducting of an interview with the client. This can be a lengthy and expensive process over several months. To get these big fish, you have to get it all right.

Is it more difficult doing environmental or print work?
EGD is more complex to me, not more difficult. There are many, many fingers in the EGD pie. The client group can include the architect of the building and the owner or institution that is the ultimate client. These both may have several representatives on the project. An owner's representative may be managing

the project. Presentations to ten or fifteen people are not unusual.

How do you go after clients?
Mostly we answer the phone. We're not proactive enough, but many great opportunities come to us because we're now well-known and have been around for almost twenty years. A good deal of our work comes from the architects of the buildings and developments that need signage. We keep in touch with those who are actively giving us work right now.

Do you have a specific approach to hiring designers?
We get resumes all the time; we're in some great books about design; we have contacts with the schools.

What do you look for in new designers?
I look for a sense of personal vision and commitment to design and am also interested in a personable, poised individual who can collaborate with her peers in the office and deal with clients. I assume the designer has a graphic design education.

What does someone who is dedicated to environmental design need to know?
Patience to deal with long-term projects, an interest in complexity, and, most importantly, an understanding of the third dimension—how communication works in space rather than on a two-dimensional surface.

TITLE: Baltimore Waterfront Promenade Signage Program DESIGNERS: David Gibson, Doug Morris, Julie Marable CREATIVE DIRECTOR: David Gibson COMPANY: Two Twelve Associates, Inc. CLIENT: Baltimore Harbor Endowment ARCHITECT: Cho, Wilks & Benn PHOTOGRAPHER: Jake Wyman TYPEFACE: Futura YEAR: 1992

TITLE: Massachusetts General Hospital Wayfinding System DESIGNERS: David Gibson, Cindy Poulton, Sylvia Harris CREATIVE DIRECTOR: David Gibson COMPANY: Two Twelve Associates, Inc. CLIENT: Massachusetts General Hospital ARCHITECT: Stubbins Assoc. TYPEFACE: Minion YEAR: 1998

Effect on the World

Principal, The Office of Michael Manwaring, San Anselmo, California

>> **You do print and environmental design. What is the difference?**

In general, environmental graphic design (EGD) is a slower process than print or digital graphic design. Most of the people in the field right now are early to late middle-age. Of course, it does not have to be this way. If you want to create graphic design that hangs around for a longer time period, and you love craft and materials and have some degree of patience, then EGD might be for you. EGD can be as simple as choosing wall colors or adding a sign on the front of a store. It can be more complex if you change the position of the walls to redefine the space, or make the walls into shapes, or make the space into figures, or make the walls a sign, or make the space a sign, or make the whole front of the store a symbol that then becomes known as its sign. It can also be how a store relates to the public space in front of it—landscaping, street furniture, lighting, paving patterns, lighting shadow shapes, sounds, and smell.

What about this interests you?

What interests me is working in public space. This can involve street signing, trail maps, history walks, exhibits, memorials, monuments, and design of festivities. Working in public space means being engaged in the world; it can shape space, perceptions, and consciousness. There is so much potential here for design-

ers to have a useful and positive effect on the world and simultaneously feel that they are part of it.

What advice would you give to someone who is interested in environmental design?

Even though I feel EGD has not really defined itself clearly, to me there are a few things that should be canon:

· Whatever you create, you should think of it in a cultural sense: Are you contributing to your culture, or are you making things worse?
· Make things well. Nurture a love for materials and how things are made. Think of tectonics.
· From time to time, make something with your hands—preferably out of doors.

TITLE: Downtown Plaza Signage DESIGNERS: Michael Manwaring, David Meckel, Tim Perks COMPANY: The Office of Michael Manwaring CLIENT: The Hahn Company YEAR: 1991

TITLE: Silicon Graphics Signage Program DESIGNERS: Michael Manwaring, Tim Perks COMPANY: The Office of Michael Manwaring CLIENT: Silicon Graphics Computer Systems TYPEFACE: Univers Family YEAR: 1996

TITLE: Irvington Gateways DESIGNERS: Michael Manwaring, Bruce Anderson, Jay Claiborne COMPANY: The Office of Michael Manwaring CLIENT: City of Fremont, California TYPEFACE: Futura YEAR: 1993

DESIGNING IN PUBLIC SPACES

SHEILA LEVRANT DEBRETTEVILLE has a special interest in the environmental design of public spaces that give something to the community. A recent project, funded by the Department of Cultural Affairs of the City of New York, for a library in Flushing, Queens, is called Search: Literature. "I searched for a visual metaphor that would have to combine a basic and immutable aspect of Library," she says, "as well as a major aspect of the Flushing Community—historically a place where immigrants come in search of freedom, in search of a better life. I identify with this quest as I am the daughter of Polish immigrants for whom reading and education were the path to becoming viable citizens." Her idea involved placing the titles of what she refers to as "search narratives" at the base of the new library. Narrative literature, stories in which a person seeks out a truth, exist in every culture and are handed down by grandparents and parents, or read in school. DeBretteville talked to many people in the neighborhood serviced by the Flush ing Library, and each related a story that they said was known to virtually everyone in the community.

DeBretteville chose titles commonly known to the people of the country in which they were told and written. She then etched the titles into the granite risers of the stairs in much the same way

names of famous thinkers are cut into the stone of civic buildings. Her hope was that at least one title would be recognized by pedestrians and that their interest in the titles they did not recognize would lure them into the library. "Each title I chose because of an aspect of search in the nature of the story told," deBrettville explains. "Searching for something you do not have at home appeared to me to be an apt metaphor both for immigration and for the experience of going to a library. Many of the people in the street do not come from cultures with public libraries, but all of them either recognize their language or the names of one or more of the stories whose titles I had cut into the stone steps when they were still in the Georgia quarry."

Regarding design for public spaces, deBretteville says, "I do permanent public work now, usually at the edge of cities, and usually involved with immigrant populations. As my parents were immigrants and I grew up in an extended family of many aunts, uncles, and grandparents, I have an affinity for the experience of immigrant populations. And I like to talk to people about their neighborhood's history. It is a terrific opportunity for me to be able to go to a site and propose what it is I think makes sense both to me and to the neighborhood."

TITLE: Biddy Mason: Time & Place
DESIGNER: Sheila Levrant deBretteville
CLIENT: Community Redevelopment Agency, Los Angeles, Power of Place
PHOTOGRAPHER: Annette Del Zoppo
TYPEFACE: Goudy
YEAR: 1990

VIII. INTERACTION

THE TERM *new media*, which represents Web site, CD-ROM, PDA, and wireless interface design, is neither precise nor accurate. What was indeed new a decade ago has become commonplace. Now the operative terms are *interactivity* and *user experience*. Virtually all businesses and nonprofit institutions have dedicated Web sites, which means that many design studios and firms are engaged in designing and maintaining them. Although a large percentage of Web sites are designed by freelancers or design consultancies, in-house staffs are employed where they never existed before. Businesses that have small sites usually rely on freelancers to revise and update them regularly; larger companies with continually changing contents require consistent, daily design attention. This may not be *new* anymore, but it is a burgeoning field. For those who seek jobs in this area, working for a dedicated Web design firm, a graphic design studio with a Web design component, or at an in-house staff position in a corporate Web design department are all viable options. The better your experience, the more competitive you are for the most challenging jobs.

A few years ago, the population of designers involved in new—or what practitioners called *multi-* or *time-based media*—was comparatively low. The only way to get experience was on the job. Today, virtually every significant art and design school includes courses on Web design and other digital media. A large percentage of student portfolios include at least the requisite home page designs and, usually, fully developed Web sites with advanced navigational systems and links to supplementary pages. A few years ago, the technology did not allow for sophisticated design nuances. Today, advanced software programs have increased the potential to such an extent that

> *DESIGNERS CAN NOW CREATE MOVIES, TELEVISION SERIES, INTERACTIVE GAMES—THERE IS NO LIMIT (ONLY TALENT AND SKILL).*

student work is sometimes on a par with professional accomplishment. In addition, a growing number of students are launching actual sites as virtual portfolios, both to show off their talent and to develop content on their own.

The opportunities afforded designers in this realm of communication far exceed the imagination of even a decade ago. Designers can now create movies, television series, interactive games—there is no limit (only talent and skill).

New, advanced programs have made it relatively simple for a non-designer to master this medium. In an age when even grade-school children can effortlessly create their own or classroom Web pages, adults without design training do some surprisingly competent layouts, but these must not be confused with skilled and professional designs. As is the danger with desktop publishing, it is not enough to know a few type fonts or to be able to import a picture onto a page—this is not designing, it is constructing. A Web designer must have the talent to bring aesthetic taste and navigational acuity to the construction site. The designer is often both bricklayer and architect—but more often, these days, the designer is solely an architect, leaving the mechanical aspects of Web page construction to programming and production experts.

Because this is a highly technical medium, designers must know, or at least understand, the technological parameters and potentials involved in making site, CD, PDA, or wireless interfaces. While it is also true that print designers should understand prepress and printing limitations, a print designer can actually make do without ever seeing the inside of a press room. The multimedia designer, however, must work directly with the technology to achieve results. While the new media designer does not have to be fluent in programming code, it is useful to be able to converse in this language, if only to ensure that designer and programmer are on the same track. Numerous inter-

The Planets

342.3560
Specially Priced Youth Tickets $3.00
For children 12 & under with accompanying adult

November 19 and 20 at 8 p.m.
Orpheum Theater

Omaha Symphony

TITLE: The Planets CLIENT: Omaha Symphony DESIGNER/CREATIVE DIRECTOR: Jason A. Tselentis YEAR: 2000

mediate and advanced design and programming courses are available for virtually every level of multimedia activity, from brief intensives to extended graduate studies. Those who are interested in becoming proficient in this field should explore investing in one or more of the available courses.

Within the Web site and digital media job market, the possibilities are vast. All the major mass-media corporations—newspapers, magazines, television, book publishers—have Web site divisions. While the Internet is still considered a complement to the primary media, and, with most companies, online content is taken directly from the newspaper or television programming, nevertheless, more original material is being developed every day. Web creative departments are

also growing. The Internet offers media consumers many more options than the conventional outlet, including interactivity, archiving, and purchasing capabilities. Some Web sites are solely informational, while others are designed to engage the consumer/viewer/reader in specific activities and offerings. With such a large variety of uses, designers are constantly challenged to develop interfaces that are aesthetically and functionally alluring—and rapidly changing to retain the audience's interest.

All graphic designers must work collaboratively. Some designers may have a personal style, but none can be an island without bridges to clients, production personnel, or other designers. Web and wireless design require even more intense collaboration. Like movie and television producers, multimedia designers cannot achieve their goals without writers, producers, programmers, and technicians. A single designer can take on many of these roles and act as an auteur, but the completion of the project would require unlimited time. Owing to the immediacy of the medium, Web design (and, to a lesser extent, CD-ROM) is rarely afforded a leisurely schedule. With so much competition for attention, a site must be launched quickly and revised frequently for it to be a destination of choice.

Web sites are governed by demographics, which means that each is aimed at specific segments of the online population. This also means that Web sites do not

TOO MANY COOKS?

Multimedia requires multiple skills and talents. Even if you have been a desktop Web designer in your own home and of your own site, that does not mean that in the real world you can do it by yourself. Once in the professional arena, many people are required for, and often imposed on, a multimedia project. In addition to the interface designer are directors, producers, programmers, and other technical support staff. While it is useful to be well-versed across the board, total authorship in the digital realm is rare. The best work is a mixture of different chefs with distinct ingredients. Of course, this could mean too many cooks—but with the right collaborators, the project will turn out fine.

conform to the same few design codes. As in print design, some designers are better suited for one type of content than another. Designers for the *New York Times* site may not be qualified for the Cartoon Network site; the aesthetics and sensibility required for each style are certainly incompatible. Therefore, designers looking for work in this area should show prospective employers their most relevant work.

Web and wireless design hier-

TITLE: *Supermarket Bag* DESIGNER: *Randy J. Hunt* CLIENT: *Supercorp*

archies are not very different from those in the print environment. Depending on the makeup of the firm, studio, or in-house design department, the designations are the same: *design director*, *art director*, *senior* and *junior designer*. Most Web offices also employ a large number of *interns*. Internships offer the best way to get hands-on experience in a real-time situation. Freelancers are routinely hired to fill out the creative and production teams; often, a good freelancer is permanently hired. A few years ago, Web design directors and art directors did not necessarily need to have prior Web experience. Today, however, the proliferation of the medium makes it necessary for designers on every level to be trained in the tools of the trade. But, if ever there was a graphic design industry that was welcoming of newcomers, this is definitely it.

This is one of the fastest-growing media for the graphic designer and, therefore, the standard for good work is fluid. Those looking for jobs as Web site or CD-ROM designers are encouraged to present work in both printed and digital forms to at once show the quality of the graphic interfaces and the intelligence of the navigational system.

Entry Level

School assignments and personal projects are expected. Because this medium can be practiced by anyone with access to the appropriate software, it is presumed that mastery even at this level is higher than comparable print forms.

CONTENTS

    a.   Various printout versions of user interfaces

    b.   Working screens on Zip Disk or CD-ROM

    c.   Links to sites already up and running (if available)

    d.   Photographic and illustration styles

Advanced

Projects should be fairly advanced. Not only is the design of the interface, agents, and navigational tools important, but examples of navigational systems should be prominently displayed.

CONTENTS

    a.   Printout versions of user interfaces (a wide range of approaches from a signature to a utilitarian style)

    b.   Working screens on Zip Disk or CD-ROM

    c.   One or two speculative projects (if available)

    d.   Typography, either in digital or print formats

    e.   Links to sites already up and running

    f.   Related multimedia projects

Format

The best presentations are CDs, DVDs, or actual Web sites. You may show printouts as well, but the actual medium is more persuasive.

TITLE: *The War of the Worlds* CLIENT: *Science Fiction Museum and Hall of Fame* DESIGNER/CREATIVE DIRECTOR: *Jason A. Tselentis* YEAR: *2004*

| # The Zen of Just Enough

Interaction Design Director, Etsy, and Founder, Citizen Scholar, Brooklyn, New York

>> **How long have you had your own studio?**

I started Citizen Scholar as a design studio in 2005, so it's been going for 5 years. Two years ago I partnered with a client to form Supercorp, where we build e-commerce tools and create online marketplaces.

What are the changes in practice you have seen and experienced since you began?

Changes in practice have been pushed out to the edges of the design profession. When I first started designing, there were specialists and generalists. Now there seems to be a huge set of designers that fall in between. We're experts in a few areas and then have varying levels of experience in many, many others. Today there can now be a multifaced designer, with skills and experience in many aspects of design (for example, motion graphics, logo design, identity systems), and yet there are many times as more other areas that they haven't had experience with (say, interaction design or book design).

How have these changes impacted your work?

The vast majority of our work is for interactive projects now. When I started, we'd get a call about doing an identity, and a simple Web site. Now we get calls about Web sites, which evolve

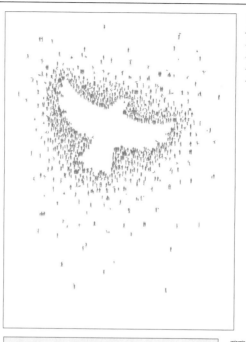

TITLE: Peace Poster
ART DIRECTOR: Randy J. Hunt
DESIGNER/ILLUSTRATOR: Ross Pike

TITLE: Art for Asia
DESIGNER: Randy J. Hunt

>>

into other design projects. These changes have made our work more flexible. From the beginning, almost every choice is weighed against how it might play out in other media in the future. Even if that illustration, say, is going to be on a poster, will it be too detailed to also look good on screen at a modest size?

Would you say that you have a particular style or character to your design? If so, how would you define it?

If anything I think it would be a character of "just enough." Sometimes that means an economy of colors, or paper choices, but it also translates into careful copywriting and the right choices of media to begin with.

What about graphic design is the most challenging for you?

What is most challenging, but also most rewarding, is the process of selling or explaining ideas to other people you need to get behind it, whether they're clients, sponsors, or collaborators. It is truly another art to be able to talk about design, and it is a constant learning process.

What are the projects that most satisfy your aesthetic sense?

I most enjoy projects that can be stripped down to one or two very simple design ideas. I love when typography takes the leading role and it supports very well-written copy. I very much enjoy the process of writing and designing simultaneously, so the language and form can play off of one another.

What, in this current technological and economic climate, does the future hold for you specifically, and graphic design in general?

Currently, a majority of my time is spent developing Web-based and physical products. It appears that this trajectory will continue to the point where we're defining most projects and offering them as products to customers rather than deliverables to clients. I think this is happening in many areas of graphic design and will continue to grow. In some cases, this will become the sole practice of a designer, but in many more instances I think it will become a natural, integral part of design businesses that are engaged in many different activities. For the discipline in general, I think it's the ideal time to take risks and experiment. No one is quite sure where technology, the economy, trends in globalization and politics will take us, but I'm hopeful. Those designers who can make a place for themselves now will be poised to have wide-reaching influence in the future.

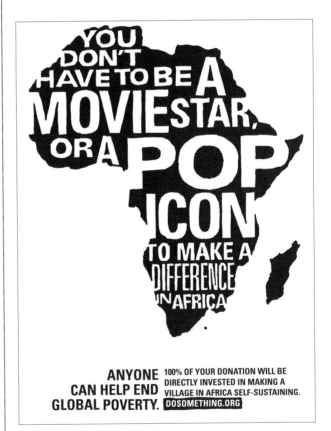

TITLE: Do Something for Africa DESIGNER: Randy J. Hunt CLIENT: DoSomething.org

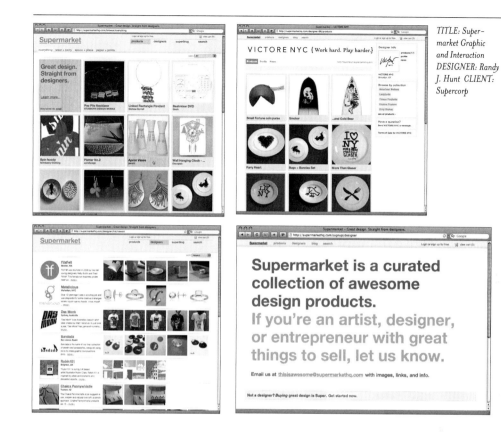

TITLE: Supermarket Graphic and Interaction
DESIGNER: Randy J. Hunt CLIENT: Supercorp

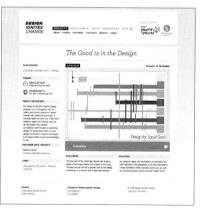

TITLE: Design Ignites Change WEB SITE DESIGNERS: Randy J. Hunt, Ross Pike, Nina Mettler (Worldstudio) INTERACTION DESIGN: Randy J. Hunt ART DIRECTOR: Mark Randall (Worldstudio) CLIENT: Design Ignites Change/Worldstudio

An Immature Medium

Principal, The Office of Clement Mok, San Francisco

>> **What made you choose new media as a focal point?**

My introduction to graphic design was through technology. The printing press was the new medium for an impressionable fifteen-year-old kid twenty-five years ago. Since that first encounter, the graphic design industry has gone through continuous changes and realignments. I don't see the new media focus as unusual; it is a continuation of my self-learning process.

How would you describe new media in relation to print?

To date, the new media resemble a game rather than a book where structured discourse or opinions can be presented. There are no rules. The arena is immature, incredibly restrictive, and driven primarily by technology. It's addressing these weaknesses that I find compelling. It's in these weaknesses that a designer can have the most profound effect. This is the area where one can establish standards and develop new benchmarks for others to follow. The new media truly engage all aspects of design thinking.

You have often talked about the changes in graphic design since entering the field. What are these changes?

The changes are both in processes and in the things we create. The

TITLE: *ups.com* DESIGNERS: *Matt Coulson, Guthrie Dolen, Samantha Feutsch, Gregg Heard, Mark Liguameri, Michael Vizzina* CREATIVE DIRECTORS: *Samantha Feutsch, Gregg Heard, Clement Mok* COMPANY: *Studio Archetype* CLIENT: *United Parcel Service* YEAR: *1997*

TITLE: *NetObjects Fusion* DESIGNERS: *Vic Zanderer, Sal Arora* CREATIVE DIRECTORS: *Clement Mok, Sal Arora* COMPANY: *NetObjects, Inc.* CLIENT: *NetObjects, Inc.* YEAR: *1996*

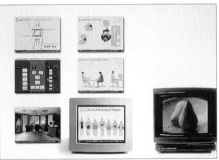

TITLE: *The Aeron Chair* DESIGNERS: *Clement Mok, Claire Barry, Paula Meizelman* CREATIVE DIRECTOR: *Clement Mok* COMPANY: *Studio Archetype* CLIENT: *Herman Miller* ILLUSTRATOR: *Ward Schumaker* PHOTOGRAPHERS: *Stan Musleik, Terry Heffernan* YEAR: *1995*

visual differences are self-evident. The most notable changes have to do with the overall characteristics of the work.

Would you explain?

Implicit versus explicit: Print graphic design is a mature medium with an established lexicon between the author and the reader. Structures and systems are well-established, so deviation from the norm is expected if the work is to challenge and to compel. Implicit is good and explicit is common or everyday—done by amateurs. Screen-based graphic design is still in its infancy. The medium has many interdependencies and functions that are inherently absent from print—for example, hyperlinks, searches, and animation. The aesthetic is both visual and functional.

Without an established lexicon that's understood by many, graphic design in the new media has to work at a more explicit level than its print counterpart. For computation and processing needs, graphical user interface principles drive the aesthetics, leaving very little room to inspire, compel, and engage. For ephemeral thoughts, the new discipline of typokinesis and the language of film have been coopted into this medium to compensate for the design requirements of functional needs.

Text is difficult to read off the screen, hence graphics is the driver. Graphics has to carry a heavier burden of distilling large, complex ideas than when text and graphics were equal partners in the print world. Only when audio is used are words and pictures on the same footing.

Control versus influence: Except with editorial projects, the ink does not dry in the new media. Ideas, thoughts, and product features are updated, upgraded, and revised continuously. Absolute is a moment in time. The designer's notion of absolute control over the user experience does not exist in the liquid new media. Context and usage are often broad—hence a tailored approach to design is rare, if not inappropriate. The variables are numerous and cannot be accounted for in advance. An ideal solution for digital media is a design that is flexible and able to scale and adapt with change. Providing all things to all people is a dangerous edge designers are skating on—we either succeed or fail miserably.

Do you still consider yourself a graphic designer? Does another term better apply to your work?

How about *designer*? My firm now competes with advertising agencies, Web development firms, and system integrators.

TITLE: *The Visual Symbol Library*
DESIGNERS: *Joshua Distler, Clement Mok*
CREATIVE DIRECTOR: *Clement Mok*
Company: *CMCD, Inc.*
CLIENT: *CMCD, Inc.*
PHOTOGRAPHERS: *Mario Parnell, Steve Underwood*
YEAR: *1994*

TITLE: *The Aeron Chair*
DESIGNERS: *Clement Mok, Claire Barry, Paula Meizelman*
CREATIVE DIRECTOR: *Clement Mok*
COMPANY: *Studio Archetype* CLIENT: *Herman Miller*
ILLUSTRATOR: *Ward Schumaker*
PHOTOGRAPHERS: *Stan Musleik, Terry Heffernan*
YEAR: *1995*

Grand Master Flash

Principal and Chief Creative Officer, hillmancurtis.com, Inc., New York City

≫ What do you like most about working on the Web?

It's constantly changing and offers so many opportunities for growth as a designer. Perhaps not everyone will agree with me on this, but I also think it's a very nurturing environment for designers. There's a pretty supportive community out there. Plus it offers that great combination of the visual and the technical. Sometimes it can drive you crazy—bandwidth, CPUs, new/old browsers, different platforms, css, Java, JavaScript—all of that stuff you have to understand at least on a basic level, but it appeals to me because you have to design things that work. Web designs have to work at communicating first, but they have to function, and how well they function directly impacts the communication. It's this great big ball of form-follows-function bouncing around in a constantly changing environment. And so much of the functionality appears to be invisible. I often find myself explaining excitedly about how small a file is, how quick it loads, even though the client is on a T1 [a high-speed telephone connection] and, at least on the surface, doesn't seem that concerned. It all matters, though. If you use the limitations of the Web to your advantage you become, like I did, a better designer.

What do you need to know now about Web design that you did not need to know, say, last year?

Usability has always been important, but for the last year and a half there was a trend that favored wild experimentations in usability. You know— floating, gravity-sensitive navigation elements, palettes that you can drag all over the browser, rollovers for the sake of rollovers, browsers that maximize and take over your desktop with no clear way to minimize back. Some of it was brilliant. Then you had these ridiculous debates between academics and punk designers,

one waving the flag of standardization and the other innovation. It's still happening, but now I feel the collective focus now seems more firmly fixed on finding the simplest way to design navigable, functional, and compelling environments. The other thing you have to be aware of is making the Web sites think, making them remember the user's name, likes/dislikes, interests. That's where it's all headed now.

Some sites today are text heavy, which seems to be what a lot of clients want. What kind of design do you feel yields the optimum site?

TITLE: *Manifestival* DESIGNERS: *Hillman Curtis, Ian Kovalik* CREATIVE DIRECTOR: *Hillman Curtis* PRODUCER: *Kiley Bates* CLIENT: *Manifestival* YEAR: *1999*

TITLE: *Roger Black's Interactive Bureau Teaser* DESIGNER: *Hillman Curtis* CREATIVE DIRECTORS: *Roger Black, Dan Roam* CLIENT: *Roger Black's Interactive Bureau* YEAR: *1999*

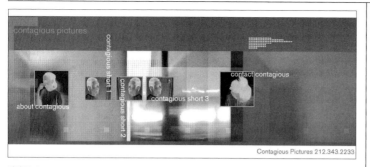

TITLE: *Contagious Pictures Web site* DESIGNERS: *Hillman Curtis, Ian Kovalik* CREATIVE DIRECTOR: *Hillman Curtis* PRODUCER: *Kiley Bates* CLIENT: *Contagious Pictures* YEAR: *1999*

TITLE: *Adobe.com* DESIGN-ERS: *Hillman Curtis, Ian Kovalik, Grant Collier, Matt Horn* CREATIVE DIRECTOR: *Hillman Curtis* PRODUCER: *Homera Chaudhry* ART DIRECTOR: *Ian Kovalik* CLIENT: *Adobe Systems Incorporated* YEAR: *2000*

TITLE: *Sky, a poem by Christina Manning* DE-SIGNER/CREATIVE DIRECTOR: *Hillman Curtis* CLIENT: *Born Magazine* YEAR: *2000*

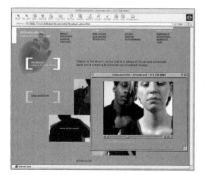

TITLE: *hillmancurtis, Inc. Web Site* DESIGNERS: *Hillman Curtis, Ian Kovalik, Matt Horn* CREATIVE DIRECTOR: *Hillman Curtis* PRODUCER: *Homera Chaudry* CLIENT: *hillmancurtis, Inc.* YEAR: *2000/2001*

I hope clients don't want text heavy, and if they do, they should call me. I would try hard to steer them away from that. It's not an effective use of the medium—don't believe anyone who claims it is. Very few people turn off graphics while surfing and if they do, the chances are they are interested in research, academic or otherwise. The very people who promote text-only also acknowledge that most users don't read on the Web. Instead, they scan and grab the last few sentences of any given paragraph. Graphic design exists for a reason. It's a visual language that everyone understands, and it offers the opportunity for communication that speaks deeper than words. Colors mean something, typography means something, layout communicates, choice of motion communicates, an image can impart a deep emotional impression—and the Web is such a wonderful place to communicate this way—simply because it knows no borders.

How much of your business revolves around the Web? How much around design? And how much technology?

About 75 percent Web, the rest a combination of broadcast, film design, and print. And it's about the same ratio for design (75 percent) and tech (25 percent). While we can program as well as the next guy and certainly can expertly work the software, we're committed to and focused on becoming a great design shop across all media.

| # Leaning Toward Smaller Studios

Principal, Kiss Me I'm Polish LLC, New York City

>> **How long have you had your own studio?**

I left my full-time post at Funny Garbage almost six years ago.

What are the changes in practice you have seen and experienced since you began?

There is a huge difference between being a freelancer and being a company and that required a significant mental adjustment for me. I am still learning how to delegate, collaborate, and let go of certain things so that my studio can function as a cohesive team, with everyone playing a core role in the process. I've also learned that if you run a small studio there has to be a balance between design and business administration, and you cannot be all things at all times. This might mean that I sometimes get to design less in a given day than I have in the past, but the ability to practice both my design and business skills is really exciting to me at this point in my career.

Why did you start your own studio?

One of the reasons is to have the flexibility to do different types of projects and not be confined to a specific type of work. Several years ago, the need for a designer to fit into a specific niche felt much stronger and while having a core focus and expertise is still extremely important today, it seems to be more acceptable that you can have more than one definition. I also feel that over the last several years,

TITLE: *Transparency—America's Problem Drugs* CLIENT: *GOOD Inc.* DESIGNER: *Josh Covarrubias* ART DIRECTOR: *Agnieszka Gasparska* FIRM: *Kiss Me I'm Polish, LLC* YEAR: *2009*

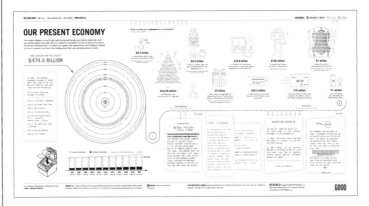

TITLE: *GOOD Sheet—Our Present Economy* CLIENT: *GOOD Inc.* DESIGNER: *Josh Covarrubias* ART DIRECTOR: *Agnieszka Gasparska* ILLUSTRATIONS: *Louise Ma, Matthew V. Caserta* FIRM: *Kiss Me I'm Polish, LLC* YEAR: *2008*

TITLE: GOOD.is website redesign
CLIENT: GOOD Inc. ART DIREC-
TOR/DESIGNER: Agnieszka Gasparska
STRATEGY/INFORMATION
ARCHITECTURE: Irwin Chen, Redub
LLC FIRM: Kiss Me I'm Polish, LLC
YEAR: 2008

TITLES: Nesuhi Ertegun Jazz Hall of Fame Kiosk + Web Site
CLIENT: Jazz at Lincoln Center ART DIRECTOR/DESIGNER:
Agnieszka Gasparska DESIGN PRODUCTION: Hollye Chapman
ANIMATION: Matthew V. Caserta PROGRAMMING: The Map
Office FIRM: Kiss Me I'm Polish, LLC YEAR: 2007-2008

>>

the landscape has been shifting in favor of smaller studios.

Not only are clients more willing and eager to work with leaner, smaller shops where teams are more accessible, flexible, and custom-tailored to the needs of the specific project, but thanks to the efficiency and convenience of high-speed Internet and wireless technology, we are all able to work together in a more open, fluid way. My studio consists of a small core staff of designers, but with a large network of dedicated collaborators with whom we partner-up on various projects, we can function as a larger team—much like a bigger company—while still giving our clients the personal attention that they would hope to get from a smaller studio. This also allows us the freedom to shift and morph from project to project without the responsibilities and overhead of having a large full-time staff. It makes every project fresh in a way.

Would you say that you have a particular style or character to your design?

I learned a lot about my style through the process of redesigning our Web site recently. I have come to learn that my aesthetic sensibility has been really greatly shaped by my background. Growing up in Communist Poland, I was inevitably infused with a certain sense of efficiency, harshness, and rigidity, which was then simultaneously offset by colorful tradition, ornate decoration, and the personal and handmade. That duality—the balance between structure and emotion—still inspires me today. The pushing and pulling of those two polar opposites is what I feel defines my style.

What about graphic design is the most challenging for you?

Running a small business I know that basically at the end of the day it all comes down to me and there's always going to be more work to be done, and there's never enough hours in the day. I've learned that I have to be able to shut off the lights and walk out the door in time to

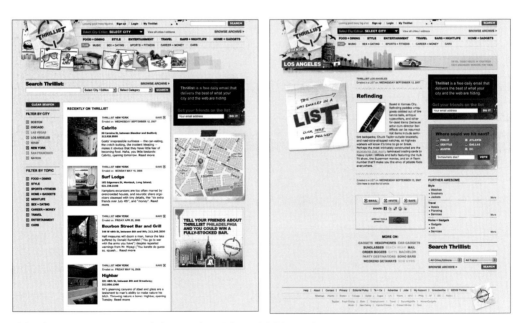

TITLE: *Thrillist Web Site Redesign* CLIENT: *Thrillist* ART DIRECTOR/DESIGNER: *Agnieszka Gasparska* DESIGN PRODUCTION: *Claire Taylor Hansen, Joshua Covarrubias* ILLUSTRATOR: *Matthew V. Caserta* STRATEGY/INFORMATION ARCHITECTURE: *Irwin Chen, Redub LLC* FIRM: *Kiss Me I'm Polish, LLC* YEAR: *2008*

have a part of the day be for me.

You have to be able to separate yourself from your business practice once in a while. And clearing your head is sometimes the best thing you can do to move forward with an idea. Creative work requires a lot of patience—every project is different and each solution is going to happen differently, sometimes in a very different time frame than the one before it. That initial phase of a project—before you get there—when you're still exploring and fishing around in the dark, can be really terrifying and frustrating. But if you give yourself the time and space to play and let things flow, you *will*

come up with something.

How important is type and typography in what you do?

To me, type is another design tool. It can play a huge role or it could recede into the background. In some projects it's going to be more clearly at the forefront as a design element, and other times it's going to be more utilitarian. It's really case-specific—based on what you're trying to do with your design—but it's always playing a role.

What, in this current technological and economic climate, does the future hold for you specifically, and graphic design in general?

I believe in not keeping all of your

eggs in one basket. Not only because it allows you to be constantly growing as a designer but because it makes for a better business strategy.

When the climate shifts and certain opportunities dry up, there are always new ones that sprout up and the more open you are to different types of projects and to new ways of working, the better you will be able to weather the storm. The growing trend toward small independent businesses which allow the team to be tailor-made to the specific needs of a given project, also gives you the ability to make changes faster and stay afloat more easily, since you're not carrying as much extra baggage.

TITLE: Cute as Hell (packaging design) CLIENT: BlueQ ART DIRECTOR/DESIGNER: Agnieszka Gasparska DESIGN PRODUCTION: Hollye Chapman ILLUSTRATOR: Tanya Thompson, aka Misery FIRM: Kiss Me I'm Polish, LLC YEAR: 2007

Good Design Is Good Design

Animation Producer and Creator of "Crank Yankers" (2002 – 2007), Los Angeles

>> **What about the Web excites you creatively?**

It's not specifically the Web that excites me, it's the whole range of design for new platforms and media. The Web is an early example of what the future will bring for designers—issues of usability, interface design, information design, application design. There are a lot of possibilities for design in all these new areas. It's a challenge for younger designers and a real kick in the ass for older designers. I also really love the idea of design not being a sovereign gesture sent from the designer to the audience. These new media allow people to customize and sometimes change designs according to their preferences and needs. This can be scary to some designers.

What about the Web makes you want to smash your computer?

Lots of things make me want to smash my computer. I cut the Web a lot of slack; it was sent out into the world when it was too young. It's growing up in public. The real problems I have with the Web are mostly inherited from general interface and application standards that have been problematic with computers and human-computer interaction for a long time. I also think it's important to make a distinction between the problems people have with browsers and

TITLE: EMP (hard media/kiosk) EXECUTIVE PRODUCER: John Carlin CREATIVE DIRECTOR: Peter Girardi PRODUCER: Sarah Shatz ASSOCIATE PRODUCER: Alec Bemis PROGRAMMER: Colin Holgate ART DIRECTORS: Agnieszka Gasparska, Matthew Canton DESIGNERS: Todd Hulin, Jesse Alexander PRODUCTION: Sharon Spieldenner, Angela Martini, Darleen Hall CLIENT: Experience Music Project YEAR: 2000

TITLE: Comedy Central (Web) CREATIVE DIRECTOR: Peter Girardi ART DIRECTOR: Jeff Tyson DESIGNER/ ILLUSTRATOR: Todd Hulin CLIENT: Comedy Central YEAR: 2001

browser-based technology and with the Web itself. The Web is a great location for information and resources of all kinds; the browsers and other technology to view the Web can really suck.

Are there any viable comparisons between the Web and print, or must you design in unique ways for each medium?

You must design for each medium in a unique way. Every medium has its own pros and cons. Designing for pixel-based delivery is quite different than designing for print-based or film/TV-based. A lot more technical issues must be considered in designing a Web site or other forms of interactive experience, both from the user's point of view and the designer's. That said, good design is good design regardless of medium. There are plenty of commonsense design lessons that should be remembered no matter what medium you are designing for.

What is the most challenging aspect of teaching design in the digital environment?

Separating the teaching of design principles from the teaching of the software. You have to know all of the software to really be able to design for this medium, but knowing all the software doesn't make you a good designer. Sometimes the opposite. It's also hard to teach all the skills it takes to be a successful interactive media designer. You have to be part graphic designer, part information designer, part interface designer, and part programmer.

What have you learned about designing for the Web that is a total revelation?

How difficult it is to be part graphic designer, part information designer, part interface designer, and part programmer.

TITLE: Raptoons (Animation) DIRECTORS: Mark Marek, Ric Heitzman ILLUSTRATOR: Todd James CLIENT: Funny Garbage YEAR: 2000

TITLE: Independent Film Channel (Internet) CREATIVE DIRECTOR: Chris Capuozzo ART DIRECTOR: Matthew Canton SENIOR DESIGNER: Jesse Alexander DESIGNERS: Andrew Pratt, Kiki Lavigne, Peter Hamlin, Yi Liu, Matthew Girardi SOUND: Andres Levin, Sohrab Habibon PROGRAM-MING: Brett Webb, Kim Howe, Randy Weinstein, Asya Prikster, Jeff Jackson, Russel Simpkins EXECUTIVE PRODUCTION: Kristin Ellington, Hope Moore PRODUCERS: Susanna Graves, Dan Latorre YEAR: 2001

The Cross-Over Is Coming

Principal Designer, Core77, New York City

How long have you been designing Core77?

Stuart Constantine and I designed the initial version of the site; I grew into the role of principal designer over the next few iterations of the site in 1995–1997. I've been in that role since.

Why did you cofound it?

The World Wide Web was less than a couple years old at that point, there were not many Web sites. It was a new, interesting piece of technology and it was clear it was going to be something big. Core77 evolved out of a joint project with Stuart at Pratt Institute the subject of industrial design was chosen because it was what we were studying at the time and had the most interest in.

Although it is an industrial design site, have you seen more of a merging of industrial and graphic design?

Historically, the cross-over point between these professions has been in product packaging and wayfinding systems. The closest a typical industrial designer gets to graphic design is in selecting CMF—colors, materials, finishes—for their projects. The skill set of these professions are fairly distinct. It seems like designers find a spot in one or the other generally. The cross-over projects you do see often take one of the simpler forms of the other practice; such as a graphic designer making flatware, as is the case with Robert Sambonet, or with industrial designers creating a logo such as Raymond Lowe's Lucky Strike.

What are the changes in practice you have seen and experienced since you began? How have these changes impacted design?

Interactive/new media/Web design/ interaction design have moved from the fringe to the most prominent position possible within the larger practice of design in the time we've been around. Technology is really driving much of the transition, each medium's unique set of opportunities and restrictions leading to unique forms. In step with these technological changes have been commercial marketplace changes that have created a more and more practical bent to these practices—the transition being one of information delivery to business-to-business exchange to niche mass market to broad mass market. The formal trend is an adoption of more and more market-friendly style following more cues direct and indirect from the world of advertising and the cultural landscape. In this process the medium has receded in importance—the restrictions diminished and a broader range of style, forms, voices have emerged.

What are the projects that most satisfy your aesthetic sense?

They are those projects which provide a series of opportunities to

TITLE: *Milk Crate Robot* CLIENT: *Core77*
DESIGNER: *Eric Ludlum* PHOTOGRAPHER:
Glen Jackson Taylor DESCRIPTION: *A giant robot made of Core77 milk crates for a 24-keg party in San Francisco.*

TITLE: *Bicycle Badge* CLIENT: *Core77*
DESIGNER: *Eric Ludlum* PHOTOGRAPHER:
Glen Jackson Taylor DESCRIPTION: *A bike badge for the limited edition Core77 bike.*

refine and realign meaning—projects that are in their formative stages on a number of levels, perhaps editorially, conceptually, technologically, where a designer can alter the course of an enterprise through the littlest suggestion of the form or inflection of delivery.

What, in this current technological and economic climate, does the future hold for you specifically, and graphic design in general?
With Core77 we have had more time to focus on the technological side of our operations, trying to improve our business model. Likewise, I believe that it is an opportune time for designers to focus on the fundamentals of their personal marketplace proposition—not just their personal brand—but a more fundamental examination of why they want to be a designer anyway and what they want their day-to-day existence to be.

TITLE: *Diablo Jihad* CLIENT: *Core77* DESIGNER: *Eric Ludlum* DESCRIPTION: *Our mascot, equipped here with a Webcam eye, is a Mexican wrestler with a warrior's headband.*

TITLE: *Core77 logo badge* CLIENT: *Core77* DESIGNER: *Eric Ludlum* PHOTOGRAPHER: *Glen Jackson Taylor* DESCRIPTION: *The Core77 logo in metal—a tchotchke which we give away.*

TITLE: *Core77 DIY Board Graphic Tutorial* CLIENT: *Core77* DESIGNER: *Eric Ludlum* DESCRIPTION: *A how-to for making a duotone design for your skateboard—done for Readymade magazine.*

TITLE: *Core77 T-Shirt* CLIENT: *Core77* DESIGNER/ PHOTOGRA-PHER: *Glen Jackson Taylor* DESCRIPTION: *A t-shirt design with our motto "There is no plan B."*

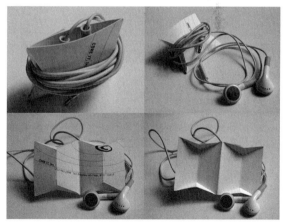

TITLE: *Business Card One-Hour Design Challenge* CLIENT: *Core77* DESIGNER: *Eric Ludlum* DESCRIPTION: *A challenge to Core77 readers to make something useful of a business card—this is our attempt.*

The Right Balance

Principal, Work Is Play, New York City

>> **As an illustrator, did you always want to see your work animated?**

I think if you grew up watching as many cartoons as I did, maybe you would. I watched a lot of Warner Brothers and Fleischer Brothers cartoons. I would make flip books and shoot short Super 8 animations with my dad's camera. Much later, I worked at a few animation studios, starting at the lowest level painting cels and eventually moving up to inking. Every project that came in had its own look or style, and the job became more about being a really good forger than anything else. I wanted to be more in control of the work I was doing, so I put a portfolio together and became an illustrator. This led to doing children's books, and eventually that led to having my own work animated. Once you've had the experience of seeing one of your ideas moving around, it's hard not to get hooked and want more.

How has the computer influenced your work in a kinetic sense?

The computer has given me more control. It makes it a whole lot easier to create animation entirely by myself. I'm interested now in getting a better understanding of the interactive side of programs like Flash. I want to create experiences that are deep and rich and, hopefully, entertaining. In the case of the TRY site, I don't think the concept would have occurred to me if it was a

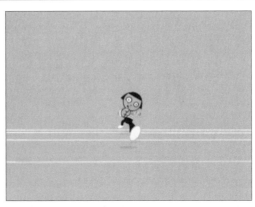

TITLE: PBS Kids
DESIGNER: Richard McGuire
CREATIVE DIRECTOR/ PRODUCER: Lee Hunt Associates
CLIENT: PBS
YEAR: 1999

print job. You are using a different set of tools, so they suggest different ideas. Even if the same idea was adapted to print it wouldn't be half as effective. Magic happens when you see the transformation trick in real time.

Are you more interested in telling stories or creating effects?

I'm developing different things. One thing I'm interested in doing is creating a longer book project that will have an animated Web component and could possibly be adapted for TV as well. When I look back at my work and see the pattern of my interests, it has never really been about story. I like systems and structures. I want to create experiences that make you see the world a bit differently after the experience. I'm also interested in pure play—making things that are for fun, with no real goal. I like the idea of creating virtual toys.

What are the most important components in animation for TV and the Web?

The most important thing about the Web is the fact that you can create something, post it, and there are potentially millions of viewers. Word of mouth can be enough. My TRY site got half a million hits with no advertising, and that amazes me. I'm always trading interesting sites with friends in the same way you pass along a good joke. It's unlike any other medium because of its direct link to an audience.

It's also cheaper than any other way of communicating to the masses. Of course, the TV audience is bigger; millions of people see my PBS Kids logos everyday. Technically, TV has different sets of problems. The broadcasting system in this country is actually pretty crude. It hasn't changed at all since color TV was introduced in the 1960s. Things like having color against color can cause shadows and vibrations unless there is a trapping line, for instance. There are color problems with the Web, too, where you have to use a limited Web palette. Then there are also the restrictions of connecting speeds with modems.

Do you work differently for TV and the Web?

Yes; they are completely different. The Web is about navigation and structure and is more like architec-ture, really. It's about being able to move around spaces where things happen. I can work with a small crew and there are, in general, fewer people to answer to. With TV, it's about advertising, shows, or branding. A lot more people are involved because the budgets are bigger. You would think this would translate to better quality, but everyone usually wants the cheapest, quickest solution. If the budget allows for a really good animator, someone who understands how to make an object look like it has weight and knows something about anatomy or the timing of a joke, it's a luxury.

What is the most challenging aspect of working in a kinetic environment?

The most challenging thing is creating the right balance. The content is crucial, but finding the right people to nurture it is also crucial. Animators are like actors interpreting the work, and their personalities show in the work. Getting the right soundtrack is crucial. The voice of a character or the music is so important it can change the feeling of everything. In Web design, I think a big challenge is to make a site inviting enough that users stay to explore it.

TITLE: www.willing-to-try.com DESIGNER: Richard McGuire CREATIVE DIRECTOR/PRODUCER: Funny Garbage CLIENT: TRY YEAR: 1999

| # The Power of Creativity

Creative Director, Juxt Interactive, Newport Beach, California

>> **Why and how did you start designing for the Web?**

I used to be an architect and had a love for visual design and computers. I got involved with graphic design and soon learned that this pursuit was much more rewarding for me personally. Eventually, I got my hands on (Macromind) Director software, and when I found the power of interactivity, I knew I had found my future. Being able to design and then bring that to life was magic to me. Soon after this, the Web came on the scene and a previous employer decided to start a shop doing home pages, as he called it. This was back in 1995. He hired me as the art director, and I worked alongside my now partner, Steve Wages. We saw the Web bloom, and we wanted to be a part of it, not just as bystanders but as part of its evolution. This compelled us to create Juxt Interactive and to focus on trying to push the envelope of the medium.

Some of your work is wildly kinetic; some is more quiet and staid. What determines how you will approach the design of a project?

The client's brand and the audience are the two major factors that drive the design. We design objective-driven projects, not style-driven projects as such. It all

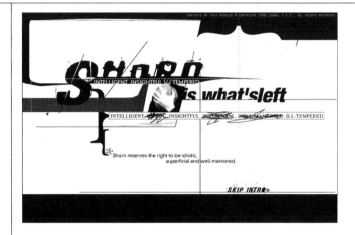

TITLE: SHORN Prototype   DESIGNERS: Todd Purgason, Ryan Holstein, Kristian Olson, Paul Nugyen, Jenn Redmond, Eva Au ART DIRECTOR: Ryan Holstein   CREATIVE DIRECTOR: Todd Purgason   PHOTOGRAPHERS: David Tsay, Todd Purgason   SOUND DESIGN: Todd Purgason   COPY: Dave Fraunces, Itay Dankner, Jordan Berman   PROJECT MANAGER: Steve Wages CLIENT: Shorn LLC   YEAR: 2000

TITLE: Building Flash
Presentation UCON99
DESIGNER/COPY
WRITER/SOUND
PRODUCER: Todd
Purgason CLIENT:
Macromedia/Self
YEAR: 1999

boils down to solving the particular needs of the client. We do have clients asking us to refer to some of our previous work as inspiration for their project, so you can see veins of style running through many projects. We also love typography—all of us do, even our programmers—so that influences our work as well.

How much of what you do on the Web is informed by film or TV? Or is there no relationship among the media?

I have not had TV for fifteen years. I hate it, it is insulting, and I'm stupid enough to watch it when it is around me, so I avoid it. But I do love film. I watch a lot of videos—probably not as many as people without children but enough to fill my mind. I love film titles, especially from the 1960s and the last five years. My wife thinks I'm a total design geek. I sit in the darkness of the theater and name the fonts in the titles, and man, if I see a font I don't have but want, I can't focus on the movie—obsessive-compulsive, I suppose.

TITLE: IPPA June 1999 Screen Calendar DESIGNER: Todd Purgason CLIENT: IPPA YEAR: 2000

What is the most challenging design problem with new media?

Browsers: They are so inconsistent, and the makers have released some real bad versions that were only published for weeks or days even that have their own obscure incompatibilities. We love Flash (although it is not totally immune to browser bugs); it is much more self-contained and consistent.

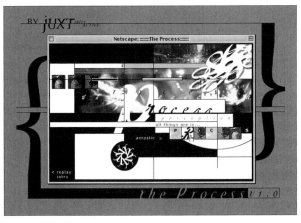

TITLE: Juxt Interactive's The Process DESIGNER/COPY WRITER/SOUND DESIGNER: Todd Purgason
PROGRAMMERS: Brian Drake, Shaun Hervey CLIENT: Juxt Interactive YEAR: 2000

Global, Immediate, Democratic, and Free

Creative Director, Google Creative Lab and Principal, Please Enjoy, New York City

>> **How long have you had your own studio?**

I never had my own studio space in a conventional way. My studio has been my laptop and I do my work on my dining table, cafes, airplanes, hotel rooms...

What are the changes in practice you have seen and experienced since you began?

When I was studying graphic design in New York in the early '90s, my design school was going through the historical transition of mechanical to digital design. In one semester I was taking classes where everything (typesetting, layout, etc.) had to be done by hand (cutting and pasting). The following semester, the school introduced its first computer lab and everything was switched to digital. This was an important transition with a huge impact on how I saw and did design. During the era of mechanical design, *print* was the predominant media. In the digital era of computers and Internet, media and other forms of communication platform have exploded, offering infinite possibilities for designers. Because of this, many graphic designers today are also filmmakers, fashion designers, artists, bloggers, etc.

How have these changes impacted your work?

I completely changed my view on design because of the Internet. Nice thing about the Internet is that it is global, immediate, democratic, and free. It's fascinating how a good

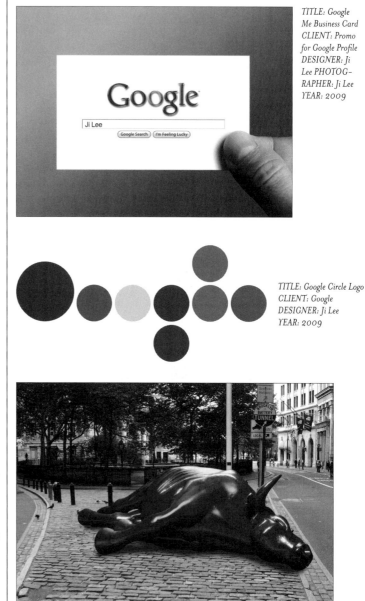

TITLE: *Google Me Business Card* CLIENT: *Promo for Google Profile* DESIGNER: *Ji Lee* PHOTOGRAPHER: *Ji Lee* YEAR: *2009*

TITLE: *Google Circle Logo* CLIENT: *Google* DESIGNER: *Ji Lee* YEAR: *2009*

TITLE: *Dead Bull* CLIENT: *Conde Nast* ILLUSTRATOR: *Ji Lee* YEAR: *2009*

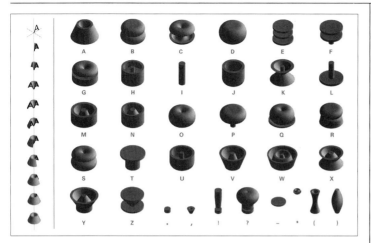

TITLE: *Univers Revolved, a 3D Alphabet* DESIGNER: *Ji Lee* PUBLISHER: *Harry Abrams* YEAR: *2009*

TITLE: *Bubble Project* PHOTOGRA-PHER: *Ji Lee* YEAR: *2009*

TITLE: *Delete Bill-board—Part of NY Street Advertising Takeover* ILLUSTRATOR/ PHOTOGRA-PHER: *Ji Lee* YEAR: *2009*

project can spread instantly to millions across the globe. A designer doesn't need money, a publisher, or a marketing plan to spread his or her project. In this sense, the Internet is a liberating and empowering tool for designers and a lot of us are taking advantage of that. When I think about a project, often I think about what's the best way to make it Web-friendly. I like to create projects as platforms which are open, simple, visual, collaborative, and scalable.

What is the allure of information and *faux* information?

Information is power and that's the allure. And Web makes it very easy for anyone to have access to information. I consume an incredible amount of information everyday: news, sports, images, gossips, Facebook updates, research for new projects, etc. The great thing is that all this information is readily available. On the other hand, I rarely go deep into any subject. I constantly surf the surface of things. I know the essence about a lot of things, but I don't necessarily know much in depth. That's why in the end I must rely on my intuition to create a project. Information is there as research material which serves as inspiration and support. The core of my creativity must come from my feelings and intuitions.

Would you say that you have a particular style or character to your design? If so, how would you define it?

I like to do work which is idea-driven, simple, witty, and thought-provoking. I grew up in Korea, Brazil, and New York. Because of the language barriers and cultural differences, I had to learn new ways to communicate. I think that's why my work tends to be ultra-simple and visual, which can appeal to lots of different people. Humor is also an important aspect in my work. I believe people are attracted to simplicity and fun.

What about graphic design is the most challenging for you?
There are lots of challenging things about what I design. One of them is to always remind myself to step outside of my own vision and see whatever I do from the viewer's perspective and see if it makes sense and works. Things always seem to make sense when I'm so sucked into a project and that's the danger of doing the work in self-absorbed inertia.

The other big challenge for me is to work in collaboration with people. To truly listen and understand my clients and colleagues and communicate my ideas clearly and constructively, so it's not about my ego or control, but all about having a positive and collaborative attitude.

How important is type and typography?
Type is very important. Type gives a voice to the piece. I spend a lot of time tweaking and perfecting type. I'm very fortunate to have had a really incredible typography teacher (Charles Nix) when I was studying design. He gave me the important basic understanding about typography which I use everyday.

What, in this current technological and economic climate, does the future hold for you specifically, and graphic design in general?
I believe our society as a whole has become design savvy and visually sophisticated. More and more people see the importance of design both in a purely aesthetical sense and also as a business solution. For many years designers have been perceived as "decorators" or "beautifiers." Today designers are playing more of a role of "problem solvers" and "inventors" which I think is really exciting.

TITLE: *New Museum Building* PHOTOGRAPHY: *New Museum*
ARCHITECT: *Sanaa* YEAR: *2009*

TITLE: *New Museum Launch Campaign, Subway Ad* CLIENT: *New Museum*
AGENCY: *Droga5* DESIGNER/PHOTOGRAPHER: *Ji Lee* YEAR: *2009*

TITLE: *New Museum Launch Campaign, Subway Ad* CLIENT: *New Museum*
AGENCY: *Droga5* DESIGNER/PHOTOGRAPHER: *Ji Lee* YEAR: *2009*

TITLE: *New Museum Launch Campaign, Calvin Klein Billboard Takeover*
CLIENT: *New Museum, in partnership with Calvin Klein* AGENCY: *Droga5*
DESIGNER/PHOTOGRAPHER: *Ji Lee* YEAR: *2009*

JASON SANTA MARIA

The Web Is Not Print

Partners, WIDEOPENSPACES, Los Angeles

>> **What are the changes in practice and form you have seen and experienced since you began?**

The work I do is mainly for the Web, and in the time since I've started the barrier to entry has dropped even lower. If you have a good idea you can just make it. You don't always need funding or anyone to help. You have access to a global audience. With that said, many times it feels like an arms race. Because the Web affords you the ability to get something out there so easily, it seems to devalue what a brand means. People try out so many new things all the time that they are just as likely to jump ship to the latest site or service.

How have these changes impacted your work?

It makes me more cautious of the kind of work I take on. I'm less likely to take a start-up company as a client because they generally seem to be a bit looser with regard to process and deliverables. This loose style works for their internal process, but can be difficult to work around in a typical client/vendor relationship.

I also try to be sure the work I do attempts to connect with people and not just be about the hot new thing. I can concede that people's interest can fade from one site to the next, but I want to try and make meaningful experiences while I have their attention.

How did you decide to specialize in Web design?

It was a bit roundabout for me. I went to school for traditional graphic design and only came to the Web when I needed a place to showcase my work. I was swept up with how fertile the Web was for design and intrigued that very few people seemed to be doing anything about it at the time.

Did you have specific training?

Other than an introduction to Web design class in college, I am completely self-taught. Looking back now, I'm glad I went down this path. I was able to bring my design education to a different medium, but one where many of the same ideals apply.

What is the biggest challenge you face regarding design and the Web?

The biggest challenge I face is helping people understand that the Web is not print. It sounds like it would be obvious, and the two mediums do overlap in areas, but they are very different in terms of the user experience. People interact with a Web site differently and the design of that site needs to be understanding of that >>

TITLE: *Typedia Web Site* CLIENT: *Self*
DESIGNER/ILLUSTRATOR: *Jason Santa Maria* PROGRAMS: *Illustrator, Photoshop* YEAR: *2009*

fact and assist the visitor at the same time. At the same time, centuries worth of design principles don't immediately transfer to the Web in the same ways. Many graphic designers think the Web is a barren place for design, when the reality is they are proclaiming they don't understand the medium.

How important is typography in what you do?

Typography is absolutely essential. The vast majority of the Web is text, and where there's text, there's an opportunity to communicate something with typography. Typography structures the user experience and is essential to every design.

Given the current economic climate and technological shifts, what is in the future for graphic design?

I think the Web is only going to gain more momentum in our industry. Every job we take on will need to have some sort of Web-related counterpoint, and designers who don't embrace it will be forced to outsource work. What's more, online connectivity will begin to creep into more facets of our lives. Eventually everything we touch will be connected to everything else, and those are new interactions that will need the help of design.

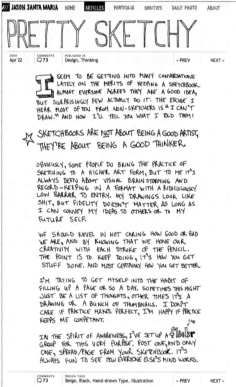

TITLE: Jason Santa Maria Web Site
CLIENT: Self
DESIGNER/ ILLUSTRATOR: Jason Santa Maria
PROGRAMS: Illustrator, Photoshop
YEAR: 2008

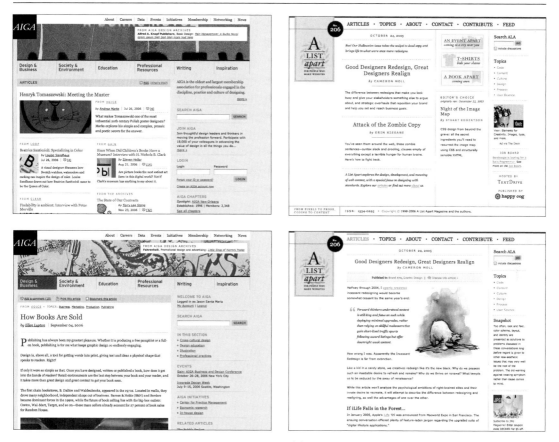

TITLE: *A List Apart and An Event Apart Web Sites*
CLIENT: *Happy Cog Studios* DESIGNER: *Jason Santa Maria* ILLUSTRATOR: *Kevin Cornell (ALA article page)* PROGRAMS: *Illustrator, Photoshop* YEAR: *2005*

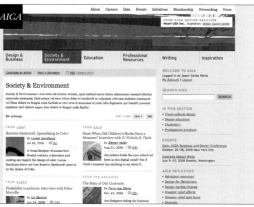

TITLE: *AIGA Web Site* CLIENT: *AIGA* DESIGNER: *Jason Santa Maria*
PROGRAMS: *Illustrator, Photoshop* YEAR: *2007*

JASON TSELENTIS

Principal, Jason Tselentis Design, Charlotte, North Carolina

The Digital Bookworm

How long have you had your own studio?

I incorporated in 1997, but I had been freelancing since 1991.

What are the changes in practice and form you have seen and experienced since you began?

It used to be that everyone wanted a logo; lately everyone wants a Web site.

How did you decide to become a graphic designer?

During my adolescent and teenage years I adored magazines, movie titles, and comic books—anything with type and image. The Macintosh Plus my father brought home in 1986 became a box-shaped laboratory where I could make those things myself.

Did you have specific training?

I committed myself to design from 1992–1994 by studying with Jackson Boelts at the University of Arizona. I finished my bachelor's degree at the University of Nebraska-Lincoln, and received mentorship outside of classes from the late Richard Eckersley. Finally, I earned my masters in visual communication at the University of Washington.

What is the biggest challenge you face regarding design in this new digital environment?

Because so many clients understand the computer and its immediacy, they want results as soon as possible.

How important is typography in what you do?

Typography is very important because as a bookworm, I like words. Formally, I begin with the message and how typography shapes meaning, structure, and rhythm.

Given the current economic climate and technological shifts, what is in the future for graphic design?

Designers have the opportunity to become entrepreneurs by doing self-initiated or market-driven work that we create on our own.

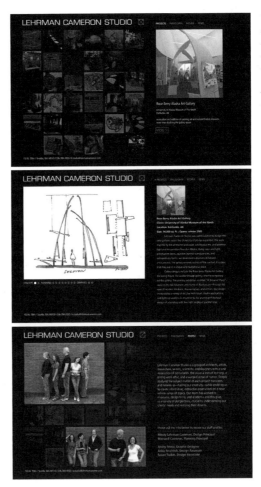

TITLE: *Lehrman Cameron Studio Web Site* CLIENT: *Lehrman Cameron Studio* DESIGNER/CREATIVE DIRECTOR: *Jason A. Tselentis* ILLUSTRATORS AND PHOTOGRAPHERS: *Lehrman Cameron Studio* YEAR: *2004*

TITLE: Bark with
the Big Dogs
CLIENT: AIGA
Charlotte
DESIGNER/
CREATIVE
DIRECTOR:
Jason A. Tselentis
PHOTOGRAPHER:
George B. Tselentis
YEAR: 2007

TITLE: Faculty Art Exhibition CLIENT: University of North
Carolina-Charlotte DESIGNER/CREATIVE DIRECTOR:
Jason A. Tselentis YEAR: 2005

TITLE: Jackson
School of International
Studies Web Site
CLIENT: University
of Washington
DESIGNER/
CREATIVE
DIRECTOR:
Jason A. Tselentis
YEAR: 2006

TITLE: Proof Poster CLIENT: Seattle Repertory Theatre
DESIGNER/CREATIVE DIRECTOR: Jason A. Tselentis
YEAR: 2001

IX. MOTION

IN THE YEARS SINCE the advent of cable TV and an increase in the number of both Hollywood and independent movies being made, graphic designers have become more integral to film and television production. Both industries have traditionally employed graphic and advertising designers to promote their wares in print, but a current surge in the use of motion designers has developed into a popular specialty.

Motion is the umbrella term for a discipline practiced by designers who create movement on either silver or LED and plasma screens. The former create film titles (the graphic cinematic sequences that introduce a movie) and trailers (promotions used to advertise a film prior to release), while the latter develop station or network identifiers, interstices, or bumpers (short promotional sequences between programs), and program openers (the main titles for a TV show). Some designers work with live action, others with animation, and most integrate type with kinetic imagery. Some work exclusively for the film or broadcast industries, but most are generalists within this specialty. Some designers are on the staffs of film studios or television stations; others are independent contractors with studios or firms. Some firms are small—based on the vision of one or two designers—and a few are very large and handle a wide variety of motion-related projects. For those with an interest in movement, this is a creatively challenging yet highly pressured field that requires considerable collaboration.

FILM

When Hollywood was in its infancy and movies were silent, generic title cards were the means to introduce a film and to caption scenes. With the subsequent advent of talkies and color, titles were designed in more ambi-

SOME DESIGNERS WORK WITH LIVE ACTION, OTHERS WITH ANIMATION, AND MOST INTEGRATE TYPE WITH KINETIC IMAGERY.

tious and dramatic styles befitting the content of the movie. In the early 1950s, Saul Bass, a graphic designer, directed the first abstract title sequence for the Otto Preminger film *The Man with the Golden Arm*; it showed the animated development of a crooked, serpentine arm and hand twisting around the names of the cast. Influenced by the art of German expressionism, this unprecedented symbolic approach was used to indicate the raw, drug-related theme of the movie. Not only did the sequence present the title and cast billing in a novel way, it established the tenor of the film through allusion rather than a live-action scene. From this touchstone, Bass and other title designers began to direct very short films. Although not all title sequences are as ambitious, the best are indeed films within films and used as shorthand introductions that ease the viewer into the story or plot of the movie.

Many classic examples are currently found on video—*Vertigo*, *North by Northwest*, *To Kill a Mockingbird*, *Around the World in Eighty Days*, *The Pink Panther*, and *Dr. Strangelove*, just to name a few of the best. And in recent years, numerous future classics have been produced—*Seven*, *Men in Black*, *Casino*, *Clockers*, and more. Everyone interested in this design discipline should watch these again and again.

In most cases, film titles are budgeted into an overall production estimate; they are also often the first thing to be jettisoned when costs run over. Low-budget films are routinely bereft of designed titles, while high-budget and blockbuster films, which can afford them, go all out. Of course, this is not a consistent rule; sometimes young designers work at cost in order to experiment with titles for independent films—but "at cost" can be costly. Title sequences are usually commissioned by film directors or producers and, depending on their level of involvement, they either micro- or macromanage the sequence. Regardless of how little or how much freedom is allowed, the title sequence designer is not hired to create an independent film but to complement, as creatively as possible, the main story.

Various optical houses based in Hollywood, which once did almost all the title work, specialize in main and end titles and employ staff designers and technicians who work anonymously on specific projects. Quite a few well-known title designers got their early training at these optical houses. However, after Saul Bass created his first title sequence, the conventions changed to include freelance designers, working alone or in studios, who were commissioned on a project basis. Today, the most inspired and memorable title sequences are designed by independent firms and studios that have their own creative and production components. Most are headquartered in Los Angeles in close proximity to the major film studios, but New York is home to others. Indeed, as more film pre- and postproduction is done in New York, it is no longer necessary to live and work in L.A. to get good film title assignments. Moreover, in addition to the dedicated film title firms, generalist graphic designers are commissioned to do the occasional film title as one part of their overall practice.

Film title assignments are commissioned in various ways. Specialists are known for their work and hired based on their portfolio (or reel) and reputation. If both director/producer and designer have a good experience, the likelihood of repeat business increases. Although the well-known specialists get the lion's share of the work, small and even untried design firms are continually tapped by directors looking for novel approaches.

Designing a title sequence is not for the neophyte. If a designer is not well-versed in the techniques of filmmaking, a strong support/production team is necessary to translate a storyboard into celluloid. The designer must, however, be able to think in terms of movement and create narrative or abstract sequences that fuse into a graphic entity. The designer should understand as much

TRAINING IN FILM, SOUND EDITING AND CINEMATOGRAPHY IS RECOMMENDED, IF ONLY TO HAVE A SENSE OF THE MEDIUM AND ITS POTENTIAL.

of the process as possible, which means a fairly extensive apprenticeship at an optical house or design firm. Training in (or exposure to) film and sound editing and cinematography is recommended, if only to have a sense of the medium and its potential. Because an increasing number of effects are done on computer, the designer should also have experience with editing programs (Director, AfterEffects, and others) for the Macintosh, Media 100, and Silicon Graphics hardware.

Film titles are concept-driven but work-intensive and require much collaboration from the design/production team. For those who want to direct sequences, it is prudent to become members of these teams. The neophyte should create both storyboards and computer-generated samples as principle portfolio components—then, once in the door, learn as much as possible. More knowledge means more options that can be brought to the screen.

Some designers who specialize in film titles also do collateral print work for the movie industry, including posters and press kits, but most of this work is done by designers in advertising agencies or design firms that specialize in promotion.

TELEVISION
Designers who work primarily in film may also work in television (and vice versa). Although the aspect ratio (the size of the image on the screen) is quite different, the basic technology is the same. Of course, a TV program introduction is rarely as long as a film title sequence, and a television bumper is no more than thirty seconds, but the creative energy and production invested in each is similar.

Once, when only three major networks reigned and a few local stations operated in regional markets, all television work, from broadcast design (such as the graphics seen behind the talking heads on the news) to on-air motion design, was stratified and restricted. In-house art departments were responsible for the majority of the work, or it was farmed out to production studios that specialized in them. However, with the advent of cable TV networks, the demand for unique approaches (rather than network clichés) led cable creative directors to commission independent designers to supplement in-house design staffs. Although this genre is not as huge as publishing, advertising, or corporate design, opportunities have increased, and the number of dedicated practitioners is growing. When one stops to think how much broadcast air has to be filled with distinctive graphics, it is clear that this is not a slacker industry.

From the 1950s through the 1970s, CBS was the major influence on television graphic design. From its iconic logo—the CBS Eye, designed by William Golden—to its print advertising and on-air promotion, designed by Louis Dorfsman, all the graphics for the "champagne network" were elegant, creative, and memorable. In addition, NBC had its peacock, ABC had its Paul Rand logo, and these were the cornerstones of design achievement. Early in the 1980s, computer technology entered the graphic arena and with it a not altogether welcome trend called the *flying logo*. State-of-the-art imaging systems, such as Paintbox, allowed designers to dimensionalize and kineticize their graphics with such ease that every network and regional station made their identifiers jump, bounce, and otherwise speed across the television screen. Soon the practice was ridiculed inside the profession as a substitute for original thinking. Today the trend is lessened, although

not entirely gone. Instead, MTV was launched in 1979 and with it an entirely new approach to on-air graphic identification. The original logo was not a simple, elegant form but an inelegant *M* with a scrawled *TV* beside it. Not only was this akin to graffiti, the mark constantly and animatedly changed its form—color, pattern, context—on the air. In addition, over time, the logo was included in bumpers and interstices that were

> TELEVISION OR BROADCAST DESIGN EMPLOYS NUMEROUS SKILLS AND TALENTS. SOME DESIGNERS SPECIALIZE; OTHERS DO NOT.

miniature animated movies. With the busting of television graphic convention, the floodgates were opened to a wide range of creative possibilities throughout the cable industry. Today, diverse approaches contributed by a new generation of TV designers are found on Nickelodeon, Lifetime, American Movie Channel, Comedy Central, E!, Bravo, and HBO.

Television or broadcast design employs numerous skills and talents. Some designers specialize; others do not. Here is a brief summary:

1. In-house graphic designers or graphic artists for news broad- casting: These are the designers who produce breaking news and generic graphics that highlight or introduce a news subject and are most commonly seen behind the newscaster's talking head. These designers are proficient in drawing and graphics software.

2. In-house graphic designers or graphic artists for station identifiers: All large and most small broadcast operations employ staff designers to create on-air bumpers, promos, and common identifiers. The more ambitious work might be contracted to independent design/production firms.

3. In-house art departments for program openers: Most of these are contracted to independent designers but, in some larger design departments for stations or networks that generate their own programming (like certain public broadcasting stations), this is considered something of a perk. It usually requires an art director working with a production crew (cameraman, animator, etc.), depending on whether the film is live action or animated. Program openers are not restricted to type on a screen.

4. Independent design firms for on-air promos and identifiers: Graphic design studios are getting an increasing amount of choice on-air assignments, and the ratio of experienced film or broadcast designers to those without track records in this area is fairly balanced. MTV Networks (including Nickelodeon, Nick at Nite, and Cartoon Network) have turned to young designers, illustrators, and animators in an effort to tap unknown talents. In turn, this has launched new subspecialties for firms and individuals who may have been exclusively print-oriented.

There is also a great need for advertising and program *content*. This is the prime area for animation studios, a few of which combine graphic design and illustration. Although traditional animation studios are routinely subcontracted by television and advertising art directors to produce predetermined storyboards, there is also a rise in creative animation/design firms that specialize in developing their own ideas. For some of these, it is important to have experienced animators, producers, or directors, while others supplement a core staff of experts with neophytes who are unfettered by constraints. With more advertising spots using animation, and with the advent of cable programming devoted to new animation (experimental programming) as well as a desire among the funkier stations to push the limits of on-air identification, creative animation teams are finding a receptive clientele.

To enter the motion design discipline, it is useful to have some film and television training, which can be obtained in special school courses or through internships (even local low-power TV stations are a good place to begin, if only to become acquainted with broadcast technology). Today, it is not as daunting or difficult to enter the field as it used to be. Indeed, knowledge of key programs (which change frequently, so stay informed) allows you to try your hand at this medium and to determine whether or not you have the talent to pursue a career.

This area includes any kind of film- or television-based media. While some motion designers also engage in Web or CD-ROM design, others do not. The emphasis should be on film or television title sequences, television interstices, bumpers, videos, and other related practice.

Entry Level

School and speculative assignments are acceptable, along with any design or artwork that contributes to sequential motion graphics.

CONTENTS

    a. Printout versions of on-screen designs

    b. Screen grabs on Zip Disk or CD-ROM

    c. Videocassette (if available), featuring motion graphics, animation, pencil tests, etc.

    d. Two or three storyboards

Advanced

Projects should be fairly advanced. Individual or collaborative live assignments should be combined with speculative work.

CONTENTS

    a. Printout versions of on-screen designs

    b. Screen grabs on Zip Disk or CD-ROM

    c. One or two speculative projects as storyboards or realized

    d. Videocassette with professional-quality work

    e. Two or three storyboards or preparatory work

Format

CD and DVD in the following formats: Flash, PowerPoint, and iPhoto. Online portfolios are also encouraged. Avoid digital tricks. Keep it as straightforward as possible. Anything that crashes the viewer's computer will hamper appreciation of your work.

TITLE: Monsoon Wedding DESIGNER: Jasmine Jodry ART DIRECTORS: Jakob Trollbäck, Antoine Tinguely ILLUSTRATOR: Laura Ljungkvist TYPEFACE: Din CLIENT: Mirabai YEAR: 2003

RANDALL BALSMEYER | Lights, Camera, Design

Principal, Big Film Design, Inc., New York City

» How did you become a film title designer?

I was working as a graphic designer when a friend asked me if I could design the titles for a documentary she had just made. It sounded like fun, so I gave it a try. Next thing I knew I was designing more titles, which led to learning about animation, cinematography, and opticals. It was the first time that my interests in photography, design, film, and computers all clicked together. It was very satisfying to create these kinds of images. I've always been both left- and right-brained, and this was the first time that both sides were happy.

What is the key difference between designing for film and TV?

The principal difference between film and TV (aside from aspect ratio) is pacing. TV is about getting through material as quickly as possible, before the viewer clicks his remote control. It's also about selling the show. The goal in TV is to grab the viewer's interest and hook him into watching the rest of the show. Films are a bit more leisurely. You can take the time to set a mood, build a rapport with the viewer. You don't have to sell the movie because the viewer has already bought his ticket and has committed to watching the picture.

What about the difference between motion and print?

TITLE: *The Big Lebowski* DESIGNER: *Randall Balsmeyer* CLIENT: *Working Title Films* TYPEFACES: *Mesquite, Magneto* YEAR: *1997* Copyright: *© Polygram Filmed Entertainment*

TITLE: *The First Wives Club* DESIGNER: *Randall Balsmeyer* TYPEFACES: *Hairspray, Cafeteria* YEAR: *1996* Copyright: *© 1996 Paramount Pictures*

TITLE: *Kundun* DESIGNER: *Randall Balsmeyer* CLIENT: *Refuge Productions* TYPEFACE: *ITC Viner Hand Italic* YEAR: *1997* Copyright: *© 1997 Touchstone Pictures. All rights reserved.*

TITLE: *Jungle Fever* DESIGNER: *Randall Balsmeyer* CLIENT: *40 Acres and a Mule Filmworks* YEAR: *1991* Copyright: *© 1991 Universal City Studios, Inc. Courtesy of Universal Publishing Rights, a Division of Universal Studios, Inc. All rights reserved.*

In both TV and film, designers dictate the pace at which the piece is seen. In print, the viewer controls the pace and chooses whether to explore the piece in depth, skim for meaning, or just turn the page.

Is this field open or closed to newcomers?

Film graphics is now more open than it ever has been. The technical changes of the last few years have taken design out of the Iron Age and made it more accessible to anyone with a good idea. The downside of this is that a lot of really terrible work shows up because now anyone can do it. We now frequently see technique masquerading as an idea.

How much technology must you know to achieve your goals?

I live with one foot in the design world and one foot in the visual effects world. By necessity (and choice), my inclination is to be fluent in the available technology. On one hand, I try not to think about the means of execution when I'm coming up with ideas. On the other hand, I need to know how to actualize something once a design is agreed upon. We invented a character, my alter ego, the Technoslut (someone who is easy for technology). We gave him a tongue-in-cheek slogan, "Complicated Is Better," which we hope communicates the sense of humor with which we view the technology we're so dependent upon.

You work with assistants; what do you look for in a portfolio?

The work should be idea-centric. It should not be about its own means of production. It should be bold, not precious. It should be a strong, original means of communicating an idea. If it breaks rules to do that, great! But the work should not be about breaking rules, because it then becomes self-referential. If it's a thesis on kerning, don't bother sending it.

TITLE: *Short Cuts* DESIGNER: *Randall Balsmeyer* CLIENT: *Short Cuts Productions* TYPE-FACE: *Journal* YEAR: 1993 *Copyright: © 1993 Fine Line Features. All rights reserved.*

TITLE: *Naked Lunch* DESIGNER: *Randall Balsmeyer* CLIENT: *Recorded Picture Company* TYPEFACE: *Futura* YEAR: 1991 Copyright: © 1991 Twentieth Century Fox

The Art of Storytelling

Director, Prologue Films, Hollywood, California

》 What have been the major influences on your work as a film title designer?

Saul Bass's main titles for *The Man with the Golden Arm*, *Take a Walk on the Wild Side*, and *Seconds*, which I saw in 1985. I was also influenced by R. Greenberg's titles for *Altered States, Goldfinger*, by Robert Brownjohn, and *To Kill a Mockingbird*, by Stephen Frankfurt. Of course, I also loved *Star Wars*, but what impressed me the most was the editing and the juxtaposition of images. Paul Hirsch and George Lucas really made an impression on me. George Lucas seems very aware of the editorial aspect of a film and what that can bring to the movie.

Do you have a personal style in your film titles?

I heard someone say once that having a style is like being in jail. I do not agree, but I try to approach each design differently; one style is never appropriate for all jobs. The visual approach I take for a main title sequence should establish a tone—encapsulate, and generate excitement in people about what they are about to see. My work is sometimes seen as experimental; I do like to keep up to date with what is new in graphic design and film, but I think that under everything I have done is an attempt to solve a specific communication problem. With each title sequence, a problem has to be solved. I need to understand the content of the film. The type is often like an actor, always

behaving in a way that would help explain the small story.

What is the most fulfilling aspect of your job? The least?

The most fulfilling aspect of my job is being able to combine my interests in film, typography, technology, and storytelling. There are limitless options in the production process. I can integrate almost every medium imaginable. The least is probably when we try to do too much work at once or go into something without a plan. I also do not like when people try to separate the main title from the movie and critique it as a separate piece. A main title, ideally, should seem like an integrated part of the film.

How have technological advancements affected your work?

A great deal. Technology allows us to do complex things more simply and in less time. Take *The Island of Dr. Moreau*, for instance. We used Adobe Illustrator to do things with type—stretching end points to create violent shards, sharpening, deconstructing, reconfiguring. It's the kind of graphics that would have to have been hand-painted ten years ago. Technology allows us to execute almost anything we imagine.

Do you have a specific approach to hiring designers?

We look for people who are good thinkers, typographers with a good film sense first. I do lean toward good typographers, however. I like to give people a chance to try something they may not have done before. Often this means bringing in incredibly talented print graphic designers and introducing them to motion graphics. It is really an ongoing process of constantly being open to meeting and seeing the work of interested designers and interns.

TITLE: *Sphere* DESIGNERS: *Olivia D'Albis, Mikon Van Gastel* CREATIVE DIRECTOR: *Kyle Cooper* ART DIRECTORS: *Mikon Van Gastel, Kurt Mattila* COMPANY: *Imaginary Forces* CLIENT: *Warner Bros.* PHOTOGRAPHER: *Norbert Wu* TYPOGRAPHER: *Mikon Van Gastel* YEAR: *1998*

TITLE: *Donnie Brasco*
DESIGNERS: *Kyle Cooper,
Kurt Mattila, Adam Bluming,
Olivia D'Albis* COMPANY:
Imaginary Forces CLIENTS:
*TriStar Pictures, Mandalay
Entertainment* YEAR: *1997*

TITLE: *Mission: Impossible* DESIGNERS: *Kyle Cooper, Jenny Shainin* CREATIVE DIRECTORS: *Kyle Cooper, Peter Frankfurt*
COMPANY: *Imaginary Forces* CLIENT: *Paramount* YEAR: *1996*

TITLE: *The Island of Dr. Moreau* DESIGNERS: *Kyle Cooper, Karin Fox, Chris Do, Scarlett Kim, Vince Abogado*
ART DIRECTOR: *Karin Fox* COMPANY: *Imaginary Forces* CLIENT: *New Line Cinema* TYPEFACES: *Mason, Caslon* YEAR: *1996*

JACOB TROLLBÄCK | All about Kinetic Energy

Principal, Trollbäck + Company, New York City

» What prompted a graphic designer to become expert in motion—film and video?

I find graphic design very formal when it is static. There can be an amazing energy in a printed piece, but it is what a physicist would call potential energy. It is what makes print design hard—to find the expression that hits the energy level where it works just right. Motion, on the other hand, is all about kinetic energy. It moves within the linear passing of time and creates tension and rhythm patterns in its flow. In my twenties I was a music freak and a DJ, and used graphics to promote events. Ultimately I realized that I was even happier when I could apply my skills as a DJ and mixer to a flow of images.

What is the most challenging aspect of creating visuals in time and space?

Having them mean something. Ninety percent of all graphics that I see doesn't mean anything. It's frivolous and ultimately bores me.

Do you tell stories or make design?

If you want to make people feel in a special way, you have to be very particular about what you design and how you present it. For anyone to understand what you try to say, you need to work inside (or outside) a set of social and cultural values. This is why good motion design is a close relative to storytelling.

There are times when a client just

wants something new, and the whole idea is to create something that nobody has seen before. This can be a great challenge and force you to search all kinds of cultural expressions for unique voices. But in the end, without the story (however convoluted) it will never really move anyone.

How did you learn to work in this medium? How much is craft, and how much is design intuition?

I was always pretty good with technical things and felt at home with all kinds of software, which helped tremendously. I spent years learning to move things around on a screen. This is the craft, to understand how to shoot, animate, and edit something in order for it to feel in a certain way—heavy, doughy, airy, cold, angry, happy, etc. Then you need to invoke some magic to find that unseen angle that makes it unique.

What is the most satisfying piece that you've done?

This is a hard one. There's a lot of work through the years that I am very happy with, but obviously, running a company means that I'm not always as much hands on, which in the end is most satisfying to me.

I'm very happy with the live-action spots that I directed for Lifetime, and some branding work, like AMC and TNT. I still like the numerous openings that I've done for the TED conferences, and I keep

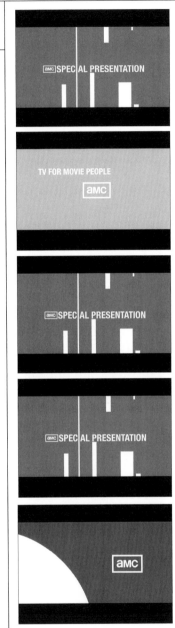

TITLE: AMC DESIGNERS: Antoine Tinguely, Laurent Fauchere, Todd Neal, Greg Hahn ART DI-RECTOR: Jakob Trollbäck TYPOGRAPHER: Max Miedinger CLIENT: Rainbow Media YEAR: 2003

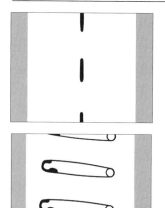

TITLE: *Night Falls on Man-hattan* DESIGNER: *Todd Neal* ART DIRECTOR: *Jakob Trollbäck* TYPEFACE: *Sabon by Jan Tschichold* CLIENT: *Night Falls on Manhattan* YEAR: *1996*

looking back on the main titles for *Night Falls on Manhattan* with joy.

Given your trajectory, how would you suggest that designers enter the motion field?
With passion. There is no substitute for it.

But specifically, what are the necessities that a motion designer must have?
Rhythm. Syncopation. Listen to Bill Evans's piano on Miles's *All Blues*. Especially what he is doing under the solos. You got to try to be totally in tune with the piece, and at the same time be as joyfully unpredictable.

It's a true gift, and I believe that the link between music and motion is here, right now.

Once you understand this and can feel the rhythm, you take your idea and go to work with your toolbox of images, color, type, art, culture, and patience.

Anything else?
Magic is very rare, but it does happen.

TITLE: *Volvo Safety* DESIGN-ERS: *Antoine Tinguely, Laurent Fauchere* ART DIRECTORS: *Jakob Trollbäck, Antoine Tinguely, Laurent Fauchere* TYPEFACE: *Volvo Custom Font* CLIENT: *Volvo* YEAR: *2003*

TITLE: *TED8* DESIGNER/ART DIRECTOR: *Jakob Trollbäck* TYPOGRA-PHER: *Max Miedinger* CLIENT: *The TED Conferences* YEAR: *1997*

| # Designing on Air

Vice President of Design and On-air Creative, MTV, New York City

---

» What is your role at MTV, and what are your responsibilities?

I'm responsible for all on-air graphics and show opens. I do all the packaging for the channel and for shows, and I'm also in charge of all the print work, which ranges from business-to-business stuff to consumer stuff to licensing and consumer products. I have currently about thirty-five people on my staff. It's a big in-house group.

MTV is the hot medium; how do you address the problems you are given?

I think the biggest challenge is constantly trying to have a philosophy, as much as possible, and to reinvent yourself and trying to keep moving, and to not get caught up in visual redundancy. In that way, whether people see your work on air or in the print materials, they feel that there's a continuity but also an evolutionary process going on. Sometimes we live in a world of fashion and pay attention to what's going on, but you have to change with the times, too.

Being in the vortex of the most fashionable designing for a youth culture, do you lead, follow, or echo?

It's a combination. We really don't want to echo, but at the same time we have to pay attention to what's going on and what kids are reacting to and what their world is about. We really can't impose our own visual agenda on them. We tend to look

TITLE: American Illustration 16 DESIGNERS: Jeffrey Keyton, Stacy Drummond, Tracy Hoychuck COMPANY: MTV Design CLIENT: Amerulis, Inc. ILLUSTRATOR: Geoffrey Gran TYPEFACE: Helvetica YEAR: 2001

at fashion trends and pay attention to music kids are listening to. In the time of Nirvana, when everything was grunge, the graphics had a little bit more of that type of look and feel, but now, with the current fragmentation in music, a youth might be listening to the music of Puff Daddy and Celine Dion. You can get away with more eclecticism and probably go a little cleaner and more minimal, as it seems to be a more conservative time. That's just in the last couple of years. Sometimes I feel if I look at too much stuff it could affect me subconsciously. I'll skim enough to know what's going on; I don't want to feel like I'm out of it. I think it's important to know what your peers are doing, but not to the point where you study it. So if I am following, it's more fashion and music trends than design trends.

When hiring designers, do you have a specific approach?

First and foremost, we're always looking for someone with basic design skills and at how well she can decorate. We'd prefer someone with an interesting, slightly unusual approach rather than a classical, traditional approach because that's not necessarily the most appropriate style up here. Being an in-house department in a corporation, we are influenced by interpersonal skills. Is she going to be a good communicator? In small studios, you can get stuck in a back room and not come out. You can't really get away with that in a corporation. And, of course, conceptual thinking is always good, too.

TITLE: On-air Design SEQUENCE DESIGNER/ART DIRECTOR: Catherine Chesters CREATIVE DIRECTOR: Jeffrey Keyton COMPANY: MTV Design CLIENT: MTV

TITLE: On-air Opens for Sports and Music Festival DESIGNER: Greg Hahn CREATIVE DIRECTOR: Jeffrey Keyton ART DIRECTORS: Todd St. John, Greg Hahn COMPANY: MTV Design CLIENT: MTV ILLUSTRATOR: Packorn Buppahavesa YEAR: 2003

JONATHAN NOTARO

JONATHAN NOTARO | Typographic Justice

Principal, Brand New School, Santa Monica, California

>> Why did you decide to work in new media?

I'm a designer of things. I don't necessarily work in new media. Sure, I've done plenty of "new media" projects for companies and self-promotion, but I guess I'm a graphic designer who just happens to be working in motion right now, until something else interests me, or I get bored, whatever comes first.

How much does typography play in your design scheme?

Typography plays a huge role in my work. On the page, typography is one thing, but it goes so far beyond that. I explore its relationships in space and environment—how it reacts, mimics, or negates identifiable relationships in physical space. Ultimately, I suppose, it carries a whole new set of connotations, not to mention an evolution of form. The majority of work I do is for ad agencies; they love to see their precious copy receive typographic justice.

Do you integrate design for the digital realm with print?

We've seen so much of this lately, where the constraints of Flash [vector-based image making] influence the print aesthetic, and things start to carry a poor 1970s lithograph nostalgic vernacular. The mysticism of the digital realm has been unveiled, so I think its design has become much easier.

Or has it? It's always interesting to see what spills over to the other side, formally and conceptually. The old limitations of the Web have forced designers to think simply yet still attempt to be interesting with information. I think the biggest fear designers should have is managing aesthetic differences based on the functional differences of variation in media.

Do you allow enough time for research, development, and experimentation? How so?

That's one of the perks of owning my own company. As a design director, part of my job is choosing the right projects, determining how much time to allocate for research, development, experimentation, and assessing what resources the project may demand.

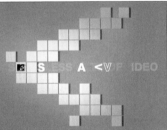

TITLE: Senseless Acts of Video—show package DESIGNER: Jonathan Notaro CREATIVE DIRECTOR/PRODUCER: Jonathan Notaro PRODUCER: Casey Steele CLIENT: MTV Networks YEAR: 2000

TITLE: *MTV Fashionably Loud Week—Show Package* DESIGN-
ERS: *Jonathan Notaro, Jens Gehlhaar, Sean Dougherty* CREATIVE
DIRECTOR/PRODUCER: *Jonathan Notaro* PRODUCER: *Angela
de Oliveira* CLIENT: *MTV Networks* YEAR: *2000*

≫ How does your firm integrate print, Web, and motion into a holistic practice? Or are these totally separate activities?

Mulder: They are not totally separate activities. They just require separate considerations. For example, broadcast design work general exists in a low-resolution format like NTSC. The way you can handle type and line is very different from what is possible in print. Therefore, your visual solutions have to be flexible enough to change for each medium.

Doing work in all three genres is challenging. It usually takes a day or so to switch gears when going from a large motion project to a print project. But I think it keeps us on our toes because we are influenced by that many more people and ideas.

Schneider: Creatively, these factors all seem to melt together. Of course, sensibilities change with each media type but, often, one creative solution will spur ideas in other areas. This seems particularly evident in dynamic online media such as Flash and its comparisons to Film/Broadcast. It's becoming quite cyclical.

As graphic designers, did you have to acclimate yourselves to motion? What was the learning curve?

Mulder: I did for sure. Because of the greater freedom that designing over time gives, you need to be a better manager of time and assets. It was really overwhelming at first. You have the ability to vary an infinite amount of factors in seemingly infinite numbers of ways at infinite points in time. Technically, there is a learning curve of specialized knowledge for broadcast and film work. But the technical knowledge isn't any more or less complex than you would find for print or interactive; it is just different.

What is the most important design issue for film?

Mulder: The single most important design issue for film or

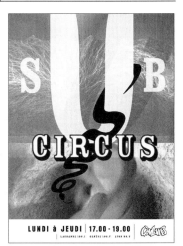

TITLE: Couleur 3 Poster Series
DESIGNER/ART DIRECTOR: Matthew Mulder AGENCY: WGR Lausanne, CH CLIENT: Swiss State Radio YEAR: 1999

TITLE: I AM
DESIGNERS/
DIRECTORS:
Matthew Mulder,
Paul Schneider
CLIENT: CODEX 3
YEAR: 2001

TITLE: WIDEOPENSPACES Postcards DESIGNERS: Matthew Mulder, Paul Schneider
CLIENT: WIDEOPENSPACES YEAR: 2001

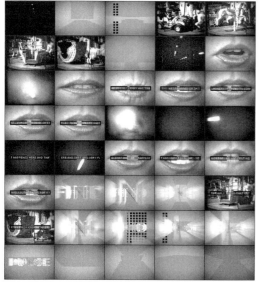

TITLE: The Pulse
Lets Me Know I Am
Alive DESIGNERS/
DIRECTORS: Matthew
Mulder, Paul Schneider
CLIENT: Belief Studios
YEAR: 2001

TITLE: Rossignol
Snowboard Video
DESIGNER/
DIRECTOR:
Paul Schneider
CLIENT: Rossignol
Skis and Snowboards
YEAR: 1999

any other motion-based medium is understanding narrative and dramatic structures. This is completely overlooked in graphic design education currently. We should look to our film school brethren, for whom understanding an audience and how to engage them is beaten into their brains as students. I also think that the concept of editing is important. In the beginning, I would try and fit everything into a single moment because that was what I was used to doing in print. **Schneider:** Telling a story over time utilizing conflicts created between imagery, sound, and graphic. It is important for a designer working in such media to realize this in order to react/interact in a desired manner.

How important is a typographic or cinematic style?

Mulder: I believe that each project should develop its form based on its context and goals, so I wouldn't place a relative value on one style. It all depends. Hopefully, you can avoid relying on a single style to drive your designs. Of course, this is a catch-22 for all creatives. If you have some success with a certain piece, then often you are approached to provide a client with the same treatment. Personally, I try to avoid doing too much of the same thing. Working in a variety of media helps.
Schneider: The thought process for different media is varied, so identifying original style becomes a dubious proposition.

Motion Control

Creative Director, Media and Entertainment, Razorfish, New York City

≫ What changes in the broadcast environment have you experienced that affect your design?

More than I could reasonably mention here. I began my career in the BBC graphic design department in a nondigital age. As I look back on those years, I have cause to think how primitive it all was. Whilst we did not have the bag of tricks that are now available, we certainly had to be very creative with not much at all. The basic principle of idea first and technique second has provided me with a fantastic grounding.

So what specific changes have affected my work? I will list them in more or less chronological order. Don't forget this list represents changes over approximately twenty years. Most of the changes have happened within the last five to ten years.

1. Motion control: This meant we were able to shoot multiple passes on a subject. Each pass matched exactly, so we were able to achieve effects not previously possible.

2. Computer graphics [CG]: Although poor at the beginning, CG became another way of creating original images for designers wishing to explore the third dimension. Many CG techniques have been developed over the years.

3. Telecine steadygate: This got rid of film weave and allowed for multiple layering.

4. Digital paint systems: Suddenly, design is pitched into the spotlight. No longer did we have to create artwork traditionally, then record it onto film or tape. Paint systems like Quantel Paintbox revolutionized the TV design world.

5. Digital editing online: Multiple passes can now be achieved without the degradation caused by analog editing. These early machines were developed from digital paint systems and allowed bad directors to save their careers with retouching!

6. Digital editing offline: Suddenly, the world of cutting a film together is revolutionized. No more strips of film stuck together with tape. More alternative cuts can be worked in a much quicker time.

7. Desktop software: Suddenly, a simple Apple Mac is able to do the job that the previous generation of expensive high-end paint and digital editing systems did. A single designer working from home is able to do what an army of specialists previously did.

8. Internet: We can send still and moving images from one continent to another instantly. This has allowed me to more easily work for international clients.

What is more important, the narrative or the effects?

That deserves an unequivocal answer: The narrative.

TITLE: A&E Biography—Show Open
DESIGNER: Dana Yee CREATIVE DIRECTOR:
Bob English CLIENT: A&E Network YEAR: 1998

TITLE: 48 Hours—Show Open
DESIGNER: Chun Chien Lien
CREATIVE DIRECTOR: Bob English
DIRECTOR: Bob English CLIENT:
CBS YEAR: 1997

TITLE: Court TV—Channel Rebrand
and Relaunch DESIGNER: Kylie
Matulick CREATIVE DIRECTOR: Bob
English PHOTOGRAPHER: Chris Amaral CLIENT: Court TV YEAR: 1999

Do you feel that you have developed a style? An approach?

I see myself as a chameleon. I try to avoid a specific style, because each client's requirements are different. I tend to work at a much more conceptual level, in any case, and enjoy collaborating with people who have the unique talent and style that I think is appropriate for each project.

How would you like to see motion design progress in the near future?

I would like to see motion designers given the flexibility to work in different media. Broadband will offer many possibilities for the future. I would like motion designers to be a little more open to different techniques. Too many designers are designing on computers. This, in my mind, is dangerous. Free thought and inspiration should be allowed to evolve away from the confines of a screen.

How much of your work is determined by client intervention? How free have you been to develop on your own?

This is a difficult question to answer, as I regard myself as a designer, not a fine artist. I would prefer to have a relationship with a client that allows for work to develop in partnership. In reality, this doesn't always happen and depends on the mindset of the client. Occasionally, I have been asked to do my own thing. These times are wonderfully liberating and, I suppose, have produced my most innovative work. I tend to do my own thing outside of TV design to truly express myself.

TITLE: CMT— Channel Relaunch DESIGNER: Stephen Fuller CREATIVE DIRECTOR: Bob English DIRECTOR: Chris McCumber CLIENT: Country Music Television YEAR: 1999

TITLE: ZDF—Channel Rebrand and Relaunch DESIGNERS: Bob English, Reg Squires, Jason Fisher Jones, Jodelle Reed, Thom Hallgren CREATIVE DIRECTOR: Bob English DIRECTORS: Jurgen Bolmyer, Jason Fisher Jones, Wolfgang Jaiser, Jodelle Reed, Thom Hallgren CLIENT: ZDF YEAR: 2001

TITLE: Arte—Channel Redesign DESIGNER: Bob English CREATIVE DIRECTOR: Bob English DIRECTORS: Thierry Rajic, Sylvie Pere CLIENT: Arte YEAR: 2000

Sequential Format

Blind Visual Propaganda, Inc., Santa Monica, California

» Why did you open a firm devoted to motion design?

Motion graphics is an extremely challenging and compelling field, adding a dimension to design that is fertile for discovery. It combines the principles of graphic design, typography, filmmaking, animation, and photography. Working and thinking in a sequential format opens up new variables and opportunities not available in traditional two-dimensional print design.

What were your influences in this field— film, type, animation, or all?

I think it is important for designers to draw from a pool of experience, ideas, and images outside of the design world. For this reason, my influences come from all fields of study. I am inspired by other designers and artists, including Robert Rauschenberg, the Starn Brothers, Herbert Bayer, Marcel Duchamp, David McKean, Jan Tschicold, Tadeo Ando, The Brothers Quay, Joseph Muller-Brockman, Paul Rand, Joel-Peter Witkin, Andy Warhol, Joseph Cornell, John Pawson, Morphosis, and Bradbury Thompson.

Do you feel that you've developed a style or an attitude in your work? Can you explain what either is?

Our philosophical approach to design is centered around the notion that all problems are different and

TITLE: Archipelago
DESIGN DIRECTOR: Chris Do
2-D ANIMATORS: Nic Benns, David Ko, Calvin Lo
3-D ANIMATORS: Colin Strause, Brian Bell, David Ko AGENCY: Fallon McElligot, MN
AGENCY ART DIRECTOR: Bobby Appleby Agency CREATIVE DIRECTOR: Scott Vincent CLIENT: Archipelago SOFTWARE: Maya, Flame, Inferno YEAR: 2001

TITLE: Ultimate TV
DESIGN DIRECTOR: Chris Do
DIRECTORS: Steve Pacheco, Tom Koh EDITOR: Chris Do EFFECTS PHOTOGRAPHER: Rick Spitznass ANIMATORS: Lawrence Wyatt, David Ko AGENCY: Foote, Cone & Belding, SF Agency ART DIRECTOR: Jay Gnospelius CLIENT: Ultimate TV Microsoft SOFTWARE: AfterEffects, Henry, Media Composer YEAR: 2001

require an appropriately unique solution. Only by examining a particular project and its parameters can we determine the merit of a solution. This fundamental belief is used to guide our design and thinking.

What is the most important aspect of design that you bring to motion?

Our love of letterforms and typography in both its formal and symbolic application, our uncompromising pursuit of creative expression, combined with our unique brand of design.

Is storytelling a key part of what you do? Or are effects more central?

Great design occurs when an idea and a design are inseparable. They are naturally complementary components. In essence, the solution comes from the content. We use design, images, and typography as a means to communicate an idea or to tell a story.

What does the future hold for motion design?

Motion graphics is still far from reaching its potential. As tools become more powerful and affordable, de-

signers are more liberated to express their creative vision, unbound by the machines they use. Small design boutiques are able to produce incredibly experimental and interesting work. At the same time, the general public is much more visually aware and sophisticated. As a result, companies are more receptive to new ideas that may help them connect to their audience. Motion graphics is still relatively contemporary in that rules and boundaries haven't been established; we like to push that envelope.

TITLE: LAFF DESIGN DIRECTOR: Chris Do DESIGNER/ DIRECTOR/ANIMATOR: Tom Koh EDITOR: Erik Buth COMPOSER: Adam Sanborne DIRECTOR OF PHOTO-GRAPHY: Joe Maxwell CLIENT: IFP/West Los Angeles Film Festival MEDIUM/SOFTWARE: 35mm Film, After Effects, Flint, Media Composer YEAR: 2001

TITLE: Dogtown DESIGN DIRECTOR: Chris Do DESIGNER: Tom Koh ANIMATORS: Tom Koh, Calvin Lo, David Ko, Wilson Wu ANIMATION EDITORS: Chris Do, Tom Koh FIRM: Agi Orsi Productions CLIENT: Stacy Peralta SOFTWARE/ MEDIUM: AfterEffects, 35mm, 16mm, Super 8 Film Elements YEAR: 2000

GARSON YU | Film Is Storytelling

Principal, Yu + co., Hollywood, California

>> **Did you start as a filmmaker or a graphic designer?**

I came from a traditional graphic design background. If I were a filmmaker, my works would be very different. As a graphic designer, it is important to have diverse knowledge of different disciplines, such as architecture, art, film, and music. I was always interested in art and architecture as well as graphic design when I was in design school. But ever since one of my classmates introduced Eisenstein's film montage theory to me, my interest and passion in film has grown exponentially. After I graduated, I worked as a freelance designer at RGA in New York. I have been learning more about filmmaking since then.

Does designing film titles draw upon your traditional design training or require all new skills?

Design is about problem solving. It is also about communication. Film is storytelling. Conveying a thought, to me, is communication. We still need to design in our mind before we communicate to others. Most people think film title design is just dealing with fonts, which is not totally accurate. Typography is only a minor part of film title design; the main part is storytelling, setting up the tone and emotion. When we say traditional graphic design, does that mean two-dimensional design? In that case, do we deal only with

TITLE: *Passion of Mind*
CREATIVE DIRECTOR/
DESIGNER: *Garson Yu*
DESIGNER/ANIMATOR:
Ying Fan PRODUCER:
Ty Van Huisen
CLIENT: *Paramount
Classics* YEAR: *2000*

TITLE: *Hanging Up*
CREATIVE DIRECTOR/
DESIGNER: *Garson Yu*
DESIGNER/ANIMATOR:
Ying Fan PRODUCER:
Jennifer Fong CLIENT:
Columbia Pictures
YEAR: *2000*

shapes, colors, and all pictorial formal issues? When we deal with images transforming over time, then we need a different mindset and require all new skills because we need to make an image into an event: What's before? What's after? And what's the beginning? How does it end?

A title sequence is often a film within a film. How do you view your role as title designer?
Although it is often a film within a film, a good title sequence should seamlessly blend into the film. It is the title designer's job to tell the background story, setting up the tone and letting the audience get ready for the film. I am particularly interested in using animated title sequences to reflect or hint what the film is about.

How much do you actually have to know about the technology with which you work?
Everything is possible nowadays because of the technology. It is all about imagination. If I don't know how to do something, I will surround myself with good, knowledgeable people. Technology gives me possibilities and options. But the key is the concepts and ideas. Knowing the technology will surely broaden my options.

As you continue to work in motion, can you see a new design form emerging? How would you describe it?
Motion is the fourth dimension that we are dealing with in design in the context of time and space. In the twenty-first century, things are getting virtual, and artificial intelligence has become a major topic. What those contribute to are interactive in design. We always want to find ways to control the behaviors of images. Images respond and react to what we like them to in real time. It is quite exciting to see this new form of design emerging.

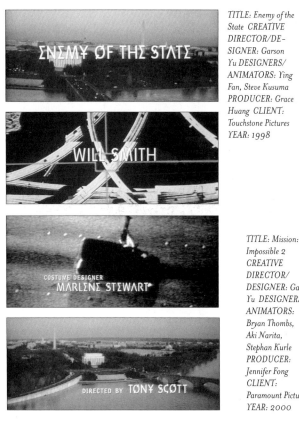

TITLE: Enemy of the State CREATIVE DIRECTOR/DESIGNER: Garson Yu DESIGNERS/ANIMATORS: Ying Fan, Steve Kusuma PRODUCER: Grace Huang CLIENT: Touchstone Pictures YEAR: 1998

TITLE: Mission: Impossible 2 CREATIVE DIRECTOR/DESIGNER: Garson Yu DESIGNERS/ANIMATORS: Bryan Thombs, Aki Narita, Stephan Kurle PRODUCER: Jennifer Fong CLIENT: Paramount Pictures YEAR: 2000

STEFANIE BARTH, JULIE HIRSCHFELD, JOAN RASPO

Principals, Stiletto NYC, New York City

Message Matters

>> **How and why did you form a studio that deals in multiple media?**

Some things just happen. When we met, we were working in different media and countries, but we connected creatively and wanted to work together. The studio evolved out of that.

Of these media, what are your primary tools?

Well, right now, we are back to handcrafting and using things like crayons. But tool number one is still our computer.

How do you handcraft in this digital environment?

It's about going back to precomputer methods—replacing the mouse with the pencil.

To do motion design well, how much do you rely on narrative versus technical skill?

For us, narrative drives every project. The idea drives the execution. We try not to let technical skill drive the concept. First we come up with the idea, then we figure out how to do it.

What is your most ambitious narrative to date?

Joan cocreated and directed the animated series "Avenue Amy" on Oxygen.

Do you try to have a studio style? Or do you flow with the needs of the commission?

We tend toward a certain sensibility because we relate to the same things and look at the same influences. We hope that we never develop a signature style. Our aim is to continue evolving and not be defined by anything described as Stiletto style. It would suck if a client wanted that certain thing we did in project x for client y.

What is the greatest challenge for you as a designer in today's new media?

Outsmarting the young designers.

What is more important for you—message, attitude, or effects? Or are these completely interconnected?

We'd say message matters. Effects are the least relevant. They feel dated really quickly and seem kind of cheap.

TITLE: Fresh Poster
ART DIRECTORS/DESIGNERS: Stefanie Barth, Julie Hirschfeld, Joan Raspo FIRM: Stiletto NYC ILLUSTRATOR/ PHOTOGRAPHER: Lisa Carville CLIENT: AIGA YEAR: 2001

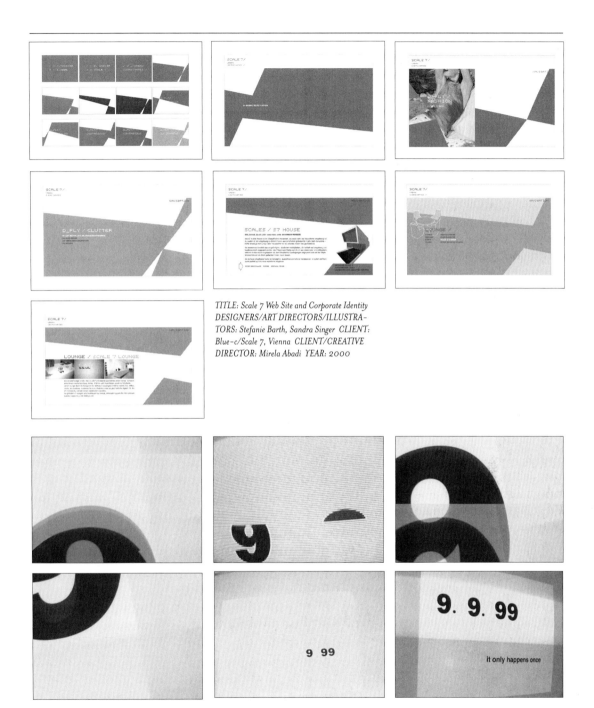

TITLE: Scale 7 Web Site and Corporate Identity
DESIGNERS/ART DIRECTORS/ILLUSTRA-
TORS: Stefanie Barth, Sandra Singer CLIENT:
Blue-c/Scale 7, Vienna CLIENT/CREATIVE
DIRECTOR: Mirela Abadi YEAR: 2000

TITLE: 9.9.99 DESIGNER: Julie Hirschfeld CREATIVE DIRECTOR:
MTV—Jeffrey Keyton ART DIRECTOR: MTV—Romy Mann
ANIMATOR: Bennett Killmer CLIENT: MTV YEAR: 1999

Illustrating with Film

Principal, Mirko Ilic Corp., New York City

≫ You began as a pen and ink illustrator. Why did you turn to the computer?

As a traditional illustrator and designer, you are always looking for new tools. Something new and dramatic comes along only every ten or fifteen years. Seeing the development of the Macintosh, I bought my first computer in 1990 or 1991. I figured out that it would allow me to operate in the capacity of a studio (combining the roles of typographer, keyliner, etc.) and still remain an individual.

What influenced you to turn to motion design?

In the 1970s, I was publishing a lot of comics while working at Zagreb Films as a freelance animator. As an illustrator and as a designer, you must tell a story in a single image. But in comics, I found my first opportunity to tell a story in multiple images, a visual essay. The computer is the next logical step. It condenses to a few the once large array of roles necessary to produce traditional cell animation. In 1992, I bought my first Silicon Graphics computer. But for most of the time, in the beginning, I used it only to create illustrations. From the narrow U.S. corporate point of view, you are only able to produce things like you've already done, so I was commissioned for editorial illustration only. It took time to make the transition.

As an illustrator, you work by yourself; with movie titles, you must collaborate with many people—directors, programmers, etc. How does this affect what you do as an artist?

Tell me in what country an illustrator works without collaborating, and I'll move immediately there. From my experience in the United States, illustrators 99 percent of the time must collaborate with art directors, designers, editors, and even writers. Being an illustrator, in most cases, means constant compromise. It's true that in movie titles, a few more people are involved, but it's a more expensive and complicated procedure. It's a logical extension that more people are required; the dynamic is essentially the same.

What do you need to know to work in this medium that you did not know before?

The thing you really need to know is that the technology is constantly advancing. It's important to know when to get new equipment, when to upgrade, and when to stop. You could spend your whole life buying little gadgets.

What do you think is your most valuable asset in terms of motion design?

I didn't come to motion design from the usual path: from graphic designer to motion designer. I came to it from both this and an illustration base. I think about motion design differently. If graphic design was my only

TITLE: Scout's Honor ART DIRECTORS: Walter Bernard and Mirko Ilic DESIGN FIRMS: WBMG, Inc. and Mirko Ilic Corp. CLIENT: Neil Leifer YEAR: 1999

experience, I would take photography or illustration and place type over it in Illustrator or Photoshop, then using whatever filter is most up to date, I'd manipulate the forms. But coming also from an illustrator's point of view, I consider type in a more illustrative way, as a character on the stage, so to speak, fusing this

with the narrative. In the case of the title for *You've Got Mail*, we created the whole environment on the computer, and made it into a little story. I was able to do this because of my illustration skills.

How difficult is it to get good commissions?
It's extremely difficult to get any commissions in such a narrowly

divided, compartmentalized field. Moving from one genre to another (in this case, movies) is hard. Every movie studio has its own system. Different people make decisions. With most key people in California, it's a big challenge finding the right person's hands to put your reel into.

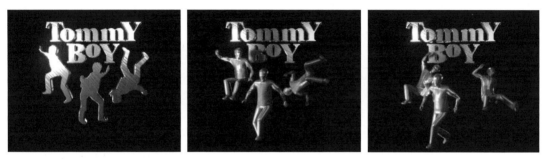

TITLE: Tommy Boy CREATIVE DIRECTION: Mirko Ilic MOTION DESIGN: Lauren DeNapoli
DESIGN STUDIO: Mirko Ilic Corp. CLIENT: Tommy Boy Records YEAR: 2001

TITLE: Zen Stories CREATIVE DIRECTION: Mirko Ilic MOTION DESIGN: Mirko Ilic and Heath Hinegardner DESIGN STUDIO: Mirko Ilic Corp. CLIENT: IMG Media YEAR: 2000

Narrative Design

>> **As a graphic designer with a print background, what do you think is fundamentally different about working in the television medium?**

Well, the most obvious answer is music and sound design. That is a huge challenge because even though moving type is obviously different from setting it on a piece of paper, it still works under the basic principles of design. You are still trying to get your audience's attention by using scale, placement, and visual stimuli. With motion, you also have the added layer of sound, which is something I didn't learn in school, so my approach to it is basically instinctual.

Do you find that working in sequential media requires storytelling ability?

Being a good storyteller is important in any art or entertainment work, be it commercial, fine art, music, literature, babysitting, or cooking, to name a few. Success is all in the timing and the delivery.

Are you more concerned with the narrative or the design?

The narrative is definitely the thing that drives the work. It is from the narrative that the idea is born and, as far as we are concerned, the design can only come from that, not the other way around. You are trying to connect with your audience, and the narrative helps you do that.

How many fingers are in this particular pie?

Hmmmm. All of them?

What has been your most challenging on-air project, and why?

Our most challenging project was not exactly on air in that it was made for high schools across the country. We were hired by the Josten's Corporation to make a short film about the millennium. The directive was to give kids a sense of why the year 2000 should be important to them and to do it by showing the history of the past thousand years and the possibilities of the next thousand years, and to do it in a way that was smart, funny, hip (but not too hip), inspiring, entertaining, cool (but not too cool), global, and local, and able to be shown in every high school in America. Oh, and it should be about six minutes long. We made a moving timeline and are very proud of the piece.

Can you describe the perfect marriage of design and motion?

The scene in *Take the Money and Run* where Woody Allen plays the cello in the marching band. Also, almost anything by the Basses, Maurice Binder, Pittman Hensley, Bureau, and Buster Keaton. Doing this must require senses that are unnecessary in print—music and sound, for example.

Was this something you had to learn, or was it an innate talent?

Sound design is hard. As I said earlier, it's not something we learned in school. But over time, you get a feel for how to work with

TITLE: Saturday Night Live DESIGNERS/ CREATIVE DIRECTORS: Emily Oberman, Bonnie Siegler COMPANY: Number Seventeen CLIENT: Saturday Night Live TYPEFACE: Engraver's Gothic YEAR: 1997

music and sound, so it is both innate and learned.

Would you say that time and space require considerably more skill than print?

Nope. Just slightly different skills. And the difference is narrowing every day.

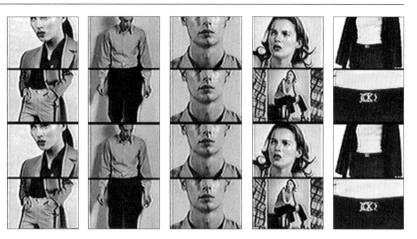

TITLE: Calvin Klein In-store Display DESIGNER: Keira Alexandra CREATIVE DIRECTORS: Emily Oberman, Bonnie Siegler COMPANY: Number Seventeen CLIENT: Calvin Klein YEAR: 1997

TITLE: MTV Animated Logo DESIGNERS: Keira Alexandra, David Israel CREATIVE DIRECTORS: Emily Oberman, Bonnie Siegler COMPANY: Number Seventeen CLIENT: MTV Productions YEAR: 1996

TITLE: American Dreamers DESIGNERS/CREATIVE DIRECTORS: Emily Oberman, Bonnie Siegler COMPANY: Number Seventeen CLIENT: Schaffer TYPEFACE: Clarendon YEAR: 1997

X. TYPE AND LETTERING

NOT TOO LONG AGO, type design was almost an airtight profession. Only the very skilled and highly motivated were allowed entry. One reason was the intense amount of time that it took to design a typeface in its various weights and point sizes. Another was the expense involved in making metal fonts. A third was that type foundries were major industrial operations, and although they commissioned a fair number of novelty typefaces to supplement the classics, they relied on either proven and experienced staff designers or respected freelancers. Breaking into this realm of design required years of apprenticeship.

Today, the computer has changed all that—some argue for good, others for ill. Type design software has increased the capability of serious type designers to create many more custom and proprietary typefaces and has made it possible for neophyte and fly-by-night designers to develop personalized type. Somewhere between these two extremes, graphic designers who are interested in or passionate about typefaces have entered the field, either developing the occasional face, which they then sell or license to a digital type foundry, or establishing their own digital type foundries. The computer has broken down the barriers between designer and craftsperson, and the Internet (shareware, free programs offered on the Web) has democratized the distribution networks. Of course, today more laypeople know the once arcane term *font* than ever before, and many even know the names of a few typefaces (as if they were rock groups).

And yet, type design is definitely not a profession for amateurs. Indeed, many of the novelty faces are too eccentric and quirky for continued use. These faces may be

> *ALTHOUGH IT CAN BE ENJOYABLE TO INVENT A TYPEFACE, TO MAKE IT FUNCTIONAL REMAINS THE PROVINCE OF THE TRAINED TYPE DESIGNER.*

fun to use as display type for the occasional poster or advertisement, but it is unlikely that they will have legs over the long haul and for diverse applications. For type to work effectively, it is not enough to simply draw an alphabet; rather, it is necessary to know how the letterforms will function together on both aesthetic and utilitarian levels. Although it can be enjoyable to invent a typeface, to make it functional remains the province of the trained type designer.

So what is a trained and skilled type designer? There are two answers. A type designer is someone who has devoted the better part of a professional life to knowing the history of type, drawing letterforms precisely, having aesthetic values and practical savvy, and a vision of the overall application of type in the print environment. A type designer is also someone who is gifted with a keen sense of aesthetics and function and can draw with complete precision. The former takes many years and considerable practice (internships, apprenticeships, and scholarly study); the latter comes at birth and yet requires all of the former to make a truly effective type designer. This is not to say that the generalist designer cannot design one perfectly utilitarian typeface—and never design another. In 1896, Bertram Goodhue, an architect, designed Cheltenham, one of the most commonly used American typefaces. But the majority of good typeface designers are dedicated to their field—and dedication is exactly what it takes.

For those inclined to choose type design as a career choice, the best idea is to seek a position at a digital type foundry (or type shop) that both licenses other designers' and produces its own typefaces. In the 1990s, many such foundries were established and can be found listed on the Internet. Even an entry-level job at a good foundry provides exposure to and, perhaps, hands-on experience with the entire type design process, from inspiration to distribution. (Incidentally, those foundries that are not good are the ones that routinely pirate other designers' original work or license inferior typefaces without first testing their viability.) Another entry point is an apprenticeship with an experienced type designer; here you can learn as much as possible before either becoming a freelance type designer or joining a company. Yet another approach is to enroll in a type design class with a master type designer and then attempt one or all of the above.

At the same time, the technology is available for a neophyte to experiment at designing typefaces on the desktop and then testing its applications in real documents. Never before in the history of type design and type founding has this been so technically and financially accessible.

Lettering is another indispensable component of graphic design. Lettering is the design of one-of-a-kind, often limited-use typographic or calligraphic compositions. The letterer is not necessarily a type designer, and vice versa, but the skills of one are certainly useful to the other. Letterers are most often used to develop signs, logos, book titles, package labels, and other custom needs. Lettering classes are common in most art and design schools and are the only efficient way to learn the methods of the craft. Although much lettering begins as hand-drawing, the computer is used as a tool for detailing and finalizing work.

Type design is fairly straightforward. Full or partial alphabets and the drawing that go into making them are the ideal portfolio contents for both entry-level and advanced typeface designers.

Entry Level and Advanced

School assignments and personal projects, either drawn or composed on the computer, are ideal samples.

CONTENTS

- a. One or more complete alphabets
- b. Example of typefaces application
- c. Drawings used in the development of a typeface or family of faces

Format

35mm slides (in tray) are still applicable, but increasingly this method is being phased out in favor of CD and DVD in the following formats: Flash, PowerPoint, and iPhoto. Online portfolios are also encouraged. Avoid digital tricks. Keep it as straightforward as possible. Anything that crashes the viewer's computer will hamper appreciation of your work.

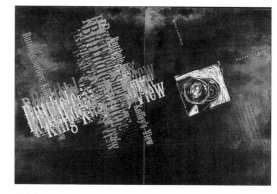

TITLE: Butthole Surfers Spread DESIGNER/CREATIVE DIRECTOR: Joshua Berger COMPANY: Plazm CLIENT: Plazm Media ILLUSTRATOR: Joe Sorren TYPEFACE: Stele Bevel, Onyx YEAR: 1995

Type design is an extremely time-intensive field; the designer may work for many months on a single family, style, or even weight. Type designers who create custom faces for publishing, corporate, or institutional clients also spend a large sum of time in revisions as well. The letterer works on a specific project, usually for a fixed period of time. This is not to imply that one field is more satisfying than the other, but if type and lettering are desired specialties, it is important to evaluate the investment required for each of these.

Designer and Letterer, Toronto, Canada

>> **How long have you had your own studio?**
I've been on my own since 2004.
Before that I owned a studio with
a partner since 1994.

**What are the changes in practice you have
seen and experienced since you began?**
The biggest change was in myself,
and the way I work. In 2004 I left
the method of strategic design, and
began working in a more personal
way, which I call Graphic Art. Fortunately for me, my interests in ornament coincided with the beginning
of a rise in ornament in general, so
I was able to ride a wave (sometimes
even at the crest) that was very suitable for me and what I was trying
to achieve. But my entire view of
design, what makes good design, and
what's important has changed since
I got my head out of the Vancouver
sand and started looking around the
world. This is an ongoing thing, but
the work that is coming out of con-
tinents other than North America—
particularly Europe—is much more
imaginative and experimental than
anything I had seen before; and I'm
still convinced we have a lot to learn
over here. Much progress needs to
be made in how we communicate.
We are just starting to resurrect our
creative skills. I once thought that
design was no place for an artist, and
I'm starting to think that's not true.

How have these changes impacted your work?
The more "art-based" work is ac-

TITLE: "Cake" MEDIUM: Cake, Icing Sugar
CLIENT: Creative Review YEAR: 2008

TITLE: Saks Fifth Avenue
Valentine Heart
MEDIUM: Vector Art
CLIENT: Saks Fifth
Avenue YEAR: 2008

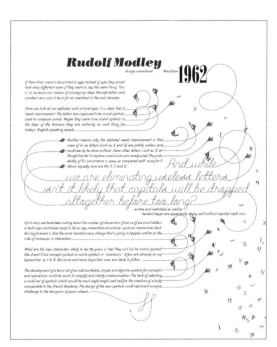

TITLE: "Print
Magazine" (one of
8 pages) MEDIUM:
Vector Art CLIENT:
Print Magazine
YEAR: 2006

cepted in the design environment, the more opportunity there is for me to keep pushing it. It's very difficult, but very important to move beyond "style," and just make new forms and new ways of communication. I think the environment is much more open to that now than it was ten or fifteen years ago.

Would you say that you have a particular style or character to your design?

Yes and no. Although I'm known for my "beautiful," elegant lines, if you look at my work, it's actually really varied in form. But what it does usually have is complexity. If it's complex, and beautiful, but structured it might be mine.

What about graphic design is the most challenging for you?

Dealing with money, doing paperwork, managing difficult clients—all the stuff that is not actually conceiving and making.

What are the projects that most satisfy your aesthetic sense?

The open brief. Those rare few where I am hired for my quirky ingenuity rather than the style of anything I've done in the past. I actually do have a brain and I prefer to use it. I don't like the term "problem solving" at all, but I do like to figure things out—often this means adding complexity to the process in order to get a surprising result.

How important is type and typography in what you do?

Extremely important when I'm designing. I spend hours on my typography, and despite twenty-five years of experience, I don't actually think I'm that good. Doing elegant, classical typography is easy; but I'm not used to typographic acrobatics—it's very hard to do well, but I keep trying. I have a terrible time choosing typefaces; it's one of my weakest links.

What, in this current technological and economic climate, does the future hold for you specifically, and graphic design in general?

I may regret saying this, and must knock on wood while doing so, but I think I'm in a really good position because my work is personal and creative and hard to emulate. I think that those who practice standard corporate design will run into a lot of competition from (a) other designers, (b) template software, and (c) outsourcing. Art and creative thinking is something I really think will become increasingly valuable in the years to come. I know I'm good at what I do, so I have hope.

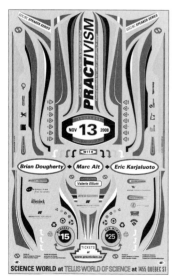

TITLE: "Practivism" MEDIUM: Vector Art CLIENT: Society of Graphic Designers of Canada/ BC Chapter YEAR: 2008

TITLE: "Design Ignites Change" Poster MEDIUM: Laser Cut from White Paper CLIENT: Academy for Educational Development (AED) YEAR: 2008

TITLE: "Valentines 2009" MEDIUM: Pen and Ink CLIENT: Self YEAR: 2009

The Informal Air

Designer, Puccino's Coffee Bar, London, UK

» What is the advantage of using hand-lettering in your work?

I usually write the copy and my style is colloquial, so it makes sense to use my handwriting. For the client, I suppose there is a feeling that they are buying something slightly more personal than usual.

You produced a fair number of package designs. Doesn't handwriting rather than type give too informal an air?

For Puccino's, this informal air has worked to their advantage. They were keen to keep the feeling of a small, friendly company as they grew larger.

How difficult is it to design in this raw manner for companies that are trying to appear professional?

It depends how brave the company is. If they have confidence in their products and services, then they can afford to be more daring with their design. Small companies have less to lose, so are willing to take bigger risks.

Do clients ask you to work in a certain manner? And what is it that they ask?

I get a lot of my work from people that have seen my stuff for Puccino's. They usually just want me to do my stuff—a hand written, cartoony approach. Most importantly, they are interested in humorous copy.

Where did you train as a graphic designer, illustrator, or typographer? Do you know

the official rules of design?

I did a degree in advertising, graphic design, and illustration at Buckinghamshire College in England. I've just been interested in it since I was young and have looked at lots of it. I also draw—I think that can teach you a lot about design.

Do you feel you are in or out of the mainstream of design?

I suppose the fact that everything I do starts out on paper and is scanned in is fairly unusual.

Would you suggest that young designers just starting out present unorthodox approaches, or should they be safe?

You should always push it as far as possible. Doing something that the client doesn't expect will earn you the freedom to be adventurous next time. If you are cautious and do what you think the client is expecting, there's a good chance he'll want you to play it safe every time.

TITLE: Cola Is for Wimps DESIGNER/ART DIR-ECTOR/PHOTOGRAPHER/ILLUSTRATOR/TYPOGRAPHER: Jim Smith CLIENT: Puccino's Ltd. YEAR: 2003

TITLES: Bin, Biscuit, Schadenfreude DESIGNER/ART DIRECTOR/PHOTOGRAPHER/ILLUS-TRATOR/TYPOGRAPHER: Jim Smith CLIENT: Puccino's Ltd. YEARS: 2001–2004

From PostScript to Type 1

Principal, Schwartzco, New York

≫ How long have you had your own studio?

I've been working on my own since 2001, but I wouldn't really say I had my own studio until late 2003 or so, when I started getting more steady work and stopped freelancing in other people's studios. I started collaborating on many projects with London-based designer Paul Barnes in 2004, starting with our work on an extensive custom typeface family for *The Guardian*. In 2007 we decided to jointly form a new type foundry called Commercial Type, mainly to publish our own work and to occasionally release typefaces by outside designers as well.

What are the changes in practice (and form) you have seen and experienced since you began?

I think the biggest change in my field has been the transition from PostScript Type 1 fonts, which had a character set strictly limited to 256 glyphs (meaning individual characters—a letter, number, or symbol), to OpenType fonts, which can include over 65,000 glyphs. The biggest change for me personally has been the transition from working as a freelance type designer to running a business with a partner, a full-time designer, and a part-time administrator. I've really had to learn on my feet, and the hardest thing has been learning to let go of things

when I need to—there's a fine line between being helpfully hands-on with what other people are working on and interfering with getting things done.

How have these changes impacted your work?

My customers expect a lot more out of a font than they used to. Support for Central European languages like Czech and Polish; fractions; multiple kinds of numbers; and alternates for setting text in all-caps, for example, are now seen as de rigeur, but they used to be a luxury. Unfortunately for me, the price of a font, or the

Punxen els estudis tècnics i d'humanitats

DESERCIÓ · Un 40% dels universitaris abandonen per desmotivació o per dificultat d'aprovar **ÈXIT** · L'àrea de salut, la que té menys abandonaments **P32**

'El Cèntim'

Alguns vinaters ja afronten el canvi climàtic · **Suplement**

TITLE: Amplitude DESIGNER: Christian Schwartz COMPANY: Font Bureau YEAR: 2002

204 | ARCHITECTURE

Book: Concrete Toronto

IT'S A SIGN of changing times when a city starts to boast about its concrete content—in decades past few urban areas felt the need to inform the world about their aggregate-based architecture. *Concrete Toronto* is a bold celebration of the city's best structures, part guide book, part historical document.

TITLE: ADAO 11 Poster DESIGNER: Christian Schwartz

TITLE: FF Unit Slab COMPANY: FontFont DESIGNERS: Christian Schwartz, Kris Sowersby and Erik Spiekermann YEAR: 2009 ≫

Vertigo:
Aus dem Reich der Toten

TITLE: Graphik Poster CLIENT: Adam Art Gallery in Wellington, NZ DESIGNERS/ ILLUSTRATORS: Duncan Forbes and Elaina Hamilton, The International Office YEAR: 2007-09

uncorked

HAUT WITHOUT HAUTEUR

HAUT-BRION IS THE BORDEAUX OF POETS AND PHILOSOPHERS, ELEGANT, APPROACHABLE, AND LONG IN THE WING.

TITLE: Neutraface Slab COMPANY: House Industries DESIGNERS: Kai Bernau and Susana Carvalho ART DIRECTOR: Christian Schwartz YEAR: 2009

EMPIRE STATE BUILDING
LOBBY
Mezzanine
Observatory

TITLE: Empire State Building DESIGNERS: Christian Schwartz, Paul Barnes COMMISSIONED BY: Laura Varacchi at Two Twelve Associates CLIENT: Empire State Building YEAR: 2007

Life in mono

From Bach to Led Zeppelin, music has always had a powerful emotional pull for critic **Nick Coleman**. But since he lost hearing in one ear, listening is agony and his favourite artists no longer move him. Will the magic ever return?

TITLE: Guardian Egyptian COMPANY: Commercial Type DESIGNERS: Christian Schwartz, Paul Barnes CREATIVE DIRECTOR: Mark Porter CLIENT: The Guardian YEARS: 2004–2005

budget and schedule for a custom typeface project, have not scaled along with character sets, so I've had to become a lot more clever in finding ways to speed up and in some cases to automate portions of the work. I am lucky to know type designer/programmers like Tal Leming and Erik van Blokland, who have created many tools that are now part of my everyday process.

I think working with Paul has really improved my work. Between the two of us, we seem to be able to distill solutions for design problems much more quickly than I ever did on my own. I think it really helps that we have different backgrounds (mine more in newspapers and corporate design and Paul's more in magazines and graphic design) but largely overlapping taste. Adding another designer to the team has been interesting as well, because he's a bit younger than we are and brings a different set of references to the mix.

How did you decide to specialize in type?
Honestly, it happened by accident. I started drawing type as a hobby in high school (nerdy, I know) but didn't really get serious about it until the summer after my first year of college, when I cold-called Tobias Frere-Jones, who was working at the Font Bureau in Boston at the time, to see if they had any openings for summer interns. I spent the summer unlearning what I knew about drawing and spacing type and learning how to do it properly, and also got a crash course in type history.

Did you have specific training?

Besides my apprenticeships at Font Bureau and MetaDesign, I am not formally trained as a type designer, but I do have a degree in Communication Design from Carnegie Mellon University. My background in graphic design and typography has been extremely valuable in my work, even though I barely ever use type anymore, because I like to think it keeps me grounded in reality: able to think like a graphic designer and draw type that graphic designers would want to use.

You do many proprietary faces, do you see this has been a wise career move?

This was more a pragmatic decision than a strategic one—when I was first starting out, people who were familiar with my retail fonts and my history at Font Bureau contacted me to see if I could do custom type projects and I said I could. I didn't promote myself as a custom type specialist until much later.

What are the projects that most satisfy your aesthetic sense?

I'm kind of an aesthetic omnivore, so I don't really have a genre that I especially like to work in, although I do have a weakness for British type from the nineteenth century and early twentieth-century German and French type, and I tend to go back to borrow from these sources again and again.

What, in this current technological and economic climate, does the future hold for you specifically, and graphic design in general?

I don't know what the future holds for Commercial Type specifically. As I write this, we are about to launch a new Web site with online ordering, and there is a debate raging on the future of embedded fonts on the Web. I don't know how either of these things will turn out, but they are both going to be key in shaping the future of my company, and the second will play a big role in shaping the next ten to fifteen years of type design as well. If we get the embedding thing right, we will have a new renaissance in screen fonts, which will be very exciting.

TITLE: ADAO 11 Poster
DESIGNER: Christian Schwartz

TITLE: Giorgio and Giorgio Sans Giorgio released by Commercial Type, CLIENT: Both commissioned for T, *the New York Times Style Magazine ART DIRECTOR: Chris Martinez YEAR: 2008*

Principal, Hoefler + Frere-Jones, New York City

>> **How did you decide to be a type designer?**

I was always fond of geometry; it was one of my favorite classes in high school—aside from the art classes, obviously. Drawing type lets me indulge my fascination in ratio, interval, curvature, etc. Although I love to draw, I was never very good with perspective or color. Happily for me, type design rarely involves either of those.

As a type designer, do you exhibit a personal style?

I'm sure I do, though I prefer not to think about it too much. Ruminating on one's own style can be a dangerous activity. I prefer to just draw what pleases me and let someone else describe the style. Being a hardcore believer in self-education, it seems that the more styles and motifs I work in, the more I'll learn.

With so many typefaces extant, what determines what faces you devote your time to?

Generally, those ones that attract me are the ones that satisfy me. I have no delusions about changing the course of design in any significant way—I do this because I think it's fun. For my personal projects (that is, the ones with no client directly attached), my own enjoyment always comes before potential sales. Some of the faces I've drawn sank like a stone in the retail market, but I don't care that much, because I enjoyed the

TITLE: Interstate DESIGNER/ART DIRECTOR: Tobias Frere-Jones COMPANY/ CLIENT: The Font Bureau YEAR: 1993–1994

TITLE: Reiner Script DESIGNERS: Imre Reiner, Tobias Frere-Jones ART DIRECTOR: Tobias Frere-Jones COMPANY/ CLIENT: The Font Bureau YEAR: 1993

TITLE: Poynter Oldstyle DESIGNER: Tobias Frere-Jones ART DIRECTORS: Tobias Frere-Jones, Mike Parker, David Berlow COMPANY/CLIENT: The Font Bureau YEAR: 1997

TITLE: Stereo DESIGNERS: Karlgeorg Hoefer, Tobias Frere-Jones ART DIRECTOR: Tobias Frere-Jones COMPANY/CLIENT: The Font Bureau YEAR: 1993

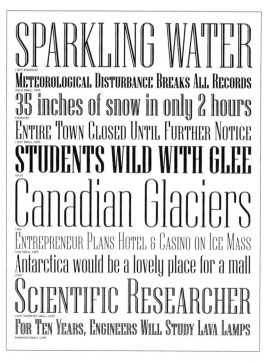

TITLE: Niagara DESIGNER/ART DIRECTOR: Tobias Frere-Jones COMPANY/ CLIENT: The Font Bureau YEAR: 1994

design process. It may be simply having some entertaining forms to draw, like Stereo or Reiner Script, or it may be the challenge of taking on something new, like Poynter Oldstyle and Gothic.

How much time, on average, do you devote to designing new or reviving old faces?

This is a tricky one to answer, as the line between purely original and straight revival is not sharp. Besides, I don't think it's possible to say that one kind of work is better or more valuable than another. I'm always drawn to projects that will educate me but also to ones that will offer users new options. If I can show that the old standards aren't the only way of getting a job done, I'd find that very pleasing. In that context, I don't worry so much about what category of sources I'm working with.

Is there room in the business for more type designers?

That's hard to say, because the number of designers and the number of users are expanding simultaneously. One hundred years, or fifty years, or even fifteen years ago, nobody would know what to do with so many type designers. Having said that, I think there are two general classes of designers: ones who work in a careful, measured approach, and those who work only in the mode of the moment. In other words, there are ones who ignore the fads and others who are driven by them. If there's room for more, it's with the classicists.

A Restrictive Design Form

Principal, Terminal Design, New York City

>> **How long have you had your own studio?**

I opened Terminal Design in 1990. I was working in a packaging design studio during the day, doing freelance design work at night, playing bass in a rock band, and studying and teaching martial art. Something had to give, so I quit my day job!

What are the changes in practice you have seen and experienced since you began?

Certainly the maturing of the personal computer as a serious tool in 1989 was the biggest change. Doing work digitally instead of by traditional methods was the major readjustment. Losing the handmade, but gaining a much higher level of finished product still bothers some designers. I don't want to go back to hand-inking letterforms. But I think at this point the personal computer is such an integral part of a design work flow that I would have to say that the ubiquitousness of broadband Internet and email has had the most profound change on the way I work. What used to take weeks now takes days. What used to take days now takes hours.

How have these changes impacted your work?

Before the computer, type design was part of a larger manufacturing process employing many people and requiring many months of work. Most clients could not have afforded custom typefaces under these circumstances, and I certainly would not have been an independent type

Collins:Geometric Thin
Showing off that ever so friendly colon.

Collins:Geometric Light
Showing off that ever so friendly colon.

Collins:Geometric Regular
Showing off that ever so friendly colon.

Collins:Geometric Medium
Showing off that ever so friendly colon.

TITLE: Collins Geometric (custom typeface) CLIENT: Collins Design Research ART DIRECTOR: John Fulbrook TYPE DESIGN: James Montalbano YEAR: 2009

TITLE: Enclave Specimen (original typeface) CLIENT: Terminal Design ART DIRECTOR: James Montalbano TYPE DESIGN: James Montalbano YEAR: 2007

Puzzled women bequeath jerks very exotic gifts.
ENCLAVE THIN — PUZZLED WOMEN BEQUEATH JERKS VERY EXOTIC GIFTS.
Puzzled women bequeath jerks very exotic gifts.
ENCLAVE THIN ITALIC — PUZZLED WOMEN BEQUEATH JERKS VERY EXOTIC GIFTS.
Puzzled women bequeath jerks very exotic gifts.
ENCLAVE LIGHT — PUZZLED WOMEN BEQUEATH JERKS VERY EXOTIC GIFTS.
Puzzled women bequeath jerks very exotic gifts.
ENCLAVE LIGHT ITALIC — PUZZLED WOMEN BEQUEATH JERKS VERY EXOTIC GIFTS.
Puzzled women bequeath jerks very exotic gifts.
ENCLAVE BOOK — PUZZLED WOMEN BEQUEATH JERKS VERY EXOTIC GIFTS.
Puzzled women bequeath jerks very exotic gifts.
ENCLAVE BOOK ITALIC — PUZZLED WOMEN BEQUEATH JERKS VERY EXOTIC GIFTS.
Puzzled women bequeath jerks very exotic gifts.
ENCLAVE MEDIUM — PUZZLED WOMEN BEQUEATH JERKS VERY EXOTIC GIFTS.
Puzzled women bequeath jerks very exotic gifts.
ENCLAVE MEDIUM ITALIC — PUZZLED WOMEN BEQUEATH JERKS VERY EXOTIC GIFTS.
Puzzled women bequeath jerks very exotic gifts.
ENCLAVE DEMIBOLD — PUZZLED WOMEN BEQUEATH JERKS VERY EXOTIC GIFTS.
Puzzled women bequeath jerks very exotic gifts.
ENCLAVE DEMIBOLD ITALIC — PUZZLED WOMEN BEQUEATH JERKS VERY EXOTIC GIFTS.
Puzzled women bequeath jerks very exotic gifts.
ENCLAVE BOLD — PUZZLED WOMEN BEQUEATH JERKS VERY EXOTIC GIFTS.
Puzzled women bequeath jerks very exotic gifts.
ENCLAVE BOLD ITALIC — PUZZLED WOMEN BEQUEATH JERKS VERY EXOTIC GIFTS.
Puzzled women bequeath jerks very exotic gifts.
ENCLAVE EXTRABOLD — PUZZLED WOMEN BEQUEATH JERKS VERY EXOTIC GIFTS.
Puzzled women bequeath jerks very exotic gifts.
ENCLAVE EXTRABOLD ITALIC — PUZZLED WOMEN BEQUEATH JERKS VERY EXOTIC GIFTS.
Puzzled women bequeath jerks very exotic gifts.
ENCLAVE BLACK — PUZZLED WOMEN BEQUEATH JERKS VERY EXOTIC GIFTS.
Puzzled women bequeath jerks very exotic gifts.
ENCLAVE BLACK ITALIC — PUZZLED WOMEN BEQUEATH JERKS VERY EXOTIC GIFTS.

designer. The computer, and font editing software, has made it possible for me to do the work I do, and for my clients to be able to afford it. It has also added the ability to be speculative. Rather than waiting for a client to underwrite a new design, I can take a personal idea and develop it as a typeface and release it to the design market. It could be a hit, or it could just sit there and attract no attention at all. In a way, the type business is beginning to resemble the music business.

What about type design is the most challenging for you?

Almost everything about type design is challenging. It is a very restrictive design form. It requires a lot of stamina to complete a font. With the emergence of the OpenType font format and extended language support, a font has gone from 256 characters to several thousand. Mul-

tiply that by six or ten weights and italics and suddenly that becomes an awful lot of work!

What are the types that most satisfy your aesthetic sense?

It changes depending on what I am working on. I don't look at any contemporary work. I have a vague idea what my colleagues are working on but I don't pay attention. I look at historical forms. I have a particular fondness for Venetian types of the mid-1500s. But that changes as well.

How important is typography in what you do?

Typography is everything I do. I got into this business via education. I was trained to be an industrial arts teacher. I spent a lot of time hand-setting foundry type and doing letterpress printing. When I was in graduate school, I discovered that there was this thing called graphic design. I used type and typography

to solve all my design assignments. I wasn't an illustrator and all of my classmates could draw so beautifully, I couldn't compete, so it was type to the rescue. I started working in NYC in type shops. I specified type and did copy fitting. It has always been all about typography.

What, in this current technological and economic climate, does the future hold for you specifically, and graphic design in general?

It is all about the Web. Type makers are trying to come to terms with allowing their fonts to be used on the Web given the insecure nature of it. Piracy has always haunted type designers, and some are having a hard time coming to grips with the lack of security for their fonts in this environment. As for graphic design in general, I think it is the same answer: The Web, and interactivity. It is all very exciting and a little nerve-wracking as well.

TITLE: *Vanity Fair Logo* CLIENT: Vanity Fair *Magazine*
ART DIRECTOR: *David Harris* LETTERING DESIGN: *James Montalbano* YEAR: *2001*

TITLE: *Barneys New York* CLIENT: *Barneys New York* ART DIRECTOR: *Scott Williams* LETTERING DESIGN: *James Montalbano* YEAR: *2009*

TITLE: *PW Show Daily* CLIENT: Publishers Weekly *ART DIRECTOR: Clive Chiu* LETTERING DESIGN: *James Montalbano* YEAR: *2004*

TITLE: *Lucky Logo* CLIENT: Lucky Magazine *ART DIRECTOR: Eleftherios Kardamakis* LETTERING DESIGN: *James Montalbano* YEAR: *2006*

Type for Now and the Ages

Principal, CipherType, Los Angeles

>> **Why did you become a typeface designer?**

I was designing two posters and related collateral for a promotional campaign for a fashion school. In order to tie all the pieces together and express the theme of the event, I wanted a unique typeface, but I couldn't find anything that came close, so I designed the typeface I needed. After that I was hooked. I wanted to see if I could design typefaces that reflected contemporary ideas, attitudes, and emotions. I like the challenge: A typeface can be as simple or complex as you want to make it; you can design one in a few minutes or a few years.

Do you have a personal style?

I think all designers exhibit a personal style to some degree. I am sure I do too, but I am probably not the best judge of what it is or what its merits may be.

With so many typefaces extant, what determines what faces you devote your time to?

It takes a lot of time to develop and refine a typeface, so the last thing I want to do is design one that is too similar to one that already exists, particularly if it's not an improvement. So if I know the face is sufficiently distinctive, the next thing I ask is, would anyone want this? Does it fill a need or create a need? Would I like to use

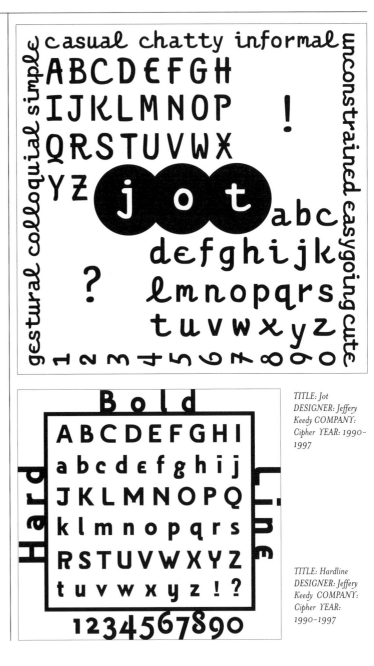

TITLE: Jot
DESIGNER: Jeffery Keedy COMPANY: Cipher YEAR: 1990-1997

TITLE: Hardline
DESIGNER: Jeffery Keedy COMPANY: Cipher YEAR: 1990-1997

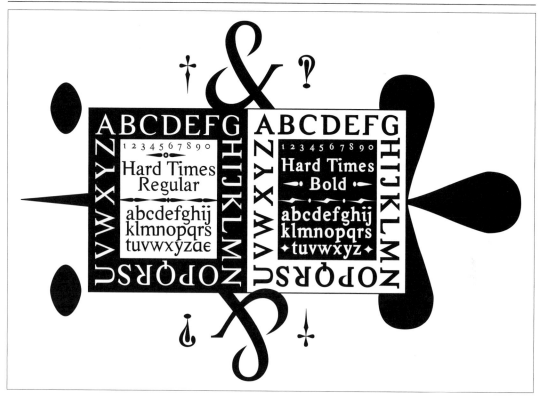

TITLE: *Hard Times* DESIGNER: *Jeffery Keedy*
COMPANY: *Cipher* YEAR: *1990–1997*

TITLE: *Glide*
DESIGNER: *Jeffery Keedy*
COMPANY: *Cipher*
YEAR: *2005*

≫

this and see it on the streets, in magazines, on television? In the end, it comes down to being committed or obsessed enough to see it through to the end.

How much time, on average, do you devote to designing new or reviving old faces?

Technically, all typefaces are revivals, in that they are all based on existing typefaces and the alphabet. I'm not very interested in designing revivals that are copies of old typefaces that have fallen out of use or fashion. In designing new typefaces, I know they will become old soon. I'm interested in expressing our current era in all of its complexity and contradictions.

Is there room in the business for more type designers?

There is always room in this business for more type designers, but it is not easy to make a living on type design alone. Unless you have continuous commissions and a way to sell a lot of typefaces directly, or you get royalties from a big distributor, you won't make much money. Only a few designers survive on type design alone. For most graphic designers, type design is an excellent skill that helps improve typography and logotype design, and a few popular typefaces can be good for self-promotion.

TITLE: Manu Sans DESIGNER: Jeffery Keedy COMPANY: Cipher YEAR: 1991

TITLE: Keedy Sans DESIGNER: Jeffery Keedy COMPANY: Cipher YEAR: 1990-1997

Doing His Thing

Principal, Illustration, Letters and Art, Halifax, Nova Scotia, Canada

>> **How long have you had your own studio?**
I've been working on my own doing illustration and art full-time for three years. I was part of a design and illustration coop for two years prior to that but then split off on my own. We still share the studio space though, which is nice—especially in a recession.

Your work is focused largely on lettering. How did this interest come about?
When I was in design school I thought I would either end up in type design or book design, because my main interest was in typography. I wasn't very good at computer-based type design though. I enjoyed the preliminary phase, the sketching and ideation, but when things got taken to the computer I kind of lost interest. I have patience and am willing to work hard, but adjusting bezier points in the type software just killed the buzz completely, and when you aren't passionate about something it obviously shows up in the work. I was more drawn to idiosyncrasy, to seeing some letterform filtered through my own abilities, than I was to perfecting anything. So I went with that.

So, you were drawn to design?
I was initially drawn to type itself. I feel like I'd have to go to therapy to understand that because it's something deeply felt. I could

intellectualize it and say I'm fascinated by language, but that's not it entirely. I suspect that because I love writing and drawing equally, I'm attracted to a form that allows for both to happen at once.

Currently you are attempting to transition out of illustration into fine art. Why?

After years of design and illustration, I'm convinced that I have a lot more potential in fine art. I love illustration, but I think art will allow me more room to explore my own ideas and develop in a way that plays to my strengths. My background is interdisciplinary, which I've ignored for quite

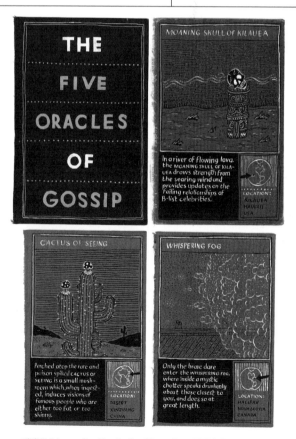

TITLE: Selections from Five Oracles of Gossip Comic DESIGNER: Ray Fenwick
CLIENT: Comic for Fantagraphics' Mome Anthology YEAR: 2007

>>

some time, and I'd like to have the option to choose whichever form best suits the concept. If something doesn't make sense as a drawing, I want to be able to try writing it, or performing it. I don't think of it as transitioning out of illustration though, because my plan is to do both. Even though my focus will be on developing as an artist, that's going to have an effect on my illustration work, which is exciting.

Your lettering and illustration is so much about your own personality. Did you feel that was a limitation in commercial practice?

It can be a bit difficult if someone has some misconceptions about my sensibility. People will say things like just do your thing, and then I do, but my conception of my thing doesn't match up with theirs, and it gets hilariously awkward. No no no they'll say, your thing. Your thing. Do that. It's no different than a personal relationship though, and when it works, it's a great experience. Sometimes you connect with someone, and there is flawless communication, and other times it's like trying to plug a lamp into an ice-cream cone, which just doesn't make any sense.

Do you have a particular style or character to your design? If so, how would you define it?

Oh, for sure. As you mentioned earlier it's definitely personal, or at least representative of the more palatable aspects of my personality. I think it's also idiosyncratic, ridiculous, loose, and anxious—

which are also ways I would describe myself to someone.

What about graphic design is the most challenging for you?

After eleven years working first as a designer, then an illustrator, you would think I would have developed a thick skin when it comes to critique, but I haven't. I still take

things personally when I shouldn't. You asked earlier about personality being a limitation, and this is one of the areas where that issue pops up. When the work is personal, even just a little bit, it can feel like someone is attacking you as a person when all they're doing is giving notes. It's completely immature and unprofessional, but I usually

TITLE: Selections from Drama Club Comic *DESIGNER: Ray Fenwick*
CLIENT: Personal Work YEAR: 2007–2008

TITLE: Selections from Hi: 30 Postcards *DESIGNER: Ray Fenwick CLIENT: Chronicle Books YEAR: 2009*

hide it pretty well, so it's OK. Only my studio mates experience my hissy fits and riotous weeping.

What are the projects that most satisfy your aesthetic sense?

I would say any project that allows for a sense of authorship, or real collaboration. Anything I can bring myself to care about. Those are the times when the work feels less like a service and more like an engaging activity. That's what I'm working toward in general.

What do you think the future has in store for you?

I don't have anything resembling self-confidence, but I have this almost religious belief in my own potential. It's a very confusing contradiction, but it gets me up early and motivates me so I'm not going to try and solve it. The present is always messy, because I'm working on several things at once, but it does all feel like it's leading somewhere great, so the mess and confusion will be worth it.

TITLE: Title Pages for The Great and Only Barnum Book DESIGNER: Ray Fenwick CLIENT: Schwartz and Wade BOOKS ART DIRECTOR: Rachael Cole YEAR: 2009

TITLE: Illustrated Life of Mystery Poster DESIGNER: Ray Fenwick CLIENT: Tiny Showcase YEAR: 2008

TITLE: "Face Race" Pattern DESIGNER: Ray Fenwick CLIENT: Personal Work YEAR: 2009

TITLE: Selections from Artwork The Final Campaign DESIGNER: Ray Fenwick CLIENT: Personal Work YEAR: 2008

Principal, Thirst Type, Barrington, Illinois

>> **Why did you decide to become a type designer?**

Type design is but one of the things that I do. In the service of communication, I find myself a designer, writer, photographer, and sometimes type designer. Often I just tweak a typeface for a given project. But when the type design muse does pay a visit, I abide by her, whatever she may ask me to do. As a result, I do not have an area of type design. I do whatever comes, when it comes.

As a type designer, do you exhibit a personal style?

There are probably hints in each of my typefaces that would allow a typo-archaeologist to trace them all back to the source. It may be the way that my ampersands look, or the placement of accents over lowercase i's. Perhaps once I have a proper, sizable body of work to analyze, I will be able to link it all up.

With so many typefaces extant, what determines what faces you devote your time to?

I have been working on some titling caps faces, both sans and with serifs. One is being used in its unfinished state in signage and other stuff for the Lyric Opera of Chicago. There is also a face based on a typo-joke based on real-life events: Shirley Temple, and its

WHUZZAT

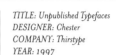

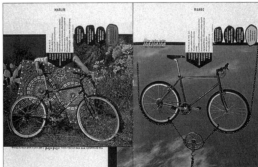

TITLE: Unpublished Typefaces DESIGNER: Chester COMPANY: Thirstype YEAR: 1997

TITLE: Whuzzat? DESIGNER: Chester COMPANY: Thirst TYPEFACE: Info Text YEAR: 1996

TITLE: You Gotta Start Somewhere DESIGNER: Rick Valicenti, Chester COMPANY: Thirst CLIENT: Gary Fisher Mountain Bikes PHOTOGRAPHER: Rick Valicenti TYPEFACE: DIN, Zeus's Hammock YEAR: 1996

TITLE: *Past, Present, Futures: 1997 ANNUAL REPORT DESIGNER: Rick Valicenti, Chester COMPANY: Thirst CLIENT: Chicago Board of Trade ILLUSTRATORS: Thirst, William Harrison, Ann Evanson PHOTOGRAPHER: Rick Valicenti, ARCHIVE TYPEFACE: Traitor, Rheostat YEAR: 1998*

TITLE: *Crystal Lake, IL DESIGNER: Chester COMPANY: Thirst CLIENT: Friends of Gilbert: Gilbert Paper PHOTOGRAPHER: William Valicenti, Chester TYPEFACE: Trade Gothic Bold Condensed YEAR: 1996*

TITLE: *Change Is Good DESIGNERS: Rick Valicenti, Chester COMPANY: Thirst CLIENT: Gary Fisher Mountain Bikes PHOTOGRAPHER: Rick Valicenti TYPE-FACE: Interstate YEAR: 1997*

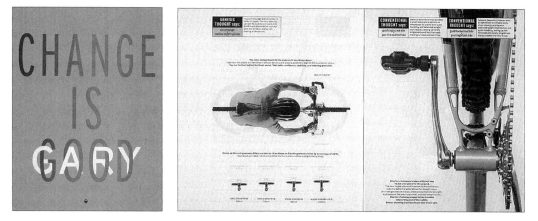

companion heavy face Shirley Temple Black. (Have you ever seen *The Bachelor and the Bobbysoxer*? It's a great movie with Cary Grant, Myrna Loy, and the teenage Shirley Temple.)

Is there room in the business for more type designers?

I kind of liked it in the old days, when I was just getting started designing type and there were perhaps a few hundred professional type designers. Now that the world has discovered Fontographer, a lot more type amateurs are playing at being professional. But there are also the real talents who, thanks to access to Fontographer, are able to get their ideas out into the world. If I may draw an analogy, type designers are like musicians. The world is full of music, but a new voice, a new musical style comes along from time to time, and it enriches a lot of lives. We do not actually need more typefaces, but a fresh new idea is wonderful to behold.

Type Is Passion

Principal, Hoefler + Frere-Jones, New York City

>> **Why did you decide to become a type designer?**

I recognized early on that an infatuation with typography isn't really enough to make a good graphic designer. A series of book jackets where I paired immaculately lettered titles with boxes marked "author photo to come" didn't really endear me to my publishing clients, and the fact that I'm red-green color-blind suggested that art-directing photo shoots might not be in my future. But I've also always been fascinated by the history of design, the history of typography specifically, and as a practicing graphic designer I suspected that I wouldn't have the opportunities to dwell on the things I find so rewarding. Research is an important part of type design, and writing is an important part of running a foundry; I'd miss these things too much if I were a graphic designer.

With so many typefaces extant, what determines what faces you devote your time to?

My clients, for one. When I'm commissioned to develop a new typeface, it generally means that someone has spotted something lacking in existing faces, and the opportunity to address some of these lacunae in typography is what keeps me going. There are also areas of personal importance

TITLE: *Catalog of Typefaces, No. 2*
DESIGNER/CREATIVE DIRECTOR: *Jonathan Hoefler* COMPANY/CLIENT/ILLUSTRATOR: *The Hoefler Type Foundry* YEAR: *2008*

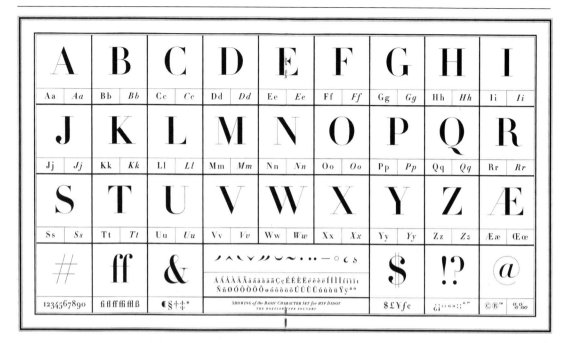

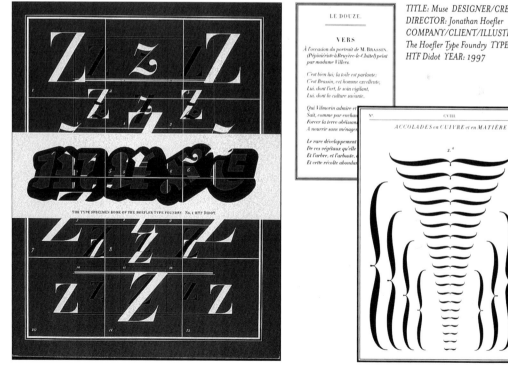

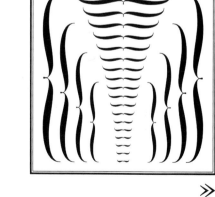

TITLE: Muse DESIGNER/CREATIVE
DIRECTOR: Jonathan Hoefler
COMPANY/CLIENT/ILLUSTRATOR:
The Hoefler Type Foundry TYPEFACE:
HTF Didot YEAR: 1997

to which I try to devote some time; there are always things I'm coming across that I think warrant further investigation, discoveries that sometimes result in a pretty good idea for a new typeface.

Is there room in the business for more type designers?
Of course. But I hope that both working graphic design-ers and future type designers will recognize that rampant font piracy is seriously threatening the industry. I hope that anyone who's enthusiastic enough about typography to consider a career in it might start by recognizing that collecting fonts on disk—how a lot of us get our most rudimentary education—is a dangerous pastime that endangers the livelihood of practicing designers and encour-ages the benighted idea that fonts are somehow free. Type designers are already regarded somewhat suspiciously by art directors, and that we're now fighting a rising tide of passed-around fonts makes it even harder to do what we do. You're welcome to join the party, but enter at your own peril.

TITLE: *Catalog of Typefaces, No. 2*
DESIGNER/CREATIVE DIRECTOR: *Jonathan Hoefler* COMPANY/ CLIENT/ILLUSTRATOR: *The Hoefler Type Foundry* YEAR: *2008*

Writing with Toothbrushes

Principal, Bernard Maisner, New York City

>> **How long have you had your own studio?**
From the day I graduated college, I have run my own studio. I have always been self-employed, or worked on a freelance basis. It is simply my temperament and I have never been an employee of a company. There is a saying: "Why work eight hours a day for someone else—when you can work eighteen hours a day for yourself?" Of course there are good and bad sides to this, but we all must follow our nature. Other than making signs for local stores or small lettering jobs as a kid, my real business began in 1977 by writing names onto place cards and nametags for large, corporate functions. I was paid one dollar per nametag. I could earn my month's rent, $100, in a few hours. The rest of my time was spent as an artist, making paintings. There were many corporate meetings and I lettered many place cards and nametags. (There were no label maker machines or laser printers in those days. The IBM Selectric typewriter was new and a really big thing with changeable font balls at the time.) The only way to make a nametag was to write it out by hand.

What are the changes in practice (and form) you have seen and experienced since you began?
In every way but one. I still create all lettering using eye and hand, but the technical means and methods in the preparation of lettering for reproduction are radically different,

and the styles and breadth of usage for creative hand lettering expanded dramatically. When I started in the business, most lettering seemed pretty straightforward. It was more like sign painting on a small scale. Skilled letterers used dip pens, created flowing brushwork, made bold swashy headlines. It was following, more or less, the kind of beautiful

hand lettering you can see in movie titles and credits during the 1930s through the 1950s. Social lettering, such as calligraphy for nametags and place cards, addressing envelopes for weddings, or doing lettering for the wedding invitation itself was also pretty straightforward and prescribed as well. There were pre-existing historic styles of calligraphy

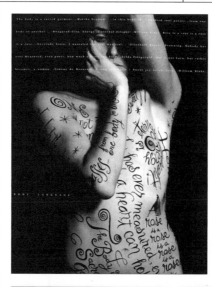

TITLE: *Body Language*
DESIGNER/ILLUSTRATOR:
Bernard Maisner
CLIENT: *Self* TYPE: *Custom*
YEAR: *2009*

TITLE: *Notecards* DESIGNER/ILLUS-
TRATOR: *Bernard Maisner* CLIENT:
Self YEAR: *2008*

TITLE: *Mr. & Mrs. Gold*
DESIGNER/ILLUSTRA-
TOR: *Bernard Maisner*
CLIENT: *Mr. and Mrs.*
Gold TYPE: *Custom*
YEAR: *2007*

(from thousands of years of model samples), and we calligraphers were taught them. You did a medieval style (gothic) or a Renaissance style (Chancery cursive) or whatever, but there were model books and/or alphabets to follow. You could do it well or you could do it poorly, but you knew what it was supposed to look like and you tried your best to make it look that way.

How have these changes impacted your work?

I started using and creating all sorts of tools to do writing with—toothbrushes, twigs, foam balls, cotton swabs, eyedroppers, syringes—anything that would hold paint or ink in a different way than traditional writing implements did. This was all in a quest to get new effects, new forms, new feeling. Then I made hundreds of phone calls and went to hundreds of meetings, with my portfolio, at the art departments of different companies; publishing companies, record companies, advertising agencies, etc. In the old days you could literally call a company switchboard, ask for the art director's name, be transferred over, introduce yourself, and set up a time and day that you'd stop by and personally show your portfolio of work to the art director. The big buildings in midtown NYC, now on the Avenue of the Americas, (but then known simply as Sixth Avenue), in the 1970s were being built at that time—and I remember being so scared and intimidated walking into these huge and impressive marble lobbies—but you met people, you got bold, you gained experience, you learned things. It was great. It was exciting. Changes in the industry

TITLE: *The Cheatin' Art* DESIGNER/ILLUSTRATOR: *Bernard Maisner* CLIENT: *Self* TYPE: *Custom* YEAR: *2008*

TITLE: *My Body Is a Little Too Heavy?* DESIGNER/ ILLUSTRATOR: *Bernard Maisner* CLIENT: *Self* TYPE: *Custom* YEAR: *2008*

TITLE: *Bon Appetit!* DESIGNER/ILLUSTRATOR: *Bernard Maisner* CLIENT: *Self* TYPE: *Custom* YEAR: *2009*

TITLE: *Wedding Announcement* DESIGNER/ILLUSTRATOR: *Bernard Maisner* CLIENT: *Mare Elarde and Anda Smith* TYPE: *Custom* YEAR: *2009*

TITLE: *Bernard Maisner* DESIGNER/ILLUSTRATOR: *Bernard Maisner* CLIENT: *Self* TYPE: *Custom* YEAR: *2009*

were coming, and I was forced to change and adapt my business. New font technologies must have made a difference.

Fonts were being created with new Fontographer program. Handwriting could now be digitized and easily made into a font that people could keyboard into existence. Lots of previously original hand-made lettering was copied and modified and made into a font. Whereas in the past a hand letterer might be hired to do lettering for a book cover and be paid $1,000, art directors turned to substandard hand-lettered-looking fonts for $50. Otherwise talented designers would type out the headlines (no matter how crummy it looked), accept it and leave it the way it popped out of the computer, and go to press happy as clams. If a hand letterer had handed in similar art, the art director would have sent it back and said to correct it. To my eye, most hand-lettered-looking fonts are horrid fast-food versions of hand lettering. Spacing, grace, letterform relationships, natural variations of a repeated given letter—all was lost to repetitive, lifeless fonts. But they were cheap! Because of this growing trend I was losing work and income at a fast clip. It was similar to what had happened to photographers and illustrators with "stock" pictures and illustration. But things change and we must too. I looked for gaps in what could be improved upon yet still benefit from custom hand lettering in other fields. Social stationery was it for me—fine engraved wedding and party invitations and personal correspondence stationery. The engraving method of printing (i.e., intaglio, like artists etchings are) is a very classic, mechanical, and manual method of printing, and still holds an esteemed position in the luxury market. I worked hard at developing a calligraphic style that would stand out from the rest. It was a modern blend of the historic Copperplate and Spencerian styles, with a modern aesthetic added in to it. I still did creative advertising lettering, but turned to building a fine stationery business, creating custom stationery, as well as developing a retail line of products to complement it.

Finally, I am now considering creating hand-lettered fonts of my own brand. "If you can't beat them, join them" is where I find myself now. But I will try to break barriers and make the best hand-lettered-looking fonts out there.

TITLE: *Environmentology* DESIGNER/ILLUSTRATOR: *Bernard Maisner*
CLIENT: *Self* TYPE: *Custom* YEAR: *2009*

TITLE: *Wedding Announcement* DESIGNER/ILLUSTRATOR: *Bernard Maisner* CLIENT: *Alexi Maria and David M. Leuschen* TYPE: *Custom* YEAR: *2007*

BERNARD MAISNER · LIVE WRITING ON CAMERA
FOR FILM AND TELEVISION
MEMBER SCREEN ACTORS GUILD (S.A.G.)

TITLE: *Live Writing on Camera* DESIGNER/ILLUSTRATOR: *Bernard Maisner* CLIENT: *Self* TYPE: *Custom* YEAR: *2009*

Poring over Type

Co-Principal, Plazmfonts, Portland, Oregon

>> **Why did you become a partner, along with Joshua Berger and Niko Courtelis, in Plazm Digital Type Foundry?**

This was the coming-together of a few factors: It was a way to create the typefaces that we wanted to use; because of the distribution of Plazm magazine, other designers began sending us their own type experiments; and lastly, we saw the foundry as a way to support our magazine habit.

What level of training did you have in the art and craft of type?

I really had no bona fide training as a type designer in the traditional sense. However, when I first discovered type, I was all over it, poring over every font I could find.

The very first type class I had, we cut out type from photocopies and hand-kerned different words. We also would painstakingly paint letterforms on ten-inch square boards. I remember thinking how crazy it seemed to spend so much time just painting letterforms, but I really enjoyed the process and making the letterforms and words look perfect. Now I make my students do similar exercises, but it's even harder for them to understand why it's so important to work with the type with their own hands. Slowly, after hours spent working with type this way, they start to appreciate the value of the exercise.

Did you also have experience in hot type and letterpress?

adiHAUS regular
adiHAUS italic
adiHAUS semibold
adiHAUS semibold italic
adiHAUS bold
adiHAUS bold italic

adiHAUS
designed exclusively for adidas.

adiHAUS condensed light
adiHAUS condensed italic
adiHAUS condensed bold

ABCDEFGHIJKLMNOPQ
RSTUVWXYZ abcdefghi
jklmnopqrstuvwxyz
1234567890 !@#$%^&*{ }

TITLE: adiHaus, commissioned by Adidas CREATIVE DIRECTOR: Pete McCracken DESIGNERS: Pete McCracken, Gus Nicklos, Long Lam, Carol Ambuen YEAR: 2002

TITLE: 3000, a Typeface for the Next Millenium DESIGNER: Pete McCracken YEAR: 2000

Inky-BLACK.
Over inked. Poorly
printed and over
done.*
Perfect.
© pete mccracken 1994
*RISD didn't want me in their design dept.

TITLE: Inky-black – Created at the Rhode Island School of Design, Letterpress Shop DESIGNER: Pete McCracken YEAR: 1994

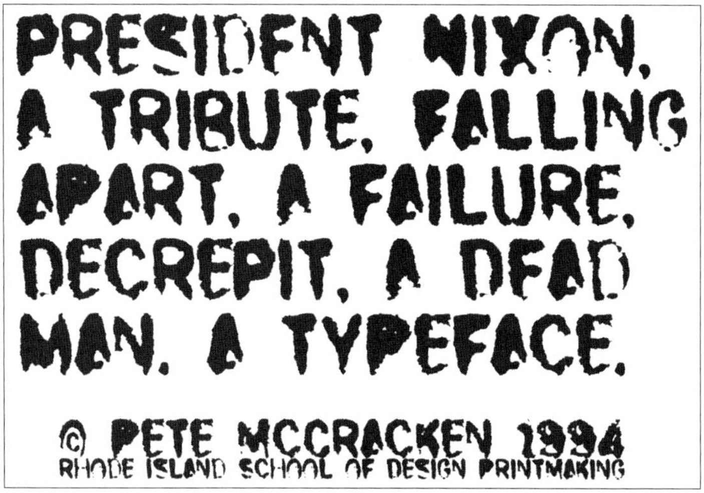

PRESIDENT NIXON, A TRIBUTE. FALLING APART. A FAILURE, DECREPIT, A DEAD MAN. A TYPEFACE.

© PETE MCCRACKEN 1994
RHODE ISLAND SCHOOL OF DESIGN PRINTMAKING

TITLE: President Nixon – Created at the Rhode Island School of Design, Printmaking Department
DESIGNER: Pete McCracken
YEAR: 1994

Mtvpe Round

ABCDEFGHIJKLMNOPQ
RSTUVWXYZ abcdefghi
jklmnopqrstuvwxyz
1234567890
!@#$%^£*{ }

TITLE: Mtvpe – Commisioned by MTV Networks
DESIGNER: Pete McCracken
YEAR: 1997

Petescript – currently featured on Playboy's online extravaganza of lovely ladies and on Aerosmith's album BIG ONES. Ummm.....

© pete mccracken 1992

TITLE: Petescript – Created at the Pacific Northwest College of Art, Printmaking Department
DESIGNER: Pete McCracken
YEAR: 1992

My introduction to letterpress was an important step toward learning about how type functioned physically and also gave me a better understanding of how printers/designers worked before the computer and offset litho. Once I learned how to do things right, I started to mess things up. It was about 1994, when I was studying printmaking at the Rhode Island School of Design, that I created Inky-black using over-inked presses, and also President Nixon (a typeface tribute to the old dodgy stinker when he passed away) from a child's manual typewriter I found at the Salvation Army. It said President across the front of the machine and only had uppercase keys. My technical background consists of learning and working with Fontographer, Adobe Illustrator, and now Fontlab.

What do you look for in a viable typeface?
We generally look for a typeface that has a very solid grounded structure but also has a unique quality. By grounded structure I mean a harmonious design thread tying the whole typeface together.

For a type to be commercially viable, what are the key attributes?
One of the most important attributes is that the type is mechanically sound, not only in terms of software but also spacing and kerning. Having a unique design is not enough. The type must be painstakingly tested in many applications, both physically and within current software standards.

Principal, Brightwork Press, Newtown, Connecticut

>> **You are primarily known for your illustration. How did you become interested in old wood and metal types?**

I started out in the small press world in Toronto as a printer, papermaker, and typesetter in the early 1970s. At the same time, I was doing some illustration occasionally—mostly small decorative pieces done as linocuts for poetry broadsides or books, and occasionally, I would draw some little piece for a commercial client—a doodle for a pamphlet or flyer. Some editorial illustrators I met through the printing shop encouraged me to take some of my work around to magazines, and eventually I started getting enough illustration work that I left printing behind. Then, around the early 1990s, after focusing on illustration for years, I started doing more and more writing and self-publishing—posters and calendars and broadsides—but I was hiring or collaborating with designers to do the type and printers to print them. It wasn't long before the various small hassles drove me to figure out a way to do more of that part myself and to find a small tabletop proofing press around 1994.

Would you say that your retro style of typography was intentional or a function of your interest in vintage type?

I think my love of nineteenth-

TITLE: *I Don't Give a Rat's Ass DESIGNER/ART DIRECTOR/ILLUSTRATOR/TYPOGRAPHER: Ross MacDonald CLIENT: Self YEAR: 1997*

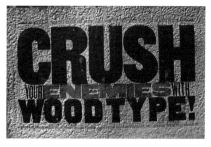

TITLE: *Crush DESIGNER/ART DIRECTOR/TYPOGRAPHER: Ross MacDonald CLIENT: Self YEAR: 1998*

TITLE: *Enemies of the Church (Movie Prop) Cover and Interior Pages DESIGNER/ART DIRECTOR/ILLUSTRATOR: Ross MacDonald TYPOGRAPHER: Kirsten Sorton CLIENT: Tornado Productions/The Legend of Zorro YEAR: 2004*

century (and earlier) type and design has had a huge influence on my work. Even back in the 1970s, display typography and big broadsides had been the things I was most interested in. As I started discovering nineteenth-century type and design, I felt like I had hit the mother lode. Of course, we have all seen lots of this stuff, but until I really started studying it I never understood or appreciated it. I take a lot of my cues from the first half of the nineteenth century, but I also find myself trying out things that I see in fifteenth-century books or on eighteenth-century tobacco wrappers. Those things influence me, but I don't try to ape them blindly. Also, since I often use nineteenth-century wood type, my stuff can't help but have a certain period look, but I try to use the old type in new ways.

You have created a couple of illustrated children's books, and in addition to your artwork, you have illustrated it with cacophonies of old type. Do you plan integrating more typographics into your work?
I'm working on the third book now, and although it won't have much wood type beyond the cover and title page, I will be doing a lot of hand-lettering on the pages. Next I want to do a book called Always and Never, a parody of the old didactic children's books of the early part of the nineteenth century, like Struwelpeter. I want to make it a smaller two-color book, and set all the pages in different fonts.

You are an illustrator who designs, and a designer who prints using old presses and type. Is this something that all students and young professionals should do?
It depends on the person. Some people are more focused on one thing, and that's great too. I think you really have to work from your strength.

TITLE: Dead Eye Comics DESIGNER/ART DIRECTOR/ILLUSTRATOR/TYPOGRAPHER: Ross MacDonald CLIENT: Self YEAR: 2001

TITLE: Hand Made DESIGNER/ART DIRECTOR/ILLUSTRATOR/TYPOGRAPHER: Ross MacDonald CLIENT: Self YEAR: 2002

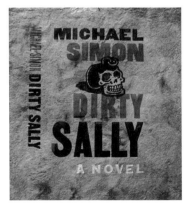

TITLE: Dirty Sally (unpublished) DESIGNER: Paul Buckley ART DIRECTOR/ ILLUSTRATOR/ TYPOGRAPHER: Ross MacDonald CLIENT: Viking YEAR: 2003

TITLE: Nobody's Perfect DESIGNER/ ART DIRECTOR/ ILLUSTRATOR/ TYPOGRAPHER: Ross MacDonald CLIENT: Self YEAR: 2001

What advice do you have for an aspiring graphic designer?

"Look at everything for influence and inspiration; don't limit yourself. It is also very important to have an understanding of the history of art and design. And it is very important not to let people discourage you." —*Kyle Cooper*

"HAVE MONEY BEHIND YOU, BECAUSE THE DESIGN FIELD IS VERY, VERY TOUGH TO BREAK INTO."

—*Dennis Barnett*

"When going for an interview, do your homework: Know what that firm has done in the past, what kind of work they do. Be very familiar with who you're talking to." —*Kent Hunter*

"Look at cultural history, really look at art history and understand it. Anything anthropological is a valuable reference for a graphic designer, so I'd say really hit that world in a big way. I would also look at the history of architecture, anything in the history of printing, anything that provides the map of how people solved problems in the past."

—*Michael Patrick Cronan*

"A DESIGNER NEEDS A BROAD EDUCATION THAT IS NOT TOO NARROWLY FOCUSED ON DESIGN. A DESIGNER NEEDS TO HAVE A SKEPTICISM ABOUT DESIGN, A SLIGHT SENSE OF REMOVE FROM IT, OR IT WILL SWALLOW HIM UP."

— *J. Abbott Miller*

"Unless you have a huge flair for self-promotion, it's going to be tough to get recognized. It's hard for somebody who's just getting started. I guess I would say that you should look at every possible magazine and book and European publication to try to see everything that's being done, now and in the past." —*Rita Marshall*

"Look at a range of design possibilities. Investigate and explore where graphic design can fit in, so that if you have interests besides doing brochures, you find a way of bringing that into what you do. I think you should investigate the whole world, read widely, see lots of things, collect things. I'm a collector, always have been. Now I let my collecting be part of my process. It's natural to me." — *Martin Venezky*

"Try and eke out some fun. This is supposed to be a creative job. If it ain't, then why the hell are you doing it? Go out and get a real job that pays well, one for which you won't have to sit up late at night answering questionnaires. What do designers need to be successful? What is successful? They need to figure that out."

—James Victore

"1. Fire in the belly
2. Intellectual curiosity
3. Visual sensitivity
4. Guts of steel
5. Thick skin
6. Stamina
7. The ability to listen."

—Deborah Sussman

"In a college situation, I don't think it's important if somebody decides after a couple of years to drop out and do an entirely different subject. I think art school is a splendid general education. At the same time, if you are serious about continuing after two or three years in college, you need to start meeting designers and spending time on an internship or something of that sort, actually meeting circumstances in the environment." —Richard Eckersley

"It is difficult to give advice in general; patients should be cured individually. However, we think that graphic design is the organization of information in a sensitive, exciting, and creative way. Therefore, we do not think that graphic design is a second-class art form and we try to clarify that in students' minds. I think the most important skill in a graphic designer is the capability of a quick diagnosis that gets to the core of the problem." —Massimo Vignelli

"Don't concentrate on technical skills. Learn to see. Learn to think. Learn to listen to everything going on in the world around you. Design follows from ideas, not the other way around. The best design does not come from knowing two thousand typefaces and six Macintosh programs by heart. It comes from having a life and being observant and involved in the world at large."

—Randall Balsmeyer

"To be a graphic designer is fundamentally to be in the service of others. It doesn't mean to be blindly in the service of others, but it does mean that we play a role in society for which we are trained to think, to analyze communications problems or social problems, and to provide options, and so if someone is considering graphic design, the perspective that I offer them is: Are you willing to serve? And if their goal, their desire is other than to serve and to learn what it means to serve, then I think that they are really misconstruing what design does in society."

—David Peters

"Be culturally literate, because if you don't have any understanding of the world you live in and the culture you live in, you're not going to be able to express anything to anybody else. And don't become a designer unless you're good. We don't need any more mediocre designers."

—Paula Scher

The beauty of Rajae's art is complex. It is bathed in the love of a passionate soul, it shines with the hopes & dreams of an idealist, it bleeds from the wounds of an UNJUST WORLD, it marches forward with the courage of a revolutionary, it carries the infinite wisdom of a learned sage, it laughs with the innocence of a blissful child, it flies with the freedom of an enlightened spirit. It is rock, it is jazz, it is pop, it is drum 'n bass, it is Arab, it is European, it is native, it is foreign, it is poetry, it is philosophy, it is unique, it is beauty in every word, every chord and every beat. The spirit of Rajae now flows to the world through her art as her songwriting, composing, producing and singing have given birth to a form of music that is truly her own

TITLE: Promotional Posters
Rajae CLIENT: Rajae El
Mouhandiz DESIGNER/ART
DIRECTOR: Tarek Atrissi
YEAR: 2006

Changes in technology have not changed the way to enter the field. The recommended first step to getting started in the design business is to find an internship or staff job in one or some of the areas outlined in the preceding section. Learn as much as possible, do as much hands-on work as you can, and become an experienced practitioner in your chosen field(s). Pretty simple, right?

Right! Yet not every young designer is content to be an employee—or at least to be employed at the same job for an extended period. Nonetheless, it is prudent to have the experience of a staff job. Before deciding on an opportune time to leave it, you should make certain that you have developed the talent and acquired enough skill to move forward. If there is no such forward movement after a year or two, the situation should be reexamined and questions like these should be asked: Is there more to be learned in the present position? Does the job offer opportunities for advancement? Does this

SECTION ②

Design Businesses

situation provide enough challenges? Am I taking advantage of the challenges? If the job does not equal your ambitions, it is time to move on. If your ambition is to be more directly responsible for the work being done, then it is possible that working for someone else will never satisfy you.

The graphic design profession is composed of staffers, freelancers, and proprietors. The first category is discussed throughout the previous section. The second includes hired hands who work independently but may be employed as either temporary (or casual) staff (without the benefits and perks of a full-time staff member) or on a job-by-job basis based on need. The third group is designer-managers who are proprietors of small, medium, or large studios, firms, or offices. Work done in this category is developed and produced on the proprietor's premises and using the proprietor's staff. The following are more detailed descriptions of the common divisions of labor.

Freelancers are hired as production support for identified assignments. They are hired to design or art-direct specific projects (newsletters, letterheads, posters, magazines, etc.). Moreover, freelance advertising art directors are a staple of that industry. Virtually every kind of design operation uses freelancers in at least one of these capacities: In-house art departments employ them to supplement insufficient full-time staff, and independent design studios hire them when particular projects demand more attention.

The graphic design profession relies heavily on freelancers with both creative and production experience. In turn, highly skilled freelancers command relatively substantial hourly rates. For the less experienced freelancer, this is an excellent opportunity to be tested prior to being hired in a full-time position (or used regularly as a freelancer). Some young designers use their freelance status as a way to sample options and determine which jobs they prefer. Some designers simply prefer working as freelancers because they are not locked into predetermined schedules.

For the freelancer with the ambition of opening a proprietary design studio, firm, or office, this is a very effective way to establish a reputation and develop the beginnings of a solid client base. Most designers do not open offices straight out of school but allow some time wherein they acquire experience and contacts. Freelancers who develop numer-

FREELANCERS: WORK FOR HIRE

Not all independent contractors are called freelancers, but all freelancers are independent contractors. They may be specialists in particular disciplines or generalists hired for various jobs. They may have formerly held staff jobs and decided that they are better suited to being their own boss (with all the freedom and limitations that implies). Freelancers may work in a home office, small studio, or on the client's premises. Often, a freelancer's workweek is spent shuttling among several work environments. Freelancers may rent a studio with other freelancers and share basic utilities and hardware (such as copier and water cooler), or may lead a solitary existence without the benefit of sustained human contact. A freelancer may employ other freelancers to help produce certain projects but, more likely, she works without assistance.

ous clients put themselves on a good trajectory for the next professional stage. More clients equals more work, and more work usually requires an overarching management structure—which, in turn, means opening a studio, firm, or office.

SMALL STUDIO: BUSINESS BABY STEPS

There is nothing mysterious about starting up a small studio. It is essentially a natural outgrowth of being a freelance practitioner who already works out of a home or outside office. The requirements are minimal: computer (with modem), telephone, copy machine, flat files, desk(s), and an ergonomic chair. Oh yes, and a title, which can be a proper name (Jane Doe Design), a clever name (World Domination Design), a corporate-sounding name (Apex Communications), or an enigmatic name (TypeSet Ltd.). A freelance or full-time assistant is commonly employed to help with production and traffic as well as design. It is also more prudent than ever to retain an accountant or bookkeeper to keep track of income and outlay and to help formulate a business plan.

The first question to ask is not "How do I set up a small studio?" but "Why?" Some freelancers are much better-suited to working alone on a job-by-job basis than running a small business. Most designers are interested in making design, not worrying about the pressures of business, while others are capable of (in fact revel in) both. For those freelancers who are so endowed, the desire to start a small studio is the result of need—*and* success. More work equals more demand on one's time equals the need to have an assistant (or more). Thus a studio is born. The term *studio* suggests a primarily creative group, often working in general practice. *Firm* indicates a fusion of creative and business and may very well be a multidisciplinary or specialist practice. *Office* is a more brisk-sounding way of describing a studio or firm. Generally, a small studio consists of a principal (or a couple of partners) and approximately one to three employees. This number may include senior and junior designers, a production artist, and an intern. The team might also include a receptionist to answer phones and manage traffic. The reasons vary for why small studios are started. Here are a few typical possibilities:

Experience: A designer at a company or design firm who has gained enough experience as a staffer decides to become an independent practitioner.

Clients: A freelancer develops one or more regular clients and, therefore, enough income to make a studio financially feasible.

Ambition: A designer with only

IMAGE ISN'T EVERYTHING, BUT IT HELPS

A graphic designer must prove his capabilities through work. Nonetheless, it helps to have sophisticated promotion that presents a positive image. Clients are impressed by quality and the way in which the work is presented enhances the image. You can promote yourself in print, on CD-ROM, and on the Internet, and can employ both novel and traditional formats, including booklets, posters, and portfolios. A promotion piece serves two immediate functions: It presents a current sampling of work, and it reveals taste and imagination. The former is obvious, but the latter requires investment. To present a memorable image, create an unforgettable promotion designed in accordance with your aesthetic and conceptual values. Do not skimp on promotion, but do not be ostentatious, either. This piece is possibly the most revealing work you will ever do.

All business arrangements, especially partnerships, should be built on a solid legal foundation. Partners must consider safeguards to ensure that the emotional needs of each are seriously considered, but equally important is the legal and financial structure of the business, which must be protected from problems that may (and probably will) arise between the partners. While great mutual benefit is to be gained from the marriage of talents and energies, neophyte partners must be aware that this kind of business requires maturity.

a few years of experience decides that independence is the key to success, and a studio is a way to achieve that goal.

Partnerships: Two or more like-minded individuals agree that by pooling their talents and skills (for example, creative and business) they can achieve success as a single entity. Getting those all-important initial jobs is accomplished in a variety of ways. Here are a few common scenarios:

Existing clients: The designer is given hand-me-down jobs from a former employer (which is different than the unethical practice of stealing clients). This may include being subcontracted in certain aspects of a job that the primary designer is no longer interested in doing.

Referrals: The vast amount of job-getting is done through word of mouth. A potential client may not have a large enough budget or does not have the right kind of assignment for a larger studio or firm and is therefore referred to another. (Because of this, it is always a good idea to maintain good relations with former employers, as some important early referrals may come from this direction.)

Advertising/Promotion: Promotional kits and advertisements featuring samples of past work serve as the first line of attack in making contact with clients. Frequent mailings are recommended, and entry to design annual competitions is an excellent idea.

Reviews: Potential clients may approach many studios (the names of which are obtained through referrals, promotional materials,

WHAT NOT TO NAME YOUR STUDIO

A studio by any other name is not the best maxim. Not every name is a suitable or smart way to win clients and influence people. A studio should be given a name that represents its mission not only to other designers but to clients. Some studios use clever names simply to be clever, without an eye or ear to the real world. Depending on the quality of the work, this may not be a problem, but a name like Boo Poo Bee Doo Studio usually defeats the purpose of attracting long-term, intelligent clients. Hair salons can afford cute names, but serious design studios cannot. The rule of thumb is to think hard before committing resources (letterhead, mailing labels, promotion) to a name that you may want to change in a year's time.

Which is not to say that something offbeat is entirely taboo. Many design firms have metaphorical or symbolic names that are conceptually smart. So let *smart* be the watchword. If you can't think of a name that expresses a characteristic of your practice, or is a play on or anagram of your name or your partners' names, then go the conservative route: Call your studio by your name. You can always add an identifier (Jane Doe Design, Jane Doe Communications, Jane Doe Office, Jane Doe Visual Communications, Jane Doe Graphics, Jane Doe Limited, or Jane Doe and Associates).

and work found in the design annuals). Bidding and proposals (an itemization of costs and services rendered) are usually solicited if the client is fundamentally interested in the studio's work.

Representation: Some small and many large studios or firms use representatives or salespersons (who often work on a commission basis) to approach clients. When properly managed, this is a good way to make initial contacts—if not for a specific job, then for future possibilities.

The small studio may be an end in itself or a stepping stone to the next professional stage, which may be a medium-size studio or larger firm. Some studio proprietors prefer not to expand to the point

where additional clients require the hiring of more employees, which means greater overhead. Growth also means that the principal spends more and more time managing than designing. Therefore, design commissions are scrutinized and weighed (as much for profit and loss as for time expended and ultimate satisfaction) before acceptance. However, if a small studio is a stepping stone, the principal(s) seek the most demanding and ambitious commissions in order to lay the foundation for the larger studio or firm. Those designers with good management skills make the transition from small to medium-size firms without difficulty. The problem to avoid is becoming overextended; the solution must be an individual business decision.

In deciding to go from small to intermediate or large studio, various decisions must be weighed. How much design versus management is required? How much of that is within the principal's ability? Will it require additional assistance? At this juncture, it is also useful to consider whether a sole proprietorship or a partnership is a more effective direction.

PARTNERSHIPS: MARRIAGE WITHOUT CHILDREN?

A young designer can build an independent business either as a sole proprietor or in conjunction with one or more partners. Partnerships are often an efficient way of easing into the business of graphic design by sharing responsibilities in a collegial environment. This is certainly among the best ways to mitigate the inevitable insecurity of starting a new business. Partnership is also one of the most difficult relationships to engage in, short of marriage. In fact, it is somewhat analogous to marriage.

Partnerships are based on the common interests of two or more individuals. They often grow from design or art school friendships or collegial relationships made at staff jobs. Some even involve married couples who manage, often against the odds, to balance home and office life. Some are marriages of convenience—acquaintances whose particular specialties complement each other and add value to the overall business. The reason for a partnership to exist is that the sum of the parts equals a whole that is potentially greater than each of the individuals alone could achieve. If one partner is better at editorial work and another is best at multimedia work, then the result is a more diverse studio or firm. If one partner is the creative engine and

TITLE: *Moby Wait for Me Album* CLIENT: *Moby* DESIGNER: *Chris Ritchie* ART DIRECTOR/ ILLUSTRATOR: *Moby* YEAR: *2009*

the other is more talented at sales and promotion, then the result is combined strength in those areas. Partnerships come in many configurations and sizes, depending on the perceived needs of the whole.

Of course, the wedding of two or more personalities is potentially problematic, but the best partnerships are based on mutual respect for each other's talents, mutual tolerance for each other's weaknesses, and mutual goals that allow individuals to forge respect and tolerance (and perhaps even a certain amount of fondness) into a viable business.

In any partnership, the strengths of each partner must be funneled into the reputation of the studio or firm, while at the same time the individual must be able to preserve his uniqueness. Invariably there are alpha and beta partners (suggesting dominance and subservience). Because an individual may be subsumed by the partnership, accommodations must be made (and there are no established guidelines for this; they each must be addressed individually). Some partnerships grow into long-term, well-balanced associations, while others unravel in time. Like any human relationship, the partnership should be nourished for mutual gain, but when, if ever, signs of distress appear, the issues should be addressed immediately. Although no definitive statistics are available, many partnerships face problems within the first three years.

Partnerships are found in all strata of the design business, in small, medium, and large studios, firms, and offices. Some partnerships are intended to remain small and easily manageable; the partners complement one another nicely and form a tight, self-contained unit. Others are more ambitious and spin off into many directions wherein the partners take on different tasks and responsibilities in the management of the larger entity. Medium- and large-sized firms may involve a managing partner or office manager who oversees the daily operation.

Clean, Witty, and Easy to Understand

Principal, Craig Frazier Studio, Mill Valley, California

>> **How long have you had your own studio?**
Twenty-nine years.

What are the changes in practice (and form) you have seen and experienced since you began?
The demise of type houses, the integration of the computer into the studio, the proliferation of digital photography, the ability to modify photographs (Photoshop), the ability for anyone to publish and participate in design practices, however unqualified, the virtual demise of any system of mentoring, the proliferation of studios and small design businesses, the saturation of imagery giving yield to stock houses, and the Internet as a publishing destination.

How have these changes impacted your work?
The Internet has made it possible to work anywhere in the world as an illustrator, though the pace is quicker. It is easier to be recognized for doing simple, clean imagery because of the proliferation of poorly conceived and crafted design. There are many more businesses desiring design in order to remain competitive.

Would you say that you have a particular style or character to your design? If so, how would you define it?
Simple, clean, witty, and easy to comprehend. I think I am a good problem solver with a sense of how to communicate to a client's audience. I tend to help a client see past their own preconceptions and communicate clearly.

What about graphic design is the most challenging for you?
Finding clients that are willing to pay for and endure the process of making good work.

What are the projects that most satisfy your aesthetic sense?
Early in my career, I was learning to art direct, so projects where I worked with great photographers were very satisfying. Trademarks are very satisfying because they require competent drawing skills. The last twelve years I have been primarily illustrating, so compelling assignments such as the *NY Times* or *Harvard Business Review* require good thinking and are likewise satisfying. Occasionally, I work on a package or a poster where I illustrate and design, which is extremely satisfying.

How do you feel education has changed in the past decade?
The ability to produce very polished portfolios has taken the place of teaching good verbal, written, and hand skills. There is too much emphasis placed on finished product and less on the objectives of how to communicate effectively.

TITLE: Love Stamp CLIENT: USPS DESIGNER/ILLUSTRATOR: Craig Frazier ART DIRECTOR: Carl Herrman YEAR: 2006

TITLE: LucasArts Trademark CLIENT: George Lucas DESIGNER/ILLUSTRATOR: Craig Frazier YEAR: 1994

TITLE: In the Realm of Absurd Possibilities CLIENT: Realm Cellars DESIGNER/ART DIRECTOR/ILLUSTRATOR: Craig Frazier WRITER: Kirk Citron YEAR: 2008

TITLE: *Steelcase Corporate Ad Campaign* CLIENT: *Steelcase/Saatchi & Saatchi*
DESIGNER/ART DIRECTOR: *Craig Frazier* PHOTOGRAPHER: *Rudi Legname*
WRITER: *Michael Wright* YEAR: *1989*

What, in this current technological and economic climate, does the future hold for you specifically, and graphic design in general?

We all have to work smarter and be more effective for our clients. As every business holds the same vehicles such as brochures and Web sites, we have to work harder to draw out and communicate their competitive differences. We have to help clients rise above (or below) the noise of modern business. I personally am drawn to companies and projects that I have a personal connection with in terms of their people and purpose. I want my job to remain intellectually challenging and fun.

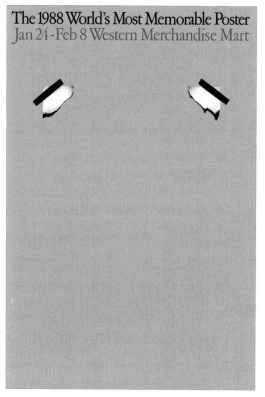

TITLE: *UNESCO Poster Exhibition* CLIENT: *UNESCO*
DESIGNER/ART DIRECTOR/ILLUSTRATOR/PHOTOGRAPHER:
Craig Frazier YEAR: *1988*

TITLE: *Sant Cruz Guitar Company Poster* CLIENT:
Santa Cruz Guitar Company DESIGNER/ART DIRECTOR/
ILLUSTRATOR: *Craig Frazier* YEAR: *2003*

| # Organized Humanist

Principal, Coa Design, New York City

≫ How long have you had your own studio?
Since April 2007.

What are the changes in practice you have seen and experienced since you began?
The most significant changes I've noticed in the past few years involve new technology and client expectations. As about half of the work we do is Web-based, we've realized that most clients now understand that their site cannot just be a singular project that can be designed, launched, and then finished. But, that it is more of a constantly evolving organism that must be shifted and updated to show that the company is on the pulse of their respective industry. The other aspect of practice that's been shifting in my opinion is many clients' expectations regarding the perceived value of design work. With competition growing every year among studios, but also the advent of online bargain-basement design bidding sites and automated template services, the design industry has a bit of an identity crisis on its hands. I've found that the process of demonstrating to clients what the difference is between professional, thoughtful, personalized (and more expensive) design work, and cookie-cutter, uniform, unfitting (yet less pricey) design work, is sometimes an arduous task.

TITLE: Recast Circulite Poster CLIENT: Recast DESIGNER/ ART DIRECTOR/ ILLUSTRATOR/ PHOTOGRAPHER: Chris Ritchie YEAR: 2005

TITLE: David Zaveloff Photography Web Site CLIENT: David Zaveloff Photography DESIGNER/ ART DIRECTOR: Chris Ritchie ILLUSTRATOR/ PHOTOGRAPHER: David Zaveloff PROGRAMMING: Noél Méndez YEAR: 2008

TITLE: *Manhattan New Music Project Homepage* CLIENT: *Manhattan New Music Project* DESIGNER/ ART DIRECTOR: *Chris Ritchie* PHOTOGRAPHER: *Various, courtesy of the musicians* YEAR: *2009*

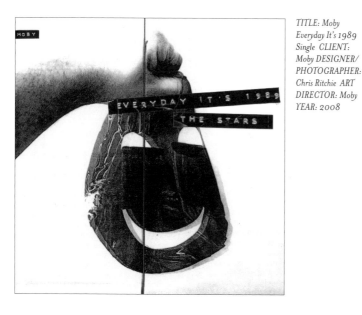

TITLE: *Moby Everyday It's 1989 Single* CLIENT: *Moby* DESIGNER/ PHOTOGRAPHER: *Chris Ritchie* ART DIRECTOR: *Moby* YEAR: *2008*

How have these changes impacted your work?

In order to adapt to these changes we try to offer our clients plans of how to develop and expand their ideas beyond just one aspect and try to establish more of a long-term partnership with them. We want to understand their business and become more strategic collaborators rather than just subcontractors who arrive after the important decisions are made to put visuals to their concepts.

Would you say that you have a particular style or character to your design?

I would define my design style as organized yet humanistic. I think design decisions should be made with a reasoning that supports the main purpose of the project and I believe that the best solutions are not obvious but often simple. I also have a curiosity and willingness to attempt a variety of work and styles because I feel that it broadens what I offer as a designer (even if some attempts end up being unsuccessful).

What about graphic design is the most challenging for you?

Finding new ways to look at things— new perspectives. Composing a strategy, idea, or concept that archives a perfect balance of newness and familiarity, tradition and irreverence, beauty and function.

How important is type and typography in what you do?

Essential to every project I do. Typographical sensitivity—whether it's formulating the visual hierarchy to a page, selecting a combination of typefaces that complement and balance each other, or simply executing the mechanics of letter-spacing or re-ragging a block of copy—is a fundamental skill that can never be overlooked and always improved upon.

What, in this current technological and economic climate, does the future hold for you specifically, and graphic design in general?

As the economic climate changes, design is going to continue to get more competitive and more specialized. With change comes new opportunities, however, and as new industries grow (e.g., alternative energy, healthcare, social networking), graphic design is still going to be a major factor in their success and impact. More companies now realize how design and public perception can rapidly affect their bottom line, and many are making design a top priority in their development process.

So, I think as the economic climate shifts there will continue to be opportunities as designers. We are planning to promote to specific specialized industries using our expertise from previous work in those fields. We are also continuing to keep our skills diverse and varied so we can make money with long-term client relationships as well as with internally developed consumer products that we sell.

TITLE: Five Dutch Days, Proposed Logo CLIENT: Five Dutch Days DESIGNER/ ART DIRECTOR/ILLUSTRATOR: Chris Ritchie YEAR: 2009

TITLE: Salsa! Client: Noél Méndez DESIGNER/ART DIRECTOR/ILLUSTRATOR: Chris Ritchie YEAR: 2009

TITLE: Moby Last Night Album CLIENT: Moby DESIGNER: Chris Ritchie ART DIRECTOR: Moby PHOTOGRAPHER: Dale May YEAR: 2008

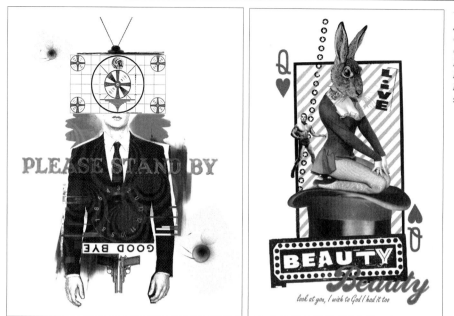

TITLE: Seven Deadly Sins T-Shirt Line CLIENT: Trinity Design Group DESIGNER/ILLUSTRATOR: Chris Ritchie ART DIRECTOR: Erika Mark YEAR: 2008–2009

TITLE: Donkey Product Packaging CLIENT: DonkeyNY DESIGNER/ART DIRECTOR: Chris Ritchie ADDITIONAL INFO: Bags made from old NYC billboards YEAR: 2008

TITLE: Jewish Home Lifecare Newsletters CLIENT: Jewish Home Lifecare/Winkleman Company DESIGNER/ART DIRECTOR: Chris Ritchie PHOTOGRAPHER: Courtesy Jewish Home Lifecare YEAR: 2008

TITLE: HOPE Survey Volunteer Fieldguide CLIENT: City University of New York, School of Professional Studies DESIGNER: Chris Ritchie ART DIRECTOR: Chris Ritchie ILLUSTRATOR: Eva Reese YEAR: 2009

A Business of Her Own

Principal, Louise Fili Ltd., New York City

≫ **What was your first "important" job, where you were able to exercise your own design sensibility?**

Being art director of Pantheon Books gave me the opportunity to experiment daily with many periods of design history.

Why did you leave your staff job to start your own studio?

Although I loved designing book jackets, I wanted to diversify in order to pursue my other passion: food.

What was the major difference in being bossed and being your own boss?

Under a boss, I worked very hard. As my own boss, I work even harder.

You started small and have remained small. Why?

I am a hands-on designer. If I can't design, I have no reason for being in this business. Increasing my staff would mean spending more time in meetings—more revenue, perhaps, but much less satisfaction.

What do you look for in an assistant?

A great eye for type, a passion for design, and a working knowledge of design history. A pleasant demeanor also helps.

TITLE: Grapeseed Oil Packaging DESIGNERS: Louise Fili, Mary Jane Callister CREATIVE DIRECTOR: Louise Fili COMPANY: Louise Fili Ltd. CLIENT: California Grapeseed Co. TYPEFACE: Hand-lettering YEAR: 1998

TITLE: Monzù Restaurant Identity DESIGNERS: Louise Fili, Mary Jane Callister CREATIVE DIRECTOR: Louise Fili COMPANY: Louise Fili Ltd. CLIENT: Monzù TYPEFACE: Hand-lettering YEAR: 1997

TITLE: El Paso Chile Co. Margarita Salt and
Mix Packaging DESIGNER/CREATIVE
DIRECTOR: Louise Fili COMPANY: Louise
Fili Ltd. CLIENT: El Paso Chile Co. ILLUS-
TRATOR: James Grashow YEAR: 1997

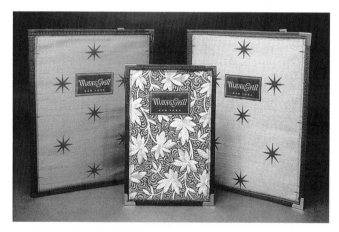

TITLE: Metro Grill Restaurant Identity
DESIGNERS: Louise Fili, Mary Jane Callister
CREATIVE DIRECTOR: Louise Fili COM-
PANY: Louise Fili Ltd. CLIENT: Metro Grill
TYPEFACE: Bernhard Tango YEAR: 1997

What has changed for you in terms of the kind of work you do over the years that you have had your own studio?

I am trying to focus on larger jobs primarily in the areas of food packaging and restaurant identity.

Do you think that small entrepreneurial studios are more effective and, for you, creatively satisfying than larger firms?

Yes!

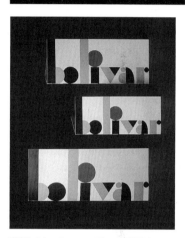

TITLE: Bolivar Restaurant Menus DESIGN-
ERS: Louise Fili, Mary Jane Callister CREATIVE
DIRECTOR: Louise Fili COMPANY: Louise Fili
Ltd. CLIENT: Bolivar TYPEFACE:
Hand-lettering YEAR: 1998

TITLE: Pulse of the Planet
DESIGNER/CREATIVE
DIRECTOR: Louise Fili
COMPANY: Louise Fili Ltd.
CLIENT: Pulse of the Planet
(Radio Program) ILLUS-
TRATOR: Anthony Russo
YEAR: 1990

Making Stories

Proprietor, Buchanan-Smith and Best Made Inc., New York City

>> **How did you become a design entrepreneur?**
My first design/publishing venture was a self-published newsprint guide to the small town in Canada where I grew up. It was a successful business model and, more importantly, an excuse to just publish something.

And not having the money to publish myself (let alone 10,000 copies of a 60-page guidebook) I approached local businesses and informed them that they had been selected by an elite board of judges (me) to be included in a "best of" book. After flattering their socks off, I laid on the guilt, saying that the only way this book will be published (and their greatness recognized) was if they took out a generous ad. Most of them signed on the dotted line.

Your first entrepreneurial project was your book *Speck*. How did this come about?
Speck was the manifestation of years of looking too closely at and seeing value in the small, unimportant things in life. *Speck* was also a way to exercise my eagerness to have my name on the cover of a book. After some dead-end jobs in New York, I enrolled in the MFA Design program at the School of Visual Arts. It was there that I was encouraged to roll my creative interests and entrepreneurial instincts into one, and the

TITLE: Speck Designer/ ART DIRECTOR/ TYPOGRAPHER: Peter Buchanan-Smith CLIENT: Princeton Architectural Press YEAR: 2001

TITLE: Ganzfeld 3 DESIGNER/ TYPOGRAPHER: Peter Buchanan-Smith ART DIRECTORS: Peter Buchanan-Smith, Dan Nadel YEAR: 2003

result was *Speck*. I think P.T. Barnum did it best: Take something of seemingly no value, give it a story, and then sell it for buckets of money. Barnum was also wise enough to not try and make his money publishing books.

What kind of design work did you do before starting your business?

I was the art director of the op-ed page at the *New York Times*. It involved very little design and much more art direction: working with illustrators, coming up with big ideas, and then trying to sell them to an editor. It was the greatest human pressure cooker you can imagine. Funnily enough, what kept me going were my side projects (*Speck* and *The Ganzfeld*). The *Times* was a wonderful introduction to the world's great designers, illustrators, and artists, most of whom not only ended up on the op-ed page but also on my little side projects!

How would you describe the key difference between your first business, PictureBox, and now?

Designing for someone else and designing for yourself are two entirely different things. Design »

TITLE: Wilco: Book Tomaselli DESIGNERS: Peter Buchanan-Smith, Dan Nadel ART DIRECTOR/ TYPOGRAPHER: Peter Buchanan-Smith YEAR: 2004

TITLE: Wilco Cover DESIGNER/TYPOGRAPHER: Peter Buchanan-Smith ART DIRECTORS: Peter Buchanan-Smith, Dan Nadel PHOTOGRAPHER: Michael Schmelling YEAR: 2004

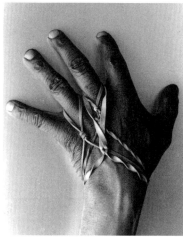

TITLE: Harry Kitt DESIGNER/ ART DIRECTOR/TYPOGRA- PHER/PHOTOGRAPHER: Peter Buchanan-Smith YEAR: 2004

pre-PictureBox was more about straight-up design. Now design is a little more complicated: It's not only about making a page pretty, telling a story, communicating visually (all things I used to think design was), but, more meaningfully, design is the process whereby I gather, assemble, and release months of our work and thousands of our dollars into something that ends up being a book (hopefully on someone's shelf). In this sense, design (and all aspects of publishing) have become more empowering.

Self-publishing is not easy. How have you succeeded with *The Wilco Book*?

It's impossible to think of doing a project like this completely on my own, without my business partner, Dan Nadel. We have also learned how invaluable others can be (from employing interns to hiring a publicist).

Start by assuming that all publishing ventures are basically ludicrous to begin with. Then once you've come up with a brilliant idea for a book, you must have the willingness to basically sacrifice all for the sake of the insane project at hand. You must be incredibly persistent to make it happen. The idea of *The Wilco Book* was sold to the band on our previous work (mainly *Speck* and *The Ganzfeld*). Neither of these publications paid off financially, but they've earned their keep in the amount of interest and confidence from others that they've been able to generate. You could say they are extremely elaborate promotional devices.

The nuts and bolts of how we succeeded with this book was to: (1) make lots of beautiful dummies that would spark interest from contributors and investors alike, (2) endear ourselves to everyone at every step of the way, (3) develop a solid understanding of how books like this are made and seek out all the opportunities available to you (connections, publishing techniques, etc.), (4) find talented and nice people to work with, (5) find a really good distributor who you trust (someone who will pay on time and understands your product), and (6) continually calculate and assess the best possible angle that maximizes your enjoyment, creative fulfillment, and moneymaking potential.

Is there a plan you follow to determine how much of your work will be design for clients versus entrepreneurial?

There is no plan. At this stage, we take whatever we can get but always

TITLE: *Speck: Eddie Simon's Collection of Earth, Air and Water* DESIGNER/ ART DIRECTOR/ TYPOGRAPHER/ PHOTOGRAPHER: *Peter Buchanan–Smith* CLIENT: *Princeton Architectural Press* YEAR: *2001*

TITLE: *Speck: The Backs of Famous Paintings (Franz Kline)* DESIGNER/ ART DIRECTOR/ TYPOGRAPHER: *Peter Buchanan–Smith* PHOTOGRAPHER: *Adam Yates* CLIENT: *Princeton Architectural Press* YEAR: *2001*

keep our own projects at the top of our list. Hopefully someday that list will just be all our own projects, with a few hand-picked client jobs for good measure—but that's a long way away. In the beginning, the client work is what has sustained us.

What would you say to a designer who is looking to do what you've done?

· Abandon being a designer and assume a much more abstract, frightening role in life.

· In the beginning, have a steady stream of freelance/client work. If things get good, you can easily scale those back.

· Don't do it unless you have a huge list of ideas to sell and are eager to make lots of money from them—but at the same time are willing to possibly make no money from them at all.

· Always think of design as an integral part of some bigger machine with many other important moving parts, all of which you should have your eye on at all times.

· Always aspire to be the pilot of that machine mentioned above.

· Because it is often your money and time at stake, you have to be able to do an exacting and tireless job of everything. It can't be in your nature to take shortcuts, because it's ultimately your ass on the line.

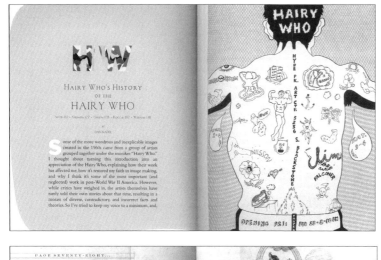

TITLE: Speck: Lipstick DESIGNER/ART DIRECTOR/ TYPOGRAPHER: Peter Buchanan-Smith PHOTOG-RAPHER: Stacy Greene CLIENT: Princeton Architectural Press YEAR: 2001

TITLES: Ganzfeld 3: Ballets, Battles and Bridal Showers; Ganzfeld 3: Hairy Who's History of the Hairy Who DESIGNER/TYPOG-RAPHER: Peter Buchanan-Smith ART DIRECTORS: Peter Buchanan-Smith, Dan Nadel YEAR: 2003

The Art of Adaptation

Principal, Eleven19, Omaha, Nebraska

>> **How long have you had your own studio?**

I incorporated Eleven19 in early 2002 with a business partner, and I give that as my official studio date. Before that, I had been doing freelance and contract work almost immediately after graduating from the University of Nebraska at Kearney in December 1997.

What are the changes in practice you have seen and experienced since you began?

A few years ago people saw computer monitors as constantly getting larger, and changing how we design Web sites, but with small laptops and iPhones becoming more and more adopted, we also have the opposite happening at the same time. I started my business during the recession in 2002, and a larger one seems to be happening now in 2009. There are always going to be ups and downs in business. I try to keep as much focused on the long-term as much as possible, and let some of the things that are easy to get wrapped up in (like the markets or the price of oil), but I have no control over, work themselves out on their own.

What about changes in form?

As for form, the styles and colors that are popular today are out-dated tomorrow. Trends come and go, and get revisited. When

TITLE: Voting Is Sexy (Poster) CLIENT: AIGA DESIGNER: Donovan Beery ART DIRECTORS: Donovan Beery, Drew Davies, Heidi Mihelich, Tom Nemitz, Nate Voss PHOTOGRAPHER: Geoff Johnson DIGITAL IMAGING: Kate Heller YEAR: 2004

TITLE: Be a Design Cast: Live at Boise State CLIENT: Be a Design Cast DESIGNERS: Donovan Beery, Nate Voss YEAR: 2007

TITLE: *Chip Kidd: A Lecture (Poster)* CLIENT: *AIGA Nebraska* DESIGNER/ ILLUSTRATOR: *Nicole Blauw* ART DIRECTORS: *Donovan Beery, Nicole Blauw* PRINT-ING: *Mike Weihs* YEAR: *2008*

TITLE: *RIA Compliance Consultants Identity (1) and Marketing Kit (2)* CLIENT: *RIA Compliance Consultants* DESIGNER: *Donovan Beery* YEAR: *2005/2008*

TITLE: *Touch (Poster)* CLIENT: *Life in Abundance* DESIGNERS: *Justin Ahrens, Donovan Beery, Steve Hartman, Christine Taylor, Nate Voss* PRINTING: *Spark Stationery* YEAR: *2009*

I started out, grunge design was popular, followed by a period of earth tones and muted colors. The past few years have brought us bright colors, and currently a lot of green (and I am told this is now moving to yellow). The style of the day has brought us a lot of hand-rendered DIY-looking work, which I refer to as the "Juno" look, due to the style really hitting a peak with the collateral from that movie. Where the trends go next I am not sure, and if anyone tells you that they do, well, they are either lying or they work for Apple.

How have these changes impacted your work?

Adaptation. It's a constant learning cycle when working with interactive media. And I always try to network with people whose services may be needed in the future. I can't do everything, so I need to make sure I have people I can work with if needed.

Would you say that you have a particular style or character to your design? If so, how would you define it?

I have been lucky to have found a number of clients who work well with the design I like to do the most: solid colors, lots of type, and projects that span a variety of different smaller projects, all growing off of each other with subtle variations and changes throughout.

What about graphic design is the most challenging for you?

It is a constant challenge to push myself to do better at all times. It's easy to let the client tell me things are good enough, and to get too worked up in daily projects and deadlines to really grow as a designer. Not all projects are served by the most creative solutions, and forcing a style you want to try onto a piece better served by what it needs can be a bad idea. A lot of projects I would like to work on may never come my way naturally. And without certain projects, I will never get the chance to learn the things that really interest me, or would give me the opportunity to have a chance at some of these projects. I find creating my own projects to do works well because the timelines are more lenient, and because I am the client, the client doesn't get bothered if things take more tries than they need.

How important is type and typography in what you do?

I have heard people describe what they do in this profession as that of telling a story. I have heard that it's about conveying the message and idea to the end user in a way they can relate to. I have heard numerous mentions of design being about problem solving. Regardless of story, or message, or problems that need answers, a vast majority of this is done with language. We communicate with design and people understand words.

What, in this current technological and economic climate, does the future hold for you specifically, and graphic design in general?

Information is, and has been, becoming more accessible by the day. The tools of our trade have, and will continue to become easier to afford and use, and the general public is going to, continue to see more information each day. With so much information being seen, things need to communicate properly. The world is also becoming more integrated, and information needs to be presented in ways that can be understood by more than just one culture.

I see the profession as having more specialization as technology creates even more options. No one person can do every aspect of a company's creative. To stay as a small creative agency, you will need relationships with others that you can outsource these specialties to.

*TITLE: Eleven19 Stationery CLIENT: Eleven19 DESIGNER: Donovan Beery
WRITER: Donovan Beery YEAR: 2007*

*TITLE: Heinrichs'
50th Anniversary
Invitations
CLIENT: Arnold
and Mary Heinrichs
DESIGNER:
Donovan Beery
YEAR: 2008*

The Small Studio Boom

Partners, Helicopter, New York City

How long have you had your own studio?

ET: Eight years—we started in 2001.

What are the changes in practice you have seen and experienced since you began?

ET: When we started it felt like the beginning of the small studio boom.

Computers, the Internet—it all allowed anyone to start their own studio in their living room without much hassle. The only problem with being a "print designer" was access to a printer. We spent all our first two paychecks on a small color printer which changed our lives—we were real, no more Kinkos or asking friends to print at their offices. Now it seems like we never turn it on. It's all electronic. I used to think "oh I could never be a Web designer because it never exists beyond the screen." That thought feels like from another century now. The more we work, the less it matters whether it's print, Web, ideation—it's all design and it's all required.

JL: Because of the rise of the small studio there were a lot more of "us" out there and clients were also much more aware and involved in "the design." In the beginning we were simply thrilled to get any work we could get. But over the years, we have learned to stop seeing design as a physical deliverable and to start asking the right questions and invite a much larger conversation, making the

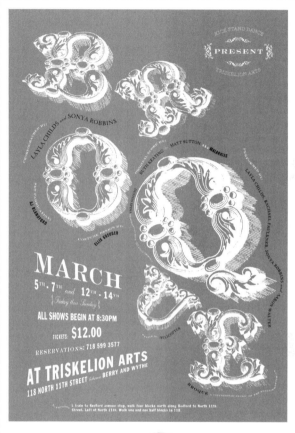

TITLE: BROQUE
DESIGNER: Ethan Trask
CLIENT: Robbinschild
TYPEFACES: Found Letters, Engravers, Swiss
YEAR: 2004

TITLE: STANDARD AMENITIES
DESIGNERS: Stacy Barnes, Josh Liberson, Ethan Trask
PHOTOGRAPHER/ ILLUSTRATOR/ CLIENT: ANDRE BALAZS PROPERTIES
TYPEFACE: Trade Gothic
YEAR: 2008

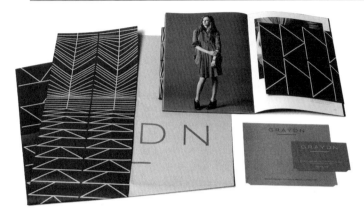

TITLE: Graydn DESIGNERS: Stacy Barnes, Johnny Taing, Ethan Trask PHOTOGRAPHER: Susanna Howe CLIENT: Todd Magill TYPEFACES: Bell Gothic, Din, Garda Titling YEAR: 2008

TITLE: Domino Magazine Cover DESIGNERS: Ethan Trask, Josh Liberson CLIENT: Condé Nast YEAR: 2005

TITLE: Standard Ad DESIGNERS: Justin Thomas Kay, Ethan Trask PHOTOGRAPHER: Getty Images ILLUSTRATOR/CLIENT: Andre Balazs Properties TYPEFACES: Trade Gothic YEAR: 2007

TITLE: Balazs Book Set DESIGNERS: Josh Liberson, Ethan Trask CLIENT: Andre Balazs Properties TYPEFACES: Fairplex and Akzidenz Grot YEAR: 2007

TITLE: Mary Boone Identity DESIGNER: Ethan Trask CLIENT: Mary Boone Gallery TYPEFACE: Copperplate YEAR: 2007

project focus on the objectives and not the object.

How have these changes impacted your work?

JL: Small projects can get larger. If you keep the goals in mind you can offer more than what is routinely thought of as services provided by a design studio.

ET: There is a lot more talk about collaboration. Solution finding is more subjective so the designer as expert is fading and designer as team member is rising.

Would you say that you have a particular style or character to your design? If so, how would you define it?

ET: Considered. Editorial. Typographic.

JL: I think our style, if we have one, is the way we approach the work—our problem solving. We tend to see everything as a system

and then apply a highly stratified vocabulary to articulate the different notes and nuances.

What about graphic design is the most challenging for you?

JL: Helping the client to make the right choice.

ET: Believing what you are thinking and making is vitally important on some level and knowing that 95 percent of it is trivial.

What are the projects that most satisfy your aesthetic sense?

ET: Anything where I can do large system thinking and use big type off the grid.

JL: Projects where the design and the execution are inextricable.

How important is type and typography in what you do?

ET: I was once referred to as a type slut. I feel very anthropomorphic

about type. I can use three different sans serifs in a design because they all have different qualities that I feel express the essence of the project. One I like the all caps, one the lowercase, and one the bold is more extended or condensed.

JL: It's true, we're type enthusiasts.

What, in this current technological and economic climate, does the future hold for you specifically, and graphic design in general?

ET: All the new technologies are just different platforms that allow a concept or idea to be more dimensional. Thinking can now be more complex and design can flow like language moving through and taking advantage of a different parlance. I feel the designer, if he/she wanted, could be the smartest person in the room who can see all the information visually and know how to express it, sculpt it, design it til it sings.

JL: It is our belief that the kind of thinking we do is arguably more critical now than ever before. As new media channels continue to expand and diversify, products and information are competing for attention in ever-complicated environments. Thoughtful graphic design offers clients a way out of the morass.

To do this most effectively we have forged strategic relationships with individuals and groups to facilitate the array of products and services required to support our clients' business needs.

TITLE: Joe Zucker, Plunder DESIGNERS: Johnny Taing, Ethan Trask PHOTOGRAPHER/ ILLUSTRATOR: Joe Zucker CLIENT: Nyehaus, Tim Nye TYPEFACES: Hand-drawn, Black Swan, Electra YEAR: 2008

TITLE: Keith Haring DESIGNERS: Stacy Barnes, Ethan Trask CLIENT: Rizzoli Books TYPEFACES: Apex Serif, Bell Gothic, Din, Lubalin Graph, Swiss YEAR: 2008

Specialization = Death

Principal, James Victore, Inc., Brooklyn, New York City

>> **How did you decide on your area of specialty in design?**

I never decided, and I never will. Specialization equals death.

You are the principal of your own one-person studio; do you run it?

I don't think I run my studio. At least I don't run it well. Maybe someday I will get good at that. Let me put that on my list.

How would you describe a good work environment?

A good work environment? For me? James Brown and ideas flying everywhere. Being tired at the end of the day and excited about getting back the next.

How have technological advancements affected your work?

I don't think about technological advances. They are something to learn to live with.

Do you have a specific approach to hiring?

I have a small shop. I need to hire good, interesting people who are nice to be around. I get a lot of very slick, polished, suited-up designers who come to us straight from schools with very fancy portfolios and huge egos. We give them directions to Pentagram. I need nice, eager intelligent folks who don't mind a good lashing occasionally.

TITLE: *E-Pluribus* DESIGNER/CREATIVE DIRECTOR/ PHOTOGRA-PHER/ILLUSTRATOR: *James Victore* COMPANY: *James Victore, Inc.* CLIENT: *De Paul University* TYPEFACE: *Hand-lettering* YEAR: *1998*

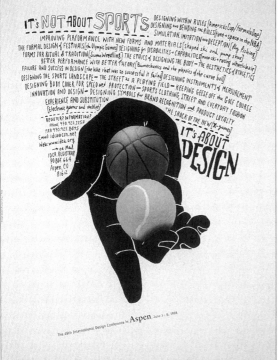

TITLE: Aspen Design Conference DESIGNER/CREATIVE DIRECTOR: James Victore COMPANY: James Victore, Inc. CLIENT: IDCA ILLUSTRATORS: James Victore, Rodrigo Honeywell TYPEFACE: Hand-lettering PHOTOGRAPHER: Stock YEAR: 1998

TITLE: Ignorance/Intolerance DESIGNER/ILLUSTRATOR: James Victore COMPANY: James Victore, Inc. CREATIVE DIRECTOR: Roger Pfund PUBLICATION: Aujourd'hui Pour Demain CLIENT: World AIDS Day TYPEFACE: Univers YEAR: 1998

TITLE: Use a Condom DESIGNER/ILLUSTRATOR: James Victore COMPANY: James Victore, Inc. CREATIVE DIRECTOR: Koichi Yano PUBLICATION: Dai Nippon CLIENT: DDD Gallery PHOTOGRAPHER: Bela Barsodi TYPEFACE: Hand-lettering YEAR: 1998

TITLE: Shit Shinola DESIGNER: James Victore CREATIVE DIRECTOR: Gimma Gatti COMPANY: James Victore, Inc. CLIENT: Portfolio Center PHOTOGRAPHER: John Stormont TYPEFACE: Sabon, Officina YEAR: 1996–1997

Principal, Design & Typography, Burlington, Vermont

>> **How long have you had your own studio?**

I registered my studio in 2002, almost right out of Parsons. And, while I cut my teeth as an art director at Mucca Design, my design business was always on in the background, allowing me a degree of creative promiscuity.

What are the changes in practice you have seen and experienced since you began?

Over the past decade people have become more design savvy in the United States. As a result of these general cultural and market shifts, publishing houses that have traditionally not paid much attention to design are increasingly expected to utilize more sophisticated concepts and typography in order to be competitive. To a great extent, however, design is a reflection of the current cultural forces. The technological shift to the Web (and all that that has brought—interaction, motion, and the necessity for complex information architecture and design) has introduced those same sensibilities into the print world. And, as always, the incorporation of youth (sub) cultures adds new spice to the pot.

How have these changes impacted your work?

Because design is in many ways a reflection of the zeitgeist, designers more than ever need to be plugged in to popular and underground culture, art, music, and social trends, or risk obsolescence.

Would you say that you have a particular style or character to your design?

I love type and color, and use any excuse I can to have fun with them. However, as any design educator would probably tell you, *style* is in some ways a dirty word: A well-rounded designer should be able to communicate in many ways. That said, I believe deeply in having a perspective—a spirit—from which your work originates. I was an activist for years before becoming a designer, developing a sensibility based on social justice, understanding history, and organizing community. In my professional life, I've been lucky enough to make things that generally don't hurt people. Additionally, I like to think that the information design work I've done has helped to elucidate problems and offer a new understanding of them.

What about graphic design is the most challenging for you?

By far, the most difficult part of the design process for me is the work it takes to come up with a fresh idea. I contort into various shapes creatively, intellectually (and sometimes physically)—always trying to push myself to reach down emotionally while also staying open to serendipity. When it works well, there's a deep sense of creative satisfaction.

TITLE: Pop! CLIENT: HarperCollins DESIGNER: Jean-Marc Troadec ART DIRECTOR: Erica Heitman-Ford YEAR: 2007

TITLE: Forgotten New York (paperback) CLIENT: HarperCollins DESIGNER: Jean-Marc Troadec ART DIRECTOR: Erica Heitman-Ford Illustrator TYPE: Jean-Marc Troadec YEAR: 2006

TITLE: *Arabia* CLIENT: *Rizzoli Publishing* DESIGNER: *Jean-Marc Troadec* ART DIRECTOR: *Matteo Bologna* YEAR: *2006*

TITLE: *Il nome di Marina ("Marina's Name")* CLIENT: *Rizzoli Publishing* DESIGNER: *Jean-Marc Troadec* ART DIRECTORS: *Matteo Bologna, Cristina Ottolini* ILLUSTRATOR: *Jean-Marc Troadec* YEAR: *2005*

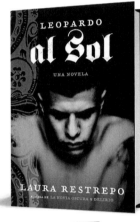

TITLE: *Series – Dulce Compañía, La Isla de la Pasion, Leopardo al Sol* CLIENT: *Rayo/HarperCollins* DESIGNER: *Jean-Marc Troadec* ART DIRECTOR: *Andrea Brown* YEAR: *2005*

What are the projects that most satisfy your aesthetic sense?

Research tends to play a role in the work I enjoy the most. I love geeking out, discovering the most historically appropriate blackletter or well-drawn script. And with information design, fully understanding the content is a given for creating the best structure to communicate it. If you're not learning, what's the point?

How important is type and typography in what you do?

I take to heart Eric Gill's maxim, "Letters are things, not pictures of things." Good typography is the foundation for good design, and I love playing with a new typeface, discovering its unique characteristics, and then using it in unforeseen ways.

What, in this current technological and economic climate, does the future hold for you specifically, and graphic design in general?

Designing book jackets still gives me a lot of pleasure, but I'm also expanding into marketing, branding, and design strategy. In the larger scheme of things, graphic design can't help but be influenced by technological innovation, even in (and perhaps even more so by) the current economic downturn. As a result, brilliant young designers will continue to emerge and push the creative envelope, and the best clients will take risks on them because they won't have any choice but to innovate.

Rule Britannia

Former Partner of Ph.D, Principal, Air Conditioned, Los Angeles, California

>> **First off, why did you call your studio Ph.D? Did you have aspirations for high academic certification?**

Well, my last name is Piercy. My partner's name was Hodgson. . . and we're designers. But it has more to do with the way we approached the work. Ph.D was a pompous, anonymous, corporate-sounding name, but our work was the opposite of that. I liked it that way.

How difficult was it to come from the United Kingdom and open a design studio in the United States? Were there any language difficulties?

Americans think that everyone from England is directly descended from royalty, so it's a huge advantage to be English over here. And there are language issues every day. In a nutshell, Americans believe that they are speaking English when they talk. We do not agree.

How do you segment your work? Some of what you do is totally client-oriented, but you also author your own.

The vast majority of our work is for clients. Occasionally you produce something for them that doesn't get used properly or that sparks a different idea, and that then begins to fuel some of the personal work. I'm a big believer in making things for no other reason than the fact that you want to do something. What it ends up being should be immaterial at first.

TITLE: *Eight!*
DESIGNER: *Clive Piercy*
CLIENT: *Primary Color*
PHOTOGRAPHER: *Anonymous*
YEAR: *2003*

TITLE: *Tunelito* DESIGNER: *John Hughes* CLIENT: *Nike* YEAR: *2004*

TITLE: Lucky DESIGNER: Clive Piercy CLIENT: Melcher Media YEAR: 2003

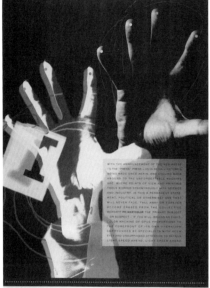

TITLE: P310 DESIGNER: Clive Piercy CLIENT: Primary Color PHOTOGRAPHER: Ron Slenzak YEAR: 2003

TITLE: Pretty DESIGNER: Clive Piercy CLIENT: Chronicle Books PHOTOGRAPHER: Clive Piercy YEAR: 2003

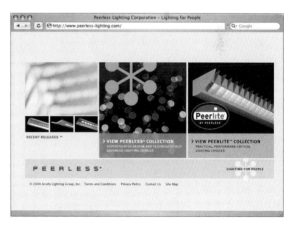

TITLE: Peerless Web Site DESIGNER: Emily Morishita CLIENT: Peerless Lighting PHOTOGRAPHER: Various YEAR: 2004

TITLE: Primary Color DESIGNER: Clive Piercy CLIENT: Primary Color YEAR: 2004

≫

Do you believe you have a style? And how does it manifest?

I have a style, I believe. It has been described as simple, strong, elegant, and witty (sometimes). I work in the mainstream and approach our work traditionally, but always try to put a spin on whatever solutions we come up with.

Must a studio have its own accent to survive?

No. Not necessarily. But the good ones must.

As partners, did you collaborate on work, or were you separate but equal?

I was the creative director. I worked on the front end of virtually all of the jobs that came in, and then with the various designers at the studio, I worked on the implementation of those assignments. I also had a number of clients/accounts that I did everything for, myself. My former partner, Michael, was the operations director, and he kept the studio running smoothly. He was also a designer and had a number of clients that he worked exclusively with.

What do you look for when you hire designers?

It's the most important word in my working vocabulary: S-O-U-L.

TITLE: AIGA
DESIGNER: Clive Piercy
CLIENT: AIGA National
PHOTOGRAPHER: Jeremy
Samuelson ILLUSTRATORS:
Various YEAR: 2003

Making and Thinking

Partner, AdamsMorioka, Los Angeles, California

>> **What are the changes in practice you have seen and experienced since you began?**

We started AdamsMorioka during the recession of the 1990s. At that time, we took a Modernist approach to less is more and sharing the responsibility of the success of the work by collaborating with our clients. At the time, design was "mysterious" and the designer was considered an "artist." Now designers consider themselves "strategists" that position and brand companies.

How did you decide to become a graphic designer?

I'm the youngest of three girls. My older sisters were not only high achievers, but were also articulate debaters. Even to this day, I don't think I can get my point across orally, so I turned to graphic design to help create a "voice" for myself. From an early age my parents were influential in forming my opinions about composition and style. In my senior year in high school, my older sister, Marian, suggested that I consider graphic design.

Did you have specific training?

After attending San Jose State for a couple years, I realized that design was not only about being good, but being able to execute great ideas with great talent. I searched out several schools and

THE ACADEMY
OF MOTION PICTURE ARTS AND SCIENCES

TITLE: AMPAS Identity and Academy Awards Poster CLIENT: Academy of Motion Picture Arts and Sciences DESIGNERS: Monica Schlaug, Sean Adams, Doyald Young CREATIVE DIRECTORS: Sean Adams, Noreen Morioka ILLUSTRATOR/PHOTOGRAPHER: Doyald Young YEAR: 2009

>>

chose CalArts. Since I felt I had the skills to execute ideas, I wanted to be in an environment that taught me to think conceptually. CalArts was extremely challenging and the teaching squad was intense: Lorraine Wild, Laurie Haycock, Scott Makela, Ed Fella, Jeff Keedy, and Lou Danziger.

If you are serious about becoming a designer, it is important to understand that our profession is based on pedigree and the school you choose will be the start of building that reputation.

What is the biggest challenge you face regarding design in this new digital environment?

I love technology. I wish I had more time to take in more.

How important is typography in what you do?

Typography is one of the keystones to great work. Educating yourself to the history, usage, structure of typography is the divide of the professional and the amateur. Then again, I'm still studying typography.

Given the current economic climate and technological shifts, what is in the future for graphic design?

We no longer can be about "making," but need to forward our profession's reputation to include "thinking," "strategic positioning," "data analysis," and most of all "business acumen." We need not be enslaved by business, but lead it.

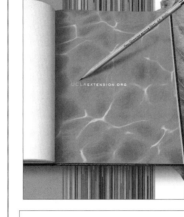

TITLE: UCLA Executive Education Custom Brochure Cover CLIENT: UCLA Executive Education DESIGNER: Monica Schlaug CREATIVE DIRECTOR: Noreen Morioka YEAR: 2009

TITLE: UCLA Extension Fall 2001 Catalog Cover CLIENT: UCLA Extension DESIGNER/ CREATIVE DIRECTOR: Noreen Morioka COMPANY: AdamsMorioka YEAR: 2001

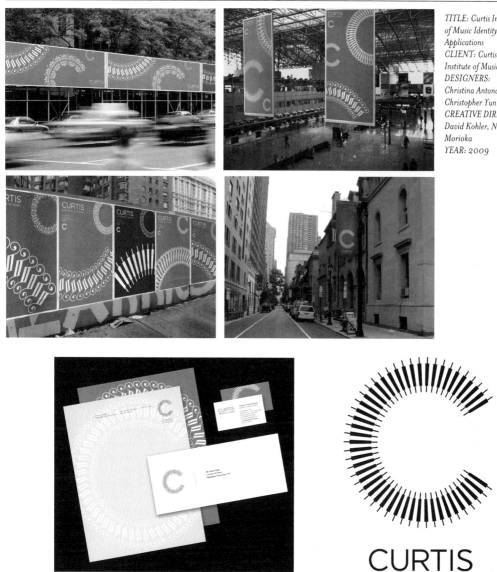

TITLE: *Curtis Institute of Music Identity and Applications*
CLIENT: *Curtis Institute of Music*
DESIGNERS: *Christina Antonopoulos, Christopher Yun*
CREATIVE DIRECTORS: *David Kohler, Noreen Morioka*
YEAR: *2009*

CURTIS
INSTITUTE OF MUSIC

TITLE: Sundance—Sundance Film Festival 2004 Poster, Sundance Film Festival 2007 Poster, Sundance Channel Outloud Poster 2003 CLIENTS: Sundance Institute, Sundance Channel DESIGNERS: 2004 Poster - Volker Dürre, Cynthia Jacquette; 2007 Poster - Volker Dürre, Monica Schlaug, Chris Taillon Outloud Poster - Noreen Morioka CREATIVE DIRECTORS: Sean Adams, Noreen Morioka ILLUSTRATOR (2004 Poster): Robert Sherrill YEARS: 2004,2007, 2003

TITLE: Philip B DESIGNERS: Noreen Morioka, Volker Dürre CLIENT: Philip B Hair Care YEAR: 1998

TITLE: USC Viewbook Cover CLIENT: University of Southern California DESIGNER: Christopher Taillon CREATIVE DIRECTORS: Noreen Morioka, Sean Adams YEAR: 2006-2007

TITLE: Meat Poster Japanese Meat CLIENT: Self DESIGNER/ CREATIVE DIRECTOR/ ILLUSTRATOR/PHOTOGRAPHER: Noreen Morioka YEAR: 2009

Designy and Illustrative

Principal, El Jefe Design, Derwood, Maryland

>> **How long have you had your own studio?**

El Jefe Design has functioned in one form or another since 2003 when I started at the School of Visual Arts in NYC. But according to the IRS, I did not become an "official" company until 2006.

What are the changes in practice you have seen and experienced since you began?

In my work with rock posters I am amazed at the change from "poster as advertisement for show" to "POSTER as merchandise to sell at show." A few years ago a poster was used primarily to advertise a show and notify the public that their new favorite band was coming to town. The poster would be hung in the venue, around town, possibly hung on lamp posts (if your city wouldn't arrest you for it), and distributed as a JPEG on the Internet. It was possible to sell a few posters at the shows and the bands did not mind as it was cool for them to see their name on the paper and get a few for keepsakes. Now with the rise and popularity of concert posters many bands see the potential of posters as money makers. Some bands no longer want the posters used as advertising and even ask that the poster not be displayed or mentioned before the show.

How have these changes impacted your work?

The biggest change is that I now have to produce something that

TITLE: My Morning Jacket—DC CLIENT: My Morning Jacket ART DIRECTOR/ ILLUSTRATOR: Jeffrey Everett YEAR: 2008

TITLE: My Morning Jacket—PA CLIENT: My Morning Jacket ART DIRECTOR/ILLUSTRATOR: Jeffrey Everett YEAR: 2008

TITLE: Devo - Q: Are We Not Men? Show Poster CLIENT: DEVO DESIGNER/ART DIRECTOR: Jeffrey Everett PHOTOGRAPHER: IStock.com YEAR: 2009

TITLE: Devo - Freedom of Choice Show Poster– CLIENT: DEVO DESIGNER/ART DIRECTOR: Jeffrey Everett PHOTOGRAPHER: IStock.com YEAR: 2009

>>

will sell—that people will desire and spend their cold hard cash on! Some designers think that doing concert posters must be easy as there are few guidelines to be followed (actual quote from a former boss: "It is so easy doing posters 'cause you can do anything you want.") On the contrary, having limitless possibilities and options is the most daunting situation of all as there is nothing to serve as a guideline.

Would you say that you have a particular style or character to your design?

I don't know if I can define my style. I try to be creative and make something individual for each client. Some pieces look more "designy" and some look illustrative. Some pieces rely on heavy concepts and inside themes to drive the design yet some other pieces use skulls and sexiness. I would say that

I try to make each piece fun and something that can be hung on a wall and stared at for years.

What about graphic design is the most challenging for you?

Being authentic is always tough. Not in the sense of telling the truth but making sure that what I do is serving my clients and myself well, being honest to myself and family and focusing on what is best for everyone. I don't want to hack out some work for a paycheck—which I am sure *everyone* has been guilty of on occasion—but I really want to do work that suits me and that does not burn me out. I once had a boss who held up a Design Annual and went around asking which pieces were cool or not. She had lost touch with her own design sensibilities and was so desperate to stay "relevant" that she became

dishonest with herself. I never want to be like that. I figure when that happens I will go back to working at a bookstore.

What are the projects that most satisfy your aesthetic sense?

I get excited when I work with a client who gives me a lot to be inspired by. My posters are truly a collaboration between two artists—designer and musician—I just happen to be working off the band's imagery. The more compelling the music and the richer the lyrics, the more it satisfies me to find that one concept that fans will pop for. Bands like Wilco who take an active part in the design make me happy because I know that they appreciate what I am producing and want to get the best piece out of me. It is all about mutual respect.

TITLE: *Atmosphere* CLIENT: *The Nightclub 9:30* ART DIRECTOR/ ILLUSTRATOR: *Jeffrey Everett* YEAR: *2008*

TITLE: *The Lucha Library* CLIENT: *El Jefe Design/Max X. G. Everett* ART DIRECTOR/ ILLUSTRATOR: *Jeffrey Everett* YEAR: *2008*

How do you feel education has changed in the past decade?

I graduated from college with a BA roughly a decade ago (American University, Class of 1999). I was taught how to draft and comp by hand and how to use a computer to flesh out concepts.

I knew how to make a book, screen print flat colors, ink a logo with Plaka Paint, and become a samurai with an Xacto knife. I could also create style sheets in Quark, trace a scanned logo in Illustrator, and tweak photos in Photoshop. I was trained specifically for Print design and felt I could master any aspect in that world.

Now students start right on computers with little-to-no hand training. I am amazed that I have seniors who have never comped boards or used an Xacto. They are more students who are "jacks-of-all trades" where they know enough of print and Web to get a job from Craigslist, but not enough to be truly knowledgeable in one field. I do believe students need to be able to talk and design in multiple fields but I don't think four years is enough time to master both Web and print. Each is a highly demanding and complex field with many aspects of study that cannot be fully taught in a mere four years.

What, in this current technological and economic climate, does the future hold for you specifically, and graphic design in general?

I think there will be a bigger turn to hand-done design and that pieces created away from the computer will be sought even more. Whether or not selling design as a product can hold up during a global recession has yet to be seen. With the resurfacing of DIY culture and the rise of sites like gigposters.com and etsy.com people are craving something that is not pixilated. I find that people who collect my posters always appreciate feeling the grit and weight of the paper, enjoy the little printing errors and off registrations, and seeing that an actual person touched each and every piece that goes to the public. Each poster is custom made and individual, no one truly has the same piece. There is a sense of personality and time. Art Chantry said it best, "I don't create art—I create artifacts." You cannot get that from a 72 dpi JPG.

TITLE: A Place to Bury Strangers CLIENT: The Nightclub 9:30 ART DIRECTOR/ILLUSTRATOR: Jeffrey Everett YEAR: 2008

TITLE: The Raveonettes Show Poster CLIENT: The Raveonettes DESIGNER/ILLUSTRATOR/ART DIRECTOR: Jeffrey Everett PHOTOGRAPHER: IStock.com YEAR: 2009

Words and Language

Partner, karlssonwilker inc., New York City

TITLE: Storytime
CLIENT: PUMA
DESIGNERS: Hjalti
Karlsson, Jan Wilker
COMPANY: karlssonwilker
inc. YEAR: 2007

>> **How long have you had your own studio?**

Hjalti Karlsson and myself started *karlssonwilker inc.* in late 2000, which seems like a different lifetime now.

Are you happy with what you do?

The answer is easy, and it's a definite yes. We are enjoying every single day we have in the studio, where we talk, work, and laugh a lot.

Are you happy with what is going on in the design field?

My view of the "design field" is quite limited; we like to live in our little studio bubble. So with this in mind I would answer *yes* and *no*. The *yes* is for all the small studios out there that stake out their claims and produce fantastic forward-thinking work; the *no* is for all the designers out there who feel ashamed for being designers and not life-saving doctors or full-time environmentalists—have a little confidence, otherwise it's time to change.

TITLE: Hugo Boss Prize CLIENT: Guggenheim Museum DESIGNERS: Hjalti Karlsson, Fabienne Hess, Jan Wilker COMPANY: karlssonwilker inc. YEAR: 2006

What are the changes in practice you have seen and experienced since you began?

Very small design studios or even one-man-shows are not only starting points or little seeds to grow from anymore, they are sustainable, desirable ends in themselves. What actually changed form-wise, I have no idea, although I wouldn't think too much.

TITLE: TIME *magazine*
YEAR: 2008 CLIENT:
TIME, Inc. DESIGNERS:
Hjalti Karlsson, Jan Wilker
COMPANY: karlssonwilker
inc. YEAR: 2006

How have these changes impacted your work?
Since I stated above that there weren't (m)any changes regarding *form*, I don't know how to answer this question.

Would you say that you have a particular style or character to your design? If so, how would you define it?

Yes, we do have a particular style or character. We are interested in words and language, since English is both our second language and we had to learn it fast and on the go. Furthermore, we use humor in our work whenever possible; it makes our days less stressful and keeps us curious and exploring.

What about graphic design is the most challenging for you?
It has been most fascinating from the beginning: To create something that surprises yourself, and then learning from it why.

What are the projects that most satisfy your aesthetic sense?
The projects that communicate more feeling than facts seem to allow more space for aesthetic exploration.

How important is type and typography in what you do?
With us, there were times in the past when type had an inferior role toward the image. Overall I would say that although our education in type and typography was very good, we became very sloppy in the "entertainment-focused" New York (*en contraire* to something like "craftsmanship-admiration").

What, in this current technological and economic climate, does the future hold for you specifically, and graphic design in general?
Hjalti and I are still floating around, without a specific long-term goal. We take on the jobs that get thrown our way, and we try to do them as good as we can. If that stops one day, whatever the reason, we will do something else. And what will happen to graphic design in general? I wouldn't believe it if someone told me.

TITLE: Buildings of Disaster CLIENT: Boym Partners, Inc. DESIGNERS: Hjalti Karlsson, Jan Wilker COMPANY: karlssonwilker inc. YEAR: 2002

TITLE: HATTLER—Visual Cuts CLIENT: HATTLER DESIGNERS: Jan Wilker, Nicole Jacek COMPANY: karlssonwilker inc. YEAR: 2005

>> **How long have you had your own studio?**
We [and partner Colleen Miller] were doing freelance projects together right out of school in 1999 and were also both working full-time at design studios. In 2006, we finally worked up the confidence to start our own studio.

What are the changes in practice you have seen and experienced since you began?
There is a lot less print work than there was in the beginning. Most clients are looking for a very strong digital presence. This is especially true for identity design. Today, most of the identity projects that we take on lead with the Web site and digital communication pieces. This certainly makes sense as a Web site is the most public-facing form of communication that businesses and individuals can have right now. And for the logo, we still need to keep print in mind, however, it's not nearly as necessary as it used to be. Many clients don't even want or need a print component. Rather than having print constraints when creating a logo, we now need to think of possibilities involving motion and interaction.

How have these changes impacted your work?
Technology has had a huge impact on what we do and how we do it. First, it's readily available and affordable, so now, anyone can essentially call themselves a designer

TITLE: Design Jargon: A primer   CLIENT: Chronicle Books   COMPANY: Landers Miller Design

CLIENT: Hackensack Medical Center Announcement/Invitation COMPANY: Landers Miller Design

TITLE: *Becoming a Digital Designer* CLIENT: *John Wiley & Sons* COMPANY: *Landers Miller Design*

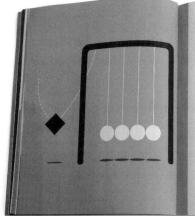

CLIENT: *Street Sweets NY Identity design* COMPANY: *Landers Miller Design*

(and many do). And secondly, the speed at which we need to work is very demanding. We really need to work hard at proving to our clients that hiring us as designers is a valuable investment. We are not simply here to push a mouse around and understand software to get the job done, but that our ideas are really worth something and that we can help them to communicate to their audience or solve their problems beyond making something look nice. More and more, we go into meetings with clients who have their laptops open to something they created in Photoshop and they say they just need us to execute it the right way. We really need to be on top of our game to think quickly and suggest ways that we can improve on what they have done or suggest that the initial idea can be thought through more completely. It's quite clear that the role of a designer is changing very quickly. Now, it's very much about the idea and translating the idea into business speak.

How has the technology impacted the time it takes to do a job?

The speed at which we are asked to work is really a huge difference between working today and when we first started out. With everything being digital, and email being accessible 24/7 from anywhere, clients really expect a lot in a very short period of time. The speed of technology and its availability really keeps us on our toes. This is particularly hard for us, as we prefer to work on something, put it down, and pick it up the next day, fine tune it, and really keep massaging it until we feel right about it. Having to work quickly also has its benefits—it serves as a reminder to stick to the fundamentals of design process by sketching out ideas and really thinking things through before trying to execute them on the computer. We don't want to waste valuable concept time trying to work out ideas on the computer (which can make any idea look better) that aren't truly great ideas. It's very true that you can think of so many more things with a pencil in your hand and a blank piece of paper. The limitations aren't there and the process of knowing how to execute your vision on the computer isn't standing in your way of getting the right idea down. So while technology has had an impact on what we do and how we do it, the fundamentals of design and process have remained very much the same.

Would you say that you have a particular style or character to your design? If so, how would you define it?

No, we don't really have a particular style that we work with, we look at this as being a very positive attribute to our work. One size doesn't fit all. We really let the client's personality define the style that is most appropriate. Every project and client is different, finding the client's voice and establishing a style that matches up best with who they are and what they have to say or who they are trying to communicate to is part of the overall challenge of being a designer. It's also really important to us to find and create solutions that are truly unique to us, mean-

ing a style that we haven't worked in before and that is unique to our client's market.

What about graphic design is the most challenging for you?

Pushing oneself is very difficult to do, standing back and looking at a solution that you have created in an objective manner and really questioning what you have spent a lot of time and energy working on and asking, "Does this solve the problem? Is this solution the best that I can do? Is this truly unique?" It's hard to have to scrap what you have done and start over. Sometimes it's the best thing in the world and ultimately leads to a great solution, but other times, especially when you have worked really hard or felt really strongly about a solution, and to have to let it go, it's a very tough pill to swallow.

Is design universal or personal?

Design is very subjective and personal; you have opinions and likes, the client has feelings about what they are seeing and then both parties are trying to figure out what would work best for the audience. As a designer your job is to be very aware of and contribute to visual culture. When a client who may not be as involved in that same culture or understanding questions our experience, it's frustrating. It's an important lesson to learn that everyone is working toward a common goal, that it's not "us versus them."

What are the projects that most satisfy your aesthetic sense?

The best and most exciting projects

are those where a client has established a niche in a market, or enters into a market, where design has not really been used to leverage the business. The projects seem much more wide open with more possibilities. Having limitations is a great thing, it helps to get the project finished, but sometimes, it's great to not have to worry about what the competition is doing. It's almost like we get to set the bar for how design is used.

How important is type and typography in what you do?

Type is everything. Even though the whole technology thing is making it easier for everyone to have access to the same tools that we use, having an understanding of the power of type is still certainly one of those skills that will always separate a designer from a d-ziner or someone who "does design on the side."

We deal with a lot of clients who simply do not have a budget for imagery—illustration or photography—and this is where having a real solid foundation in type can make all the difference in the world. It's very rewarding when a client recognizes the impact that really well-set and considered typography can have on a project. A lot of times once they see beautiful type, they realize that what is said will actually be read and suddenly content does really matter!

In this current technological and economic climate, what does the future hold for you specifically, and graphic design in general?

Economically, businesses are being more careful about their decisions. They want to be confident that hiring a designer or a studio is going to be *the* solution. Designers need to be able to speak the language of business and they need to be fluent in it. Talking about fonts and colors, it's a waste of time. CEOs and marketing managers don't want to hear it. They want to hear ideas that will keep their business alive and running ahead of the curve.

We try to immerse ourselves in designing solid user experiences for our client's clients. We are constantly trying to learn more about human behavior to help solve the poor experiences that exist, especially with evolving digital technologies that are so prevalent in our society. If we can understand the interactive products that people want to use, we as designers can map and connect that experience in practical ways. Graphic design, information architecture, Web design—they are coming together into the new realm of interaction design and we need to be a part of it!

CLIENT: KIWI *Magazine* PHOTOGRAPHER: Michael Brian COMPANY: *Landers Miller Design*

CLIENT: *School of Visual Arts MFA in Social Documentary Film Web site* COMPANY: *Landers Miller Design*

CLIENT: *Kidfresh Project Identity* DESIGNER: *Addis Creson* COMPANY: *Landers Miller Design*

Thriving on Differences

Principal, Giampietro+Smith, New York City

>> **What common interests caused you and your studio partner, Kevin Smith, to join forces?**
The interests we share are probably the same interests that many design collaborators share: a love of typography, a love of books and bookmaking, and a shared interest in design as a tool for learning about the world and about our collaborators. But while many designers may share these interests, we are probably partners today because of complementary skill sets, similar ways of working, cohesive stylistic sensibilities, and common objectives for our practice. Basically, we just work together really well.

Who has what strengths and weaknesses?
While we're very similar in our tastes—the kinds of design that inspire us, the kinds of projects we want to execute, even the kinds of music we like to listen to during the day—we're somewhat different in what we do well, what we struggle with, and what we enjoy doing most. Our practice thrives on these differences, and it makes for a working experience that is much more diversified than a sole proprietorship would be in either of our cases. Generally, in any situation, one of us is more technically savvy, one is more process-oriented, one is more visually obsessed, and one is happier than the other to answer the phone.

Do you plan on staying small, or is growth in your future?

TITLE: AIGA Web Site Poster DESIGNERS: Giampietro+Smith CLIENT: AIGA YEAR: 2004

TITLE: 50 Sound Stories + 466 Decibal Readings DESIGNERS: Giampietro+Smith CLIENT: Design Institute at the University of Minnesota YEAR: 2003

TITLE: A Force for Change: The Global Fund at 30 Months DESIGNERS: Giampietro+Smith CLIENT: The Global Fund to Fight AIDS, Tuberculosis, and Malaria YEAR: 2004

We see it as able to grow, shrink, bend, and stretch according to the needs of a project and our goals as a partnership. We've never envisioned Giampietro+Smith as a large global studio, but we'd certainly feel comfortable putting together a large team to tackle a large, ambitious project. In terms of goals, we just want to keep making work that's engaging, keep pushing ourselves to take risks and try new things, and keep meeting new people whose projects stimulate and excite us.

What role does a Web site play in your overall studio image?

When we started our studio, a friend told us, wisely, "You won't get any new business through your Web site." He was right and wrong. While no one is going to pull us off Google like a needle in the hay, the next step from a word-of-mouth referral is usually a visit to our site, and we've found that this secondary encounter helps to support what people have already heard. It puts our best foot forward and says, "This is what we're about." Some sites start with a splash page; ours starts with a mission statement. The work is shown clearly, humanely, and in context. We appreciate these qualities in our clients, so we've applied them to our site. In making it, what began as a way to get organized—photographing our best work in the best way possible—became a vision for the kind of practice we wanted to create.

Much of your work is print. Do you see your-selves expanding into other media?

We never frame the discussions we have about our practice around a given medium. We've both been teaching at Parsons, New York, in the Communication Design Department, and we've found the name to be increasingly apt in describing what we do. We're communication designers; we apply design to the communication between our collaborators and the audiences they seek to engage. In doing so, we're not limited to any single medium, which is what makes a life in design very hopeful for us these days.

Is it important to apprentice before going it on your own?

Absolutely. We've been really fortunate in our evolution as designers to work with some of the most inspiring designers around. William Drenttel and Jessica Helfand took a chance on us both and introduced us to one another, and we've found tremendous mentors in Michael Bierut, Janet Froelich, and Patrick Seymour, just to name a few. We've also had great teachers like Bethany Johns, Paul Elliman, and Michael Rock. Design is both a way to structure your thinking and an intricate craft, and as designers we know how important it is to cultivate ourselves in both directions. Our practice is built on the generosity of our mentors, who've taught us everything from how to kern a headline to how to run a small business in New York.

TITLE: *Cindy Sherman: Centerfolds* DESIGN-ERS: *Giampietro+Smith, Stella Bugbee* CLIENT: *Skarstedt Fine Art* YEAR: *2004*

TITLE: *Topic Magazine Food Designers: Giampietro+Smith, Stella Bugbee* CLIENT: *Topic Magazine* YEAR: *2003*

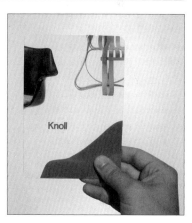

TITLE: *Knoll Space* DESIGNERS: *Giampietro+Smith* Client: *Knoll* YEAR: *2004*

MEDIUM FIRM: BIG COMMITMENT

How do you know when you are ready to graduate from small to medium? For some studios, it just happens: After working on a number of comparatively low-budget jobs, you bid for the big one—and, to your surprise, you get it. Now don't get too nervous yet. Certain reality safeguards are in place. The really big corporation is not going to willy-nilly bestow a multimillion-dollar account on a small studio. But you just may find that the quality of your work is such—and your bid is competitive enough—that you are given the commission for a job or campaign that involves many more components over a longer time span and with a lot more responsibility than you are used to. Here are your options regarding growth.

1. Stay small: Use this opportunity to test whether expanding the size of your studio is viable. Hire freelancers to work on the big job while maintaining design control. Refrain from taking on too many other large jobs at this time.

2. Seize the moment: Use this opportunity to expand in a responsible way. Budget what it will cost to hire additional staff, buy or rent additional hardware, and otherwise take advantage of a good cash flow to increase the studio's potential.

Incidentally, sometimes small studios are asked to bid on a larger project, but the principal does not feel that the studio is adequate for the needs of this client. There is no shame in turning down an invitation to submit a proposal.

A medium-sized firm includes a principal (or partners) and an average of fifteen employees (including senior and junior designers, production personnel, receptionist, traffic manager, and probably a full-time accounts person or bookkeeper). Obviously, how the size of a design studio or firm is measured is not necessarily comparable to other professions. In graphic design, however, maintaining a payroll of around fifteen full-time employees as well as a few freelancers suggests a respectable client base

A MEDIUM-SIZED FIRM ATTRACTS CLIENTS THAT A SMALL FIRM DOES NOT, WHICH MEANS HIGHER BUDGETS, MORE VISIBLE ACCOUNTS, AND, AS A RESULT, PERHAPS GREATER SATISFACTION.

and a creditable cash flow.

Designers who run medium-sized firms are able to hire administrators and need not turn their attention exclusively to management; a good office manager (or managing art director) can efficiently run the day-to-day operation and allow the principal to continue to focus on designing. But client meetings are one of the key responsibilities for a principal or proprietor of any size design business. For the small studio principal, meetings can eat up considerable portions of the day, so multiply that for the medium-size firm, which by its nature must accept more clients to meet increased overhead. Clients who engage medium firms are usually not content to work directly with the senior or junior designer on substantive matters, which means the principal spends increasingly more time managing the overall commission than actually designing it. While this is not always the case, it is probable that the balance of time expended between business and design will tilt toward the former.

On the positive side, a medium-sized firm attracts clients that a small firm does not, which means higher budgets, more visible accounts, and, as a result, perhaps greater satisfaction. For the principal or proprietor who savors the art of business as much as the art of design, this structure is a good way to wed those interests. It may also serve as another stepping stone to a still larger business.

Using the Very Best

Principal, Remolino, New York City and Buenos Aires

≫ How long have you had your own studio?

Remolino opened for business in Buenos Aires in 2004 and then two years ago they started to win business in New York. I officially joined Remolino in January 2009 and launched their office here in NYC.

What are the changes in practice you have seen and experienced since you began?

Clients are obviously a lot more cost conscious. Before they even walk through the door in New York or Buenos Aires they have a figure of how much they can spend on design and there's little room for negotiation. The challenge has been to convince clients that intelligent investment in good design today will reap rewards tomorrow.

Is this across the board in print and Web design?

Most of the projects we work on are Web-based. Some clients have produced print pieces but the majority are focused on interactive work.

How have these changes impacted your work?

The immediate thing we did when budgets fell was to analyze how we could streamline all of our working practices in New York and Buenos Aires so that the lower budgets would not affect the high standard of work we want to produce.

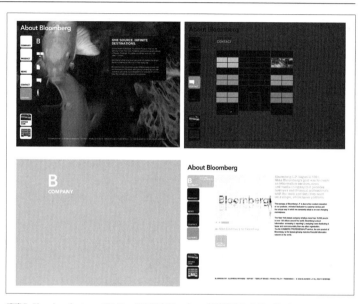

*TITLE: Bloomberg Corporate Web Site CLIENT: Bloomberg DESIGNER: Delfina Venditti
ART DIRECTOR: Raquel Tudela PROGRAMMERS: Tomas Lucadamo YEAR: 2008*

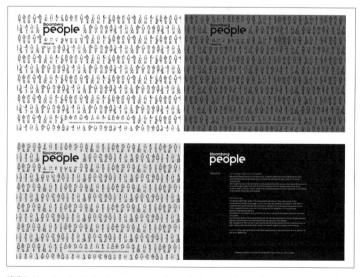

*TITLE: Bloomberg People Conferences Web Site CLIENT: Bloomberg Ventures DESIGNER/ ILLUSTRA-
TOR: Delfina Venditti PROGRAMMER: Tomas Lucadamo ART DIRECTOR: Raquel Tudela YEAR: 2009*

≫

How do you do this?

It's made us get out there and research a lot more—for instance, we now know we're using the best printer for the job, the best t-shirt manufacturer, the best bloggers, the best marketing companies, and so on. This then leads to new work and new projects as you become known for doing more with less.

Would you say that you have a particular style or character to your design? If so, how would you define it?

Well, firstly you have to understand that it's a challenge to put this into words, as it has always been about how my work makes me feel rather than the actual font, color, image, etc. but let's try… I guess my Latin American roots have influenced me. I like design that has a hand-made feel. Sometimes it's about cutting and pasting—real cutting and pasting. I like to bring humor, an edge, I tend to like things that sometimes verge on being cheeky, a bit offensive, maybe—these are the kinds of things that come through in my work.

What about graphic design is the most challenging for you?

The copy. Although I am a designer, I love copy. It usually frustrates me because I am searching for words when I design, that's why I need to work with writers who not only give me what I need but also understand where I am coming from.

What are the projects that most satisfy your aesthetic sense?

I like integrated projects that go beyond what is thought of as traditional design. We work with

TITLE: Home Hotel Branding CLIENT: Home Hotel DESIGNER/ ILLUSTRATOR: Delfina Venditti ART DIRECTOR: Raquel Tudela YEAR: 2008

clients who have enabled us to take a holistic approach to their brief and not only produce online, print, and premium pieces but also come up with the name of their building development or restaurant. These projects tend to be the most satisfying as you are involved at every level and can really work alongside the client throughout the process.

How important is type and typography in what you do?

The type can help me deliver the tone in the same way the actual words can. We have learned a lot of what translates well across multimedia and print, so typography is always a major consideration in our projects.

What, in this current technological and economic climate, does the future hold for you specifically, and graphic design in general?

It's no surprise that the majority of design projects now involve online work, so we have made sure Remolino has a very strong group of Web designers and programmers. Our graphic designers have become Web designers in many ways, they still create the logos, the layouts, and many pieces of the project, but they have to work in tandem with programmers to produce the best solutions. Clients approach us to help them with their branding, they have an interest in getting it right, and we need to embrace these people, work alongside them and steer them toward the best solutions for their business. Now, more than ever, the world needs intelligent integrated design.

TITLE: EME Hotel Branding
CLIENT: Eme Hotel
DESIGNER: Delfina Venditti ART DIRECTORS: Raquel Tudela, Paco Savio
YEAR: July 2008

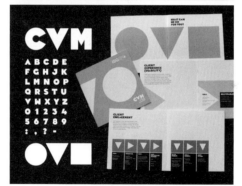

TITLE: NYC Service Report
CLIENT: City Hall
DESIGNER: Pilar Gomez
ART DIRECTOR: Raquel Tudela
YEAR: April 2009

TITLE: World Bank Brochure
CLIENT: Client Value Management, a World Bank Division DESIGNERS: Delfina Venditti, Raquel Tudela ART DIRECTOR: Raquel Tudela
YEAR: June 2009

TITLE: GIK Notebook
CLIENT: Remolino
DESIGNER: Natalia Avalos
ILLUSTRATOR: Delfina Venditti
YEAR: 2008

Do-It-All Approach

Principals, RED, Brooklyn, New York

>> **How long have you had your own studio?**

SAM: In October of 2006.

STUART: Actually, we started in September but Sam went on a beer-tasting tour of Germany that month so he doesn't remember anything before October.

What are the changes in practice (and form) you have seen and experienced since you began?

SAM: The do-it-all approach to design continues to grow. More and more firms have capabilities in Web, motion, print, packaging, signage, etc. A large part of that comes from technological availability, but I think it's also a growing interest in designers to apply their thought processes to different media.

STUART: Definitely true. We've expanded our services since we started. On the flip side, we've become more aware of the areas we work in and tried to focus our expertise in specific markets. At first, we wanted to be everything to everyone, but we realized that clients really want to work with people who understand their business.

How have these changes impacted your work?

STUART: Expanding our capabilities has definitely given us more confidence, especially when we're working on a branding project where the client needs us to produce a wide range of materi-

TITLE: *Safe: In Our Own Words Invitation*
CLIENT: *Safe Horizon* DESIGNER: *Stuart Rogers* YEAR: *2008*

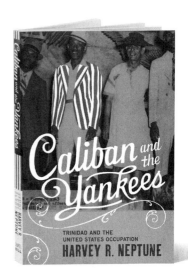

TITLE: *Caliban and the Yankees Book Jacket*
CLIENT: *UNC Press* DESIGNERS: *Stuart Rogers, Sam Eckersley* YEAR: *2007*

TITLE: *The New Group 07/08 Season* CLIENT: *The New Group*
DESIGNER: *Jane Huschka* ART DIRECTORS: *Sam Eckersley, Stuart Rogers*
PHOTOGRAPHER: *Monique Carboni* YEAR: *2007*

TITLE: Passing Strange Poster
CLIENT: The Public Theater
DESIGNER: Jane Huschka
ART DIRECTORS: Sam Eckersley,
Stuart Rogers YEAR: 2007

TITLE: MFA-Z Encyclopedia CLIENT: School
of Visual Arts MFA Design DESIGNERS: Stuart
Rogers, Brian E. Smith, Kirsten Sorten, Randy
J. Hunt, Sam Eckersley ART DIRECTORS:
Steve Heller, Lita Talarico, Esther Ro-Schofield.
YEAR: 2009

TITLE: Brooklyn Food
Conference Campaign
CLIENT: Brooklyn Food
Conference
DESIGNERS: Stuart
Rogers, Sam Eckersley.
YEAR: 2009

als. Once you do away with the mystery of producing something intimidating, like the front of house signage for a show, you begin to have more and more confidence in your ideas because you know they will work.

Would you say that you have a particular style or character to your design?
STUART: Because our work typically needs to reach a mass audience it usually feels accessible, and our ideas are straightforward. We don't do cerebral or abstract. If there is a continuous visual style to our work it's defined by our shared preference for things that feel rich and textural so our solutions usually have some sort of layered quality.
SAM: We love nothing more than to get away from the computer and get our hands dirty. You should see the mess our intern is making right now.

What about graphic design is the most challenging for you?
SAM: The client presentation. There is a real skill in getting clients to approve your designs and so much of it comes down to your ability to read people. I love the process, but it's almost always a challenge.
STUART: I completely agree. Persuading clients is the most challenging part of design. Like Sam says, you need to read people and know what and what not to say. The client presentation is where so much can be lost or gained. We have been guilty in the past of winging it and that rarely works out. It's much better to prepare and practice so you feel totally confident going into the meeting.

≫

What are the projects that most satisfy your aesthetic sense?

SAM: Posters and book covers offer a really nice playing field to get ideas across. It's all right there for the audience to figure out.

STUART: I agree. I also love doing identities because there are so many applications like banners, Web sites, and signage. I like seeing it all come together.

How important is type and typography in what you do?

SAM: It's what the game is all about. You can get so much across in the way you lay out type.

STUART: Without type we would be mediocre artists at best.

What, in this current technological and economic climate, does the future hold for you specifically, and graphic design in general?

STUART: In the short term, sadly, it means working twice as hard for half the money, especially with the types of clients we have in publishing and nonprofit. In the long term, we need to be more deliberate about the type of work we do so that we attach ourselves to growing industries. There are amazing new challenges in our field and the designers who set aside the time to research what's emerging will be in the best position in the future.

SAM: Yes, in certain ways, this economic slow-down has been a blessing in disguise for us. It's taught us to keep an eye out for these growing industries, and to never get too comfortable with the type of work we currently do.

TITLE: Free Night of Theater Campaign CLIENT: Theatre Communications Group DESIGNER: Jane Huschka ART DIRECTOR: Stuart Rogers, Sam Eckersley. YEAR: 2008

TITLE: RED Self-promotional Card DESIGNER: Sam Eckersley YEAR: 2009

LARGE FIRM: CAN'T GET ANY BIGGER

Most designers prefer designing to business and, therefore, choose to limit the size of their studios and firms. This deliberately small type of business forms the bedrock of the graphic design profession. Nevertheless, in the current age of multi- and interdisciplinary design, many ambitious designers have either solely or with partners branched out into areas that demand large support staffs and teams. Few designers actually enter the profession with the goal of building a megafirm because too many variables are unknown. Nevertheless, circumstance and ambition do combine to make large firms happen. At times, before you know what is happening, a client base is in place and mergers with other disciplines are possible.

A large firm essentially comprises a principal or partners (two or more) with a staff of over fifteen and as many as several hundred. Some large firms are exclusively domestic; others are international (with offices in other cities). The infrastructure of a large firm is as hierarchical as any corporation, from the principals, who guide the design identity and philosophy, to the senior designers, art directors, and project managers, who work on specific projects, to the technical, production, and bullpen staff, who manufacture the work. Depending on whether or not a principal micro- or macromanages, a large firm has various levels of oversight. But it is the principal who must represent the firm to existing and potential clients.

Large firms usually are not specialized. Some do focus their attention, especially on multimedia, but they may also include print, advertising, and other ancillary components to provide a fuller service. Others may be devoted to, say, retail product package design, but may

FEW DESIGNERS ACTUALLY ENTER THE PROFESSION WITH THE GOAL OF BUILDING A MEGAFIRM BECAUSE TOO MANY VARIABLES ARE UNKNOWN.

also include a branding division that involves multimedia. Still others may cater to Fortune 500 corporations, with emphasis on corporate identity, but include a division that handles, say, industrial or corporate films or Web sites. Most large firms are general in outlook. Some even go beyond today's fairly broad definition of graphic design and integrate architecture, interior design, or environmental design into what is offered to clients.

The division of labor, or how assignments are apportioned, in large firms varies as much as the firms themselves. When the firm is a sole proprietorship, the work may be assigned to individual project managers by the principal or the managing designer. In certain partnerships, each partner commands a subsection of the firm, responsible for its own clients and billing. In other partnerships, each partner dips into the common well. There are no standard rules that govern this.

For the average reader of this book, starting a large design firm is not going to happen now or ten years from now, but working in one is probable and advancing in one is possible. Rather than be concerned with how to reach the top rung on the business ladder, it is prudent to address how to join a large firm and learn what working in such an environment has to offer. It may be the best launch pad for opening your own business.

TITLE: *Design Ignites Change Promotional Button* CLIENT: *Adobe Youth Voices and Worldstudio* DESIGNER: *Luba Lukova* ART DIRECTOR: *Mark Randall* YEAR: 2009

Radical Maturity in the Market

Principal, Spunk Design Machine, Minneapolis, Minnesota

>> **What are the changes in practice you have seen and experienced since you began?**

The industry barriers for entry from design discipline to discipline have evaporated. The clients are hip to the fact that if you, as a designer, have a creative voice, you have the ability to speak in a range of media—motion, interior, print, fashion, etc. It is their expectation that you, as a designer with a "Capital D," have something of value to say. This is an incredibly valuable change in the market. What this means for a creative designer is that you have to continually reinvest into your creative voice. I have returned to school to learn new skills three times as a creative director to better speak to my clients' needs.

How have these changes impacted your work?

It's blown open the doors to possibility. As I type this, I'm currently directing the rebranding of a local architect, a Middle Eastern bank with a large motion component, an international bank with a full range of media applications, a fair trade banana project where we are silk screening banana costumes in our basement print shop right now, and a new ID for a publishing company that will have a large interior design component. It used to be only the renaissance men and women

TITLE: *Redux Pictures: Promotion Notepad*   CLIENT: *Marcel Saba/Jasmine DeFoore*
DESIGNER/ILLUSTRATOR: *Justin Martinez* CREATIVE DIRECTORS: *Ben Pagel, Jeff Johnson*
PHOTOGRAPHERS: *Various Redux Represented Photographers* WRITER: *Ben Pagel* YEAR: *2008*

at places like Eames design studio that were expected to do this kind of cross-disciplinary work—now it's the norm, and that is incredibly positive. Remember, we run a boutique studio with offices in New York City and Minneapolis, and to have that level of design thinking be the *expectation* is a radical maturity in the market.

Would you say that you have a particular style or character to your design?

A style is a straight jacket that your clients don't deserve. The client has a unique problem, it deserves an unrestricted solution. That being said, I think you could look at our work and see some sensibilities that show up over time. That's an asset in my thinking.

What about graphic design is the most challenging for you?

Making sure that the business side of our design is respected. We expect that our design company is financially rewarded for our creative vision. Not surprising to anyone, most designers suck rocks when it comes to the nuts and bolts of running a business. After thirteen years, I still am learning the ropes on this. We get better year after year. By the time I die, I will be great at it.

What are the projects that most satisfy your aesthetic sense?

I would put our recent rebranding of the University of Minnesota College of Design at the top of this list. It has the spirit of transformation that I feel is key to the design process. I would also put our recent work for the NYC-based Redux Pictures on the top. Getting some surprising and engaging design in relation to pure image work was a challenge, and I love where this project landed. I tend to have a love affair with every project we do. The most recent love affair is our Fairly Traded Banana project with the great folks at Equal Exchange. After our research we discovered that the banana is the world's funniest fruit. Nobody "Goes Apples" or "Goes Oranges,".... They "Go Bananas!"

How important is type and typography in what you do?

We spend a ridiculous amount of money on new typography. Both type we author and code for our clients, and new fonts we buy from agencies like Fountain, House, Chank, Youworkforthem, Test Pilot Collective, and Process Type Foundry. The world of emergent type is vast and incredibly healthy. There is, of course, a ton of crap being made as well. As we look for the most unique solution to our clients' work, having this range of foundries working and producing today is an incredible advantage.

>>

TITLE: *University of Minnesota College of Design: New Brand Identify Materials* CLIENT: *Laura Weber, Tom Fisher* SENIOR DESIGNER: *Steve Marth* DESIGNERS: *Andrew Voss, Jeff Johnson, Peet Fetsch, Ross Bruggink, Justin Martinez, Lucas Richards* CREATIVE DIRECTORS: *Andrew Voss, Jeff Johnson, Ben Pagel* ILLUSTRATORS: *Steve Marth, Ross Bruggink, Andrew Voss* PHOTOGRA-PHERS: *Steve Marth, Ross Bruggink, Andrew Voss, Ben Pagel* WRITER: *Ben Pagel* YEAR: *2008*

What, in this current technological and economic climate, does the future hold for you specifically, and graphic design in general?

It's awesome. Yes, there is a radical constriction of capital that we are experiencing right now—and our shop has certainly felt the pinch. But take into consideration the larger picture on how designers have the advantage in the emerging market. The traditional way for manufacturers and business scions to speak to their markets revolved around the advertising model of distraction.

Print ads, commercials, billboards, etc. It was a constant stream of interruptions in what people *really* want to do. Because of tech like Tivo, iTunes, Craigslist, XM, etc., there are just too many great interruptions. Consider that the juggernaut of cash—the classified ad—was destroyed by one Web site: Craigslist. This has sent newspaper revenue into a free-fall and crushed that medium. If you build your information business on the ability to sell used goods, you have a seriously flawed model. Designers are trained in the arts of seduction, distinction, and reward. Those skills will be in higher and higher demand as the decades move on. The same manufacturers and business scions will want to speak inside the realm of commercial speech. We, as designers, have the distinct advantage here.

Partner, with Randy Hunt, Worldstudio, New York City

>> **How long have you had your own studio?**

We started talking about the idea for Worldstudio in 1993 and by 1995 we were up and running. We launched Worldstudio Foundation first and then shortly thereafter started the for-profit side of the business Worldstudio, Inc.

What are the changes in practice you have seen and experienced since you began?

Ideas were always critical to the profession but they are more important now. Before everyone became computer savvy, clients relied on designers because they could not do design work themselves. Now that the secretary can produce a newsletter on his or her computer—and take the photos with a digital camera—design has been de-valued. More and more I see our clients thinking "gee, if we do this ourselves think of all the money we'll save." What they still can't do is "design think," they can only use design to implement a solution—and usually a really bad solution. They do not have the ability to use design thinking to come up with the ideas to solve a problem effectively.

How have these changes impacted your work?

It has forced us to be more strategic in what we offer our clients. We no longer just provide design services but we pitch ourselves as marketers and design thinkers. We develop robust solutions for our clients, many of which do not even

TITLE: *Design Ignites Change Logo* CLIENT: *Adobe Youth Voices and Worldstudio* DESIGNER: *Nina Mettler* ART DIRECTOR: *Mark Randall* YEAR: *2009*

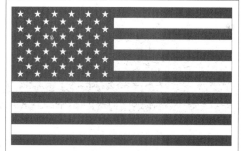

TITLE: *Pride Flag Redesign* CLIENT: *Studio 360* CONCEPT: *Mark Randall* YEAR: *2009*

TITLE: *Pride Flag Redesign* CLIENT: *Studio 360* DESIGNER: *Nina Mettler* ART DIRECTOR: *Mark Randall.* YEAR: *2009* Over 3,000 people voted on the Studio 360 Web site for their favorite new pride flag design. The white flag with gradient rainbow ring was the clear winner.

>>

contain traditional design elements like a brochure or poster. The emphasis is on strategy and ideas first, which are then supported by design.

Your work is devoted to social advocacy. Has this been a difficult road?

In a word, yes. But it's a road that we gladly travel since it is driven by passion and a belief in what we do. When we started in the mid-1990s, many in the design community would make pandering comments about those "do-gooders" over at Worldstudio. Now that social responsibility is all the rage—and rightly so—it has become easier for us. People see value in what we bring to the table. From our vantage point the time is right for the creative community to step up to the plate to really make a difference—and to make a living doing it.

How does graphic design impact society?

I like to think of graphic design in terms of the butterfly effect—which is about the notion of sensitive dependence in chaos theory. Small variations in a dynamic system may produce large variations in the long-term behavior of that system. Graphic design is about communication, it is one of the initial flaps of the butterflies' wings, it can set a chain of events in motion that can have long-term effects and large-scale impact.

The world we live in is shaped by design at every level. The work of designers can sell, it can persuade, it can educate, and it can inspire. As designers, we are trained to address projects and problems in creative and innovative ways. We get excited about pushing the envelope for our clients. If we can unleash this creativ-

TITLE: Design Ignites Change Web Site CLIENT: Adobe Youth Voices and Worldstudio DESIGNERS: Nina Mettler, Worldstudio, and Randy Hunt, Citizen Scholar ART DIRECTORS: Mark Randall and Andréa Pellegrino YEAR: 2009

Founding Partners:

TITLE: Design Times Square Poster CLIENT: Times Square Alliance DESIGNER: Mark Randall ART DIRECTOR: Mark Randall YEAR: 2005

DESIGN TIMES SQUARE

THE URBAN FOREST PROJECT

TITLE: *The Urban Forest Project Logotype*
CLIENT: *Times Square Alliance* DESIGNERS:
Alan Dye and Omnivore PROJECT CONCEPT:
Mark Randall PROJECT PARTNERS:
Worldstudio and AIGA NY YEAR: *2003*

TITLE: *The Urban Forest
Project Totebags* CLIENT:
*Times Square Alliance
TOTEBAG DESIGNER:
Jack Spade* PROJECT
CONCEPT: *Mark Randall*
PROJECT PARTNERS:
Worldstudio and AIGA NY
PHOTO CREDITS: *Mark
Dye* YEAR: *2003*

TITLE: *The Urban Forest Project Banner and
Totebag* CLIENT: *Times Square Alliance* DE-
SIGNER: *Rob Alexander* TOTEBAG DESIGN:
Jack Spade PROJECT CONCEPT: *Mark Ran-
dall* PROJECT PARTNERS: *Worldstudio and
AIGA NY* PHOTO CREDITS: *Mark Dye*
YEAR: *2003*

TITLE: *The Urban Forest
Project Banner*
CLIENT: *Times Square
Alliance* DESIGNER:
Goodesign PROJECT
CONCEPT: *Mark Randall*
PROJECT PARTNERS:
Worldstudio and AIGA NY
PHOTO CREDIT: *Mark
Dye* YEAR: *2003*

ity and innovation on pressing social problems, the possibilities for positive change are endless.

What is the most challenging for you?

I think there are two kinds of "challenging": There is the "fun" challenge and the "painful" challenge. Both are difficult. The painful challenge is finding the work to keep the studio running. I personally am more interested in the creative aspect of design, so I find the business of running a business a challenge. Often clients and their problems can be very challenging—but to me this is the "fun" challenge. I am a great believer in the idea that the journey is the destination. Clients can be difficult and it can be hard to find a solution that you both like, but the process of design is the fun part.

Design is a service business; it is not an exercise in self-expression. If you like blue, but the client likes green—and it supports their message—trust me, it's going to be green. I see so many young designers get frustrated and discouraged by this reality.

What are the projects that most satisfy you?

A project soars when it not only solves a difficult problem but when it is beautifully designed as well. The combination of great content beautifully executed I find the most rewarding.

You are involved in education, how do you feel it has changed in the past decade?

The most noticeable change is around how much schools want to get their students engaged in social issues. It seems like every design program has embraced the idea of combining

»

design and social change. Education is the great incubator of ideas. I believe that when these students graduate, and bring this new type of social thinking into the marketplace, profound and positive changes to the design profession will take place.

What does the future hold for you specifically, and graphic design in general?

We need to be more entrepreneurial about generating ideas around social change. Often what holds a designer back is the prevailing attitude that executing social work only falls under the category of pro-bono. "Giving back" is an altruistic idea, but with limited time and resources it's often not realistic. This attitude has to change in order to create a sustainable model that not only promotes this type of work, but also encourages it in the marketplace. As creative professionals, we should be compensated for the time and effort that we put into solving not only our client's projects, but even for the projects we may create ourselves around social issues.

By creating and executing our own projects around the issues we care most about, we will do a number of things:

- Allow ourselves the freedom to use design thinking in new and innovative ways without the constraints of a client—just the constraints of the problem at hand.
- Build case studies for new modes of design thinking that demonstrate the power of design to impact change.
- Begin to create a sustainable market for ourselves to perpetuate this work.

TITLE: Sphere: The Tolerance Issue
CLIENT: Worldstudio Foundation
DESIGNER: Daniela Koenn ART DIRECTORS: Mark Randall and David Sterling
EDITORS: Peter Hall and Emmy Kondo
YEAR: 2003

TITLE: Design Times Square CLIENT: Times Square Alliance DESIGNER: /ART DIRECTOR: Mark Randall YEAR: 2005

TITLE: Sphere: The Tolerance Issue CLIENT: Worldstudio Foundation
COVER DESIGNER: Santiago Piedrafita ART DIRECTORS: Mark Randall and David Sterling EDITORS: Peter Hall and Emmy Kondo YEAR: 2003

From Living Room to Office

Principal, Sam Potts Inc., New York City

≫ How long have you had your own studio?
Sam Potts Inc. was incorporated in the State of New York in June 2002.

What are the changes in practice you have seen and experienced since you began?
The biggest and best thing to happen is that after working in my living room for three years, which went by very fast, I moved into a proper office. To be able to go home from work is a really good thing. I'm still a one-person operation, so other than trying to do bigger projects for more money more efficiently, my practice isn't all that outwardly different from Day 1.

How have these changes impacted your work?
Moving from home to an office certainly affected my way of working much more than the creative aspects of my work. I've found that taking the subway twice a day is an important part of gestating a project. If I can see a project as something whole in my mind and it makes sense, that's as good as sketching. The subway is perfect for this kind of designing, much better than the short walk from the kitchen to the computer.

Would you say that you have a particular style or character to your design? If so, how would you define it?
I would not say I have a particular style. In fact I would run screaming from this question for fear that any

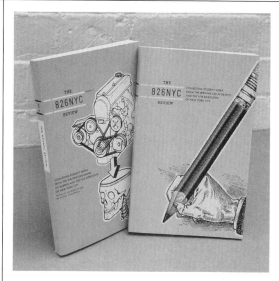

TITLE: *The 826NYC Review* (1st ed.) and (2nd ed.) CLIENT: *826NYC* DESIGNER: *Sam Potts* YEAR: *2005-2006*

TITLE: *Nine Novels by Younger Americans* Client: *826NYC* DESIGNER: *Sam Potts* JACKET IMAGE: *Jason Fulford* YEAR: *2006*

TITLE: *Aix Restaurant Identity*
CLIENT: *Philip Kirsh* DESIGNER:
Sam Potts YEAR: *2002*

TITLE: *Brooklyn Superhero Supply*
Co. Packaging CLIENT: *826NYC*
DESIGNER: *Sam Potts* YEAR: *2005*

TITLE: *Areas of My*
Expertise (2005)
and More Informa-
tion than You Require
(2008) CLIENT:
Dutton DESIGNER:
Sam Potts YEAR:
2005/2008

TITLE: *Bed, Bed,*
Bed Title Page
(book by They
Might Be Gi-
ants) CLIENT:
Simon & Schuster
DESIGNER: *Sam*
Potts ILLUSTRA-
TOR: *Marcel*
Dzama
YEAR: *2003*

deliberate consideration of my own style would make me self-conscious to the point of becoming fetal. I love typefaces and cannot draw—perhaps we can leave it at that? In the matter of whether to specialize or generalize, I'm very much a generalist. Generalizing suits whatever aesthetic style or overall approach I may have and allows me to change my approach and be as nimble as much as possible.

What about graphic design is the most challenging for you?

Let's not kid ourselves: The most challenging things are far and away the mundane things—primarily keeping up with email. Also writing up specs for print jobs, tracking down resources, waiting for clients to make decisions. These things are challenges in the sense of being exhausting and a huge drag, necessary though they are to maintaining a business.

There's a great anecdote in Danny Meyer's book *Setting the Table*, in which Irving Harris tells Danny, "The definition of business is problems." That's all of it right there. As a designer, you think the problems of the job are coming up with concepts and making a piece work and staying creative. In fact all of those things are the easy part, which is because they are the fun part. The challenge is realizing that the fun and creative making of things isn't the whole endeavor.

What are the projects that most satisfy your aesthetic sense?

If my style were more distinct (see above), it might be easier to point to a specific aesthetic that is my "thing." But why be limited in one's taste? To love lots and lots of different things costs nothing and there's no downside. By the same token, the stuff that offends me is the stupid work, the blatantly cynical and easy work: where a designer picks a font for its name, or uses irony without any point behind it, or just about every commercial ever made for beer, cosmetics, or pick-up trucks. If every project is a chance to have an idea, to actually be real and true, it's just a shame to see so much uninventive, lifeless work get made.

How important is type and typography in what you do?

A very basic and literal definition that I use on the first day of my classes at SVA is: Anything that has type on it is graphic design. No type? Then it might be illustration or calligraphy or arc welding. Every profession solves problems and works with ideas, but graphic design is the only one that deals with type to address ideas and problems. So type to me is what blood is to the surgeon or atoms to the physicist or gravity to the parachutist.

What, in this current technological and economic climate, does the future hold for you specifically, and graphic design in general?

In terms of technology, the important thing is to enjoy it. To actually revel in what software can do. It's absurd how easily comput-

ers now allow us to do things that used to require real training and skill, like drawing five perfect circles evenly spaced apart or setting a nice page of Caslon. Now: easy! The problem for me is a software glass ceiling: I stopped caring very much about new features and updates. I do think this is a creative liability. It's a way of saying "What I know is good enough," which if you actually believe it is a very bad thing to say if you're trying to stay creative. It's always better to be curious, to be open, to adapt.

The economic weather is like the regular weather: It'll always be there and always be changing. You've just got to be sure you've got dry socks, a clean shirt, and a warm coat. And of course, comfortable shoes.

TITLE: IFC Center Logo
CLIENT: IFC DESIGNER:
Sam Potts YEAR: 2005

TITLE: Geek Love (Op-Ed
Art) CLIENT: New York Times
DESIGNER: Sam Potts
YEAR: 2008

Picky About Clients

Partner, Doyle Partners, New York City

>> **You worked at a number of staff design jobs. Why did you decide to open your own firm?**

The reasons for starting Drenttel Doyle Partners with Bill Drenttel and Tom Kluepfel in 1985 was to get the inevitable failure of our own shop behind us. None of us actually expected to succeed but thought we had better get the notion out of our systems. That's the emotional base from which we were operating. Intellectually, we thought it was high time to blur some of the distinctions between design and advertising and marketing. We thought with our combined backgrounds of advertising (Bill), institutional design (Tom), and editorial (me) that some interesting fusion might result if we were to approach design and marketing for our clients as a cohesive force.

How did the partnership succeed?

One of the most gratifying things about running a company like ours is that we are constantly in a position to learn about new businesses (from the inside) as well as to meet new clients and friends in all categories, from art and publishing to filmmaking, retail, corporations, and other areas. It is wonderfully voyeuristic to be able to peer into so many industries and to participate in them as we do.

How have you structured your firm?

For the last dozen years, we have employed between ten and thirteen people. This is intentional; we want

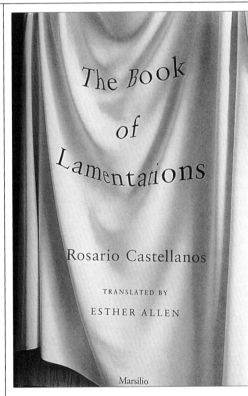

TITLE: The Book of Lamentations DESIGNERS: Stephen Doyle, Gary Tooth CREATIVE DIRECTOR: Stephen Doyle COMPANY: Doyle Partners CLIENT: Marsilio PHOTOGRAPHER: Stephen Doyle TYPEFACE: Sabon YEAR: 1996

TITLE: Was/Saw Poster CREATIVE DIRECTOR: Stephen Doyle COMPANY: Doyle Partners CLIENT: American Center for Design TYPEFACES: News Gothic, New Baskerville YEAR: 1995

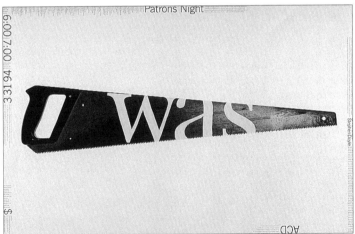

to keep the firm sized so that it feels right to the partners and core design team. In order to strike that marvelous balance of managing projects and designing them, this small team is able to turn around a lot of work, handle large projects, and is small enough to constantly be turning away work. We can be picky about which jobs we take on, and we can keep the partners designing as well as managing. We are careful to avoid the trap of trying to take care of all of the clients' needs. This would have us mushrooming in size to meet this deadline or that, and we would be designing and managing things that really don't merit our input. Often would-be clients actually come back to us later, with bigger or more strategic projects, after we turn them away the first time.

How do you operate creatively?

I have never, ever told a designer not to work on something, not to get carried away, or not to contribute to a project. I do say things like "I hate that color," or "Make the type bigger," or "Did you just come from a David Carson lecture?" Remember, design is not a solitary process; it is wholly collaborative, except for those rare flashes of onanistic brilliance that we all hope pepper our years. Clients come to us not for a certain look but a certain approach, and we are careful to try to give enough attention to all of our projects that our approach is considered and consistent. So designers can't get carried away with some personal vision thing. (Neither can the partners, for that matter, but for rare exceptions.) On the other hand, no one is ever held down if he is able to contribute to a project. Our teams are variable, so you don't get stuck with one particular client unless you want to. We work on wildly diverse projects, all at the same time: books, packaging, signage, identities, film titles, and exhibition graphics, so nobody has the chance to get bored.

Do your designers have autonomy?

Certainly not. What would be the point of working at Doyle Partners if you wanted autonomy? I'm not interested in being a rep for a bunch of designers—writing contracts, making phone calls, going to meetings so some designer can sit in my office and design. A designer who wants autonomy should do what we did: emotionally and financially prepare herself for failure and open shop.

TITLE: XIX Amendment Installation DESIGNERS: Stephen Doyle, Lisa Yee ART DIRECTORS: Stephen Doyle, William Drenttel, Miguel Oks COMPANY: Doyle Partners CLIENT: New York State Division for Women PHOTOGRAPHER: Scott Francis Architectural DESIGNER: James Hicks PROJECT MANAGER: Cameron Manning YEAR: 1995

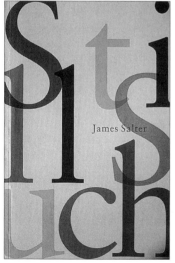

TITLE: Still Such CREATIVE DIRECTOR: Stephen Doyle COMPANY: Doyle Partners CLIENT: William Drenttel New York PHOTOGRAPHER: Duane Michaels (interior) TYPEFACE: Sabon YEAR: 1992

TITLE: Phaedra Poster DESIGNER: Katrin Schmit-Tegge CREATIVE DIRECTOR: Stephen Doyle COMPANY: Doyle Partners CLIENT: Creative Productions TYPEFACES: Orator, Futura YEAR: 1995

Partner, Project Projects, New York City

>> **How long have you had your own studio?**

I began Project Projects with Prem Krishnamurthy in January 2004, five and a half years ago. Prior to this, I ran a one-person studio for a year and a half. So across these two situations, I've had my own studio for seven years.

What are the changes in practice you have seen and experienced since you began?

It's hard to comprehensively say, as my view of the graphic design scene seems to have shrunken somewhat during that time. I remain aware of the activities of my friends and colleagues, but have lost some of the broader view that was easier to maintain from a greater distance. That said, my sense is that the 2000s have been a time of increased interdisciplinary activity, as designers seek to connect with parallel fields and practitioners (this following the far more inward-looking graphic design experiments of the 1990s). More designers appear to be engaged with the pragmatics of generating not just form, but entire situations. This broadening of boundaries is certainly enabled by the ease-of-use and speed of current software and hardware. Additionally, the international design scene has become far more thoroughly networked, so styles which may have previously remained local idiosyncrasies are now instantly broadcast and frequently replicated. I think this is basically healthy, though,

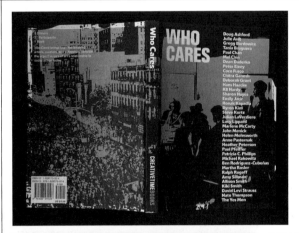

TITLE: Who Cares
CLIENT: Creative Time
DESIGNER: Adam Michael YEAR: 2006

as style can be recognized more clearly as a communicational means to an end, rather than as the signifier of individual artistic expression.

How have these changes impacted your work?

In terms of technology, I'm constantly amazed by how much can be done quickly by a small working group with a modest infrastructure. Regarding the accelerated distribution of style, this has only reinforced the belief at my studio in producing form based upon the analysis of a situation's context and content.

Would you say that you have a particular style or character to your design? If so, how would you define it?

I would say that there's a consistency of approach, but that the results vary substantially from project to project.

What about graphic design is the most challenging for you?

Graphic design is a staggeringly broad term, and most of what would fall under that rubric is very much beyond my skill set. However, one pleasure of running a studio is that I can be involved in producing nearly anything, through the assembly of collaborative teams.

What, in this current technological and economic climate, does the future hold for you specifically, and graphic design in general?

My sense is that it's a good time to run a small studio such as mine, as we can keep costs low, expand or contract based upon available work, and be quickly responsive to changing circumstances.

TITLE: Values & Variety: Shopping on Fulton Street CLIENT: The Center of Urban Pedagogy DESIGNER: Adam Michael YEAR: 2005

TITLE: Compass in Hand CLIENT: The Museum of Modern Art, New York DESIGNER: Adam Michael YEAR: 2009

Designing In Arabic

Principal, Tarek Atrissi Studio, Amsterdam, The Netherlands

» How long have you had your own studio?

I was heavily freelancing since being an undergraduate student. I registered my business in 2000 in the Netherlands, yet it was still somehow virtual and "Web-based" since I was still traveling around and I did decide to go to the School of Visual Arts in New York to do the two years MFA Designer as Author graduate program. It is in 2003—after finishing SVA—that I relocated once and for all in Holland and started with the small design studio setup that we still follow until today.

What are the changes in practice you have seen and experienced since you began?

The technological advances are what affect our discipline the most. On one hand, communication has been redefined with the new emerging Web trends of social networking, and much of design has shifted its focus to accommodate this. Not only are we designing for new mediums (mobile devices, iphone applications, redefined Web platform), but the graphic style emerging often associated with some successful new Web trends (such as Web 2.0), has affected a wider range of traditional graphic design practice, beyond just the Web and screen design.

How have these changes impacted your work?

More than ever we have to be a multidisciplinary studio, to accommodate the work possibilities

TITLE: Poster Designs – Arab Movement for Women Arising for Justice DESIGNER/ ART DIRECTOR: Tarek Atrissi YEAR: 2005

TITLE: Promotional Posters Rajae CLIENT: Rajae El Mouhandiz DESIGNER/ART DIRECTOR: Tarek Atrissi YEAR: 2006

The Ghad TV font (above) comes in two weights, Regular and Bold, and was designed specifically for usage on TV screen (ATV-the new Jordanian TV station). The font was based on an earlier version designed in one weight for Al-Ghad Newspaper (below).

TITLE: *Typeface Design, Al-Ghad Arabic Font* CLIENT: *ATV Jordan* DESIGNER/ART DIRECTOR: *Tarek Atrissi* YEAR: *2006*

TITLE: *Motion Graphics MTV Arabia* CLIENT: *MTV* DESIGNER/ART DIRECTOR: *Tarek Atrissi* YEAR: *2007*

resulting out of this change and to keep up with all developments that visual communication is witnessing. We are also forced to constantly look at the big picture, and to be critical toward the trends in the profession and in trying to see what is coming up, and analytical to the design approach we follow.

Would you say that you have a particular style or character to your design?

My visual design follows a specific line of work. My initial focus in work was on creating a modern Arabic graphic design language, focusing primarily on the use of Arabic script in design in a contemporary approach and without falling into the predictable traditional Islamic visual style, often associated with Arabic visual communication. My work then combined an inspiration from the rich Arabic visual heritage with the modern approach to Western graphic expression. The challenge lay then in creating a new Arabic (or bilingual) typographic expression, because most references were rather calligraphic than typographic. The focus on the Arab world and Arab market expanded quickly to become a focus on cross-cultural design because I realized that many of the Arab-flavored projects were actually in one way or another bridging some aspects of East and West. And by being a designer who comes from Lebanon, lives in Holland, and has worked and studied in New York, Dubai, and Qatar, I benefited from my cultural experience as a working designer in these different environments ⟫

to expand further my focus on cross-cultural design. To put it in few words then, I would say my style is typographic, simple, cross-cultural, and contemporary.

What about graphic design is the most challenging for you?

The fact that it is a business at the end of the day. So actually the nondesign aspect is the most challenging. There is a lot more that needs to be done in order to get your good design out there: setting up a business model; doing a good promotion and marketing of your services and getting clients; managing the daily work and building sustainable business models; being a profitable business; and of course, keep enjoying the process and keep on creating solid design work.

What are the projects that most satisfy your aesthetic sense?

Three types of projects are actually the most satisfying. First, projects with a strong cultural focus because these are at the core of my focus and most of the time this is where typographic solutions are welcomed by the client. Second are very large projects that are highly visible, typical, and become a significant part of the visual culture of a specific environment (and most of the time these happen to be the most profitable projects). Third are self-initiated projects, which fall under the design entrepreneurship approach where you conceptualize a project and become your own client in creating it, developing it, and making it a commercially viable product.

TITLE: Various Typographic Design Logos DESIGNER/ART DIRECTOR: Tarek Atrissi YEAR: 2000–2009

TITLE: Poster Design Arabic Graphics Exhibition CLIENT: De Levante DESIGNER/ART DIRECTOR: Tarek Atrissi YEAR: 2008

What, in this current technological and economic climate, does the future hold for you specifically, and graphic design in general?
We will just focus as a studio to keep on doing good business while creating meaningful graphic design work. The economic crisis to be honest is a good test; it tests the validity of your business model and its sustainability against an economic climate that is naturally going to be turbulent every now and then. Technology will keep forcing us to reinvent some of our work focus and working methods. The future of graphic design I think will give more importance to local graphic design scenes and for design in emerging economies as a reaction to the risk of globalization of graphic design styles and trends.

TITLE: Streets of Arabia —
Prints on Canvas
CLIENT: www. arabictypography. com DESIGNER/ ART DIRECTOR: Tarek Atrissi
YEAR: 2008

Words and Ideas

>> **What do you like best about being a graphic deisgner?**

I like working with words and ideas. I'm not that interested any more in finding out a new way to lay out the pages of a sixteen-page brochure. Instead, I like to put the brief aside and sit down with a client and talk about what we're trying to achieve. Who is the audience? What is the message? This turns into my favorite kind of process—one where the collaboration is open-ended and the outcome is anyone's guess. That, more than anything, makes me suspicious of specialization, which I think forces a designer to frame every problem in terms of a predetermined solution.

What media are most creatively satisfying?

Because I like words and ideas, I suppose I am biased toward books and magazines. But a pictorial logo, when it's done right, can be more charged with more ideas than a 496-page book. Any medium, potentially, can be satisfying.

How do you design? Are you concept-driven? Or does what you do depend on the project?

Sometimes the project has a lot of constraints built into it; in those cases, if I'm lucky, I define the problem and shake it hard enough to make the solution fall out. Other times, the situation is wide open,

TITLE: The Good Diner
DESIGNERS: Michael
Bierut, Lisa Cerveny
CREATIVE DIRECTOR:
Michael Bierut
COMPANY: Pentagram
Design, Inc. CLIENT:
Gotham Equities
ILLUSTRATOR: Woody
Pirtle YEAR: 1992

TITLE: Minnesota
Children's Museum
DESIGNER: Tracey
Cameron CREATIVE
DIRECTOR: Michael Bierut
COMPANY: Pentagram
Design, Inc. CLIENT: Ann
Bitter and Jeanne Bergeron,
Minnesota Children's
Museum PHOTOGRA-
PHERS: July Olausen,
Michael O'Neill (hands);
Don F. Wong (documenta-
tion) YEAR: 1994–1995

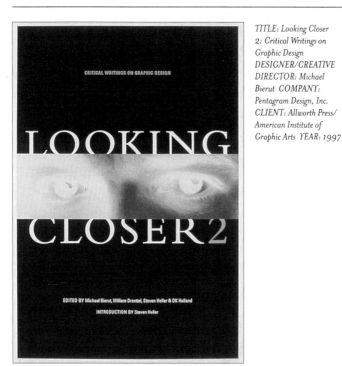

TITLE: Looking Closer
2: Critical Writings on
Graphic Design
DESIGNER/CREATIVE
DIRECTOR: Michael
Bierut COMPANY:
Pentagram Design, Inc.
CLIENT: Allworth Press/
American Arts of
Graphic Arts YEAR: 1997

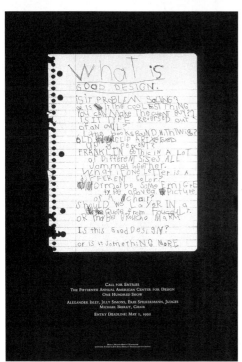

TITLE: What Is Good
Design DESIGNER/
CREATIVE DIRECTOR:
Michael Bierut COM-
PANY: Pentagram Design,
Inc. CLIENT: American
Center for Design TYPE-
FACE: Hand-lettering—
Elizabeth Ann Kresz Bierut
YEAR: 1992

and it takes more intuition to get to the solution. In either case, I usually try to get as far as I can by thinking it through beforehand. Often, by the time I put pencil to paper, I've gone a lot of the way toward the solution in my head.

Has working as a principal of a large firm increased or confined your creative output?

I work in a big firm, but my design team is similar to a small design office: me, an administrative assistant, four full-time designers, and an intern or two. I work fast, and I like to work on a lot of projects at once. At any one moment, chances are that I've got at least thirty projects going on. These range from an invitation to a benefit event at a museum to a book to a signage project for a public space to an international corporate identity project. Working as a partner of Pentagram has fed my hunger for more projects and more varied projects.

Are clients more concerned with business than aesthetics?

I am always surprised by how few clients, in the end, have any ability to distinguish good design from bad design. Instead, most clients are primarily concerned with their own business success. Usually, I define my solutions to a problem not in aesthetic terms but in terms of my client's objectives. Successful designers figure out a way to align the client's business goals with their own personal goals.

Equal Among Partners

Partner, Pentagram Design, Inc., New York City

>> **You've worked in the music industry as a record jacket designer; now you are the partner in one of the largest international design firms. What made you become a designer?**
I stunk at everything else.

What do you look for in a partner?
Somebody who brings things to the group or to the partnership that I don't already have.

How do you work with your partners at Pentagram?
In two ways: formally and informally. We work together formally if we're collaborating on a specific project, and we work together informally by the fact that we sit nose-to-nose together in a kind of kibbutz, getting involved in each other's work whether asked or not.

What is the most fulfilling aspect of your work?
I like doing things I've never done before.

What is the least fulfilling?
Doing billing.

Do you think that the business of graphic design is a good business? Is it an ethical business?
If you mean a moral business, it depends how you feel about capitalism. If you believe that the profit motive is good, graphic design is certainly as good as any other business. If you don't believe in that, then no business is good. Graphic

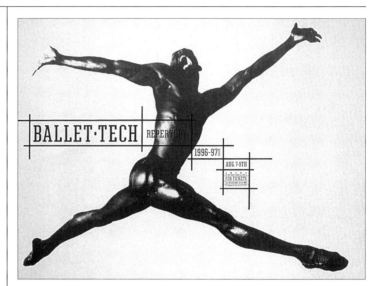

TITLE: Ballet Tech DESIGNERS: Lisa Mazur, Anke Stohlmann CREATIVE DIRECTOR: Paula Scher COMPANY: Pentagram CLIENT: Ballet Tech PHOTOGRAPHER: Lois Greenfield TYPEFACE: Constructa YEAR: 1996–1997

TITLE: Le Parker Meridien DESIGNER: Anke Stohlmann CREATIVE DIRECTOR: Paula Scher COMPANY: Pentagram CLIENT: Le Parker Meridien TYPEFACE: Gill Sans YEAR: 1998

TITLE: Showcenter Haedo DESIGNERS: Ed Chiquitucto, Lisa Mazur, Anke Stohlmann, Maria Wenzel CREATIVE DIRECTORS: Paula Scher, Michael Gericke COMPANY: Pentagram CLIENT: Maccarone Emprienditos PHOTOGRA-PHER/DOCUMENTATION: Alejandro Leveratto YEAR: 1996

design gives people a service that enables them to make themselves known in some way, whether it's through selling a product or making information accessible, or getting somebody through a complicated building, making somebody understand a film. Of course, I think it's ethically and morally sound.

Can you describe your design style?
I design things to make an emotional impact. The emotions change all the time.

How much of your time is devoted to design, and how much to business?
I used to think very little was devoted to design, because I saw myself always in meetings, but then I realized that I'm doing design and art direction in meetings. So I would say, with the exception of the time I spend gossiping, all the other time is really spent in design.

How do you know if you're a good designer?
You just work at it until you are.

What makes a good work environment?
I think a good work environment is little more than people being around people who are enthusiastic about their work. A bad work environment is being around people who are depressed about their work.

Is there anything that you'd still like to accomplish in your career?
I'd like to become much more involved in city planning. I'm starting to do that now. I'm very interested in how design marries into architecture to become environmental design. It's really more about design integrating into the cities and how large imagery and typography works within cityscapes—not in the traditional way in which we think of signage but in a more extravagant and dramatic way.

TITLE: Bring In Da Noise, Bring In Da Funk DESIGNER: Lisa Mazur CREATIVE DIRECTOR: Paula Scher COMPANY: Pentagram CLIENT: The Public Theater PHOTOGRAPHER: Richard Avedon TYPEFACE: American Wood Typefaces YEAR: 1996

TITLE: The Diva Is Dismissed DESIGNERS: Ron Louie, Lisa Mazur, Jane Mella CREATIVE DIRECTOR: Paula Scher COMPANY: Pentagram CLIENT: The Public Theater PHOTOGRAPHER: Teresa Lizette TYPEFACES: American Wood Typefaces YEAR: 1994

Has there been a major influence in your career?

"Design history is an endless source of inspiration and learning, as is the work of contemporary designers. Because design is a cultural activity, all of the other creative practices, like art, music, literature, and film, also influence graphic designers' work. How could it not?"

—*Jeffery Keedy*

"Major influences are people who do what they do with a distinctive sensibility. Animator Richard Williams's dedication to resurrecting animation has been an influence. My father, Joe Sedelmaier, a live-action director and filmmaker who is involved in every aspect of the filmmaking process, has been an influence. Classic comedians like Keaton, Laurel and Hardy, and the Marx Brothers are also reflected in stuff I do."

—*J.J. Sedelmaier*

"I would have to say that my husband, Etienne Delessert, has been a huge influence because of his connections to the European market. Through him I've been able to work with French publishers, Italian publishers—all sorts—so that now I can recognize and appreciate book design across cultures."

—*Rita Marshall*

"Teachers: Hugo Weber, Misch Kohn at the Institute of Design; Franz Kline, Merce Cunningham, and John Cage at Black Mountain College. Environment and students and interaction with avant-garde arts in Chicago. Modernism. Previously, my two years studying painting, literature, history, French, and symbolic logic at Bard College. Later influences: the Eames, Sandro Girard, international populist arts, and streetscapes."

—*Deborah Sussman*

"Fine art has been a huge influence on my design, and I think that we're at a point where there is a huge criss-crossing of design and fine art. I go to museums all the time— I'm always looking at what fine artists do." —*Janet Froelich*

"*In many ways, designing typefaces has provided me an excuse to spend time looking at historical typefaces. Increasingly, I'm finding that I'm not influenced by the look of a historical typeface but wondering about the thinking behind it. It's usually a theoretical underpinning that precipitates a new design rather than merely the look of something old.*"

—*Jonathan Hoefler*

"Modernism, postmodernism, classicism, Bauhaus, and Thomas Jefferson." —*Michael Vanderbyl*

"POSTERS, BEARDSLEY, WESSELMANN." *—John Martinez*

"The strongest influence in my life was the modern movement as interpreted by LeCorbusier, Mies van der Rohe, the Bauhaus, the Swiss graphic designers like Müller Brockman, Max Bill, and Max Huber as well as designers like Nizzoli, Ray and Charles Eames, Dieter Rams, and many others—all people I was fortunate to know personally and from whom I learned to be what I am. It was not just their style but their commitments to design, society, and ethics that I admired." —Massimo Vignelli

"The USC School of Architecture was an incredible influence. They taught me how to visualize and make presentations. They taught me to respect professionalism." *—Mike Salisbury*

"I went to a theater school within my high school, and we produced everything from the most outrageous New York happenings by Alan Caprow to *Macbeth*, from Ionesco to little-known Canadian playwrights. Having experienced the breadth of all of that, creating costumes and stage managing and producing and writing and directing and acting and having done all those roles, I come back again and again to the fundamental of theater, which is that communicating is a human endeavor." *—David Peters*

"A big early influence was a teacher I had at college named Hanno Ehses. He was pushing the study of semiotics at a time when nobody had applied it to graphic design, and students were appalled to be studying rhetoric. But it was a really great course and a great way of thinking about design and understanding how to communicate using visual language, and that had a big influence on how I looked at design and the purposes of design as a communication tool." *—Rhonda Rubenstein*

"NO SPECIFIC INFLUENCES OTHER THAN THE CLASSIC SWISS STYLE PRACTITIONERS OF THE 1960s AND, IRONICALLY, THE ENTERTAINMENT INDUSTRY IN THE 1990s." *—Wayne Hunt*

"When I first got involved with type (over forty years ago), it was still a mechanical industry in which the designing of type was separate from its manufacture. Since then, a succession of technical changes—photocomposition, digital type, desktop type—has progressively reunited the two things, designing and making, so it is now once again possible, as it was in type's early centuries, for one person to be both type designer and font maker. This development, the return of the punch cutter as auteur, blessed by the coming of open-font formats, has probably had the greatest influence on how I work and, consequently, on what I do." —Matthew Carter

"My teacher, Armin Hofmann, had by far the most influence on me. Also my entire education, deeply rooted in drawing, taught me a discipline that has guided me throughout my career. Out of the up to fifty-six studio hours per week, perhaps more than half were drawing classes." —Steff Geissbuhler

OPIUM FIVE

BAD COMPANY

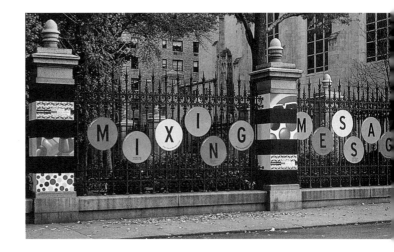

CLOCKWISE:
TITLE: *Opium Magazine,
Issue 5, Magazine Cover*
CLIENT: *Opium Magazine*
DESIGNER/ART DIREC-
TOR/PHOTOGRAPHER:
David Barringer YEAR: *2007*

TITLE: *Mesü* DESIGNER:
Jennifer Pänépinto CLIENT:
Studio Pänépinto YEAR: *2004*

TITLE: *ClearRx* CLIENT:
Target Corporation DESIGN-
ERS: *Deborah Adler, Target
Industrial* DESIGNER: *Klaus
Rosburg* ART DIRECTOR:
Deborah Adler YEAR: *2005*

TITLE: *Mixing Messages Sign*
DESIGNER: *Ellen Lupton*
COMPANY: *Cooper-Hewitt,
National Design Museum*
PHOTOGRAPHER: *Bill
Jacobson* TYPEFACE:
Interstate YEAR: *1996*

G*raphic design* is a slippery term and not entirely applicable in the current design environment. Arguably, *commercial art* is more to the point but less sophisticated than other enigmatic nomenclature. The term *graphic design* is credited to W.A. Dwiggins, a letterer, calligrapher, and type, book, and advertising designer as well as a novelist, playwright, and marionette theater impresario, who in 1922 proposed the term as a definition of his own multifaceted professional activity. The coinage was matter-of-factly proposed in an article in which Dwiggins argued that new kinds of commercial advertising methods and techniques required a new kind of *graphic designer*—a generalist proficient in wedding various media into one inclusive practice rather than a specialist in an anonymous production line. As an alternative to more specific labels—including *layout-* or *board-person*, *comp artist*, *airbrush artist*, *illustrator*, and *letterer*—*graphic designer* was certainly a broad enough term to include all these jobs and more. But now, in an age of expanded media, it is an insufficient way to define the widening range of the design profession.

SECTION ③

Design Options

During the 1930s, graphic designers who were also involved in package and product design, as well as those who engaged in industrial design, called themselves "designers for industry." At that pivotal time of the Machine Age, a new breed of cross-disciplinary, independent design firm emerged that took responsibility for the conception and production of entire projects rather than specialized aspects of the whole. These identity, packaging, and signage projects were on a fairly grand scale for corporations as large as Ford Motor and DuPont Chemical Companies, among others. The staffs of these firms included graphic, interior, and architectural specialists working together in unified teams. While team members practiced their particular specialties, each contributed to the other's goals.

In the postwar period, as dedicated design departments and so-called design laboratories developed within progressive corporations, cross-disciplinary programs grew in both popularity and necessity. Moreover, the specialists had to know how their work fit into the larger context. It was not enough for a designer to practice typography alone, for example; knowledge of how it worked and interacted in the world was equally important. Therefore, previously standalone disciplines were integrated into overall practices, and designers had to be fluent in much more than their own arcane specialties.

Starting in the 1950s, in an effort to expand and legitimize graphic design in the international business world, designers referred to themselves with more inclusive monikers: *visual communicator, visual designer, graphic communicator, communications specialist, communications consultant,* and so on. Although the majority of graphic designers continued to use conventional, though enigmatic, nomenclature, in the face of a growing shift from single- to multidisciplinary practice, the term *graphic design* lost some of its relevance as the focus of work gradually shifted from paper to three dimensions. *Graphic* suggests marks on paper (although it is really broader than that); *visual* implies images as well as graphics.

This section examines some of the options that graphic design-ers (and cross-platform designers) are offered today and analyzes the widening expectations of clients in relation to technological shifts that have allowed the graphic designer to branch away from traditional practice.

CROSSING DISCIPLINES

MANY DESIGNERS are content to design beautiful lettering, splendid pages, or smart logos for the course of their entire careers. Developing such skills over time is both personally rewarding and professionally satisfying, to be sure. But others are not as sanguine about having only a single specialty. The reasons vary: Some do not have the talent or ability to master one thing brilliantly, while others lack the patience to do so. Some view specialization as offering too few challenges and therefore explore numerous options as a matter of personal pride and preference. Still others believe that specialization equals limitation, and limitation in this expanding field is professional suicide.

As a graphic designer, the secret to longevity is not a marketable style but rather keeping abreast of shifts in all media and incorporating as many of these as possible into your own repertoire. In recent years, the widespread access to so many kinds of media (as outlined in Section 1) has both opened the job market and stretched the boundaries of this field. Crossing disciplines is no longer an exception to the rule—it *is* the rule. If one is unable to solve problems in more than one discipline, a client will probably go to someone who can. Small clients may be content with a logo and stationery—and many designers can fill those simple needs—but medium and large clients prefer one-stop shopping for a variety of print (packaging, publishing, promotion, advertising) and multimedia needs (Internet, interactive kiosk, video). One of the clearest indications of this is the addition of Web site designers to most design studio, firm, and office staffs. Some design firms are now linked to architects and interior designers, too.

Crossing disciplines means that a graphic designer must be something of a chameleon. With the inclusion of graphic design as a component of screen-based media, understanding the kinetic properties of type and image, for example, is a given. While members of the older generation may have to grapple with such media, the younger generation, weaned on the computer, deal with this tool as a fact of professional life. In fact, this kind of discipline-crossing is now routinely taught in many art and design schools, and will become inextricably tied to whatever graphic design becomes in the future.

However, other crossover disciplines are not as naturally woven into the graphic designer's education or daily routine, and these must be sought out, learned, and practiced. The most common crossovers involve aspects of television, film, video, and exhibitions, requiring both interest and skill in complementary media, including music, lighting, and editing, for example. In addition, an increasing number of

designers collaborate with architects on the graphics for building exteriors or interiors, which may include printed as well as three-dimensional executions. Architects who specialize in retail and restaurant interiors, for example, have become more aware of graphics and frequently collaborate with graphic designers on the look and feel of entire projects, not simply on the finishing touches.

Graphic designers have also become more proactive in the process of conception and management in a variety of areas. One example is city and community planning—developing visual identities, wayfinding systems, even determining the layout of streets and neighborhoods—and another example is the organization of retail and entertainment districts. Hence, the quintessential cross-

disciplinary graphic designer is not merely a subcontractor serving the needs of so-called higher-echelon designers but is an active participant in an overarching planning and design scheme, a valued member of a team that integrates several media into one entity.

A graphic designer can train to work in various disciplines through advanced study (continuing education courses are offered in virtually all complementary and supplementary professional spheres), but more likely, a designer often backs into these other disciplines by chance. Necessity is the mother of most invention, and a client's need for interrelated disciplines is often just the impetus that a designer needs to branch into previously uncharted realms.

WHO YOU CALLIN' A GRAPHIC DESIGNER?

I hate the term *graphic designer* because it's extremely limiting and it has very little to do with our profession. The word *graphic* implies printed or offset matter. Because probably less than a third of the work we do has its end product as a printed product, it just seems kind of ludicrous.

I'm a designer. On my stationery it says "A Visual Communication Consultancy." That's probably a little long, but at the same time it's more important that I distinguish this from a graphic design office. The Italians used to have a designation during the time of the Medici: *consiglieri*, people who advised on a variety of subjects, who were part of the organization but not *in* the organization. The consiglieri had an understanding of everything that was going on—of the people, of the products, of the businesses, of the culture, of the arts, of science. They had everything to do with the world and, in a sense, could bring a different voice or a point of view that may not have been considered.

That's how the design profession has evolved and will continue to evolve, because it's a personal service business. So the aesthetics are a mechanism for communication, not an end in and of themselves. I think that's part of where a good deal of the confusion about what a designer is comes from.   *- Joseph Essex*

ELLEN LUPTON | Designer as Curator

Director, MFA in Graphic Design, Maryland Institute, College of Art, Baltimore, Maryland
and Partner, Design/Writing/Research, Baltimore, Maryland

>> Why did you expand your practice to include curatorial and authorial work? Was this strategy or accident?

As someone who was always fascinated with the written word, I felt design was an ideal forum in which to develop text and image. I became a curator by accident. When I graduated from the Cooper Union in 1985, I was invited to run the just-founded Herb Lubalin Study Center for Design and Typography. It was a shoestring operation occupying a few small rooms and hallways of the Cooper Union. But it was a great opportunity to put together exhibitions and publications about design history and theory. I got hooked, and I was able to build a career as a critic and curator.

Is this cross-disciplinary activity viable in the market today, or simply a fortuitous niche that you made for yourself?

My position as a museum curator is a rare one—there is only a handful of design curators around the country, at institutions including the Museum of Modern Art in New York and the San Francisco Museum of Modern Art. However, there are more and more opportunities for designers to develop and use their skills as writers/editors/publishers and for literary people to engage the processes of design. This is a broader cultural development with relevance beyond my particular experience.

TITLE: *Mixing Messages Sign* DESIGNER: *Ellen Lupton* COMPANY: *Cooper-Hewitt, National Design Museum* PHOTOGRAPHER: *Bill Jacobson* TYPEFACE: *Interstate* YEAR: *1996*

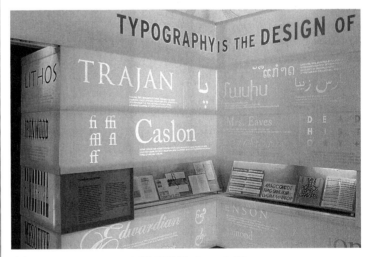

TITLE: *Mixing Messages Font Room* DESIGNERS: *Ellen Lupton, Fred Gates, Kennedy & Violich Architects* COMPANY: *Cooper-Hewitt, National Design Museum* PHOTOGRAPHER: *Bill Jacobson* TYPEFACE: *Interstate and Various* YEAR: *1996*

Would you say that your interdisciplinary practice has given your firm, Design/Writing/Research, an advantage in the competitive design market? How do you account for your success?

As partners in Design/Writing/Research, Abbott Miller and I have done a series of key projects that exemplify the ideal of combining research and writing with visual work. These are not always the most lucrative projects, however, and the studio does many projects that are executed along a more traditional design services model. The studio is primarily Abbott's undertaking—I am primarily employed by Cooper-Hewitt National Design Museum and, more recently, the Maryland Institute College of Art. Abbott is doing a marvelous job at the studio, developing the ideal of a design-research continuum while still making a living for himself and his staff.

TITLE: Mechanical Brides (installation of typographic laundry in exhibition about women, work, and technology) DESIGNER: Ellen Lupton COMPANY: Cooper-Hewitt, National Design Museum PHOTOGRAPHER: Bill Jacobson TYPEFACE: Scala YEAR: 1993

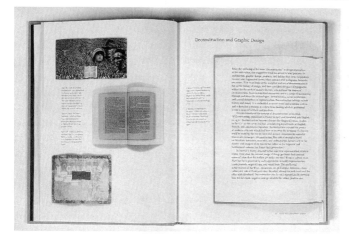

TITLE: Design Writing Research: Writing on Graphic Design DESIGNERS: Ellen Lupton, Abbott Miller COMPANY: Design/Writing/Research/Kiosk TYPEFACE: Scala YEAR: 1996

| # A Graphic Architect

Partner, Pentagram Architectural Services/Pentagram Design, Inc., New York City

>> **Your interior design has always been very "graphic." Do you think in terms of architectonics or graphics?**

I think entirely architecturally, but always with an image or a particular visual point of view to communicate, the operative word being *communicate*. I try not to get lost in the architectonics of the project but rather to use them as a language to make the design legible, accessible, and therefore, in my view, effective. This is probably not how most architects think. They prefer, in most cases, to solve the architectural problem at the expense of the accessibility of the ideas.

You often work with graphic designers. What is the dynamic of this relationship?

I love working with any creative individual. The possibility for real creative exchange, triggering of ideas, the back-and-forth of building an idea is increased when working with any visual artist, especially one whose work I respect and enjoy. It's a bit like teaching; you can tangle with ideas outside your normal realm and grow creatively.

Is being a partner in a graphic design firm with an architectural component different than working for an architectural firm?

To put it diplomatically, I have never felt the need to join a partnership of architects. This

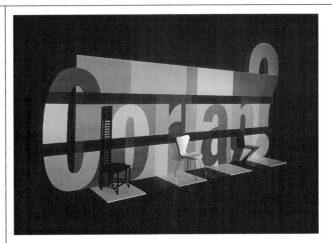

TITLE: DuPont Corian? Corian! Trade Show Exhibit ARCHITECT: James Biber ARCHI-TECT/ASSISTANT: Michael Zweck-Bronner GRAPHIC DESIGNER: Nikki Richardson PROJECT COORDINATOR: Leslie Wellott COMPANY: Pentagram Architectural Services/ Pentagram Design, Inc. CLIENT: DuPont PHOTOGRAPHER: Peter Margonelli YEAR: 1996

TITLE: The Globe ARCHITECT: James Biber ARCHITECT/ASSISTANT: Michael Zweck-Bronner COMPANY: Pentagram Design, Inc. CLIENT: Jim Heckler & Nick Polsky PHOTOGRAPHER: Andrew Bordwin YEAR: 1997

partnership, however, thrives on different ideas, different points of view, different talents. We can work together on a project, or on different aspects of a single project, with less competition (of the destructive kind), more enjoyment of each other's ideas, and, I like to think, a better process and product as a result.

Is your position anomalous, or are there many openings for this kind of cross-disciplinary relationship?

This may be one of a very few situations where a series of disciplines (at the partner level) coexist in a single firm. We don't hire talent from other disciplines as staff members; we seek them out as partners. We are a firm of equals rather than a pyramid of management, and that is a big part of why it works.

What do you look for in an assistant—architectural and graphic design expertise?

I look for a keen architectural mind, good working habits, and a great attitude. Fortunately, our office is such a cauldron of design that the graphic parts just seem to rub off on my architectural staff. They all leave with an enhanced appreciation and eye for graphic design, and I like to think that the graphic design staff learns as much from us.

Do you envision architecture and graphic design becoming a more unified profession?

Any unification will probably always exist outside the mainstream of architectural practice. The professions are different in demeanor, working methodology, fee structures, and time scales. The biggest barrier, in my view, is that most architects don't consider graphic designers their professional equals. Collaboration only works among equals. Collaboration among unequals is called *employment*.

TITLE: *I Want To Take You Higher Exhibition* DESIGNER: *Nikki Richardson* CREATIVE DIRECTORS: *James Biber, Michael Bierut* COMPANY: *Pentagram Architectural Services/Pentagram Design, Inc.* CLIENT: *The Rock and Roll Hall of Fame* PHOTOGRAPHER: *Peter Mauss* YEAR: *1997*

TITLE: *The Fashion Center Information Kiosk* ARCHITECT: *James Biber* ARCHITECT/ASSISTANT: *Michael Zweck-Bronner* GRAPHICS CREATIVE DIRECTOR: *Michael Bierut* GRAPHIC DESIGNER: *Esther Bridavsky* COMPANY: *Pentagram Architectural Services/Pentagram Design, Inc.* CLIENT: *The Fashion Center* PHOTOGRAPHER: *James Shanks* YEAR: *1996*

Mixing Fields

Principal, McCoy & McCoy, Buena Vista, Colorado

>> **In addition to being chair of the graphic design graduate program at Cranbrook for almost twenty-five years, you have worked in many design disciplines—graphic, interior, exhibition, product. Why did you combine these interests, and how do you balance them?**

I find it impossible to separate the design fields into tidy little compartments. Each has everything to do with the others. Graphic design has materiality and dimensionality, products and interior must communicate, and a large-scale exhibition combines communications, product, interiors, and even architecture. Mixing the fields comes especially naturally to me because my husband and design partner, Michael McCoy, is an industrial and furniture designer who also has a love of graphic design. Together we make an interdisciplinary design team. We also enjoy partnering with other designers, including architects and interior designers, on large projects.

What is the gratification in this?

One of the most gratifying of our interdisciplinary projects came a few years ago, when we were asked to design the office of the president of Formica Corporation using the company's products. We used Formica Colorcore to graphically mark work zones and traffic areas, combining our enthusiasm for both interiors and graphic design. The office's custom furniture integrated work surfaces and cabinetry into the walls, also with functionality markings embedded in the Formica surfaces. Before the office interior was installed, the company displayed it at the Pacific Design Center's West Week. As an exhibit, it needed a panel for fabrication and design credits. So I designed a plaque that translated the office's three-dimensional design language into a bas-relief of laminated Colorcore. The invitation for the exhibition's opening was another opportunity to translate the design vocabulary, this time into an offset printed paper piece. So what began as an exercise of bringing graphic design into an environment ended as a translation of an environment back into graphic design.

How is your graphic work enriched by other disciplinary work?

I find that other design fields are laden with fresh ideas that can enrich graphic design. For instance, architecture is a much older and more highly evolved field that has a whole body of history, theory, and criticism that can be bent to apply to graphic design as well. As postmodernism began to germinate in architecture, I found architectural thinkers like Robert Venturi gave a useful context to our experiments in graphic design.

TITLE: *Expo 2000 Hannover Poster* DESIGNER: *Katherine McCoy* CREATIVE DIRECTOR: *Egon Chemaitis* COMPANY: *McCoy & McCoy Associates* CLIENT: *Expo 2000 Committee, Hannover, Germany* TYPEFACES: *Caslon Italic, Futura Condensed* YEAR: *1997*

Do you see cross-disciplinary activity as a future trend, or is this something that is endemic to our practice?

Design projects are becoming ever bigger and more complex, both in content and technology, and require a range of expertise far greater than one person can embody.

This requires teamwork, and I see three basic types of teams. One is composed of similar professionals; this has been common for years on large-scale communications projects like corporate identity systems and annual reports. Second is an interdisciplinary team composed of a mix of design professionals; for instance, the design of a large hospital requires architects, interior designers, and graphic designers for the signage and wayfinding. The design of a piece of electronic equipment requires industrial designers for the major physical configuration; they must develop an operational interface with software interaction designers, and both must work with communications designers for the look and feel of the interface and the hard controls and brand identity. The third type of team is an overlay of the first two and positions design as a strategic component of business competitiveness. Designers are becoming involved in product development and communications planning on interdisciplinary teams that can include specialists in finance, marketing, advertising, and engineering long before a project advances to the design brief. This type of designer must know the theory and language of business and marketing, allowing equal participation on a high level in a business organization. It is increasingly common for designers to pursue MBAs in graduate schools of business management. In the undergraduate training of a designer, it is advisable to include as much marketing and business management course work as possible.

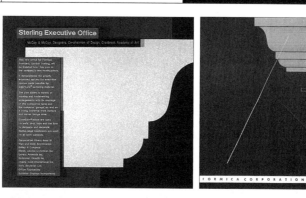

TITLE: *Cranbrook Academy of Art Catalog*
DESIGNER: *Katherine McCoy* DESIGN ASSISTANCE: *Lorraine Wild* COMPANY: *McCoy & McCoy Associates* CLIENT: *Cranbrook Academy of Art* PHOTOGRAPHER: *Steven Milanowski* TYPEFACE: *Helvetica* YEAR: 1976

TITLES: *Sterling Executive Office Design and Fabrication Credits Plaque and Sterling Executive Office Exhibition Reception Invitation* DESIGNER: *Katherine McCoy* COMPANY: *McCoy & McCoy Associates* CLIENT: *Formica Corporation, Susan Lewin* TYPEFACE: *Helvetica* YEAR: 1985

TITLE: *Sterling Executive Office; President's Office Interior, Formica Corporation* DESIGNERS: *Katherine McCoy, Michael McCoy* COMPANY: *McCoy & McCoy Associates* CLIENT: *Formica Corporation, Susan Lewin* YEAR: 1985

| # Making a Brand

Editorial Director, Martha Stewart Living OmniMedia, New York City

>> **You began as a book designer, and now you are involved in all aspects of marketing. What is the most important lesson you've learned?**

I've learned why product design has gotten to be where it is: because the people who make design decisions are the financial people. They look at what was sold last year and base their decisions on what their sales were. This totally stymies any innovation or inspiration or ability to have impromptu ideas. Martha is able to cut through that because she is a believable personality. She's got great taste and style, and she really is forcing manufacturers to think carefully about what they are doing. Just because something is discount, don't give people the bottom of the line. People who can't afford four-hundred-dollar bedsheets still deserve to have good design, even if they're only buying twenty-four-dollar sheets. It's a very populist idea.

How is the company organized?

We're trying to organize our businesses along the lines of our interests. So gardening, food, decorating, crafts, weddings, and holidays are the things that we are invested in across all media. We have experts here who work across media because they are the expert on gardening or cooking or whatever. Then each business

TITLE: Wash Day: MSL Clotheskeeping Special Issue DESIGNERS: Gael Towey, Michelle Outland CREATIVE DIRECTOR: Gael Towey PUBLICATION: Martha Stewart Living PHOTOGRAPHER: Victoria Pearson TYPEFACES: Wello Script, Humanist YEAR: 1998

TITLE: Wool—MSL Clotheskeeping Special Issue DESIGNERS: Gael Towey, Michelle Outland CREATIVE DIRECTOR: Gael Towey PUBLICATION: Martha Stewart Living PHOTOGRAPHER: Richard Phibbs TYPEFACE: Wello Script YEAR: 1998

TITLE: Figs: Glossary DESIGNER/CREATIVE DIRECTOR: Gael Towey PUBLICATION: Martha Stewart Living PHOTOGRAPHER: Maria Robledo TYPEFACE: MSL Gothic YEAR: 1997

TITLE: Peaches
DESIGNER/CRE-
ATIVE DIRECTOR:
Gael Towey
PUBLICATION:
Martha Stewart
Living PHOTOG-
RAPHER: Christopher
Baker TYPEFACES:
Garamond, MSL Gothic
YEAR: 1995

TITLE: Chickens
DESIGNER/
CREATIVE DIREC-
TOR: Gael Towey
PUBLICATION:
Martha Stewart Living
PHOTOGRAPHER:
Victor Schrager
TYPEFACE: MSL
Gothic YEAR: 1994

TITLE: Bouquets:
MSL Weddings/Spring
Issue DESIGNER/
CREATIVE DIREC-
TOR: Gael Towey
PUBLICATION:
Martha Stewart Living
PHOTOGRAPHER:
Victoria Pearson
TYPEFACE: Elzevir
YEAR: 1998

has people who work solely on that business, but they have access to all the people in the core groups who are the experts. It's a complicated structure, and what we are finding is that it's extremely difficult to maintain—but we are at an incredible advantage because we have all of our experts here and they are trained by us, and Martha's very involved personally. We have K-Mart, Sherwin-Williams, who does our paint, and now we've just signed a deal with Kaufmann fabrics to do a line of fabrics, and we're also doing gardening with K-Mart.

You created a look for the magazine that many are now imitating. How do you feel about this?

I wish they'd get a life. Find their own damn photographer. Imitation is the best form of flattery.

How did the look develop?

The first thing I did was to think about Martha herself. She's very traditional, she's classic, but she's a very modern woman, and she's very visual. Photography has always been her love and her way of communicating, so we used photography in a way that is extremely respectful. Pictures are never ripped up or put on top of one another or anything like that; they're treated in a classical and delicate way. The typography tends to take a back seat; it's not very designed, it's quiet, and it's very readable because we want the person reading the magazine to have an intimate experience and not have to struggle.

»

What is the most fulfilling aspect of your job? And the least?

One of the greatest pleasures that I have is watching people grow, and I am lucky to be in a place where we've had incredible growth. The first assistant who I hired seven years ago is now running the *Wedding* magazine, and she's in her low thirties. Because of this phenomenal growth, people are amazed at what they've been able to do and how much they've grown—to be able to have gone from magazine design to product design and so on. It's very exciting. I feel enormous pride in the teaching aspect of being an art director and seeing people excel.

The hardest part of my job right now is managing the growth and the infrastructure, because we have grown so fast. I think we are over three hundred people now, and two years ago we were eighty people. It's been horrifyingly fast and breathtaking. We are trying hard to build infrastructure right now, moving from one area of neediness to the next. I hate watching people struggle. But it's been a double-edged sword, because the people who are struggling are also the people who have grown so fast in their jobs.

You do a lot of hiring. What do you look for in a designer?

We use interns and, in fact, we've hired a number from Rhode Island School of Design. RISD students seem to acquire an understanding of texture. That's kind of a weird thing to say, but most schools don't teach photography and they don't teach storytelling. It's very hard to find people who have all of these talents. So we tend to hire people who are artists, who can go out and make stuff up, and who are interested in decorating and cooking and so on and know a lot about it, or are willing to really learn about it.

ENTREPRENEURS

AN ENTREPRENEUR IS an independent creator, supplier, or distributor who establishes a business or develops a product, identifies a market, and sells the produced wares to the public. From its inception, the United States has been a country of small and large entrepreneurs, from Lisa the lemonade stand operator to Bill the Microsoft mogul. There is no shortage of viable business ideas in the air; furthermore, depending on the state of the national economy, there is easy access to start-up capital.

So what is a *design* entrepreneur? Would not a designer who opens an independent studio, firm, or office be considered an entrepreneur?

In the strictest sense, the answer to the second question is *yes*. But to be more specific, graphic design studios and firms that offer only client services are not truly entrepreneurial because service businesses do not create, supply, or distribute their own products. Conversely, as an answer to the first question, a graphic designer who in addition to providing services also initiates products (or in the argot of today, "content") is indeed entrepreneurial. What's more, many designers who have the ability to skillfully package and promote other people's products have discovered that it is more satisfying and at times more lucrative to develop their own wares.

This concept is not new, however. Over the past decades,

TITLE: *Peaches* DESIGNER/CREATIVE DIRECTOR: *Gael Towey* PUBLICATION: *Martha Stewart Living* PHOTOGRAPHER: *Christopher Baker* TYPEFACES: *Garamond, MSL Gothic* YEAR: *1995*

enterprising graphic designers have engaged in various forms of entrepreneurism, from small cottage industries to large retail establishments, from balsamic vinegar bottling to book packaging. A graphic designer is not locked into products related to graphic design alone but rather is free to develop any kind of merchandise (see sidebar) from candy to furniture—or whatever the imagination conjures. Entrepreneurial activity is either a supplement to an existing design business or a totally independent subsidiary of one, yet in both cases new products contribute to creative and business challenges that add value to a designer's personal and professional worth. All that is required is a good idea, some capital, a simple business plan, a means of manufacturing, a method of distribution, and a modicum of chutzpah.

Being an entrepreneur is not a viable direction for the designer who lacks the confidence to test the limits of creativity or the stamina to take business risks, but it is safe to say that almost everyone with creativity has at least one idea that is worth developing as product. For the faint of heart, as an alternative to starting an entrepreneurial business, many graphic designers develop products for other businesses, and they either retain rights to or obtain royalties from the sale of their products. Although in this scenario the graphic designer is still working for a client, the result is not a framing of a client's product or idea with a brochure, package, or other service-oriented item but

rather providing the client with an entity that adds value to the product line. Some of the most common products graphic designers have been commissioned to create are watches, clocks, bed sheets, towels, greeting cards, neckties, jewelry, even furniture.

Depending on the simplicity or ambition of the product,

BEING AN ENTRE-PRENEUR IS NOT A VIABLE DIRECTION FOR THE DESIGNER WHO LACKS THE CONFIDENCE TO TEST THE LIMITS OF CREATIVITY OR THE STAMINA TO TAKE BUSINESS RISKS...

the learning curve varies greatly. While mistakes are invariably made, entrepreneurism offers the graphic designer insight into the nature of business as well as the satisfaction that simply toiling as a service provider will never generate. If the future of graphic design is greater involvement in the means and result of production, this cross-disciplinary activity is a large step in that direction.

DESIGNERS' PRODUCTS

Many graphic designers and design studios have gone into entrepreneurial businesses either for the fun of it or to supplement their income. These are some of the firms and their products:

Dana Arnett: documentary films

CSA Archive: clip art books, watches

Doyle and Partners: watches

William Drenttel: books

Emigre: magazine, books, records

Nancye Green: chairs

Guarnaccia Studio: metal sculpture

Higashi Glaser Design: children's toys

Alex Isely: refrigerator magnets

Jerry Herring Design: books

Michael Ian Kaye: soft drinks

Louise Fili Ltd.: basil vinegar

M&Co: watches, stationery supplies

Richard McGuire: children's toys

Francoise Mouly: regional map and guide

Pentagram: books, ephemera

Plazm: magazine, records

Push Pin Studio: gourmet candy

Studio Pänépinto: handbags, T-shirts, dishes

Supon Design: books

Michael Vanderbyl: furniture

Vignelli Associates: clothing

Walking Man: clothing

JIM HEIMANN | Book Man

Creative Director, Taschen Books, Los Angeles

>> **What made you, a graphic designer, so interested in producing books in an entrepreneurial way?**

I have always been interested in the whole process of putting a book together. I like to control the project from concept to finished product, not just putting a proposal together and handing it over to an agent. This control came from my college classes where we had to complete a project including the design, writing, illustration, type, and mechanical production. I found that it was hard to relinquish this control in my postgraduate world, so I blindly approached publishing from the winner-takes-all perspective. Plus the book business is all about being an entrepreneur. From gathering the material for a book to putting a proposal together, it's all about being self-motivated and going to market with your creation. Of course, if you don't have a broad skill set to produce a package, you have to farm some of these duties out. Luckily, what I didn't have I educated myself, through trial and error, some good connections, and a lot of helpful people.

Your interest in popular culture has led you to uncover designs that might be taken for granted. What is so interesting about vernacular forms?

My introduction and appreciation of vernacular imagery came from a variety of sources begin-

ning while I was in high school. The Pop Art movement had an element of exposing appreciation of the everyday. Packaging, labels, comics, postcards, tattoos, and other anonymous imagery was scrutinized and reinterpreted into art, and this stuff was very appealing to me, primarily because it was not so formal. At about the same time I entered college, Push Pin Studios was hitting its stride, and Milton Glaser and Seymour Chwast were mining and exposing vernacular elements in their art. I recall being taken by Walker Evans photographs for the Farm Security Administration in the 1930s, especially the ones that featured billboards and signage done by untrained artists. Add to that psychedelic posters from the late 1960s, which appropriated a lot of vernacular imagery, and you have the foundation of my obsession with this visual form. From there it was a slippery road to obsession ferreting out postcards, match covers, pamphlets, menus, and other ephemera that have found their place in my books.

As the creative director for Taschen Books in the United States, how much of your job is design, and how much is editing?

While I am responsible for putting together titles for my own books (anywhere from three up to ten

projects in a calendar year), I am also responsible for overseeing all content and flow of any text that is used on other projects that fall within my category. Among my other duties are: reviewing all proposals from American authors; coming up with ideas for new titles; purchasing content (photos, ephemera, etc.) for any titles that need it; connecting with the manager of our Beverly Hills bookstore and coordinating the mix of titles and staging store publicity events. As far as the design part, most of the design is done in Cologne, Germany, with the exception of a few projects. At Taschen, a general design model based on the grid is utilized for designing most of the books, resulting in a certain in-house style. Our books are very clean. One reason for this is that much of our content is heavy on the visual side, and Benedikt Taschen, our publisher, wants the visuals to drive the design and showcase the work. Taschen book design is a direct reflection of the publisher and his tastes, with the collaboration of several other people. It has been a trade-off of sorts but I respect his design sensibilities.

For some designers who turn to entrepreneurship, design becomes less important than developing content. Is this true in your case?

For my own projects, both things are equally important. I want my imprint on everything from reviewing the contract and negotiating the price to writing the text and deciding typefaces. Thus the design remains part of the game. Developing the content can be more consuming sometimes, and for me that is often the best part. Researching and compiling the material still remains a joy. Discovering little-known facts and new images still keeps me going. The development of an idea and getting it to market is still a rush.

Has desktop publishing made it easier for the designer to become the designer-entrepreneur?

Desktop publishing has made a lot of things easier from a production standpoint. The downside is that many people think that a computer equals a publishing career. However, developing content, taking an idea to market, and entrepreneurship in general are not directly affected by the digital world. A lot of that is still old-school hard work: making phone calls, knocking on doors, and coming up with ideas. So far, a computer hasn't been able to do that.

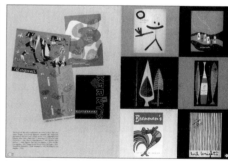

TITLE: Hula DESIGNER: Paul Mussa ART DIRECTOR: Jim Heimann CLIENT: Taschen Publishing YEAR: 2004

TITLE: May I Take Your Order? DESIGNER/ ART DIRECTOR/ TYPOGRAPHER (cover lettering): Jim Heimann CLIENT: Chronicle Books YEAR: 1998

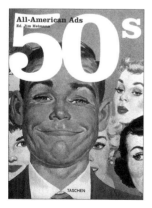

TITLE: '50s Ads DESIGNERS: Jim Heimann, Cindy Vance ART DIRECTOR: Jim Heimann CLIENT: Taschen Publishing YEAR: 2001

Bowls for Better Living

Principal, Studio Pänépinto, Ramsey, New Jersey

>> **How did your entrepreneurial endeavor begin?**

I have always wanted to be an entrepreneur. It is in the family genes. My great-grandfather started a very successful medical device company. Also, my dad, an engineer, invents all kinds of useful things, coupled with my mom (I think of her as a "life-artist"), who has shown me ways to look at the world from all angles. With this foundation, I've been able to see how starting a business and creating new things could be rewarding.

After going to Pratt Institute for my undergraduate degree, I started a company that designed handbags and T-shirts. I only stayed in business for about a year before realizing that I was more interested in designing products that would make the world a better place, rather than merely making accessories and clothing. I needed to go back to school to get a better direction. The SVA MFA was the only logical program for me because the program emphasized authorship of work and entrepreneurial focus.

While at SVA, I was planning a wedding, working a part-time job, and trying to lose some weight in the process. I had little time to prepare meals and watch what I was eating. I had been measuring my portions in a measuring cup (which I would then eat out of) for some time when I came up with the idea for mesü, a set of dishes that were pretty enough to take to the table that also measured food.

Once you developed your product, how did you find a viable market?

As an entrepreneur, it is hard to be all things to all people, and selling and marketing are my weaker skills. When mesü was ready to hit the market, I was very lucky to have a network of people who believed in me and the product. Brian Collins, my thesis professor at SVA, took it upon himself to launch mesü for me. He bought the first 100 sets, which were sent to his friends and colleagues as holiday gifts, December 2003. From this, I received all kinds of responses of praise and criticism. But there *is* one response that stands out against all others. This came from Elizabeth Talerman.

Elizabeth had been successful in advertising for fifteen years and was looking for a career shift. She approached me about starting a sort of partnership where she and a third person, Gina Paoloni, would work with me to bring mesü to market.

Because many Americans are interested in staying healthy and also with losing weight, mesü has a very broad audience. What narrows it a little is the price point of $49.95, which brings it into a higher market than, say, K-mart. After looking at the possibilities, Elizabeth and Gina went head-on into the market and

TITLE: *Mesü* DESIGNER: *Jennifer Pänépinto* CLIENT: *Studio Pänépinto* YEAR: *2004*

introduced mesü. They went after higher-end big box retailers and small gift boutiques.

Simultaneous to going after wholesalers, we started seeking editorial press, although many editors were finding us on their own as well. Magazines such as *ID*, *Step*, *How*, and *Food & Wine*, to name a few, ran features that helped to generate sales on the retail end by bringing customers to the mesü Web site. Gina was also able to secure mesü a spot on the TV show *eXtra* and the *Today* show, which increased sales as well.

How much of your project is about graphic design? And how much is about business?

My project is about making something that I needed, and then realizing that other people needed it too. I was just so tired of punishing myself, eating out of a measuring cup, while my husband ate out of a normal dish—which makes it about 20 percent me. The design of it, making it pretty enough to eat off of, for myself as well as others, and making all the collateral is about 40 percent. Getting it out there, the business part of it, to the other people who may need it, is about 40 percent.

Has being an entrepreneur added to your design craft?

Absolutely. Yes. Being able to set my own boundaries, rather than have them set for me, is precious. The project would simply not happen without the freedom and self-discipline of being an entrepreneur.

What would you advise a designer who wants to make and sell a product?

· It may seem obvious, but ask yourself, does the world really want this? What is the human element of the work?
· Believe in the project with your heart. Don't make it until you do.
· Show it to as many people as you can, take the advice you want, and rework the project and show again. Repeat as necessary until you get only excitement from those who experience it.

· Commit to investing money as well as time, but don't expect only money as the return.
· Ask for help when you need it; you don't have to do it alone.
· Understand the value of the fight, the value of making something out of nothing. And keep fighting.
· Realize that your way of seeing the world and your project is unique, and others will respect and welcome your vision.

TITLE: *Mesü*
DESIGNER: *Jennifer Pänépinto*
CLIENT: Studio *Pänépinto*
YEAR: 2004

| # Design Is Business

Art Director, Charles S. Anderson Design Co. and CSA Images, Minneapolis, Minnesota

>> **Give us an idea of the range of entrepreneurial concerns you are involved in.**

In 1995, we formed CSA Images as a separate company from Charles S. Anderson Design to concentrate on creating unique stock illustration and photography collections as well as on licensing images for use on retail products. The CSA Archive Stock CD and catalog contains over 8,000 line art illustrations. CSA Snapstock, a new collection of 7,000 illustrations, suggests the jazz/beatnik era. CSA Plastock is a new resource based on photographs of our synthetic friends: the plastic person, object, building, shot individually or in combination from our collection of 50,000 pieces of plastic to convey virtually any photo concept. After ten years of designing award-winning packaging and products for other companies, we decided to launch our own brand, Chuk A, a licensed young men's and women's apparel line. We are also currently in the process of upgrading our watch line with a Swiss manufacturer.

As the producer of a line of products, how much of your day is involved in business versus creative?

My time is split about in half. The eight employees of CSA Images spend all of their time on products.

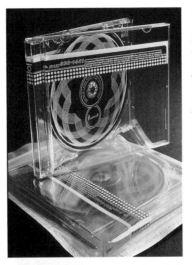

TITLE: Plastock CD Packaging DESIGNERS: Jason Schulte, Todd Piper-Hauswirth CREATIVE DIRECTOR: Charles S. Anderson FIRM: Charles S. Anderson Design Co. CLIENT: Plastock YEAR: 1997

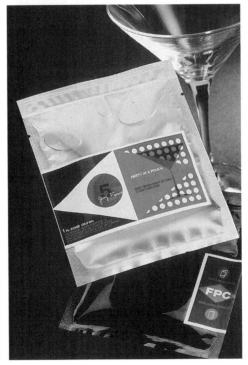

TITLE: Portable Martini (annual report survival kit) DESIGNER: Jason Schulte CREATIVE DIRECTOR: Charles Spencer Anderson COMPANY: Charles Spencer Anderson Design Co. CLIENT: French Paper Company YEAR: 1997

What do you look for in the portfolio of a designer?

We look for image-makers, people with good ideas who can convey them with strong visual concepts using either photography or illustration. We also look for people with good typographic skills. What we don't look for is someone who is attempting to knock off what they think our style is, which usually turns out to look like a bad rendition of something we were doing five years ago that we have long since moved on from.

Many talented designers have moved through your firm. Is there room for advancement? To what level?

Nearly every designer started as an intern and advanced to a designer. Todd Piper-Hauswirth was made a partner last year and is still a designer. We don't have a lot of layers or titles. Good design is what we love to do, and it's the goal of everyone here.

In my opinion, the highest job position we have, and the most impressive title, is designer. With our launch into licensed products and images, the company has the potential for change and success that could hold a lot of promise for all of us.

TITLE: *Presentation Invite* DESIGNER/CREATIVE DIRECTOR: *Charles S. Anderson* FIRM/CLIENT: *Charles S. Anderson Design Co.* YEAR: *1997*

TITLE: *French Direct Packaging* DESIGNER: *Jason Schulte* CREATIVE DIRECTOR: *Charles Spencer Anderson* COMPANY: *Charles Spencer Anderson Design Co.* CLIENT: *French Paper Company* YEAR: *1997*

TITLE: *Seinfeld Poster* DESIGNER/CREATIVE DIRECTOR: *Charles Spencer Anderson* COMPANY: *Charles Spencer Anderson Design Co.* CLIENT: *Entertainment Weekly* YEAR: *1998*

TITLE: *French Revolution* DESIGNERS: *Jason Schulte, Todd Piper-Hauswirth* CREATIVE DIRECTOR: *Charles Spencer Anderson* COMPANY: *Charles Spencer Anderson Design Co.* CLIENT: *French Paper Company* YEAR: *1997*

TITLE: *Rocket Boy* DESIGNER: *Todd Piper-Hauswirth* ART DIRECTOR: *Charles S. Anderson* COMPANY: *Charles S. AndersonDesign Co.* CLIENT: *Chuk A Apparel* PHOTOGRAPHER: *Plastock/CSA Images* YEAR: *1997*

DEBORAH ADLER | Ideas That Sell

Proprietor, Deborah Adler Design, New York City

How long have you had your own studio?

Since January 2008.

What are the changes in practice you have seen and experienced since you began?

For various reasons (environmental, social, economic), more and more people are moving away from print. Main forms of communication are through social networking and text messages. Where do we fit in? Designers have to redefine their roles and evolve in order to remain relevant to communication trends. The economy has affected many client priorities. Unfortunately, the extreme pressure on the bottom line has made design a discretionary element for many businesses.

How have these changes impacted your work?

My studio is twofold: client projects and self-initiated projects. A tough economy can lead to innovation on all fronts because it forces us to adopt a new way of approaching nearly everything we do. One of my challenges is to educate my clients on how design can be a value-added proposition for their business.

Developing my own ideas that sell is a good way to help keep my studio afloat. Not only does it have the potential to make a difference in peoples' lives, but it can also make a difference in a company's bottom line. Most important, it is also a wonderful way to keep things interesting for me.

The intersection between these two parts is where I learn the most. I take my experiences and learning from one area and apply them to the other.

Would you say that you have a particular style or character to your design?

I was taught not to trust style because it is somewhat irrelevant. However, much of my work could be defined as an attempt to change behavior through design. We are in the mysterious business of "creating an experience" for people. And when I employ design to make that experience a comfortable one, or an informative one, I have done my job.

Would you give an example?

When I began my attempt to transform the way prescription drugs are packaged for the consumer, I didn't start by researching the healthcare industry, and I didn't start by researching the pharmaceutical industry. I began my work at ground level, with my grandmother. I wanted to take a scary episode she had gone through, and change it into a safe, reassuring experience in the future. Since she is my grandmother, I really understood my customer, and empathized with her needs. And I was surprised to discover how easily my Grandma's needs translated into the needs of all Target customers.

TITLE: ClearRx CLIENT: Target Corporation DESIGNERS: Deborah Adler, Target Industrial DESIGNER: Klaus Rosburg ART DIRECTOR: Deborah Adler YEAR: 2005

TITLE: Lauren Merkin Gift Box CLIENT: Lauren Merkin DESIGNERS: Deborah Adler, Yayun Huang ART DIRECTOR: Deborah Adler YEAR: 2009

What about graphic design is the most challenging for you?

The process of developing a design solution. I have learned the best thing is to stay open to exploration, even though my instinct is to rush to a solution because I am in unchartered territory. I try to stay in that uncomfortable zone for as long as possible. This is the most challenging for me, and by far the most rewarding because it gives me the chance to learn something new.

How important is type and typography in what you do?

It is essential, but only second to truly thinking about the person who will benefit from your design/type skills, and how that design can meet their needs, and solve a very human problem.

What, in this current technological and economic climate, does the future hold for you specifically, and graphic design in general?

Designers are adapting to a new environment. We have to be flexible and eager to take advantage of opportunities. I am committed to improving safety, care, and the quality of peoples' lives, and I never forget it is a continuing and collaborative process.

TITLE: *First Aid Beauty Packaging*
CLIENT: *First Aid Beauty LLC*
DESIGNER/ART DIRECTOR:
Deborah Adler YEAR: *2009*

KIND

Rukmin Ramsuchit
Senior Project Manager

The Kind Group
27 W 24th St Suite 10-C
New York, NY 10010
Tel: 212 645 0800 x16
Fax: 212 645 0755
Mobile: 917 886 6734
rukmin@thekindgroup.com

K KIND

TITLE: *Kind Group Logo and Business Card* CLIENT: *The Kind Group* DESIGNER: *Deborah Adler* YEAR: *2007*

TITLE: *Lauren Merkin Gift Packaging* CLIENT: *Lauren Merkin* DESIGNERS: *Deborah Adler, Yayun Huang* ART DIRECTOR: *Deborah Adler* YEAR: *2009*

TITLE: *Medline Advanced Wound Care Packaging System* CLIENT: *Medline Industries* DESIGNERS: *Deborah Adler, Milton Glaser* ART DIRECTORS: *Deborah Adler, Milton Glaser* YEAR: *2007*

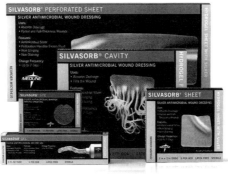

| **Too Many Ideas**

Proprietor, David Barringer Studio, North Carolina

>> **How long have you been a freelance designer?**

I have never had full-time employment at a company, but I have also never had what you'd call a studio. I'm more like an independent creative worker. I write and design from home. So over the years I've worked wherever I could find space. I've pushed my desk up against walls in apartments. I've hidden my desk in the basement of our first house. I've balanced a laptop on a countertop in a two-bedroom apartment while my kids played on a mattress in the living room. Right now I have a small study with built-in shelves for books and a cable Internet line in the floor. I've been working as a freelancer since 1992, when I sold my first article to a magazine, just before I went to law school in Ann Arbor. I was twenty-two. I continued to freelance during school, and I wrote and designed the law-school newspaper on a desktop Macintosh, printing issues at a local copy shop.

What are the changes in practice you have seen and experienced since you began?

I used to spend nights in the college computer room picking fonts for my short stories and printing them out. Today students can blog from their dorm rooms or Twitter from anywhere on campus. Creative energy today has an instant outlet. There is virtually no delay between impulse and dissemination. Your expression (in text, image, audio, video) can reach the audience in seconds. This can be dangerous for creative people. You can find a community and support for your work, but instant gratification leads to a kind of self-defeating craving for little, fleeting pleasures. I think we have to be on guard to step back, reclaim some of our private time, and imagine larger projects for ourselves, larger goals that might require more time and effort but will pay off in much greater rewards in our creative lives.

How have these changes impacted your work?

Because so much can be done digitally, I have to remind myself to incorporate the marks of humanity into my designs. So I often intentionally sneak in imperfections, scan in old book pages or botched photographs, add scribbles and scratches from my sketchbooks. Because the distance from impulse to publication can be so instantaneous, I slow down, let my work sit a while, edit and rework things carefully. I have the urge to fire things off as soon as I'm done with them, but I'm always relieved when I decide to let things sit an extra day or even a month.

TITLE: Opium Magazine, Issue 5, Magazine Cover CLIENT: Opium Magazine DESIGNER/ ART DIRECTOR/PHOTOGRAPHER: David Barringer YEAR: 2007

TITLE: "American Home Life" Book Cover CLIENT: So New Publishing DESIGNER/ART DIRECTOR: David Barringer YEAR: 2007

Do you have a particular style or character to your design? If so, how would you define it?

I do have certain intentions that recur. I try to avoid the overly literal, the literalized metaphor, the obvious. I try to avoid those sorts of designs that are real groaners or have nothing much to offer the interpretive, inquisitive mind. I try to design covers or layouts that mean something, tell a story or part of a story, deepen in mood or association as the person reads the book, novel, or magazine and then returns to consider the cover design or the typesetting. This doesn't mean the design has to be ornate or illustrative or complex. It doesn't drive the design in any particular direction or toward any particular style at all. It's meant to drive my imagination, not determine the final form of the design.

What about graphic design is the most challenging for you?

I have too many ideas, and I have difficulty choosing among the options. I can see both the virtues and flaws in anything I've created, and for that reason, I have a hard time making a final judgment. If I can't choose the best book cover out of twenty, then I figure my indecisiveness is itself the decision. In other words, if no cover jumps out of the pack, then maybe no cover is good enough yet. They're just mediocre.

What are the projects that most satisfy your aesthetic sense?

Books. I love writing and designing books. I'm an author and a designer, so the book is the perfect marriage of my two passions. I also love that tension between the object of the book itself and the imagined world created by reading the words on the page. There is wonderful drama that goes on between the visual and cerebral, the image and the word, the flat fact of the page and the deep dream of the mind. I love thinking about new ways to make books, looking for ways to combine photography and aphorism, typographic play and short stories, or illustration and poetry.

How important is type and typography in what you do?

It's critical, because I write and design books, literary journals, and other printed materials like posters, brochures, and business cards. It's the one area, in addition to Web design, in which I tell myself I really need to take a course now and then, like a continuing education course. I have learned about type slowly, in punctuated bursts, over the years, a little bit from a lot of sources, including from clients, other designers, and guidebooks. The more you know about typography, and the more experience you have working with a variety of style sheets for »

TITLE: "There's Nothing Funny About Design," Book Cover
CLIENT: Princeton Architectural Press
DESIGNER/ART DIRECTOR: David Barringer
ILLUSTRATOR: Felix Sockwell
YEAR: 2009

typesetting as well as for grammar and language style, the better off you will be when you have to make judgments as you perform the work of setting type.

What, in this current technological and economic climate, does the future hold for you specifically, and graphic design in general?

I plan to teach writing to design and art students. I will teach courses on critical thinking and writing on art, design, and culture. Students need to be able to observe, evaluate, criticize, and write persuasively. Everyone lacks these abilities until he or she decides to develop them. No one sits down at the piano for the first time ever and plays Mozart. We learn and train and practice to gain a level of competence in music or writing or design. Writing well enables you to think well. Thinking and writing critically develop your personality, improve your ability to control the design process, enable you to communicate clearly with peers, bosses, and clients, and protect you from being taken advantage of in the workplace.

Is working as a graphic designer economically difficult?

Yes, it's a tough economic climate, but that's the *national* economic climate. It doesn't mean you specifically can't work hard and get a job. It might be more difficult, but so what? Hardships of any kind won't change my advice to anyone regarding their work. No matter what, you have to stick with doing the work you love to do. If you lose a design job and you still love design, you need to stick in that industry, somehow. Some friends talk about leaving their familiar industry to find success and easy money in some other industry.

AUTHORSHIP

AUTHORSHIP IS A CURRENT buzzword for graphic designers searching for new ways to broaden the scope and increase the relevance of their cultural contribution. The term references writing, but authorship is not exclusively about writing—rather, it is about producing entire projects. Now that graphic design is at the proverbial crossroads, where new media are forcing a reevaluation and redefinition of what graphic designers do, authorship distinguishes the old commercial art from the new visual communication. Unless authorship is clearly defined in the context of what graphic designers do (and will do in the future), this, like so many other self-proclaimed titles, will have as much significance as a mail-order Ph.D.

Nonetheless, authorship is a growing subspecialty of the broader field and must be acknowledged as a viable cross-disciplinary option.

There are two kinds of graphic designer: One is primarily production-oriented, the other primarily idea-oriented. Although the two are not mutually exclusive, a byproduct of the digital revolution is a clearer distinction between those with technical skill and those with imagination. Ever since prepress production was more or less taken out of the hands of craftspeople and placed in the laps (or laptops) of designers, for designers to grow in the creative realm they

TITLE: Interior Spread Pages 90–91, Opium Magazine, Issue 8 CLIENT: Opium Magazine
DESIGNER/ART DIRECTOR: David Barringer YEAR: 2009

have to vigorously pursue all the options or get pigeonholed as production specialists. The computer has forced more responsibility onto designers to do work that was previously assigned to middlemen, yet it has also allowed for increased creative potential. The designer need not be a detached participant in an assembly line but can be the principal in a total production.

The most remarkable benefit of the computer is the potential it offers for those with vision to turn ideas into products. Of course, one does not need a computer to accomplish such feats—a human brain is good enough—but the machine houses a wellspring of possibility. As stated above, entrepreneurism is not new, yet never in the history of graphic design has there been such a huge potential for independent production.

Authorship is not a theoretical construct but rather a form of entrepreneurship where the designer takes responsibility for the quality and efficacy of a product, which can be anything from a book to an exhibition to a documentary film. What distinguishes authorship from other entrepreneurial pursuits is the marriage of word and image to whatever medium conveys it. It is closely linked to the French concept of the *auteur*, a filmmaker who is a writer, director, and, sometimes, producer.

THE WHOLE BALL OF WAX

In a typical publishing contract, the author is the creator of the work or manuscript that will be designed, printed, and published by the publisher. However, not all book publishing is done this way. Today, the so-called author may be the packager or producer of a book who is responsible for hiring the writer, designer, photographer, copy editor, prepress production manager, and even for providing a publisher and distributor with the printed product. Graphic designers are well-suited for this kind of authorship because they are already involved in all but the marketing and distribution processes. In fact, a number of graphic designers not only act as packagers but are themselves writers—and some are even production managers. Ellen Lupton and J. Abbott Miller, who are partners in Design/Writing/Research, a multidisciplinary design firm, produce books and exhibition catalogs from start to finish. As the title of their firm indicates, they control all of the creative—they design, write, and research books on the history, theory, and practice of graphic design—as well as prepress production. Knowing how to produce an entire book enables these authors to take full creative responsibility rather than be detached suppliers. Keeping control of the product allows them to control the costs and earn the most for their effort.

One may argue that authorship and entrepreneurship are distinct activities and, conventionally speaking, an author is a creator, not a manufacturer or distributor. Conversely, an entrepreneur may not be a creator but rather a facilitator of others' talents. Indeed, these distinctions are both valid and apt. But in the changing professional environment, combining these two trajectories into *authorpreneur* offers the designer increased freedom and flexibility. Authorprenuership can be accomplished solo or through an ensemble, by a few individuals or a collaborative team. There are no real bounds, but there is a defining tenet: An authorpreneur *provides* rather than merely *interprets* content.

Authorprenuership may be a tongue-twisting word to say, but it is not a convoluted notion. While there will always be those more proficient at editing than producing, or designing than writing, today's graphic designer should not be content only to design the book, magazine, or Web site. Either collaboratively or individually, the designer must be totally invested in a project and product. While there is no doubt that the graphic design field is mutating, perhaps the most meaningful shift will be when the concept of authorship (or authorprenuership) is not just a word that falsely bestows loftier status on designers but is an activity that all designers undertake.

Is it important to have a design personality?

"A design personality is what is going to get you hired, going to get you clients, going to get you acolytes (in the form of free interns). This is a personality manifest in a set of characteristics evident in your work, a stylistic obsession, an obvious focus in the subject matter, a curiosity that can be seen from project to project. Essentially, a voice."
—*Eric Ludlum*

"IT IS IMPORTANT TO USE OPPORTUNITIES TO DO MEANINGFUL WORK THAT CONNECTS WITH YOUR AUDIENCE. WE SHOULD ENTER INTO PROJECTS WITH A LOT OF PASSION, PATIENCE, EXPERIENCE, AND OPENNESS. I WOULD NOT SAY YOU NECESSARILY NEED A LOT OF DESIGN PERSONALITY."
—*Deborah Adler*

"Personality itself is actually thought of as a no-no in information circles. You know: 'Just the facts, Ma'am.' Don't have an opinion about the facts, just present them. To me that's nonsense. Everybody has an opinion, and to sit on the fence and present both sides of every argument or set of numbers leads to a numbing, even-handed approach. If you don't like my take on the numbers, go somewhere else. One thing: Don't steal anyone else's style because you like it. You'll be found out."
—*Nigel Holmes*

"CLARITY, EXCITEMENT, OR HUMOR CAN CREATE INFECTIOUS INTEREST IN DESIGN—A SORT OF 'APPROACHABILITY.' A PERSONALITY (DESIGN INCLUDED) ISN'T REALLY COMPLETE UNLESS IT IS CAPABLE OF THE FULL RANGE OF EMOTIONS— ANGER, FEAR, AND SADNESS, AND SIMPLY 'QUIET.' "
— *Michael J. Walsh*

"You want the client to know what they'll likely get. I'm usually hired because they know my work. I think all my books look different and yet if you look at them side by side, you'll see a consistency."
—*Molly Leach*

"Sure, as long as it's authentic. The age of designer as brand is here and our design personalities are often intertwined with the work itself. But is it required to create powerful, compelling work? No."
—*Masood Bukhari*

"I wish sometimes I had one; it would make decision making so much easier. It's a certain way of thinking and either you think that way or you don't. That said, I tend to have themes that run through my designs for periods of time."
— *Ethan Trask*

"Seems unavoidable? I'm not sure how my design personality might vary from my overall personality; the former can't help but be an extension of the latter. Also, the studio now has its own, constantly shifting personality, as it's become the composite of the varied people who are involved at a given time."

— *Adam Michaels*

"I think it's important to have a personality. A great deal of design is the conversations and meetings— whether it is convincing clients to trust you or convincing a young designer to rein it in. All of these things are a lot easier if you have a personality and can relate to people and communicate well."

—*Dmitri Siegel*

"Having a distinct, popular style can make you marketable, maybe even famous. However, I think what is most important is to push yourself to do great work that you are proud of. If you do this and you work for or with people that push each other creatively—the results will almost always make you happy." —*Travis Cain*

"All designers have personality; some are just louder than others. So I guess the question is, 'Do I think it's important to have a personality that is loud and prevalent in design?' I battle with this. My current answer is yes, it is important, but there are less obvious, but still effective ways you can be heard—like consistently producing great work. " —*Rodrigo Corral*

"WHATEVER YOUR 'REGULAR' PERSONALITY, IT SHOULD BE THE SAME AS YOUR 'DESIGN PERSONALITY,' OR VICE VERSA; EVERYTHING ELSE SEEMS TOO COMPLI-CATED TO ME (TEMPORARY SHOWMANSHIP MIGHT BE FINE, THOUGH)."

—*Jan Wilker*

"I actually subscribe to the old adage that the very best graphic design appears authorless— even though my own style appears to contra-dict that entirely. I guess that makes me a failure as a designer in my own estimation."

—*Art Chantry*

"I THINK HAVING A DESIGN PERSONALITY CAN BITE YOU IN THE ASS. I HAVE SEEN FAR TOO MANY ONLINE DISCUSSIONS WHERE DESIGNERS COME OFF AS ARROGANT, COMBATIVE, AND INSULT-ING. I HAVE TO BELIEVE THAT HAS COST THEM FUTURE WORK OR CONNECTIONS. I KNOW THERE ARE SEVERAL DESIGNERS WHOSE WORK I LOVE THAT I WOULD NEVER BUY FROM OR REACH OUT TO BECAUSE THEY COME ACROSS LIKE JERKS. I DON'T SEE THE USE OF BITING THE HAND THAT FEEDS OR HELPS YOU." —*Jeffery Everett*

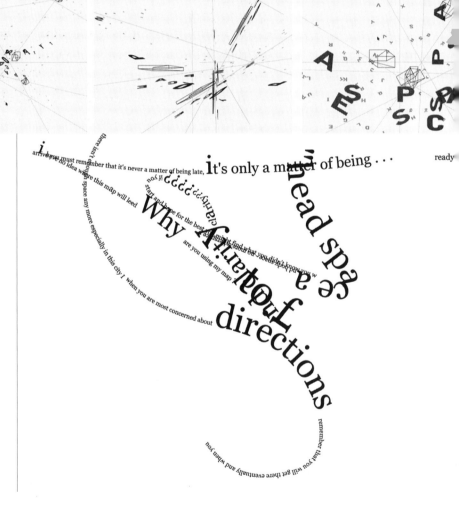

TITLE: Fractured (stills from a video by Tuan Phan of a book by Jennifer McKnight) DESIGNER/ CREATIVE DIRECTOR/ART DIRECTOR/PHOTOGRAPHER/ DIRECTOR/ILLUSTRATOR: Jennifer McKnight, PMFA VIDEOGRAPHY: Tuan Phan SCHOOL: CalArts, Valencia, CA INSTRUCTOR: Michael Worthington YEAR: 2001

TITLE: Typo Space DESIGNER: Joey Alviar, MFA 2 SCHOOL: CalArts, Valencia, CA INSTRUCTORS: Tom Bland, Ed Fella, Jeff Keedy, Lorraine Wild YEAR: 2001

TITLE: Mood Map DESIGNER/ ART DIRECTOR/ILLUSTRATOR: Emily Shaw, Parsons Design and Technology MFA student PROJECT: Student work created for the Digital Typography course INSTRUCTOR: Andrea Dezso YEAR: 2001

Two generations ago, one could convincingly argue that art or design school was not necessary to a good graphic design education. On-the-job experience was a more than adequate means of acquiring necessary skills—and, after all, talent is inborn. Today, the self-taught graphic designer is unusual. Even with all the how-to books on the market, those who acquire their interest in graphic design through working on the personal computer or through other art fields definitely require intensive training, if only to be fluent in the computer. But in order to go beyond rote computer applications to make really smart graphic design, a formal education is strongly recommended. A fundamental graphic design education can begin as early as high school. Desktop publishing at this grade level provides an introduction to the rudimentary tools and basic forms of print and screen design. Teaching kids how to design editorial and advertising pages and Web sites is an excellent way to get them interested in visual communications and it also serves as a primer for what follows.

SECTION 4

Design Education

The next step is to find a two- or, better yet, four-year undergraduate program at an art college or general university that offers a bachelor of fine arts (BFA) or equivalent degree. This is not to imply that a liberal arts education is to be ignored; liberal arts is a prerequisite that must be pursued in tandem with design instruction. However, these days, two years is barely enough time to learn the tools, theory, history, and practice of graphic design, as well as to develop a marketable portfolio. Of course, as four or more years in art or design school may be impossible for some and excessive for others, continuing education is also an option. For those with the desire and wherewithal, a graduate school education can be beneficial.

A few people possess a natural gift for graphic design and, with only a modicum of training, might turn into significant designers. But they are exceptions to the rule. Untutored designers usually produce untutored design. Although good formal education does not make anyone more talented, it does provide a strong foundation upon which to grow into a professional. While taking the occasional design class is better than no schooling at all, matriculation in a dedicated course of study, where you are bombarded with design problems and forced to devise solutions, yields much better results.

What should you look for in a two-year, four-year, or continuing education design program? The following is a general guide to undergraduate, graduate, and part-time education programs.

WHO'S GOING TO SCHOOL?

AN ESTIMATED 2,300 schools (two and four years) offer dedicated and ancillary graphic design programs and graduate about 50,000 students each year. Each year, more schools are adopting some kind of graphic design program that ranges from basic instruction of computer programs (InDesign, Photoshop) to advanced typography and layout to a range of complex digital media.

UNDERGRADUATE

Not every high school graduate knows what graphic design is. Because design is considered something of an arcane profession, most guidance counselors do not vigorously promote it as a viable career option. Prospective design students should examine the programs of as many schools as possible. Those who go to design school are introduced to graphic design, among other arts and crafts, during the foundation year. This is a time when many design and art forms are sampled prior to the student's selection of a major. Those art college students who are transfers from liberal arts programs likely go through the foundation year with everyone else (unless they specify otherwise and show a specific interest in graphic design).

Whether you decide on a dedicated art school or a state or private university art department does not matter (financial and location concerns often dictate this decision). More important is knowing the strengths and weaknesses of the chosen program. The fundamental instruction in the second year sets the tone for those to follow. Here are the areas to examine.

COMPUTER. While some design courses offer instruction in computer programs after more basic conceptual and formal issues are addressed, others dive right into the tool as vital to design practice. It does not really matter at what point the computer is taught (although most agree that it is better to understand the theory of design before attempting its practice), but computer skills must be keenly supported through individual and laboratory instruction throughout the program. It is further recommended that students have home computers or laptops so that they can practice often.

THEORY. Understanding what design is and how it works in both a philosophical and practical context is more important than doing the work, at least at the outset. If a student does not know what design is used for, how it functions, and at whom it is aimed, then making marks on paper or screen is fruitless. Graphic design is not a self-motivated fine art, and although the lessons of art may be integrated, communications theory in its various forms (semiotics, semantics, deconstruction, and so on) are the essential components of a well-rounded design education.

CONCEPT. Design is not decoration but rather the intelligent solution of conceptual problems; it is the manipulation of type, image, and, most of all, an idea that conveys a message. A strong design program emphasizes conception—developing big ideas—as a key component of the curriculum. Concept courses should include two- and three-dimensional design in all the media covered in Section 1.

TYPE. This is one of the primary means by which civilization communicates. A type font is not just something that comes installed in

PROSPECTIVE DESIGN STUDENTS SHOULD EXAMINE THE PROGRAMS OF AS MANY SCHOOLS AS POSSIBLE.

a computer. Classes in type and typography should, therefore, begin with the history of letterforms from the fifteenth century to the present—the art and craft behind them and the reasons that type conventions exist. The application of type past and present, in various media, and the purposes for which types and type families have been used should be covered. Type instruction should include a range of endeavors from metal typefounding to digital fontography. Once type has been fully addressed, typography—the design of typefaces on the page or screen context—should be thoroughly examined as both a reading and a display vehicle. Any study of typography should include intense debate about its function—legibility versus illegibility.

IMAGE. Design is about image making, and a well-rounded program includes classes devoted to photography, typo-foto (the marriage of type and picture), and illustration. Certain courses emphasize computer programs such as Photoshop, and these are indeed necessary. But a good program puts computer-generated art into perspective and, therefore, devotes more class time to traditional forms.

ADVERTISING. Some design departments segregate advertising and graphic design; others integrate the two. It is, however, useful for the graphic designer—even if book jackets or record covers are the intended specialty—to learn the techniques that go into this very public medium.

HISTORY. Most design departments are not equipped to offer more than survey courses on aspects of design history. Nevertheless, this is an integral part of design education that should continue throughout the program (and not as an elective, either). It is essential to know that graphic design has a history, and to be familiar with the building blocks of the continuum.

MULTIMEDIA. The volume of cross-disciplinary endeavors that affects designers today is only going to grow in the future. While the better part of a four-year program is devoted to training a student to design in the print or Web environment, knowledge of other media—film, television, video—is not only useful but can also be inspiring.

PRINTING. How can you design

without knowing the means of production? For a designer, being detached from the printing press is like being a doctor who never interned on a human being. Now that much prepress production is in the hands of the designer, knowledge of the final output process is more vital than ever.

BUSINESS. At the undergraduate level, few schools focus on the business of design in terms of starting a studio or firm, and all that it entails. Most design schools are concerned with developing the skills that lead to marketable portfolios, and energies are aimed at helping students get internships or jobs. Prudently, they do not encourage neophytes to start businesses immediately out of school. Nonetheless, business is an important aspect of the profession, so even if developing business plans and spreadsheets is inappropriate at this level, courses that address general business concerns are useful.

PORTFOLIO. The most important concrete result of a well-rounded education is the portfolio. Classes in how to develop portfolios usually begin in the senior year, when the student is given real-world problems in various media with the goal of creating a strong representation of talent and skill. A diploma is important, but the portfolio is evidence that a student earned it.

PLACEMENT. Schools with reputable internship programs are invaluable. Many programs have established relationships with studios, firms, and corporations throughout the United States and, often, the world. These schools place students and graduates in many working situations and monitor their development. Experience from these internships or temporary jobs (which may start in the sophomore year) is priceless and, on occasion, they lead to full-time positions. Good placement offices also keep job-bank notices and help the students prepare for these opportunities.

> *THE MOST IMPORTANT CONCRETE RESULT OF A WELL-ROUNDED EDUCATION IS THE PORTFOLIO.*

FACULTY. Let's not forget the teachers. A strong faculty is what makes all these programs work. Some schools maintain full-time faculty; others use professional faculty (part-time teachers who work full-time as designers, art directors, creative directors, etc.). Both situations are equally good. The value ultimately comes down to the individual. Inspiring teachers make the difference. Find out who they are.

GRADUATE SCHOOL

Two generations ago, only a few elite graduate schools offered programs devoted to graphic design. Today, quite a few two-year programs address aspects of the design profession. Graduate education is not for everybody, but it has become a viable means of developing areas of expertise that were ignored or deficient in most undergraduate schools. The masters of fine arts (MFA), master of arts (MA), and associate degree, which are the typical terminal degrees from graduate programs, are not necessary to obtain jobs or commissions (although if you want to teach at a university, the degree is usually mandatory), but they do indicate accomplishment: The designer has completed a rigorous course of study. For those interested in intensive instruction, the graduate school experience can be highly beneficial in creative and practical ways.

Graduate school is, however, a major investment in time and money. The average tuition is between $19,000 and $35,000. Some schools insist that students devote the majority of their time to school-related work; others are scheduled so that students can work at regular jobs or on commissions while attending evening classes.

Eligibility for graduate programs varies. All candidates must have bachelor or other degrees from undergraduate institutions (these need not always be design degrees). A few exceptions are made for work/time equivalency. Some programs accept all graduates immediately after graduating a four-year undergraduate art or design school; others seek students who have been working professionally for a year or more prior to returning to school. Portfolios and interviews are usually required, and the portfolios must include school or professional work that shows distinct talent and aptitude. Some entry requirements are more lax than others, but if the portfolio is deficient—if the prospective student shows nothing, for example, but mediocre desktop publishing work—additional training and practice is recommended before reapplying. Graduate programs are open to applicants of all ages who meet the entry requirements. Graduate school is a viable means for those who want to switch careers or to achieve greater proficiency and credentials.

If a prospective student meets all the eligibility requirements, the next step is to explore programmatic options to determine which school is appropriate to the specific educational need. Possibilities are numerous. Some programs are fairly free-form, where teachers guide a student along a self-motivated course of study. Others are more rigidly structured, with a set of specific goals to attain by the end of each study period (which may be a semester or more). Some programs are geared toward specialties; others are more general in scope. Among the specialties are corporate design, advertising design, and Internet design. A number of programs have philosophical and stylistic preferences, while others avoid ideology of any kind. Some are concerned with social activism, while others are devoted to the commercial marketplace. Some programs are better endowed than others.

Most programs have a cap on how many students are accepted annually. It is recommended that prospective students request literature from programs and visit those that are of most interest (some have open houses, others grant tours). Applicants commonly apply to more than one program, although each may require different materials. The following are programmatic concerns that should be explored before applying:

SCOPE. A graduate program is advanced study, not simply an extension of undergraduate school. While a curriculum may include components that overlap an undergraduate or continuing education course, it must go way beyond what is provided at these lower levels. When looking at a prospectus or talking with a graduate school admissions officer, determine the scope and goals of the program and the expectations it has of its students.

PHILOSOPHY. This is related to scope but demands its own category. A graduate program may require that students adhere to a particular pedagogical concept. This can be anything from minimalist (modern) to complex (deconstruction) design, or classical, or avant garde, or any other approach. It could be based on a certain iconoclasm or eclecticism. Whatever the philosophy may be, decide by talking to former students and teachers about its compatibility with your own attitudes.

TRADITION. Contemporary graphic design is as much about understanding the past as it is about diving into the future. While undergraduates are wrapped up in technology and processes that will allow them to get jobs immediately upon graduation, graduate programs should allow for greater reflection. A well-balanced program encourages students to work with their hands as well as their machines. It has a strong historical component that can be, in some way, integrated into contemporary practice.

TECHNOLOGY. A graduate program should be state-of-the-art. The design world is becoming inextricably connected to the multimedia environment, and while tradition is an important component of design pedagogy, advanced knowledge of the tools of production and creation is becoming requisite. If you are interested in becoming a producer or director as well as a designer, select a program that addresses these needs. Most contemporary graduate programs spend at least 50 percent, if not more, of class time on technological concerns, and have the hardware and labs to support thorough study.

MULTIDISCIPLINES. Graphic design graduate programs cannot afford to be specialized to the point of isolation. The more relationships with other media and genres are explored the better, even if only in survey courses.

FACILITIES. Undergraduate education is a string of related classes in a supportive environment, but graduate schools should provide facilities that encourage students to work in a more focused environment, both separately and in tandem with others. Facilities may include small studios or networked workstations in an integrated studio setting. It is important to know how you work best and in what kind of context. Some programs encourage the open studio; others simulate a design firm environment. The location of the plant is also important—for example, its proximity to other institutions or businesses. Although the graduate experience means, for some, an escape from the rigors of the quotidian, for others, it is a way to be integrated into everyday life.

FACULTY. A program is only as good as its teachers. Some graduate programs pride themselves on employing the leading practitioners in the field; others rely on full-time professors. Balancing the two is usually a good solution. In most course descriptions, the faculty members are listed along with their credentials. These should be seriously studied.

EXHIBITION. Most graduate programs are concerned that student work be tested and, ultimately, published and exhibited. Although what a student learns is most important, the quality of the results is evidence of a program's effectiveness. It is useful to examine both the means of presenting student work and the work itself. Publications are available to applicants, as are schedules of student exhibitions.

RESPONSIBILITY. A graduate program may be considered a cloistered existence. Increasingly, however, this is an opportunity for students to do the kinds of socially responsible projects that may less frequently be options in the workaday world. It is important to explore how a program contributes to the broader community.

BUSINESS. Even in a cloister, the real world must have a place, and the graduate school is indeed a good place to examine the business world. Graduate students are more likely than undergraduates to open their own businesses once they have earned their degrees. Design management and property law are important areas of concern at this level.

THESIS. The primary degree requirement is the final thesis. It is important to know what each graduate program expects of its students and how it goes about developing student thesis projects. What is involved in this process? Are there thesis classes, faculty advisers, review committees? Must the thesis be published? Ultimately, the thesis can be a portfolio or a key to a new career.

CONTINUING EDUCATION

Graduate school is not always feasible for those who must work at full-time jobs or who choose to obtain specific skills as a means to widen their career path. Therefore, the most common method of developing additional skills (and receiving inspiration) is through continuing education, also called night school. Some general colleges and universities offer programs, but usually it is the province of the art and design schools and colleges to offer a wide range of professional courses, from introductory to advanced. In addition to a potpourri of night school professional courses, some institutions offer intensive weeklong workshops with master teachers. Some of these programs are designed exclusively for working professionals (and require a fairly accomplished portfolio as a condition of acceptance), while others are open to a broader public.

Enrollees in continuing education classes run the gamut from professionals who seek to better themselves (maybe to earn promotions in their current workplaces) to neophytes who want additional career options. Classes are available for any level of expertise and are useful in acquiring knowledge, experience, and, in some cases, job opportunities.

Obviously, reputable continuing education programs are best, and they are usually offered by art and design schools. Most computer tutorials are useful, particularly as insight into common layout, illustration, photography, and graphics programs (many older professionals use these sessions to learn or brush up on new skills). A current trend is weeklong regional seminars run by either professional organizations or independent educational groups. The only rule of thumb for a potential student is to select a program that meets all needs based on the description or prospectus that is made available. Nevertheless, the financial investment is usually limited and, therefore, if a particular course does not offer enough useful or inspirational instruction, one can always try another. Still, the best continuing education programs are those that employ reputable professionals and offer a fair amount of hands-on work. Before you decide, carefully read and compare the catalogs.

Learn to Live, Live to Learn

Design Department Head, Portfolio Center, Atlanta, Georgia

>> You educate many who have entered graphic design from other jobs and disciplines. How difficult is it to teach neophytes?

Yes, the paths that lead to Portfolio Center are many and varied. Students come from dairy farms in Iowa and law firms in Mumbai. You have to imagine, though, that whatever drives them here—those corporate attorneys, performance artists, account managers, sculptors, school teachers, Olympic runners—is a strong desire to communicate ideas, the willingness to let go of preconceived notions, and the compulsion to learn a new way of thinking. They're not hard to teach; they are pliant and absorbent. They are also courageous.

What experience or fluency do you require of your students before they enter your program?

We prefer a good liberal arts education and some life experience from which to draw creatively. Portfolio Center students are generally smart, well read, and well traveled. Apparently, it is that kind of individual who is most naturally drawn to this program. If I had to say we require one thing at PC, it would be an open mind, a fluency of empathy, perhaps.

Do you find students with nondesign backgrounds are easily taught design?

It might be true that those with nondesign backgrounds are actually easier to teach, like novices in the religious sense. Besides,

TITLE: Luscious Lips
DESIGNER: Elizabeth Lippi CLASS: Publication Design
ART DIRECTOR: Melissa Kuperminc
YEAR: 2004

TITLE: Calligraphy Calendar DESIGNER: Alysia Orrel CLASS: Promotion Design INSTRUCTOR: Amy Rockhold YEAR: 2002

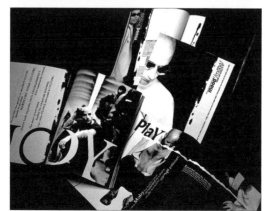

TITLE: Mood Magazine, Moby DESIGNER: Chrissy Doerr CLASS: Publication Design INSTRUCTOR: Hank Richardson YEAR: 2003

>>

they want, they are hungry for something they can't put their finger on. They're not thinking "I am a designer." Not yet, anyway; they haven't defined themselves. That's not to say students coming here with degrees in design, or people who have worked for a couple of years in the industry, don't make good students; it's just that they have to let go of some prejudices and old habits.

What makes a good design student?

In a word, curiosity. But the ability to think like a child is important. Lately, I've been pretty attached to Paul Rand's quote, "Without play, there would be no Picasso." To forget what you know, for a moment, to think like a child, is a wonderful, productive form of freedom, and the freedom to play leads to a revival of the imagina-

tion. At Portfolio Center, it is a hallmark that students work hard, but they also have fun with their projects and, later, in their work and in their lives. Play stimulates them to cope with the problems of form and content, to weigh relationships, to establish priorities, and to create stories.

Students have different levels of talent. What is the common denominator that each student has after going through your program?

No one leaves Portfolio Center without a thorough understanding of ethos, logos, and pathos. The most successful projects are a meticulous balance of all three, coming directly out of the creative's personal values, interpreted logically, and imbued with great passion.

What constitutes a viable commercial portfolio?

I can give you a general sense of what we expect in a graduate's portfolio: twelve to eighteen pieces total, including seven to ten marks and three to four handhelds, all of which should showcase superlative craft and cognitive skills. It is very important that the portfolio lean toward originality. We don't want the work to be conservative; rather, it should showcase the designer's full conceptual reach. It is much easier for a creative director to reign in a designer's imagination than it is for him or her to provide that designer more of it. Finally, what a graduate truly owns (more than the box of work) is the opportunity to change the world. It needs to be clear that, even as the work solves particular design problems, there is an individual, a soul, behind it.

TITLE: *Propa Chair* DESIGNER: *Lee Monroe* CLASS: *Modernism, Criticism, and Design History* FABRICATION: *Walter Wittman* INSTRUCTOR: *Hank Richardson*

TITLE: *Chateau Elan Winery* DESIGNER: *Elizabeth Dinerstein* CLASS: *Branding and System Design* INSTRUCTORS: *Melissa Kuperminc, Stephanie Grendzinski* YEAR: *2002*

TITLE: *Done Right Tools* DESIGNER: *Yadira Penafiel* CLASS: *Packaging Design* ART DIRECTOR: *Shawn Brasfield* YEAR: *2003*

A Humanistic Laboratory

Head of Visual Communication, Fabrica (Benetton Research & Development Communication Center), Treviso, Italy

>> **What is the goal of a Fabrica fellowship?**

Fabrica is communication and society. Fabrica is risk and utopia. Most of all, it's unique. It's a school with world-class teachers but no exams and degrees. It's a professional creative consultancy where clients accept research and errors as part of the process. It's a place where a musician can design a toilette lamp for Alessi and where a graphic designer can shoot a movie and get it in the Venice Film Festival. I would define Fabrica as a humanistic laboratory that researches new forms of communication through contemporary media. For the fifty international students receiving a twelve-month scholarship, it's an extraordinary opportunity to grow on unconventional interdisciplinary experiences in a multiethnic environment.

Students learn by working on concrete communication projects with the supervision of an international team of professionals and a training program of visiting teachers that come to Fabrica to hold workshops and lectures.

The people we attract are already very talented and well prepared. Our students almost always have a BA, and many also have work experience. Fabrica doesn't promise to train, but it guarantees extraordinary opportunities. The program is based on three parallel

TITLE: GGG Gallery Tokyo/DDD Gallery Osaka Exhibition Poster CREATIVE DIRECTOR: Omar Vulpinari ART DIRECTOR: Eric Ravelo DESIGNER: Gabriele Riva CLIENT: Fabrica YEAR: 2003

>>

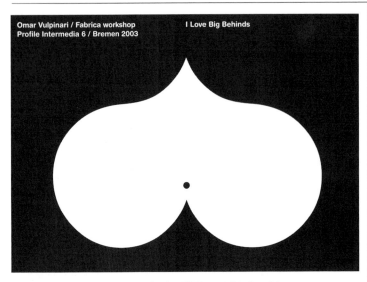

Omar Vulpinari / Fabrica workshop
Profile Intermedia 6 / Bremen 2003

I Love Big Behinds

TITLE: I Love Big Behinds Workshop Invitation CREATIVE DIRECTOR: Omar Vulpinari
DESIGNER: Craig Feinberg YEAR: 2003

TITLE: WHO Global
Violence Prevention
CREATIVE DIREC-
TOR: Omar Vulpinari
ART DIRECTOR/
DESIGNER: Gabriele
Riva PHOTOGRA-
PHER: Enrico Moro
YEAR: 2003

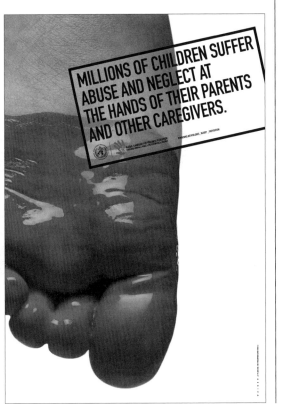

MILLIONS OF CHILDREN SUFFER ABUSE AND NEGLECT AT THE HANDS OF THEIR PARENTS AND OTHER CAREGIVERS.

activities: workshops and lectures, finalized assignments, personal research projects.

What do you expect from potential students, and what determines who is accepted?

First, we review the candidate's portfolio. If this is appropriate, the candidate is invited for a two-week trial. If this goes successfully, we offer a twelve-month grant. What do I expect after? I expect they have dreams for society, not design for designers. People who can tell stories through any media. Lateral thinkers who communicate to collective intelligence. I expect they have the courage and unconsciousness to make mistakes exploring their unknown and the intelligence to build on this. They know the rules; I want to see if they can break them in a meaningful way. This is the greatest privilege that Fabrica can offer: the luxury to commit errors in a real market process. I expect they be open to comment and anxious to understand the mysterious paths of creativity. They must be generous enough to give constructive critique and praise to others. They must be able to articulate a debate around their work. I love going to critique meetings with a perspective to share and after, leaving with new and even totally opposite beliefs.

I expect they move quickly and lightly from one task to another and back, because the more there is to do, the more gets done. And quality gains also, because a wrong idea for a certain project may be the right one for another.

How do students participate in the Fabrica community?

Multidisciplinary work is implemented, and each department ensures specific qualities. So if a writer develops a great idea for a chair, a 3-D designer will integrate the design, someone from Visual and Photography will take care of the communication, etc.

Learning by doing is the approach. It can be individually, in small department teams, in a broad interdisciplinary group mode, and even with external partners and resources. Students have the daily and direct guidance of the department heads. Teams and degrees of responsibility are defined by the project and by the people.

Do you integrate other media in your graphic design program, and to what effect?

I'm definitely not a software freak. I prefer searching for inspiration in the change of relation between media and society. For example, for some perverted reason of human evolution called consumerism, today everything has to be quick and cheap, and information is no exception. Content buying seems to be a more popular activity than content development, which is what I strive for daily.

Another interesting issue is the data sphere we live in. While we're in a meeting, we can read and send out email, type an SMS, talk with someone through a satellite on a TV screen, and answer the video cell phone, almost all at the same time. These new relations between media and man can inspire a simple visual essay but also a major multisensorial interactive exhibition.

Students attend for a year. Is this enough time to impart the necessary ethics and ethos you want them to absorb?

At Fabrica, we have the great privilege to work daily with human values, the most noble of materials. Dedicating to social issues and trying to stir up things is also a way of simply giving back for this privilege.

The most important contribution of Fabrica is in its model. A formula where everybody wins. Benetton benefits in innovation and public respect. The young people who come here learn and grow immensely from meeting the world's greatest communicators and from working in freedom on world-class projects.

One thing can be said for sure, that Fabrica is unique. I truly hope it won't be for long.

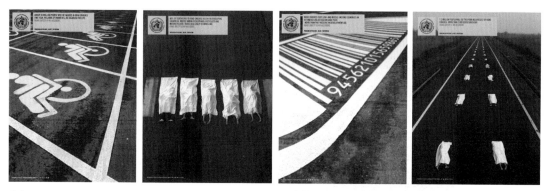

TITLE: *WHO Road Safety* CREATIVE DIRECTOR: *Omar Vulpinari* Art DIRECTORS/DESIGNERS/
PHOTOGRAPHERS: *Eric Ravelo, Gianluca Regnicoli* YEAR: *2004*

MICHAEL VANDERBYL | Training for the Workplace

Principal, Vanderbyl Design, San Francisco; Dean, Design Department, California
College of Arts and Crafts, San Francisco

>> **What is the purpose of your design program?**
To train artists and designers who
will contribute to and change our
culture.

How do you prepare students for the workforce?
We don't try to prepare them as a
trade school might; training for
the workplace can be dangerous.
Instead, we try to equip them with
the skills they need to reinvent
themselves, to adapt to the needs
of commerce, and to preserve
themselves as artists.

What do you expect them to learn from your program?
A respect for history and research,
the ability to think on a broader
cultural plane, and an awareness of
their work and influences. Also, we
hope that they will be able to find
work that nurtures them as human
beings while solving someone else's
problems. Furthermore, they
should be able to constantly reinvent their work themselves.

What makes a good student?
Passion and a broad base of education, especially in those seeking a
second degree.

What is the single most important skill a designer needs to be successful?
Reinvention.

*TITLE: Exhibitor
Show Tenth
Anniversary Poster
DESIGNER/
CREATIVE DIREC-
TOR: Michael
Vanderbyl FIRM:
Vanderbyl Design
CLIENT: Exhibitor
Magazine
YEAR: 1998*

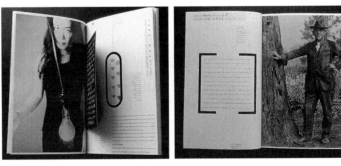

*TITLE: California College of Arts and Crafts Catalog DESIGNER/CREATIVE DIRECTOR: Michael
Vanderbyl FIRM: Vanderbyl Design CLIENT: California College of Arts and Crafts PHOTOGRAPHERS:
David Peterson, Todd Hido TYPEFACES: Agaramond, Officina YEAR: 1998*

The present is a threshold of uncertainty. Patterns unravel, paradigms shift and we discover that our concepts of order bel... an age pre... ...rochip. Before ...y to digital, ...me virtual. In ...yberspace and ...bytes and ...e only thing ...e uncharted ...ere will be no ...paradigms. And the most intelligent response to evolving patterns of "chaos" will be our readiness to adapt to changing forms as they unfold.

TITLE: Teknion Concept Brochure DESIGNER/CREATIVE DIRECTOR: Michael Vanderbyl FIRM: Vanderbyl Design CLIENT: Teknion PHOTOGRAPHER: Geof Kern TYPEFACES: Agaramond, ocrb YEAR: 1997

TITLE: Ritual (Annual Product Brochure) DESIGNER/CREATIVE DIRECTOR: Michael Vanderbyl FIRM: Vanderbyl Design CLIENT: Robert Talbott PHOTOGRAPHER: David Peterson TYPEFACE: Agaramond YEAR: 1998

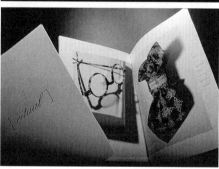

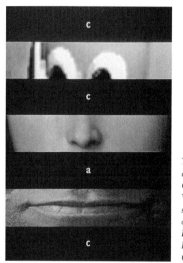

TITLE: California College of Arts and Crafts Catalog DESIGNER/CREATIVE DIRECTOR: Michael Vanderbyl FIRM: Vanderbyl Design CLIENT: California College of Arts and Crafts PHOTOGRAPHERS: David Peterson, Todd Hido TYPEFACES: Agaramond, Officina YEAR: 1998

TITLE: Robert Talbott New York Retail Store DESIGNER/CREATIVE DIRECTOR: Michael Vanderbyl FIRM: Vanderbyl Design CLIENT: Robert Talbott YEAR: 1993

Experiencing Experience

Design and Interaction teacher, New York City

≫ What is experience design?

Experience design is a complex design field for interactive media that integrates cognitive design, structural design (a.k.a. information architecture), visual design, editorial design, technical design (front-end coding), sound design, and motion design (a.k.a. multimedia). In the case of a Web site, cognitive and structural designers define what should be on the site and how the content areas should be divided. Visual designers create the visual communication, including the look and feel and information design. Editorial designers define the specific voice of the site and generate content. Sound designers create sonic identities and motion designers design animated components. Technical designers do all the front-end production, and coding, and they facilitate back-end (engineering, heavy programming, databases) integration. An experience designer can have one or several areas of expertise.

How do you teach experience design to design students?

I encourage my students to always thoroughly understand the media and its craft (whether the assignment is a book or an interactive digital interface) and the full context of their design. Who are they designing for? What purpose will the design serve? But especially because my design and technology students are less familiar with design and more familiar with technology, I also encourage them to play—and through playful exercises they quickly become familiar with the elements of design and typography.

What must a design student grasp to be a good experience designer?

First of all, the design student has to have all the skills that make a good designer in general. The student has to master the craft of design, including a solid grounding in visual communication, typography, color, composition, and style, and to be a proficient user of a range of design software. I believe that it's important for a student to have an understanding of art, design, and architecture in the context of history and society and an awareness of the current discourse in design and culture.

What differentiates print from screen design?

Verba volant, scripta manent. A printed page stays the way it was designed for eternity. A Web site, on the other hand, is a fluid construction. It allows the viewer to modify the design in many ways. Alter the default font or increase the size of the font on your browser, and you will see the page completely differently than it was designed. Screen size and resolution, different types and generations of browsers, different color settings on monitors, TI line versus 56K modem, all determine what the user experiences. Designers have to get used to working under a different set of limitations and possibilities than those for designing for print to create successful designs for an interactive environment.

That said, it is also important that the designer can work as part of an integrated team with designers from other backgrounds, engineers, and business people, in order to deliver the desired experience. Designers cannot be lonely creators. Because the work is so complex and there are usually many simultaneous work-streams that heavily depend on each other, there is a strong need for proximity.

Can a student be a viable graphic designer without knowledge of the new technologies?

I believe that for long-term viability, a graphic designer has to be familiar with the technologies relevant to her area, whatever area that might be.

As an experienced designer, I believe in the same principle. The designer needs to know what is available, what is possible, and how things are set in motion. I don't need to be able to code or program myself, but I need to have an understanding of what technology is currently available and what its implications for design are. That these technologies are constantly evolving and changing makes keeping up more difficult than in other, more established design fields, but not less necessary.

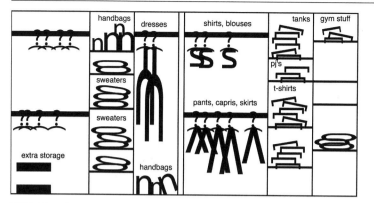

TITLE: *A Map of My Closet* DESIGNER/ART DIRECTOR/ILLUSTRATOR: *Claudia Sondakh, Parsons Design and Technology MFA student* PROJECT: *Student work created for the Digital Typography course* INSTRUCTOR: *Andrea Dezso* YEAR: *2001*

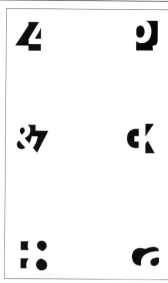

TITLE: *Form and Counterform* DESIGNER/ART DIRECTOR/ILLUSTRATOR: *Yu-Wen Chen, Parsons Design and Technology MFA Student* PROJECT: *Student work created for the Digital Typography course* INSTRUCTOR: *Andrea Dezso* YEAR: *2001*

TITLE: *Mad Cow Disease* DESIGNER/ART DIRECTOR/ILLUSTRATOR: *Rahul Siddharth, Parsons Design and Technology MFA Student* PROJECT: *Student work created for the Digital Typography course* INSTRUCTOR: *Andrea Dezso* YEAR: *2001*

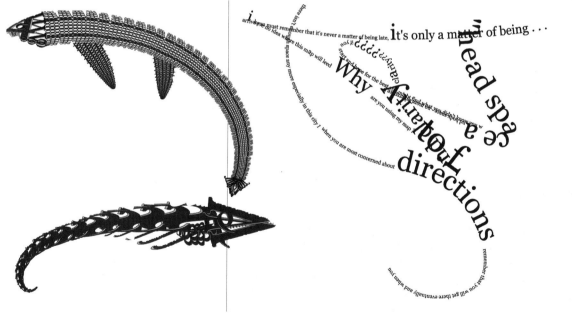

TITLE: *Type Beasts* DESIGNER/ART DIRECTOR/ILLUSTRATOR: *Michele Dubois, Parsons Design and Technology MFA student* PROJECT: *Student work created for the Digital Typography course* INSTRUCTOR: *Andrea Dezso* YEAR: *2001*

TITLE: *Mood Map* DESIGNER/ART DIRECTOR/ILLUSTRATOR: *Emily Shaw, Parsons Design and Technology MFA student* PROJECT: *Student work created for the Digital Typography course* INSTRUCTOR: *Andrea Dezso* YEAR: *2001*

Designer as Entrepreneur

Cochair, MFA/Design, School of Visual Arts, New York City

>> **What is your definition of designer as author?**

The designer as author is someone who not only controls the design—from beginning through end—but also develops the content, either alone or in tandem with a creative team. The reason the SVA/MFA Design program is called "The Designer as Author" is because we believe designers must be in a position to contribute more than aesthetics; they should be creators, implementers, producers.

Not all students want to be authors. How does this program make them better designers?

The program is an opportunity for students to explore their creativity and find different ways to express it. It is a two-year exploration whereby the students work with a variety of media with the goal of authoring in each one. This does not imply that they will never work for someone else again, but they will definitely have more confidence in their ability as thinking designers. Also, because they work in various media, the students gain knowledge of how these processes work, which will allow them to collaborate more closely with the engineer of a Web site or the director of a TV show. They can choose to be sole creators or collaborators.

What skills and talents must MFA students have when they enter your program?

Generally, students must have either an undergraduate degree in graphic design or one to two years professional experience. However, because we are a multidisciplinary program, we encourage students from other disciplines, such as film and architecture, to apply. In order for these students to be able to do the course work, we identify various courses they must take simultaneously, such as advanced typography. But we expect our students to give as much to the program as they take.

What experiences should they have when they graduate your program?

They should feel empowered to make significant things. Their thesis is a product that can (and sometimes should) go to market. Whatever they do after graduation, they will have this equity. Our definition of product is object, campaign or performance — all with a defined audience. But we will always be open to what a product can be.

What do you look for in a student?

Understanding of the visual language and the desire to use this fluency in unique and individual ways. But what we really demand is that they are committed to contributing something of value to the culture.

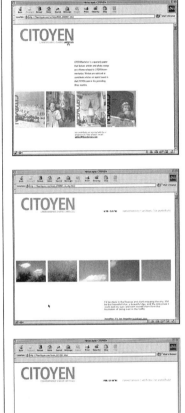

TITLE: CITOYEN Commentaries/ Diaries/Articles DESIGNER: Tania Mailangkay SCHOOL: School of Visual Arts—MFA/Design PROJECT: MFA Thesis devoted to worldwide forum YEAR: 2001

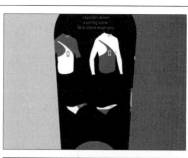

TITLE: Rayrider Web
Site DESIGNER: Rire
Nakpodia SCHOOL:
School of Visual Arts—
MFA/Design PROJECT:
MFA Thesis devoted to
Rayrider Boogie Boards
YEAR: 2001

TITLE: Backflip DESIGNER: Katy Kennedy SCHOOL:
School of Visual Arts—MFA/Design PROJECT: MFA Thesis,
online gallery devoted to artists' books YEAR: 2001

Ideas and Information

LOUISE SANDHAUS

Codirector, Graphic Design Program, CalArts, Valencia, California

How has the integration of motion and sound changed the way you teach design?

Design is still about giving structure to ideas and information, so in that sense, nothing has changed. However, motion and sound add complexity as well as possibility to the structuring. Because the sound often drives the timing and becomes the heartbeat of a motion work, the structure often needs to have some sort of relationship driven by the sound. That means designers have to think in aural structuring simultaneously with visual/information structuring while considering the connotative aspects of sound as well. No small task, but again the important thing to stress is structure and connotation, both nothing new for designers.

Is there any particular emphasis in teaching design today?

Words, the look of words, images, movement, behavior, interaction, sound: These are the elements with which communication takes place today and, thus, the fundamentals of contemporary design education. I've been thinking about the basics of visual literacy and considering that perhaps these basics need to be updated for dynamic environments (or maybe someone's already done this). Then one begins to wonder about the potential of education overload: How much can one designer not only know but also develop enough proficiency in to be useful?

Is the Web about storytelling?

Storytelling, or I'd rather refer to it as *narrative*, is actually an interesting example of a significant emphasis in design education today. There are two ways in which I feel this is important. First, when I referred to design as structuring ideas and information, that structuring is a kind of narrative. The structure, or framework, considers the raw data and turns it into something meaningful, compelling, and useful. Second, the other part of sense-making/storytelling/narrative has to do with complex projects—for instance, Web sites. These are projects of a scale where you have to communicate such that an unfamiliar audience can grasp that the idea is viable and compelling before the idea is actually produced. The designer has to consider what to show, in what order, and with what sort of narrative so that the project can be imagined. But in going through this process, the designer is also forced into reasoning ideas in ways that develop the ideas themselves. So storytelling, as I'm describing here, isn't just about selling the idea but a process that allows the idea to be coherently developed.

How much of design is now technique rather than aesthetics?

The only graphic design I know is about aesthetics—but aesthetics that have everything to do with content.

I once heard John Maeda speak, and while I don't think what Maeda does is design but, rather, art—an art form divorced from content—he was quite vocal about the need for those working in computer-related media to understand the nature of the material they're working with. In the case of the computer, he's referring to code. He stressed the importance of understanding that coding a computer is similar to creating a biologic form; it's distinct in its behavior, possibilities, and effects from any other tool or material. So technical understanding and skill is imperative to doing anything that truly might push communications into interesting new realms, but it should also be considered integral to message-making, the form of the information is the information.

What do you look for in a prospective student?

Grad students: Interest in culture in general, interest in design specifically. Formal skills, interest in inventive form. The understanding and appreciation of design as distinct from art. Strong points of view and the ability to express them. That's the ideal grad student. Undergrad students: Ideas of their own (not just life drawing or making pretty pictures—usually unicorns). The ability to draw. Understanding of graphic design. Enthusiasm. Good students.

TITLE: *Typo Space* DESIGNER: *Joey Alviar, MFA 2* SCHOOL: *CalArts, Valencia, CA*
INSTRUCTORS: *Tom Bland, Ed Fella, Jeff Keedy, Lorraine Wild* YEAR: *2001*

TITLE: *Fractured (stills from a video by Tuan Phan of a book by Jennifer McKnight)* DESIGNER/
CREATIVE DIRECTOR/ART DIRECTOR/PHOTOGRAPHER/DIRECTOR/ILLUSTRATOR:
Jennifer McKnight, PMFA VIDEOGRAPHY: *Tuan Phan* SCHOOL: *CalArts, Valencia, CA*
INSTRUCTOR: *Michael Worthington* YEAR: *2001*

TITLE: *Time Modeling
Visual Research* DESIGNER/
CREATIVE DIRECTOR/ART
DIRECTOR/PHOTOGRA-
PHER/DIRECTOR/
ILLUSTRATOR: *Petra Michel,
MFA 1* SCHOOL: *CalArts,
Valencia, CA* INSTRUCTORS:
*Johanna Drucker,
Louise Sandhaus* YEAR: *2001*

TITLE: *Sunset Strip*
DESIGNER/PHO-
TOGRAPHER/
DIRECTOR/
ILLUSTRATOR:
*Peter Bergeron,
BFA 4* SCHOOL:
*CalArts, Valencia,
CA* INSTRUC-
TOR: *Anne Burdick*
YEAR: *2000*

ART SCHOOLS AND COLLEGES: A SELECTION

The following institutions offer some of the best BFA, MFA, associate Degree, and continuing education design programs in North America. Before deciding on a course of study or institution, read and compare catalogs.

UNDERGRADUATE PROGRAMS

ACADEMY OF ART COLLEGE
79 New Montgomery Street
San Francisco, CA 94105
415-274-2200 phone
800-544-ARTS toll-free phone
www.academy.edu
Degrees: BFA, AA, MFA
Length of programs:
3–4 years UG/2 years G

AMERICAN INTERCONTINENTAL UNIVERSITY
Locations:
Buckhead, GA
Dubai, United Arab Emirates
Dunwoody, GA
Houston, TX
London, England
Los Angeles, CA
South Florida
800-846-1994 toll-free phone
www.aiuniv.edu
Degree: BFA
Length of program: 4 years

THE ART INSTITUTES
Head Office:
210 Sixth Avenue
32d floor
Admissions Department
Pittsburgh, PA 15222-2598
888-624-0300
www.artinstitutes.edu
Locations:
Arlington, VA
Atlanta, GA
Charlotte, NC
Chicago, IL
Cincinnati, OH
Dallas, TX
Denver, CO
Fort Lauderdale, FL
Houston, TX
Las Vegas, NV
Los Angeles, CA
Los Angeles—Orange County, CA
Minneapolis, MN
New York, NY
Philadelphia, PA
Phoenix, AZ
Pittsburgh, PA
Portland, OR
San Diego, CA
San Francisco, CA
Schaumberg, IL
Seattle, WA
Tampa, FL
Toronto, Canada
Vancouver, Canada
Vancouver-Burnaby, Canada
Degrees: AA, AAA, AAS, AS, AOS, BA, BS, BFA, C, D

THE ART INSTITUTE OF BOSTON AT LESLEY UNIVERSITY
700 Beacon Street
Boston, MA 02215
617-585-6700 phone
800-773-0494 toll-free phone
617-585-6720 fax
www.aiboston.edu
Degrees: BFA, Certificate
Length of program: 2–4 years
University of the Arts
320 South Broad Street
Philadelphia, PA 19102
800-616-ARTS toll-free phone
www.uarts.edu
Degree: BFA
Length of program: 4 years

ART CENTER COLLEGE OF DESIGN
1700 Lida Street
Pasadena, CA 91103
626-396-2200 phone
www.artcenter.edu
Degrees: BFA, BS, MFA, MS, MA
Length of program: 4 years UG/2 years G

UNIVERSITY OF BALTIMORE
1420 North Charles Street
Baltimore, MD 21201
410-837-4777 phone
877-APPLYUB toll-free phone
www.ubalt.edu
Degrees: BS, MFA, MA
Length of program: 4 years UG/2–3 years G

BOSTON UNIVERSITY SCHOOL FOR THE ARTS
Visual Arts Department
855 Commonwealth Avenue
Boston, MA 02215
617-353-3371 phone
617-353-7217 fax
www.bu.edu/cfa/visual/
Degrees: BFA, MFA
Length of program: 4 years UG/2 years G

BRIGHAM YOUNG UNIVERSITY COLLEGE OF FINE ARTS AND COMMUNICATIONS
Department of Visual Arts
C-502 Harris Fine Art Center
Provo, UT 84602
801-422-4266 phone
http://cfac.byu.edu/va
Degrees: BA, BFA, MA, MFA
Length of program: 4 years UG/2 years G

CALIFORNIA COLLEGE OF THE ARTS
1111 Eighth Street
San Francisco, CA 94107-2247
415-703-9500 phone
800-447-1ART toll-free phone
www.ccac-art.edu
Degrees: BFA, BArch, MFA
Length of program: 4–5 years UG/2 years G

CALIFORNIA INSTITUTE OF THE ARTS SCHOOL OF ART
24700 McBean Parkway
Valencia, CA 91355
661-255-1050 phone
www.calarts.edu
Degrees: BFA, MFA
Length of program: 4 years UG/2 years G

CALIFORNIA POLYTECHNIC STATE UNIVERSITY (CAL POLY)
Department of Art and Design
San Luis Obispo, CA 93407
805-756-1148 phone
805-756-6321 fax
art.design.libart.calpoly.edu
Degree: BFA
Length of program: 4 years

COLLEGE OF DESIGN, ARCHITECTURE, ART, AND PLANNING UNIVERSITY OF CINCINNATI
PO Box 210016
Cincinnati, OH 45221-0016
513-556-6828 phone
513-556-0240 fax
www.design.uc.edu
Degrees: BS, MDes
Length of program: 5 years UG/2 years G

THE COLLEGE OF ARTS AND ARCHITECTURE AT PENN STATE SCHOOL OF VISUAL ARTS
210 Patterson Building
University Park, PA 16802
814-865-0444 phone
www.sva.psu.edu
Degrees: BA, BFA, BS, MFA, MA
Length of program: 4 years UG/2 years G

THE COOPER UNION FOR THE ADVANCEMENT OF SCIENCE AND ART
30 Cooper Square
New York, NY 10003
212-353-4120 phone
www.cooper.edu
Degree: BFA
Length of program: 4 years

THE CORCORAN SCHOOL OF ART AND DESIGN
500 17th Street NW
Washington, DC 20006
202-639-1800 phone
www.corcoran.edu
Degrees: BFA, AFA
Length of program: 2–4 years UG

DIGITAL MEDIA ARTS COLLEGE
3785 North Federal Highway
Boca Raton, FL 33431
561-391-1149 phone
866-255-3644 toll-free phone
www.dmac-edu.org

Degree offered: BFA
Length of program: 3-4 years
Expression College for Digital Arts
6601 Shellmound Street
Emeryville, CA 94608
877-833-8800 toll-free phone
data@expression.edu
www.expression.edu
Degree offered: BS
Length of program: 4 years

UNIVERSITY OF FLORIDA SCHOOL OF ART AND ART HISTORY
302 Fine Arts Building C
PO Box 115801
Gainesville, FL 32601-5801
352-392-0201 phone
www.arts.ufl.edu
Degrees: BFA, BA, MFA, MA
Length of program: 4 years UG/ 2–3 years G

INTERNATIONAL ACADEMY OF DESIGN AND TECHNOLOGY
5225 Memorial Highway
Tampa, FL 33634
813-881-0007 phone
www.academy.edu
Degree: BS
Length of program: 3–4 years

KENT STATE UNIVERSITY
Kent, Ohio 44242-0001
330-672-2192 phone
330-672-4729 fax
http://dept.kent.edu/art/
Degrees: BA, MFA, MA
Length of program: 4 years UG/2 years G

MARYLAND INSTITUTE COLLEGE OF ART
1300 Mount Royal Avenue
Baltimore, MD 21217
410-225-2222 phone
www.mica.edu
Degrees: BFA, BFA/MAT, MA, MAT, MFA
Length of program: 4 years UG/1–2 years G

MASSACHUSETTS COLLEGE OF ART
621 Huntington Avenue
Boston, MA 02115
617-879-7222 phone
617-879-7250 fax
www.massart.edu
Degrees: BFA, Design Certificate, MFA, MSAE
Length of program: 4 years UG/2 years G

MINNEAPOLIS COLLEGE OF ART AND DESIGN
2501 Stevens Avenue South
Minneapolis, MN 55404
612-874-3760 phone
www.mcad.edu
Degrees: BFA, MFA
Length of program: 4 years UG/2 years G

UNIVERSITY OF MINNESOTA
Office of Admissions
240 Williamson Hall
231 Pilsbury Drive SE
Minneapolis, MN 55455-0213
612-625-2008 phone
800-752-100 toll free phone
612-626-1693 fax
www.umn.edu
Degree offered: BS
Length of program: 4 years

MONTANA STATE UNIVERSITY COLLEGE OF ARTS AND ARCHITECTURE
PO Box 173700
Bozeman, MT 59717-3700
406-994-0211 phone
www.montana.edu/wwwdt/
Degrees: BA, MFA
Length of program: 4 years UG/2 years G

THE NEW ENGLAND INSTITUTE OF ART AND COMMUNICATIONS
10 Brookline Place West
Brookline, MA 02445
800-903-4425 toll-free phone
www.aine.artinstitute.edu
Degree: BS
Length of program: 4 years

NORTH CAROLINA A&T STATE UNIVERSITY SCHOOL OF TECHNOLOGY
1601 East Market Street
Greensboro, NC 27411
336-334-7500 phone
www.ncat.edu
Degrees: BS, MS
Length of program: 4 years UG/2 years G
Also offered: distance learning

continued

OTIS COLLEGE OF ART AND DESIGN
9045 Lincoln Boulevard
Los Angeles, CA 90045
310-665-6800 phone
800-527-6847 toll-free phone
310-665-6821 fax
www.ojtis.edu
Degrees: BFA, MFA
Length of program: 4 years UG/2 years G

PARSONS SCHOOL OF DESIGN
66 Fifth Avenue
New York, NY 10011
212-229-8910 phone
800-252-0852 toll-free phone
212-229-8975 fax
www.parsons.edu
Degrees: AAS, BA/BFA, BBA, BFA,
MA, MFA, MArch
Length of program: 2–5 years
UG/1–3 years G

PACIFIC NORTHWEST COLLEGE
OF ART
1241 NW Johnson Street
Portland, Oregon 97209
503-226-4391 phone
503-226-3587 fax
www.pcna.edu
Degrees: BFA
Length of program: 4 years

PRATT INSTITUTE
200 Willoughby Avenue
Brooklyn, NY 11205
718-636-3600 phone
www.pratt.edu
Degrees: BA, BFA, MA, MFA, MPS, MS
Length of program: 4 years UG/2 years G

RHODE ISLAND SCHOOL OF DESIGN
(RISD)
Graphic Design Department
Two College Street
Providence, RI 02903
401-454-6300 phone
800-364-RISD toll-free phone
www.risd.edu
Degrees: BFA, BGD, MFA
Length of program: 4–5 years UG/2 years G

RINGLING SCHOOL OF ART AND
DESIGN
2700 North Tamiami Trail
Sarasota, FL 34234-5895
941-351-5100 phone

800-255-7695 toll-free phone
941-359-7517 fax
www.rsad.edu
Degree: BFA
Length of program: 4 years

SCHOOL OF DESIGN
COLLEGE OF IMAGINING ARTS AND
SCIENCES, ROCHESTER INSTITUTE
OF DESIGN (RIT)
73 Lomb Memorial Drive
Rochester, NY 14623-5603
716-475-2411 phone
716-475-7424 fax
www.rit.edu
Degrees: AAS, BFA, MFA
Length of program: 2–4 years
UG/1–2 years G

RYERSON UNIVERSITY
GRAPHIC COMMUNICATIONS
MANAGEMENT
350 Victoria Street
Toronto, Ontario Canada M5B 2K3
416-979-5050 phone
www.ryerson.ca
Degrees: MA, BTech, Ph.D.
Length of program: 4 years UG/2 years G

SAVANNAH COLLEGE OF ART
AND DESIGN
PO Box 3146
Savannah, GA 31402-3146
912-525-5100 phone
800-869-7223 toll-free phone
www.scad.edu
Degrees: BFA, MA, MFA
Length of program: 4 years UG/2 years G

STATE UNIVERSITY OF NEW YORK
(SUNY) AT BUFFALO
Art Department
202 Center for the Arts
Buffalo, NY 14260-6010
716-645-6878 ext. 1350 phone
716-645-6970 fax
www.art.buffalo.edu
Degrees: BA, BFA, MA, MFA, MAH
Length of program: 4 years UG/2 years G

SCHOOL OF VISUAL ARTS (SVA)
209 East 23rd Street
New York, NY 10010-3994
212-592-2000 phone
212-725-3587 fax
www.sva.edu

Degrees: BFA, MFA
Length of program: 4 years UG/2 years G

SYRACUSE UNIVERSITY
COLLEGE OF VISUAL AND
PERFORMING ARTS
Office of Recruitment and Admissions
202 Crouse College
Syracuse, NY 13244-1010
315-443-2611 phone
vpa.syr.edu
Degrees: BFA, BID, MA, MFA
Length of program: 4–5 years UG/2 years G

TEMPLE UNIVERSITY
TYLER SCHOOL OF ART
7725 Penrose Avenue
Elkins Park, PA 19027
215-782-2828
www.temple.edu/tyler
Degrees: BFA, MFA
Length of program: 4 years UG/2 years G

VIRGINIA COMMONWEALTH
UNIVERSITY
SCHOOL OF THE ARTS
609 Bowe Street
Richmond, VA 23284-843047
804-828-1129 phone
www.vcu.edu
Degrees: BFA, BA, MFA, MA
Length of program: 4 years UG/2 years G

2-YEAR PROGRAMS

THE ART INSTITUTE OF BOSTON AT
LESLEY UNIVERSITY
700 Beacon Street
Boston, MA 02215
617-585-6700 phone
800-773-0494 toll-free phone
617-585-6720 fax
www.aiboston.edu
Degrees: BFA, Certificate
Length of program: 2–4 years

BRIARCLIFFE COLLEGE
225 West Main Street
Patchogue, NY 11772
888-756-9900 phone
www.bcpat.com
Degree offered: AAS
Length of program: 2 years

BROOKS COLLEGE
4825 East Pacific Coast Highway
Long Beach, CA 90804
800-421-3775 toll-free phone
www.brookscollege.edu
Degree: Associate
Length of program: 2 years

COLLEGE OF EASTERN UTAH
451 East 400 North
Price, UT 84501
435-637-2120 phone
www.ceu.edu
Degrees: C (certificate), Associate
Length of programs: 1 year (C), 2 years (A)
Also offered: distance learning

COMMUNITY COLLEGE OF DENVER
Art Department
PO Box 173363
Denver, CO 80217-3363
303-556-2600 phone
www.ccd.edu/art/
Degree: Associate
Length of program: 2 years

**THE CORCORAN SCHOOL OF
ART AND DESIGN**
500 17th Street NW
Washington, DC 20006
202-639-1800 phone
www.corcoran.edu
Degrees: BFA, AFA
Length of program: 2–4 years UG

**DELAWARE COLLEGE OF ART
AND DESIGN**
600 North Market Street
Wilmington, DE 19801
302-622-8000 phone
302-622-8870 fax
www.dcad.edu
Degree: AFA
Length of program: 2 years

FERRIS STATE UNIVERSITY
The Printing and Digital Graphic Imaging
Technology Department (PDGI)
915 Campus Drive/SWN 314
Big Rapids, MI 49307
231-591-2000 phone
231-591-2845 graphic arts
www.ferris.edu
Degrees: BS, Associate
Length of program: 2 years (A)/4 years UG

**INTERNATIONAL ACADEMY OF
DESIGN AND TECHNOLOGY**
5225 Memorial Highway
Tampa, FL 33634
813-881-0007 phone
www.academy.edu
Degree: Associate
Length of program: 1–2 years

PALOMAR COLLEGE
Graphic Communications
1140 W. Mission Road
San Marcos, CA 92069
760-744-1150 ext. 2452 phone
www.palomar.edu
Degrees: C (certificate), AA
Length of program: 2 years
Also offered: distance learning

PARSONS SCHOOL OF DESIGN
66 Fifth Avenue
New York, NY 10011
212-229-8910 phone
800-252-0852 toll-free phone
212-229-8975 fax
www.parsons.edu
*Degrees: AAS, BA/BFA, BBA, BFA, MA, MFA,
MArch*
Length of program: 2–5 years UG/1–3 years G

PORTFOLIO CENTER
125 Bennett Street
Atlanta, GA 30309
404-351-5055 phone
800-255-3169 toll-free phone
404-355-8838 fax
www.portfoliocenter.com
Degree: Certificate
Length of program: 2 years

**SCHOOL OF DESIGN
COLLEGE OF IMAGINING ARTS
AND SCIENCES
ROCHESTER INSTITUTE OF DESIGN
(RIT)**
73 Lomb Memorial Drive
Rochester, NY 14623-5603
716-475-2411 phone
716-475-7424 fax
www.rit.edu
Degrees: AAS
Length of program: 2 years

SPENCERIAN COLLEGE
2355 Harrodsburg Road
Lexington, KY 40504
859-223-9608 phone
800-456-3253 toll-free phone
859-224-7744 fax
www.spencerian.edu/lexington
Degree: Associate
Length of program: 2 years

GRADUATE PROGRAMS

ACADEMY OF ART COLLEGE
79 New Montgomery Street
San Francisco, CA 94105
415-274-2200 phone
800-544-ARTS toll-free phone
www.academy.edu
Degrees: MFA
Length of program: 2 years

**UNIVERSITY OF ADVANCED
COMPUTER TECHNOLOGY**
2625 West Baseline Road
Tempe, AZ 85283-1042
602-383-8228 phone
800-658-5744 toll-free phone
602-383-8222 fax
www.uat.edu
Degree: MS
Length of program: 2 years
Also offered: distance learning

ART CENTER COLLEGE OF DESIGN
1700 Lida Street
Pasadena, CA 91103
626-396-2200 phone
www.artcenter.edu
Degrees: MFA, MS, MA
Length of program: 2 years

UNIVERSITY OF BALTIMORE
1420 North Charles Street
Baltimore, MD 21201
410-837-4777 phone
877-APPLYUB toll-free phone
410-837-4793 fax
www.ubalt.edu
Degrees: MFA, MA
Length of program: 2–3 years

continued

BOSTON UNIVERSITY
SCHOOL FOR THE ARTS
Visual Arts Department
855 Commonwealth Avenue
Boston, MA 02215
617-353-3371 phone
617-353-7217 fax
www.bu.edu/cfa/visual/
Degrees: MFA
Length of program: 2 years

BRIGHAM YOUNG UNIVERSITY
COLLEGE OF FINE ARTS AND
COMMUNICATIONS
Department of Visual Arts
C-502 Harris Fine Art Center
Provo, UT 84602
801-422-4266 phone
http://cfac.byu.edu/va
Degrees: MA, MFA
Length of program: 2 years

CALIFORNIA COLLEGE OF THE ARTS
1111 Eighth Street
San Francisco, CA 94107-2247
415-703-9500 phone
800-447-1ART toll-free phone
www.ccac-art.edu
Degrees: MFA
Length of program: 2 years G

CALIFORNIA INSTITUTE OF THE ARTS
SCHOOL OF ART
24700 McBean Parkway
Valencia, CA 91355
661-255-1050 phone
www.calarts.edu
Degrees: MFA
Length of program: 2 years

COLLEGE OF DESIGN,
ARCHITECTURE, ART, AND PLANNING
UNIVERSITY OF CINCINNATI
PO Box 210016
Cincinnati, OH 45221-0016
513-556-6828 phone
513-556-0240 fax
www.design.uc.edu
Degrees: MDes
Length of program: 2 years

THE COLLEGE OF ARTS AND
ARCHITECTURE AT PENN STATE
School of Visual Arts
210 Patterson Building
University Park, PA 16802

814-865-0444 phone
www.sva.psu.edu
Degrees: MFA, MA
Length of program: 2 years

CRANBROOK ACADEMY OF ART
39221 North Woodward Avenue
PO Box 801
Bloomfield Hills, MI 48303-0801
248-645-3300 phone
www.cranbrook.edu
Degrees: MFA, MArch
Length of program: 2 years

DIGITAL MEDIA ARTS COLLEGE
3785 North Federal Highway
Boca Raton, FL 33431
866-255-3644 toll-free phone
561-391-1149 phone
www.dmac-edu.org
Degree offered: MFA
Length of program: 2 years

UNIVERSITY OF FLORIDA
SCHOOL OF ART AND ART HISTORY
302 Fine Arts Building C
PO Box 115801
Gainesville, FL 32601-5801
352-392-0201 phone
www.arts.ufl.edu
Degrees: MFA, MA
Length of program: 2–3 years

IIT INSTITUTE OF DESIGN
3300 South Federal Street
Chicago, Illinois 60610-3793
312-567-3000 phone
www.id.itt.edu
Degree: MDes
Length of program: 2 years

KENT STATE UNIVERSITY
Kent, Ohio 44242-0001
330-672-2192 phone
330-672-4729 fax
http://dept.kent.edu/art/
Degrees: MFA, MA
Length of program: 2 years

MARYLAND INSTITUTE
COLLEGE OF ART
1300 Mount Royal Avenue
Baltimore, MD 21217
410-225-2222 phone
www.mica.edu
Degrees: MA, MAT, MFA

Length of program: 1–2 years

MINNEAPOLIS COLLEGE OF ART
AND DESIGN
2501 Stevens Avenue South
Minneapolis, MN 55404
612-874-3760 phone
800-874-MCAD toll-free phone
www.mcad.edu
Degrees: MFA
Length of program: 2 years

MASSACHUSETTS COLLEGE OF ART
621 Huntington Avenue
Boston, MA 02115
617-879-7222 phone
617-879-7250 fax
www.massart.edu
Degrees: MFA, MSAE
Length of program: 2 years

MONTANA STATE UNIVERSITY
COLLEGE OF ARTS AND
ARCHITECTURE
PO Box 173700
Bozeman, MT 59717-3700
406-994-0211 phone
www.montana.edu/wwwdt/
Degrees: MFA
Length of program: 2 years

NEW YORK UNIVERSITY
TISCH SCHOOL OF THE ARTS
Interactive Telecommunications
Program (ITP)
721 Broadway
4th floor
New York, NY 10003
212-998-1880 phone
212-998-1898 fax
www.itp.nyu.edu
Degree: MPS
Length of program: 2 years

NORTH CAROLINA A&T STATE
UNIVERSITY
SCHOOL OF TECHNOLOGY
1601 East Market Street
Greensboro, NC 27411
336-334-7500 phone
www.ncat.edu
Degrees: MS
Length of program: 2 years
Also offered: distance learning

OTIS COLLEGE OF ART AND DESIGN
9045 Lincoln Boulevard
Los Angeles, CA 90045
310-665-6800 phone
800-527-6847 toll-free phone
310-665-6821 fax
www.otis.edu
Degrees: MFA
Length of program: 2 years

PARSONS SCHOOL OF DESIGN
66 Fifth Avenue
New York, NY 10011
212-229-8910 phone
800-252-0852 toll-free phone
212-229-8975 fax
www.parsons.edu
Degrees: MA, MFA, MArch
Length of program: 1–3 years

PRATT INSTITUTE
200 Willoughby Avenue
Brooklyn, NY 11205
718-636-3600 phone
www.pratt.edu
Degrees: MA, MFA, MPS, MS
Length of program: 2 years

**RHODE ISLAND SCHOOL OF DESIGN
(RISD)**
Graphic Design Department
Two College Street
Providence, RI 02903
401-454-6300 phone
www.risd.edu
Degree: MFA
Length of program: 2 years

**SCHOOL OF DESIGN
COLLEGE OF IMAGING ARTS AND
SCIENCES, ROCHESTER INSTITUTE
OF DESIGN (RIT)**
73 Lomb Memorial Drive
Rochester, NY 14623-5603
716-475-2411 phone
716-475-7424 fax
www.rit.edu
Degree: MFA
Length of program: 1–2 years

RYERSON UNIVERSITY
Graphic Communications Management
350 Victoria Street
Toronto, Ontario Canada M5B 2K3
416-979-5050 phone
www.ryerson.ca

Degrees: MA, Ph.D.
Length of program: 2 years

**SAVANNAH COLLEGE OF ART
AND DESIGN**
PO Box 3146
Savannah, GA 31402-3146
912-525-5100 phone
www.scad.edu
Degrees: MA, MFA
Length of program: 2 years

**STATE UNIVERSITY OF NEW YORK
(SUNY) AT BUFFALO**
Art Department
202 Center for the Arts
Buffalo, NY 14260-6010
716-645-6878 ext. 1350 phone
716-645-6970 fax
www.art.buffalo.edu
Degrees: MA, MFA, MAH
Length of program: 2 years

SCHOOL OF VISUAL ARTS (SVA)
209 East 23rd Street
New York, NY 10010-3994
212-592-2000 phone
212-725-3587 fax
http://design.schoolofvisualarts.edu/
Degree: MFA
Length of program: 2 years

**SYRACUSE UNIVERSITY
COLLEGE OF VISUAL AND
PERFORMING ARTS**
Office of Recruitment and Admissions
202 Crouse College
Syracuse, NY 13244-1010
315-443-2611 phone
vpa.syr.edu
Degrees: MA, MFA
Length of program: 2 years

**TEMPLE UNIVERSITY
TYLER SCHOOL OF ART**
7725 Penrose Avenue
Elkins Park, PA 19027
215-782-2828
www.temple.edu/tyler
Degree: MFA
Length of program: 2 years

**UNIVERSITY OF ADVANCED
COMPUTER TECHNOLOGY**
2625 West Baseline Road
Tempe, AZ 85283-1042

602-383-8228 phone
800-658-5744 toll-free phone
602-383-8222 fax
www.uat.edu
Degree: MS
Length of program: 2 years
Also offered: distance learning

**VIRGINIA COMMONWEALTH
UNIVERSITY
SCHOOL OF THE ARTS**
609 Bowe Street
Richmond, VA 23284-843047
804-828-1129 phone
www.vcu.edu
Degrees: MFA, MA
Length of program: 2 years

**YALE UNIVERSITY
SCHOOL OF ART**
PO Box 208339
1156 Chapel Street
New Haven, CT 06520-8339
203-432-2600 phone
www.yale.edu/art
Degree: MFA
Length of program: 2–3 years

ONLINE SCHOOLS

THE ART INSTITUTE ONLINE
A division of the Art Institute
of Pittsburgh
420 Boulevard of the Allies
Pittsburgh, PA 15219
877-972-8869 Toll-free phone
412-291-5100 phone
www.aioline.edu
Degrees: Associate, BS

**SESSIONS.EDU ONLINE SCHOOL
OF DESIGN**
350 Seventh Avenue
Suite 1203
New York, NY 10001
800-258-4115 Toll-free phone
www.sessions.edu
Degrees: Certificate, Master's Certificate
Length of program: 1–2 years

*For more schools, contact sensebox,
a graphic design education source, at
www.sensebox.com.*

RESOURCES

DESIGN ORGANIZATIONS

**ALLIANCE GRAPHIQUE
INTERNATIONALE**
Bahnhofstrasse 11, Postfach 157
CH-9230 Flawil Switzerland
011-41-71-393-58-48 phone
www.a-g-i-.org

**AMERICAN ILLUSTRATION +
AMERICAN PHOTOGRAPHY**
1140 Broadway, 4th Floor
New York, NY 10001
917-408-9944 phone
info@ai-ap.com
www.ai-ap.com

**AMERICAN INSTITUTE OF
GRAPHIC ARTS (AIGA)**
164 Fifth Avenue
New York, NY 10010
212-807-1990 phone
comments@aiga.org
www.aiga.org
(64 local chapters nationwide)

**AMERICAN SOCIETY OF
MAGAZINE EDITORS (ASME)**
810 Seventh Avenue, 24th Floor
New York, NY 10019
212-872-3700 phone
asme@magazine.org
www.magazine.org/asme

ART DIRECTORS CLUB
106 West 29th Street
New York, NY 10001
212-643-1440 phone
info@adcglobal.org
www.adcglobal.org

**BROADCAST DESIGNERS
ASSOCIATION**
1522e Cloverfield Boulevard
Santa Monica, CA 90404
310-788-7600 phone
jessica@promaxbda.org
www.promaxbda.org

CLIO AWARDS
770 Broadway, 15th Floor
New York, NY 10003
212-683-4300 phone
www.clioawards.com

**COOPER-HEWITT NATIONAL
DESIGN MUSEUM**
2 East 91st Street
New York, NY 10128
212-849-8400 phone
http://cooperhewitt.org

GRAPHIC ARTISTS GUILD
32 Broadway, Suite 1114
New York, NY 10004
212-791-3400 phone
www.gag.org
(7 chapters nationwide)

IDEALLIANCE
1421 Prince Street, Suite 230
Alexandria, VA 22314
703-837-1070 phone
registrar@idealliance.org
www.idealliance.org

**INTERNATIONAL COUNCIL OF
GRAPHIC DESIGN ASSOCIATIONS
(ICOGRADA)**
Contact: Icograda Secretariat
455 Saint Antoine Ouest, Suite SS 10
Montreal, Quebec Canada H2Z 1J1
514-448-4949 ext. 221 phone
secretariat@icograda.org
www.icograda.org

THE ONE CLUB
21 East 26th Street
New York, NY 10010
212-979-1900 phone
info@oneclub.org
www.oneclub.org

THE SOCIETY OF ILLUSTRATORS
128 East 63rd Street
New York, NY 10065
212-838-2560 phone
info@societyillustrators.org
www.societyillustrators.com

SOCIETY FOR NEWS DESIGN
1130 Ten Rod Road, Suite E 206
North Kingstown, RI 02852
401-294-5233 phone
snd@snd.org
www.snd.org

**SOCIETY OF PUBLICATION
DESIGNERS (SPD)**
27 Union Square West, Suite 207
New York, NY 10003
212-223-3332 phone
mail@spd.org
www.spd.org

TYPE DIRECTORS CLUB
347 West 36th Street, Suite 603
New York, NY 10018
212-633-8943 phone
director@tdc.org
www.tdc.org

PUBLICATIONS

**@ISSUE: THE JOURNAL OF
BUSINESS AND DESIGN**
Corporate Design Foundation
20 Park Plaza, Suite 400
Boston, MA 02116
617-566-7676 phone
admin@cdf.org
www.cdf.org

BASELINE
Bradbourne Publishing Limited
Bradbourne House, East Malling
Kent ME19 6DZ England
011-44-1-732-87-52-00 phone
subscribe@baselinemagazine.com
www.baselinemagazine.com

COMMUNICATION ARTS
110 Constitution Drive
Menlo Park, CA 94025
650-326-6040 phone
subscription@commarts.com
www.commarts.com

DESIGN GRAPHICS
PO Box 10
Ferny Creek VIC 3786 Australia
011-61-3-9760-1200 phone
www.dgdesignnetwork.com.au

DESIGN INSTITUTE: THE KNOWLEDGE CIRCUIT
University of Minnesota
Northrop Memorial Auditorium
84 Church Street, S.E., Room 308
Minneapolis, MN 55455
612-625-3373 phone
http://di.design.umn.edu/people

DESIGN ISSUES
MIT Press Journals
238 Main Street, Suite 500
Cambridge, MA 02142
617-253-2889 phone
800-207-8354 toll-free phone
journals-orders@mit.edu
www.mitpressjournals.org/loi/desi

EYE
Eye Magazine Ltd
Studio 6, The Lux Building
2-4 Hoxton Square
London N1 6NU England
011-44-207-684-6530 phone
eye@ebsco.com

GRAPHIC ARTISTS GUILD HANDBOOK OF PRICING AND ETHICAL GUIDELINES
32 Broadway, Suite 1114
New York, NY 10004
212-791-3400 phone
www.gag.org/handbook

GRAPHIC DESIGN USA
89 Fifth Avenue, Suite 901
New York, NY 10003
212-696-4380 phone
circulation@gdusa.com
www.gdusa.com

HOW
4700 East Galbraith Road
Cincinnati, OH 45236
513-531-2690 phone
www.howdesign.com

INNOVATION JOURNAL
Industrial Designers Society
of America (IDSA)
45195 Business Court, Suite 250
Dulles, VA 20166
703-707-6000 phone
idsa@idsa.org
www.innovationjournal.org

METROPOLIS
61 West 23rd Street, 4th Floor
New York, NY 10010
212-627-9977 phone
800-344-3046 toll-free phone
edit@metropolismag.com
www.metropolismag.com

ONE. A MAGAZINE
The One Club
21 East 26th Street
New York, NY 10010
212-979-1900 phone
info@oneclub.org
www.oneclub.org/oc/magazine

PRINT
Print Magazine
38 East 29th Street, 3rd Floor
New York, NY 10016
212-447-1400 phone
800-942-0673 phone
print@palmcoastd.com
www.printmag.com

PLAZM MAGAZINE
PO Box 2863
Portland, OR 97208
503-528-8000 phone
800-524-4944 toll-free phone
editor07@plazm.com
www.plazm.com/magazine

VOICE: AIGA JOURNAL OF DESIGN
164 Fifth Avenue
New York, NY 10010
212-807-1990 phone
www.aiga.org/voice

INTERNET

AIGA
www.aiga.org

Big Cartel
www.bigcartel.com

The Book Cover Archive
www.bookcoverarchive.com

Boxes and Arrows
www.boxesandarrows.com

Communication Arts
www.commarts.com

Coroflot
www.coroflot.com

DaFont
www.dafont.com

Design Addict
www.designaddict.com

Design Charts
www.designcharts.com

Design Observer
http://www.designobserver.com/

Design Taxi
www.designtaxi.com

Design Writing Research
www.designwritingresearch.org

The Dieline
www.thedieline.com

digg labs
www.labs.digg.com

Émigré
www.emigre.com

Etsy
www.etsy.com

Font Shop
www.fontshop.com

Hoefler & Frere-Jones
www.typography.com

Kaliber 10000
www.k10k.net

Lorem Ipsum Generator
www.lipsum.com

MyFonts
www.new.myfonts.com

National Design Museum
www.cooperhewitt.org

Print
www.printmag.com

Rochester Institute of Technology
Design Archives
www.library.rit.edu/gda

Smashing Magazine
www.smashingmagazine.com

Typographic
www.typographic.com

Typophile
www.typophile.com

Unbeige
http://www.mediabistro.com/-unbeige/

Vector Jungle
www.vectorjungle.com

Veer
www.veer.com

continued

RESOURCES

BLOGS

www.backspace.com/notes
www.creativereview.co.uk/cr-blog
www.design-milk.com
www.designobserver.com
www.designspongeonline.com
www.futurefarmers.com
www.gigposters.com
www.grainedit.com
www.journal.aiga.org
www.kottke.org
www.madxs.com
www.mcsweenys.net
www.pikemurdy.com
www.posttypography.com
www.printmag.com/dailyheller
www.thedieline.com
www.themoment.blogs.nytimes.com
www.typophile.com

PORTFOLIO/SOCIAL/BUSINESS

www.creativehotlist.com
www.commarts.com
www.crowdspring.com
www.designobserver.com
www.mediabistro.com
www.coroflot.com
www.linkedin.com
www.facebook.com
www.twitter.com
www.bigcartel.com
www.etsy.com

LEARNING ABOUT DESIGN ONLINE

A selection of inspirational Web sites covering many areas of graphic design

bemboszoo.com
fun and lighthearted typographic inspiration

blog.eyemagazine.com
Eye magazine's up-to-the minute snippets on graphic design and design culture.

blog.spoongraphics.co.uk
design articles, tutorials, and resources

bookcoverarchive.com
hundreds of book covers and designers, archived for easy browsing

brandsoftheworld.com
a comprehensive resource for world famous brand logos

colourlovers.com
monitor and follow color trends across the world

core77.com
portfolio hosting, competitions, events, and more for designers

csszengarden.com
a demonstration of css-based web design

designboom.com/eng
follow the international design scene with interviews, design reports, and critique

designdump.com
a place created to share kowledge, inspire and inform the design community

designlicks.com
awards the most creative and well designed sites

designobserver.com
extensive archive of articles, interviews, and multimedia related to design

designorati.com
a creative news and information publication, updated daily

designspotter.com
dedicated to contemporary design while providing a place to share work with thousands of viewers

designtaxi.com
daily news on the creative industry; upload portfolio work

edliveshere.com
educational resource for paper, printing, and design questions

feltron.com
great resource for designers interested in information design

flashden.net
a flash resource

flickr.com/groups/type
public group posting images of typography in various mediums

flickr.com/groups/logodesign
public group for sharing sketches, drafts, and examples of logo design

ffffound.com
inspirational image bookmarking experience that allows users to post and share their favorite images on the web

gigposters.com
a massive online archive, showcasing gig posters from around the world

jumpola.com
a comprehensive list of design related links

IndesignSecrets.com
reliable online resrouce for all things Indesign

ilovetypography.com
a site dedicated to the passion for typography, type design, and lettering

kuler.adobe.com
generate and share color themes while using in tandem with Adobe Creative Suite

motionographer.com
articles, commentary, and visual resources for those interested in motion graphics

newwebpick.com
a global community for designers, showcasing portfolios of all types

notcot.com
inspiration delivered daily for creative minds

notcot.org
a digital bulletin board for designers to share inspiration

www.swiss-miss.com
Tina Eisenberg's personal resource on all things design

thedieline.com
covering and critiquing the package design industry

typegoodness.com
a showcase of anything related to typography and its use around the world

typographica.org
A review of typefaces and type books, with occasional commentary on fonts and typographic design

webcreme.com
Web design inspiration

webdesignerwall.com
design ideas, web trends, and tutorials

Andreev, Andre, and Dan Covert, **Never Sleep: Graduating to Graphic Design**, de.MO, 2009.

Baines, Phil, and Catherine Dixon, **Signs: Lettering in the Environment**, Laurence King, 2008.

Bataille, Marion, **ABC3D**, Roaring Brook Press, 2008.

Bergström, Bo, **Essentials of Visual Communication**, Laurence King Publishers, 2009.

Brody, David, and Hazel Clark, editors, **Design Studies: A Reader**, Berg Publishers, 2009.

Burke, Christopher, **Active Literature**, Hyphen Press, 2008.

Chwast, Seymour, **The Obsessive Images of Seymour Chwast**, Chronicle Books, 2009.

Donaldson, Timothy, **Shapes for Sounds**, Mark Batty Publisher, 2008.

Dougherty, Brian, **Green Graphic Design**, Allworth Press, 2009.

Eatock, Daniel, and Daniel Eatock: **Works 1975–2007**, Princeton Architectural Press, 2008.

Erlhoff, Michael, and Timothy Marshall, editors, **Design Dictionary: Perspectives on Design Terminology**, Birkhäuser Basel, 2008.

Freyer, Conny, Sebastien Noel, and Eva Rucki, **Digital by Design**, Thames & Hudson, 2009.

Gill, Bob, **Words into Pictures**, Images Publishing Group, 2009.

Glaser, Milton, **Drawing Is Thinking**, Overlook Hardcover, 2008.

Gorman, Paul, **Reasons to be Cheerful: The Life and Work of Barney Bubbles**, Adelita, 2008.

Hayes, Clay, **Gig Posters: Rock Show Art of the 21st Century**, Quirk, 2009.

Heller, Steven, editor, **Design Disasters: Great Designers, Fabulous Failure, and Lessons Learned**, Allworth Press, 2009.

Heller, Steven, and Gail Anderson, **New Vintage Type**, Watson Guptil, 2007.

Heller, Steven, and Seymour Chwast, **Illustration: A Visual History**, Abrams, 2008.

Heller, Steven, and Michael Dooley, **Teaching Motion Design: Course Offerings and Class Projects from the Leading Undergraduate and Graduate Programs**, Allworth Press, 2008.

Heller, Steven, and Louise Fili, **Stylepedia**, Chronicle Books, 2006.

Heller, Steven, and Mirko Ilic, **Anatomy of Design**, Rockport Publishers, 2007.

Heller, Steven, and Mirko Ilic, **Handwritten: Expressive Lettering in the Digital Age**, Thames and Hudson, 2007.

Heller, Steven, and Lita Talarico, **The Design Entrepreneur**, Rockport Publishers, 2008.

Heller, Steven, and Lita Talarico, **Design School Confidential: Extraordinary Class Projects from the International Design Schools, Colleges and Institutes**, Rockport Press, 2009.

Heller, Steven, and David Womack, **Becoming a Digital Designer: A Guide to Careers in Web, Video, Broadcast, Game and Animation Design**, Wiley, 2007.

Himpe, Tom, **Advertising Next**, Chronicle Books, 2008.

Jedlicka, Wendy, **Packaging Sustainability: Tools, Systems and Strategies for Innovative Package Design**, Wiley, 2008.

Klanten, R., and H. Hellige, **Playful Type: Ephemeral Lettering and Illustrative Fonts**, Die Gestalten Verlag, 2008.

Lois, George, **George Lois: On Creating the Big Idea**, Assouline, 2008.

Lupton, Ellen, **Indie Publishing**, Princeton Architectural Press, 2008.

Lupton, Ellen, and Julia Lupton, **Design Your Life: The Pleasures and Perils of Everyday Things**, St. Martin's Griffin, 2009.

Martin, Keith, Robin Dodd, Graham Davis, and Bob Gordon, **1000 Fonts**, Chronicle Books, 2009.

Müller, Lars, and Victor Malsy, **Helvetica Forever, Lars Müller** Publishers, 2009.

Munari, Bruno, **Design As Art**, Penguin Global, 2009.

Owens, Sarah, **Yes Logo: 40 Years of Branding and Design** by Michael Peters, Black Dog Publishing, 2009.

Pentagram, **Pentagram: Marks: 400 Symbols and Logotypes**, Laurence King, 2009.

Perry, Michael, **Over & Over: A Catalog of Hand-Drawn Patterns**, Princeton Architectural Press, 2008.

Poynor, Rick, **Designing Pornotopia: Travels in Visual Culture**, Princeton Architectural Press, 2006.

Roberts, Lucienne, **Good: Ethics of Graphic Design**, AVA Publishing, 2006.

Sagmeister, Stefan, **Things I Have Learned in My Life So Far**, Abrams, 2008.

Shaughnessy, Adrian, **How to Be a Graphic Designer Without Losing Your Soul**, Laurence King, 2005.

Shedroff, Nathan, **Design is the Problem: The Future of Design Must be Sustainable**, Rosenfeld Media, 2009.

Stanic, Elena, and Lipavsky Corina, **Atlas of Graphic Designers**, Rockport Publishers, 2009.

Tholenaar, Jan, and Alston W. Purvis, **Type: A Visual History of Typefaces and Graphic Styles, Vol. 1**, Taschen, 2009.

Visocky O'Grady, Jennifer, and Kenneth Visocky O'Grady, **A Designer's Research Manual: Succeed in Design by Knowing Your Clients and What They Really Need**, Rockport Publishers, 2009.

Vit, Armin, and Bryony Gomez Palacio, **Graphic Design, Referenced: A Visual Guide to the Language, Applications, and History of Graphic Design**, Rockport Publishers, 2009.

Woolma, Matt, **100s Visual Ideas: Formats, Folds & Bindings**, Angela Patchell Books, 2008